Nationalism in Stateless Nations

Nationalism in Stateless Nations

Images of Self and Other in Scotland and Newfoundland

ROBERT C. THOMSEN

First published in Great Britain in 2010 by
John Donald, an imprint of Birlinn Ltd

West Newington House
10 Newington Road
Edinburgh
EH9 1QS

www.birlinn.co.uk

ISBN: 978 1 906566 20 3

The publishers gratefully acknowledge the support of the Aarhus University
Research Foundation towards the publication of this book

British Library Cataloguing-in-Publication Data
A catalogue record for this book is available on request from the British Library

Typeset by IDSUK (DataConnection) Ltd
Printed and bound in Britain by Bell & Bain Ltd, Glasgow

Contents

Acknowledgements

I have been fortunate during the writing of this book to have had access to stimulating and constructive research environments, and I owe thanks to many individuals who have contributed to the process of carrying it to completion. I am particularly grateful to two friends and former academic mentors at Aarhus University: Hans Hauge for always being ready to challenge my hypotheses and conclusions, thus constantly inspiring me to improve the quality of the study, and Jørn Carlsen for his never-failing support and for sharing his incredible knowledge of Canadian society with me. From Aalborg University, my Alma Mater and, since recently, academic home, Henrik Halkier deserves thanks for early inspiration and constructive criticism, as does Ulf Hedetoft (currently at Copenhagen University).

Of crucial importance to the completion of this book has been time spent in research environments in Scotland and Newfoundland. A very rewarding visit to the Department of Sociology at Edinburgh University in 1999 might never have been realised had it not been for the kind interest that Dave McCrone took in my work. I remain indebted to him also for having inspired me to engage in this particular field of study – and for the phrase 'stateless nation'. The generosity and helpfulness of Jodie Robson from the British Association for Canadian Studies, the warm welcome by, and challenging discussions with, Cairns Craig, Tom Nairn, Ross Bond and others at Edinburgh University ensured that my six months in Edinburgh became an unforgettable, enlightening and thoroughly enjoyable experience. I am particularly indebted to Michael Rosie, who found time in his own busy schedule to help me secure crucial data, and who was a wonderful source of information on many aspects of Scottish society.

Equally important has been my time in Newfoundland as a research associate fellow at the Institute of Social and Economic Research (ISER), Memorial University of Newfoundland. I deeply appreciate the opportunity provided to me by ISER to conduct my research in this fascinating part of Canada. Jim Tuck, Eleanor Fitzpatrick and Darlene

Oliver provided very pleasant and supportive conditions under which to conduct my research. Susanne Ottenheimer from the Department of Sociology deserves special thanks, both for fruitful discussions about the sociology of Newfoundland and for being a very good friend to our family during our stay in Canada. Steve Tomblin from the Department of Political Science has been a patient and excellent source of information about politics in Newfoundland and Canada, and our family will always remember the warmth with which we were welcomed to St John's by Steve and his wonderful family. The amazingly knowledgeable Bert Riggs from the Centre of Newfoundland Studies was most helpful in the process of obtaining relevant data. Rose and Gus Hurley have a special place in my heart; they made their home ours, and they related to me their incredibly fascinating first-hand experience of life in Newfoundland before Confederation. Many thanks are due to Jim Overton from the Department of Sociology who gave up generous amounts of his time to discuss the Newfoundland experience with me; he remains one of my most valuable sources.

I shall remain grateful also to Andrew Bennett and Claire Campbell, wonderful hosts and good friends, for introducing me to aspects of Canadian culture and society I would never have discovered from academic books. I also wish to express my sincere gratitude to the many who kindly made themselves available for interrogation during my fieldwork in Scotland and Newfoundland: Pat Byrne, John Fitzgerald, Mark Graesser, Jonathan Hearn, Doug House, and Peter Sinclair have all patiently sat through long interviews, and have provided me with valuable information and insights, significantly adding to my understanding of Scottish and Newfoundland society and politics. Special thanks are due to former premier of Newfoundland Brian Peckford for relating to me his version of the story. Many warm thanks go to Peter Neary and Sid Noel whose work has been inspirational and who have been instrumental, through encouragement and active interest, in the publication of this book. I am truly grateful to three anonymous reviewers, who each added tremendously to the quality of the manuscript, and to Mairi Sutherland at Birlinn/John Donald publishers, who did an excellent job collecting and forging all the elements into the present form.

Although much of what is of value in this study is thus attributable to the many good people mentioned above, I claim as my own any lapses and deficiencies.

I should also like to acknowledge the important research grant I received from the International Council for Canadian Studies, which found my research worthy of funding, and thus provided the opportunity for me to collect the necessary Newfoundland data, and the generous financial support of the Aarhus University Research Foundation towards publication.

Finally, I am forever indebted to my wife for her patience and forbearance, and for accepting responsibility for the welfare and happiness of our family at times when work on the book made me more absent than present. Lene, Emil and Andreas, you have ensured that I have constantly had the most rewarding research environment I could ever wish for, and I dedicate this book to you.

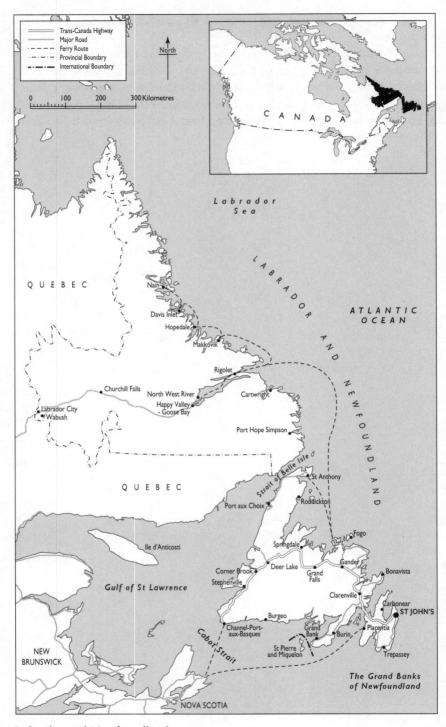

Labrador and Newfoundland

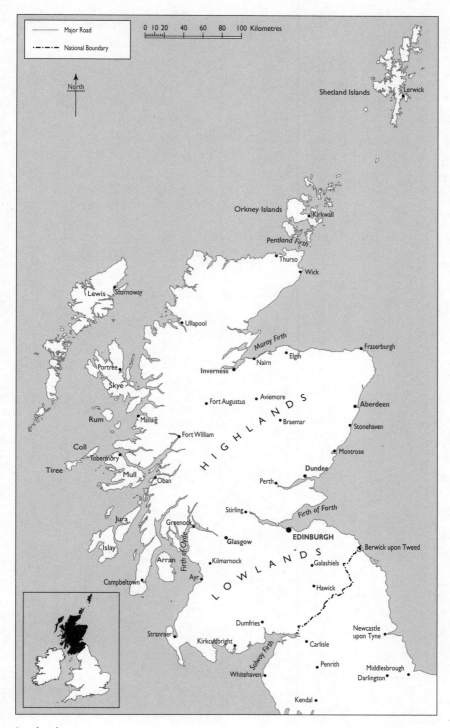

Scotland

ONE   Introduction

This book is a study of the nature of nationalism in stateless nations. Specifically, it is a study of the processes by which social actors are influenced, and in turn influence, the relationship between the national self and its 'others' in Scotland and Newfoundland.[1] The notion of 'a stateless nation' calls for clarification since Scotland and Newfoundland exist within larger polities, and both, at least since 1999, can be said to have states, albeit ones with limited powers. In this sense, these societies are obviously not stateless. However, neither the Scots nor the Newfoundlanders possess a state of their *own* – certainly not an independent one – which on many occasions has resulted in decisions by the larger states to which they belong (the UK and Canada) being made contrary to the wishes of most Scots and Newfoundlanders. In this sense, Scotland and Newfoundland are non-sovereign or, as this book suggests, stateless nations. Further on, in chapter 2, the inherent issue of 'nationhood' will be discussed at length; suffice it therefore at this point to state that both Scotland and Newfoundland are considered nations in this study, and that this perception of nationhood is shared in the periods investigated by significant proportions of the population in both societies.

Scotland and Newfoundland also resemble each other in certain other ways, all to be explored in detail in chapter 3. Geographically, both are situated in North Atlantic regions; constitutionally, both are parts of larger states which comprise several other potentially sovereign communities; and both have histories of independence coupled with a strong, widespread awareness of a unique cultural heritage and identity. Finally, both societies have been junior economic partners within their respective states. Despite these general similarities, sub-state political nationalism has followed different paths in Scotland and Newfoundland. Political nationalism as such is not a recent phenomenon in either society. Demands for autonomy have increased and decreased in strength as waves on their shores. Political nationalist movements in their current manifestations, however, are recent developments. In both cases, the surge in recent decades has been fuelled by a host of factors, some promising a brighter, more prosperous future. Perhaps the most decisive of these factors has been the promise of real alternatives to economic dependency, such as oil and gas discoveries. Yet, although a wave as powerful as the one in Scotland appeared to exist in Newfoundland in the early 1980s, political nationalism here went into hibernation in the late 1980s and 1990s, only to be followed by a strong revival in the first decade of the twenty-first century. It is both the similarities and the differences in their development that make a comparative study of the two societies relevant to the understanding of modern political nationalism.

Political nationalism, as opposed to cultural nationalism, strives to attain real change in the form of increased autonomy for the nation, most often expressed as a desire for constitutional change. The distinction between political and cultural nationalism will be discussed further on in this chapter; for now, the interesting question is: what causes sub-state political nationalism to develop? To fully answer this question one needs to address the nature of national identity, broadly defined as the sum of dominant perceptions of 'self' and 'others' in all spheres of society at any given time. The images of the national self and its others determine how national identity can legitimise political nationalism in general and sometimes its specific demands for constitutional change. The fact that the images of self and other are dynamic rather than static makes the analysis intricate – national identity is based on processes and practices rather than persistent conceptions. The analysis must therefore identify the factors and actors involved in constantly revising a particular national self-perception. For this reason, this study employs an ideographic approach, focusing exclusively on the development of national identity and nationalism in Scotland and Newfoundland from the late 1960s onwards. Without making comprehensive claims about nationalist movements in general, it seeks to show how a focus on the struggle for greater autonomy in Scotland and Newfoundland can contribute to a better understanding of the development of political nationalism in stateless nations in modern and post-modern Western societies.

NATIONALISM – PROCESS AND PRACTICE

In his introduction to Balakrishnan's *Mapping the Nation* (1996), Benedict Anderson reiterates what many other scholars working in the field of nationalism have come to recognise: there is no widely accepted definition of nationalism.² The debate on the nature of nationalism is vibrant and views are many and various. Leaving nuances aside for the moment, a general view of this debate conveys the impression of two central positions: one that maintains a perennialist stance to nations and nationalism, and one that maintains a modernist stance.

Theorists such as Anthony D. Smith, John Hutchinson and Walker Connor are often referred to as perennialists. While rejecting the primordialist claim that the ethnic roots of nations are somehow 'natural', these theorists still maintain that ethnicity remains central to all nationalisms and cannot be overruled simply as a discursive construction. Modernists such as Ernest Gellner, Benedict Anderson, Tom Nairn, John Breuilly and E. J. Hobsbawm disagree with this position. They claim that the nation is basically a modern construct, whose ethnic heritage is invented by the nationalist discourse itself. Moreover, the modernists see nationalism as the vehicle responsible for the transformation from pre-modern to modern (industrialised) society. These general positions are evidently very different, and have themselves bred many variations. Clearly, consensus is not near, neither is it desirable, as we shall see.

The perennialist and modernist positions are clearly productive contributions to the debate, but neither can claim to present the whole story about nationalism. The perennialist approach often fails to account for the development of nationalisms which have made only selective use of ethnic heritage. The modernist–constructivist approach at times seems unable to account for the emotional appeal of nationalism or the development of postmodern nationalisms in industrialised societies. Although language, territory and other more or less objective factors typically form part of the idea of the nation, they are far from definite indicators of the existence of one. In the light of the many real-life exceptions, some contemporary scholars have come to acknowledge that it makes more sense to speak of nationalism in plural. Although the many kinds of nationalisms are likely to have certain common traits, they may differ significantly in nature and content. In practice, one nationalist movement hardly ever expresses itself in the same way as another. For this reason, Rogers Brubaker argues that '"nation" is a category of "practice", not (in the first instance) a category of analysis. To understand nationalism, we have to understand the practical uses of the category "nation", the ways it can come to structure perception, to inform thought and experience, to organise discourse and political action.'³ The question that needs to be asked, therefore, is not simply 'what is nationalism?' but rather '*how* do different nationalisms *in practice* manifest themselves in different societies?' Admittedly, this makes the contours of the field more blurred, but the admission of nuances brings forth a more accurate and pertinent understanding of nationalist movements.

Brubaker's argument is easily elaborated by drawing attention to the great difference in circumstances between nineteenth and early twentieth-century nationalisms and the variants of nationalism found in today's globalised world. The world order of the Cold War has crumbled, and with it the fixed boundaries between East and West and certain nation-states. Whether one's perspective is 'globalist' or 'transformationalist',[4] globalisation is of immense importance to the way people perceive themselves and their neighbours, immediate as well as distant. The strain on traditional nation-states – produced as the importance of both supra- and sub-state entities increases – has no doubt been instrumental to a particular type of nationalist aspiration. Small semi-sovereign entities are now arguably more viable than many nation-state structures – especially if these entities have the economic resources to guarantee or improve the level of material wellbeing. Among sociologists, political scientists and scholars from many other disciplines, these new developments have resulted in much debate about the future of the nation-state. One of the many consequences of globalisation processes is the redefinition of sovereignty; separatist and semi-separatist movements around the world have been confronted with a range of more or less viable alternatives to their membership of the nation-state. Consequently, those who still favour the constitutional status quo within existing nation-states can no longer as easily brush aside group demands for greater political autonomy that are based on claims of unique national identities.

On the other hand, the goals of those advocating political and constitutional changes are in most cases no longer as radical as they used to be. Discussing Ernest Gellner's theory of the transformation of low cultures into national (high) cultures, Montserrat Guibernau observes that whereas national cultures used to strive for statehood for protection, cultural globalisation – also disparagingly known as 'McDonaldization'[5] – has made the preservation of distinctly national cultures impossible, and thus less relevant to nationalist movements.[6] At the same time, other kinds of globalisation, such as increasing supra-state control over the economies and foreign policies of nation-states by transnational institutions, seem to render the conventional goal of nationalism – the fully sovereign nation-state – more and more unattainable.

THE QUEST FOR AUTONOMY – NOT INDEPENDENCE

Since the early 1970s, the affluent states of the Western world have seen the germination and fruition of a special kind of nationalism.

'Neo-nationalism' is the prevalent label used to identify nationalist movements in Spain (in Catalonia), France (in Brittany and Corsica), Italy (in 'Padania' and Friuli), Denmark (in the Faeroe Islands and Greenland), Sweden (in Scania), the UK (in Wales and Scotland), and Canada (in Quebec and Newfoundland). These political nationalist movements are highly different, but they share two central features: an origin in wealthy liberal democracies and the distinction from classic nationalism in both content and purpose. Even though the idea of an imagined cultural community is still present, these movements are also characterised by a strong element of rationalism in the sense that they readily consider the political and socio-economic advantages and disadvantages of self-determination.

Significant factors of globalisation, such as economic interpenetration, the development of political and economic supra-state alternatives to the nation-state, and the rapid technological advances within communication have made the devolution of power a valid alternative to the status quo for many self-proclaimed national communities. In consequence, the stressing of pragmatic reasoning as much as, or even to a larger extent than, ethno-cultural affection are important features of this new kind of nationalism.

Another important point of distinction between classic and new nationalisms is the fact that for most neo-nationalists the aspiration is rarely the attainment of an independent nation-state to accommodate the *Volksgeist* of the nation, as romantic nationalism would prescribe. Neo-nationalists strive for devolution of political and economic power, but this devolution stops short of the potentially damaging status of full sovereignty. The majority of Catalan nationalists never seriously entertained the wish for an independent Catalonia.[7] Similarly, in the 1995 referendum campaign in Quebec, the supposedly 'separatist' Parti Québécois consistently spoke of *souveraineté-association* rather than a fully independent Quebec nation-state. The chief editorialist of *La Presse* in Montreal, Alain Dubuc, tellingly describes himself as a 'non-separatist nationalist'.[8] As David McCrone rightly points out 'there is *ambiguity about their aims*. Are they seeking independence or autonomy? Ambivalent terms are used in political debate, such as *"Home Rule"*, *"Autonomisme"*, *Souveraineté-Association or Consociation*.'[9]

Such nationalism, couched in what to a traditional nationalist might seem ambivalent and overly pragmatic terminology, does not comply with orthodox theories of nationalism as an ideology that strives towards national and political borders being congruent and unambiguous.[10] It suggests that some members of a nation may not see full political independence but something less as the primary purpose of their nationalist aspirations. Anthony D. Smith acknowledges that different kinds of nationalism exist and that some may not – at least in practical terms – strive for independence: 'Nationalism ideally prescribes a self-sufficiency of resources and purity of lifestyle in line with its commitment to autonomy and authenticity; failing that, nationalists strive for maximum control over their homeland and its resources.'[11] As political and economic globalisation increasingly prevents the attainment of full national sovereignty, many political neo-nationalist movements may be more accurately defined as *autonomist* movements – that is, as political movements that strive for as large a measure of national self-sufficiency (e.g., the attainment of linguistic or natural resource rights, or financial responsibility for regional development programs) as is deemed possible under the circumstances. Thus defined, autonomism accurately describes the kind of political nationalism found in Scotland and Newfoundland, and will be applied henceforth in the book.

CULTURAL AND POLITICAL NATIONALISM

For the study of nationalism in Scotland and Newfoundland, another useful distinction can be made between two closely related but nevertheless different kinds of nationalism: cultural nationalism and political nationalism. Friedrich Meinecke made a somewhat similar distinction between the *Kulturnation,* the passive cultural community, and the *Staatsnation,* the active political nation.[12] In the following, 'cultural nationalism' will refer to the apolitical celebration of the cultural history and heritage of the imagined nation and 'political nationalism' to the effective political expression of nationalist demands for change/empowerment. Described thus, the cultural–political dichotomy may appear categorical and artificially rigid, but this distinction is necessarily an approximation.[13] Cultural and political nationalism should not be seen as irreconcilable oppositions but as 'ideal' positions at either end of the same continuum. These ideal positions rarely exist in the real world. Rather, cultural nationalism often develops into a nationalism of a more political kind. Similarly, political nationalism may recede into a more cultural, apolitical form. If we think of the two types of nationalism not as separate entities but as continuations of each other, the distinction is useful in the analysis of the development of autonomism.

Cultural nationalism might exist within a particular constitutional set-up which may not be entirely just or fair; nonetheless, cultural nationalists make the conscious choice not to make any direct attempt to change an existing constitutional situation. The celebration of a distinct national identity and culture need not therefore lead to political demands for constitutional change. Logically, cultural nationalists can also be political unionists in the sense that they can favour both extensive cultural autonomy *and* the political and economic integration of their nation with the supra-national state. Cultural nationalism, in other words, is a variant of nationalism whose purpose might well be to maintain the constitutional status quo. Such a scenario differs from the perception of ultimate goals in most theories of nationalism. According to Ernest Gellner, for example, nationalism always has national sovereignty as its political goal. If one accepts this definition, one is forced to accept that a movement is only truly nationalist if its political goals are expressed as demands for constitutional change. Hence, it becomes impossible to think of nationalism as a preserving factor, unless as a political movement it has already achieved statehood for the nation. Still, it must also be acknowledged that the cultural celebration of national distinctness, even if it does not immediately translate into political demands for greater autonomy, can also be an initial step towards political nationalism.

As the analysis of Scotland and Scottish national identity features prominently in this study, it might appear relevant to use Tom Nairn's now famous term 'cultural sub-nationalism' to describe the pre-1960s Scottish situation. In *The Break-Up of Britain* (1977), Nairn used this term to describe the apolitical celebration of Scottish culture and history in the period from the Act of Union in 1707 to the 'belated' emergence of political nationalism in the 1960s: 'An anomalous historical situation could not engender a "normal" culture,' he writes. 'Scotland could not simply be adapted to the new, basically nationalist, rules of cultural evolution. But since the country could not help being affected by this evolution, it produced something like a stunted, caricatural version of it. The best title for this is perhaps "cultural sub-nationalism" . . . – a direct substitute for political action.'[14] As lucid and fascinating as Tom Nairn's analysis of Scotland's culture and identity is, the conclusions drawn from it do not correspond with the point of view that forms the basis for this study. By referring to Scottish nationalism in its apolitical phase as 'sub-nationalism', Nairn suggests that Scotland has somehow developed wrongly; that its nationalist movement has not fulfilled its potential or purpose. Seeing cultural nationalism as a mistake or an unfortunate digression on the road to 'proper' nationalism is tantamount to accepting the existence of a primordial truth about the nation and the course of nationalism. The rhetoric of nationalism is teleological, but the critical study of it should not be. Therefore, the concept of cultural sub-nationalism carries undesirable connotations which the more neutral concept of cultural nationalism does not.

As opposed to cultural nationalism, political nationalism includes the *political expression* of demands for constitutional change; it also refers to the desire for the concession of power in the shape of devolution, home rule, or independence. It is impossible to say precisely when a given variant of nationalism becomes political, but for it to be so, it will obviously have to address questions and situations politically, either within the established political party system or in other political forums. The demands of political nationalists are always based on the 'rights' of the nation, which means political nationalism will always, though to varying degrees, apply ethnic arguments in its rhetoric. Although cultural nationalism is not a precondition of political nationalism it nevertheless carries the seeds of, and often becomes instrumental in, the development of political nationalism. The ethno-cultural distinctness of the nation thus remains at the centre of political nationalist rhetoric, although, as we shall see, this is often played down in modern and post-modern political nationalist movements.

Finally, having introduced the concept of political nationalism, it is necessary to provide a distinction between it and the concept of autonomism. Political nationalism and autonomism are not synonymous concepts; rather, one is a particular version of the other. Autonomism is defined for purposes of this study as a form of political nationalism that has either an ill-defined goal or does not have an independent nation-state as its cardinal aspiration – either because this is considered an unattainable goal, or because currently independence is not seen to be beneficial to the nation. The inherent presence of the idea of the nation is what distinguishes autonomism from regionalism. Implied in autonomist demands are always the intrinsic 'rights' of the nation of self-determination, and an argument of ethnicity is necessarily present – though often applied with much rhetorical subtlety.

STRUCTURE OF THE BOOK

This introduction has sketched out the terrain of autonomism that is to be explored in two stateless nations. What remains is to provide the map that delineates the route through it. Chapter 2 will discuss national identity-building in theory and national identity as hegemonic discourse. It will also discuss and define important actors that together make up the 'nationalising domain'. The analysis of autonomism in Scotland and Newfoundland is divided into two parts. Part one comprises chapters 3, 4 and 5. Chapter 3 presents important similarities and differences between the two societies, establishing why the comparison of Scotland and Newfoundland is both relevant and useful. Chapters 4 (on Scotland)

and 5 (on Newfoundland) will invoke the theories presented in chapter 2 and analyse the changing images of self and other in each of the social spheres, covering a period of three decades from the late 1960s to the late 1990s. The analysis of this main period has been sub-divided into minor periods demarcated by important focal points or radical changes. Part two contains chapters 6 and 7. Chapter 6 analyses images of self and other in Scottish newspapers in the period 1967 to 1990; chapter 7 concerns itself with images of self and other in Newfoundland newspapers in the same period. The concluding chapter collects and discusses all findings, and draws a full a picture of nationalism in Scotland and Newfoundland.

TWO National Identity-Building

In outlining and explaining the development of nationalism in Scotland and Newfoundland, the focus in this book is naturally on the dominant collective social identity relating to a sense of belonging to a national community. That particular form of identity is best labelled 'national identity'. It may seem inappropriate to apply a concept such as national identity in an analysis of what may at certain points, to many holders of a particular collective social identity, have been perceived rather as provincial, regional or cultural identity. In other words, such a narrow concept would seem not only to refuse to acknowledge the pluralism of social identities, but also to accept the logic of nationalist rhetoric. However, what is essential here is to provide the conceptual tool that will prove most useful in analyses of this kind. It is necessary, though, to point out that Scottish national identity and Newfoundland national identity, for the meanings and connotations they carry, do not, in the period analysed, describe accurately the dominant collective social identity of *all* Scots and *all* Newfoundlanders. In fact, some will have strongly opposed the idea of anything but a British or a Canadian national identity.

Still, for the sake of clarification and conceptualisation, the concept of national identity must be used to refer to the dominant collective social identity. Furthermore, it remains not only useful but also in most respects valid. Other concepts, such as 'regional identity', do not sufficiently describe the particular ethnic element which lies beneath and legitimises political nationalism. Neither do they acknowledge the fact that the kind of belonging and conviction of inherent rights which are imbedded in the idea of the nation remain basic components of such movements.

In his article 'Being Scottish? On the Problem of the Objective Correlative' (1999), Anthony P. Cohen argues about the study of national identity: 'I may be able to specify the putative principal ingredients of national identity; but I can not generalise about what they mean to, or how they are experienced by, different people . . . We can not say what the various constructions of individuals add up to, although we may be able to speculate and generalise in gross terms about their common features.'[1]

Cohen is obviously correct. It is impossible to apply conclusions based on gross term generalisations about common features to individuals. Instead, the focus should be on commonly held images, perceptions of the self and of significant others, rather than on 'Scottishness' or the Newfoundland 'psyche'. All one can hope to do – and what will be attempted here – is to produce a multi-faceted account, resembling as closely as possible the sum of all the images, perceptions, values and beliefs which make up national identity, realising that conclusions reached in any study of this kind must necessarily be approximations.

Guibernau contends that the rational arguments of nationalism take the form of promises of a better economy, a better quality of life, etc. if the goal of a higher degree of autonomy or independence is achieved, while the emotional arguments accentuate collective identity and belonging.[2] In one sense Guibernau is right; both rational and emotional arguments exist in modern and postmodern nationalist movements, and they do indeed appear to be associated with political or socio-economic matters and a sense of ethnic belonging to a certain community or territory. Still, her distinction fails to make explicit that political traditions, economic and social circumstances may also add to or even create a sense of community. In other words, that national identity also has what might be called, in Guibernau's terms, rational sources.

In the following, national identity will be defined as the sum of collectively held images of self and other, which in the minds of Scots and Newfoundlanders define the Scottish and Newfoundland national self as culturally, politically, economically or socially distinct, and which define relations with significant others outside the national community. National identity is not, therefore, defined as the all-inclusive combination of all images in all society's spheres, but as the combination of those images which pertain to the *national* self, as opposed to other – gender, regional, occupational, etc. – identities.

The ideology of nationalism

One necessary precondition of nationalism, be it classic or new, is the desire among the majority of a population to engage in or affiliate to a collective identity – a large-scale, imagined solidarity. Ethnicity and national distinctness, however, remain constructs; it is never really a question of 'discovering' or 're-discovering' the national core, as nationalist rhetoric suggests. Numerous scholars of nationalism – from Ernest Renan in the late nineteenth century to Benedict Anderson in the late twentieth century – have presented convincing evidence against the naturalness of the nation. Despite such evidence, the development of the nationalist cause still depends on the presence of a will among a people to *believe* that such a national core exists. Consequently, proto-nationalists have to develop and nurture this illusive idea.

Although the development of autonomism owes much to a range of other aspects in the life of the nation, national identity still remains the *raison d'être* of autonomism. For people to unite in a national cause it is necessary for them to feel a sense of common destiny with their co-nationals. The success of any nationalist movement is thus largely dependent upon its ability to produce a rhetoric that can persuade a significant number of people of its legitimacy. For this reason, national identity becomes the underlying ideology of nationalism. This is not to say that an autonomist movement has no chance of success in a society which does not already have a sense of common destiny and national identity. While national identity remains at the core of political nationalism, it is also a vehicle which can be constructed and reconstructed by actors for political purposes.

The presence of uniting factors such as a common political, economic or cultural history, a common language, or common values, naturally increases any nationalist movement's chance of success. However, the nationalist cause does not rely on issues of self-identification alone. It also incorporates the dynamics of differentiation. The formulation of a national identity relies on a strong sense of demarcation between the national self and extra-national 'others'. National identity is thus constructed in the interaction between images of self and other; the combination of the two is what constitutes the reality and definition of the nation.

It is absolutely necessary for any political nationalist movement to establish its uniqueness – that which makes this particular nation different and justifies the demand for special treatment (as, for instance, a higher degree of autonomy in certain matters). To achieve this, national identity must be politicised. Coupled with the socio-economic or political problems that are deemed intolerable, the politicisation of national identity gives the cause a higher purpose. It is no longer a question of a certain class, an intellectual grouping, the business community or politicians looking out for themselves. The struggle for increased autonomy becomes a *common* national cause with the perceptions of 'natural' national differences and 'inherent' historical rights acting as vehicle. For this reason, the success of political nationalist movements depends on the widespread acceptance of common images of self and other.

Anthony D. Smith informs us that 'we can not begin to understand the power and appeal of nationalism as a political force without grounding our analysis in a wider perspective whose focus is national identity treated as a collective cultural phenomenon'.[3] Among modern scholars there is consensus about the importance of identity elements in understanding, as well as defining, nationalism and the nation as such. Few subscribe to such rigid definitions as Krejci and Velímský's: 'There are firstly five objective factors which can contribute to the identification of a group as a nation: territory, state. . ., language, culture and history. When positive answers to all these criteria coincide there can be little doubt that the respective community or population is a nation.'[4]

Many scholars adhere to less specific and fixed definitions of the nation; among the most famous of these are Ernest Renan's perception of the nation as a 'daily plebiscite',[5] and Benedict Anderson's notion of the 'imagined community'.[6] Such open definitions suggest that the nation (and nationalism) is something members of a society may or may not engage in, implying an element of voluntarism. Although this is true, one should not ignore the powerful element of inherent force. According to Ulf Hedetoft, national identity is: 'a discourse which states and demands. . ., is collective and subjective, worldly and sacred, outside and inside, political and existential all at the same time . . . It assumes that national identity exists independently of the individual will, as a natural given of the national collectivity.'[7]

This assessment is very succinct. People identify with a national identity because they want to, but also because they are expected to, persuaded as they are by the psychological bonds that bind them to their fellow nationals. Hedetoft alludes to emotive impulses when defining national identity as 'the apolitical ideology of the political community'.[8] Invoking Anderson, Anthony D. Smith puts a tighter psychological fit on his definition, arguing that nations simply cannot exist without 'a set of common understandings and aspirations, sentiments and ideas that bind the population together in their homeland'.[9] For any nationalist movement to appeal to people, it must first of all persuade them of these 'natural' emotional ties. Argues Walker Connor: 'The national bond is subconscious and emotional rather than conscious and rational in its inspiration . . . And how has the nonrational core of the nation been reached and triggered? As we have seen in the case of numerous successful nationalist leaders, not *through* appeals to reason but *through* appeals to the emotions (appeals not to the mind, but to the blood).'[10]

Although Connor points out the emotional, sub-conscious qualities of national identity, his point of view would also seem to imply that *all* that a nationalist movement needs to be able to do to be successful (i.e., to achieve the support of all potential 'nationals') is appeal to the emotions of people. This is true only to a certain extent. Emotional attachment to the nation need not in itself persuade people to support constitutional change. The more rational-minded people may want proof of improved – or at least not worsened – socio-economic conditions as a consequence of a potential constitutional scenario *before* plunging headlong into political nationalism. Such considerations also feed into the national self-definition. Consequently, national identity is not only a question of emotional attachment; it also incorporates rational perceptions of the self–other relationship. As we shall see, this is particularly important for understanding developments in Scotland and Newfoundland.

National identity is the *sine qua non* of any nationalist movement. It may be defined as *all* the combined images of the national self and its others, including emotional as well as rational factors. It follows, as McCrone argues, that 'we can not discuss ethnicity and nationality without focussing on the process of identification, on the active negotiation in which people take part as they construct who they are and who they want to be'.[11] Herein lies the key to understanding the nature and development of specific nationalist movements. Political movements do not come about in a vacuum, without incentives. Like any other political movement, political nationalism needs an ideology – a legitimising cause – and it is only when perceptions of the world change that political action can be legitimised.

DISCOURSE ANALYSIS AND THE STUDY OF NATIONAL IDENTITY

> O wad some Power the giftie gie us
> To see oursels as ithers see us!
> Robert Burns, 'To a Louse'

Several factors make discourse analysis a particularly useful point of departure for a study like the one at hand. In trying to explain social relations and social conflicts, discourse analysis focuses on the importance of *perceptions* of social reality (as opposed to structural facts), the *roles* of actors in the processes that shape society, and, in turn, collective identity. A purely post-structuralist or phenomenological approach to the study of social relations would argue that perceptions and roles are not determined by fixed structures at all. A purely structuralist approach, by contrast, would claim that structures are essential in shaping any social development. Discourse analysis as applied in this book places itself between these two positions, in a critical realist tradition, arguing there is a dialectical relationship between material and discursive practices, and that, although structures exist externally to thought, they are incapable of determining political behaviour, and they cannot adequately explain why people act the way they do. What is essential to examine is the way in which social reality is constructed by subjects interpreting, rather than describing, social structures at particular points in history. In this way, discourse analysis places itself within a hermeneutic tradition. Both discourse analysis and hermeneutics agree that interpretations are relative to their historic moment. Any perception of reality is shaped by the given social context. As Cohen points out, 'Powerlessness, centrality and peripherality are ... matters of vision and self-perception ... [T]he relativities of centrality and peripherality ... are inextricably implicated in national identities in stateless nations; and, therefore, are fundamental to their nationalisms and nationisms [sic].'[12]

Historical evidence lends much weight to Cohen's argument. The way members of a certain group perceive themselves and their situation in relation to other groups has always been at the heart of every nationalist movement. There can be little doubt that changed perceptions of the relationship between the stateless nation and the supranational state do not arise out of the blue. They are typically provoked – directly or indirectly – by political or economic structures; but even if factual conditions and events are often the initial cause, they do not create social and political movements. Perceptions and reactions do. As Laclau and Mouffe famously suggested, 'An earthquake or the falling of a brick is an event that certainly exists, in the sense that it occurs here and now, independently of my will. But whether their specificity as objects is constituted in terms of "natural phenomena" or "expressions of the wrath of God", depends upon the structuring of a discursive field.'[13]

Laclau and Mouffe's proposition can be illustrated by an example from the societies studied. That Newfoundland's northern codfish stocks declined is a fact that is difficult to deny. What is more interesting, however, is the way in which this decline and the reasons for it were constructed socially. Was it a consequence of global warming, a matter of mismanagement on the part of the federal fisheries authorities, or of greed on the part of Basque trawlers? The actions initiated in consequence of the decline in stocks claim their legitimacy from the particular interpretation of the events. Consequently, as Heywood suggests, 'legitimacy is always a "social construction" '.[14]

National identity as hegemonic discourse

One of the objectives of this book is to investigate how socially constructed perceptions change over time, reflecting how and why main ideas in society come into existence. Of particular relevance therefore is Gramsci's concept of 'hegemony'. In brief, Gramsci's notion of hegemony refers to the way in which intellectuals exercise social control by securing the voluntary consensus of the masses. For this reason, the hegemony of an idea cannot be explained as a result of force, but as a matter of popular acceptance. The concept is clearly closely related to the notion of public opinion. Hegemony needs to be persistently defended, since alternative ideologies or social models constantly contest it. At certain points in the history of any society, explains Gramsci, the authority of one group of hegemonic intellectuals and moral leaders will be seriously questioned by new groups who consider themselves more progressive and rational.[15] The reason social groups reject the existing hegemonic views of the world (and the parties promoting them) is either because of major failures in the ruling elite's political project, or because the masses have managed to unite in spite of and without the hegemonic elite.[16] Gramsci's theory of hegemony is very convincing in that it allows those who do not directly hold political power to produce successful counter-discourses that might become hegemonic over time. This is why Gramsci's notion of hegemony lends itself so well to the study of nationalist movements in stateless nations.

An ethnic group does not move through history *en bloc*. Different people obviously have different perceptions of events, but the *shared* perceptions of the world exist alongside those of the individual. If this were not so, it would not make sense to speak of ethnic, let alone national, identities at all. Most people have a pretty clear idea of the existence of a national 'us' and an extra-national 'them'. David McCrone quotes Stuart Hall as saying: 'National culture is a discourse, a way of constructing meanings which influences and organises our actions and our conceptions of ourselves . . . [I]dentities are cultural representations or discourses which both facilitate and restrict choice.'[17] As McCrone argues, if this is so, national identity can not be taken for granted, and new competing discourses about identity will always appear, ready to challenge the predominant one. It is thus fair to conclude that national identity is dynamic rather than static; it is a fluctuating amalgamation of many discourses competing to become the hegemonic national identity. Some may be more enduring and appear to occupy the scene almost permanently; others come and go, leaving little trace. In either case, the progression from one discourse to another is usually a gradual process. This ongoing transition between discourses is what characterises the dynamics of the nation. It follows that national identities are constantly in a state of construction, and the definition of national symbols and narratives is a competitive, continual process.

The anatomy of national identity: images of self and others

National and other collective identities are intelligible – they do exist, this our experience tells us – but they are never sensible: we can not directly read or measure them. All one can hope to see are the signs of national identity: images of self and images of others. Not unlike Joseph J. Thomson, the British physicist who deduced his way to the discovery of electrons by observing the glimpses they made on a fluorescent screen at the end of a cathode ray tube, this book attempts to 'read' the signs of national identity, the changing images of self and other, thereby enabling it to make conclusions at the level of national identity – and thus at the level of nationalism.

Already, images of self and images of other have been mentioned several times, and as such their meanings taken for granted. However, it is necessary to consider in more detail the nature and the function of these apparently obvious, yet illusive categories. So far, the dichotomy of images of self and other has been used almost inter-changeably with national identity, but although this has served a purpose (and is not entirely wrong) a more thorough discussion of the role of images and perceptions of 'us' vs. images and perceptions of 'them' will break down some of the inherent configurations and provide a fuller understanding of what can be seen as the anatomy of national identity.

There is consensus among both discourse analysts and theorists of nationalism that any kind of collective identity has two main purposes: to create a perception of the world for its users that makes sense, and to create a feeling of belonging.[18] For both purposes, the 'us'–'them' dichotomy is essential. Identity is one of those special terms which may denote both similarity and difference. Bruce Kapferer illustrates how the 'collectivized individual identity', which he declares the Australian nation to be, defines itself in relation to what is *not* Australian, and in the process suppresses or excludes internal differences in an attempt to assimilate, to create unity.[19] This is not unique to Australian national identity, but a general feature of national identities. Walker Connor is another scholar who stresses the essential function of images of self and other in the formation of national identity. He says: 'The essence of a nation is a psychological bond that joins a people and differentiates it, in the subconscious conviction of its members, from all nonmembers in a most vital way.'[20] Anthropologist Thomas Hylland Eriksen seconds this when he extends the argument to comprise collective identities in general: 'Every social community or identity is exclusive in the sense that not everybody can take part. Groups and collectivities are always constituted in relation to *others*.'[21]

Any person's and any group of people's national identity consists of a variety of elements, but most importantly it comprises a necessary distinction between those who belong to the national community – those who are inside – and those who are seen as belonging to another national community – those who are outside. With national identity, as with any kind of identity, the self needs an other: as it is impossible to define oneself against nothing, the very idea of nationhood implies that there are other nations. The basis of assessment of the other must necessarily be 'our' values, because in producing an image of the other, we judge and compare what 'they' have with what 'we' have. It follows that one can not perceive the other without including a perception of the self. Fulfilling this function, otherness is crucial in both national identity-building and nationalism. To discover images of self, it is therefore useful to investigate what the holders of those self-images declare they are *not*; the image of other becomes an interpretable statement about the self.

National identities are not fixed because images of self and other are by nature dialectical. Although in a national context images of the other often take the form of rigid stereotypes – especially if the other is geographically or culturally 'distant', or if for some other reason information is scarce – national identities usually contain a wide range of varying images of specific others. One perception may be the dominant discourse, but competing ones usually exist simultaneously. Images of self and other are dependent on the context. Political and economic images of the other, for instance, may be generally positive, perhaps even characterised by envy, while at the same time cultural images of the same other may be negative, characterised perhaps by condemnation. Just as a set of different images may make up the combined perception of one other, a range of different kinds of images is usually ascribed to different others. Eriksen relates how in a specific case study, a set of standardised relationships existed between different ethnic groups: 'Some groups had a "friendly" relationship, some had a "hostile" one, and yet others had "joking" relationships.'[22] This is a primitive grouping of relations between self and other but, elaborated and extended, the idea of categorising these images of the other in many cases proves useful.[23]

FOMENTING FACTORS AND ACTORS IN NATIONAL
IDENTITY-BUILDING PROCESSES

The existence of that particular part of national identity which can be described as national consciousness, the sense of national distinctness, is not in itself sufficient to solicit political nationalism. National identity can not be utilised successfully in the creation of a popular nationalist movement if those who share that national identity are also generally content with the present political, constitutional, social, economic and cultural situation. Radical changes in the images of self and other that make up national identity must first occur, and they must be utilised politically by actors with an interest in upsetting the current state of affairs.

To understand why political nationalism comes about and why it takes the shape it does, it is crucial to find out how the images of self and other, which make up a particular national identity, change; how they are utilised; and by whom. In other words, to fully come to grips with the emergence of political nationalism in Scotland and Newfoundland, it is necessary to establish: 1) what can be termed the 'fomenting factors' which cause – or are made to cause – images of self and other to change; and 2) the identity of the 'fomenting actors' who constitute the standard-bearers of the movement.

Most theories of nationalism were developed in attempts to understand the nature of classic nationalisms, and it is becoming obvious that they will not as readily explain the nature of the development of neo-nationalist movements. A list of fomenting factors with regard to neo-nationalist movements would lean heavily towards pragmatic socio-economic and political arguments and away from ethnic and cultural arguments. In the words of one theorist, Anthony D. Smith, 'several latterday nationalisms, though they may contain a romantic element, have become far less idealistic and subjectivist, preferring to base their political claims on social and economic arguments'.[24] Different theories are likely to be useful in explaining the development of nationalism in different societies. What can be stated with certainty, though, is that so-called 'ethnic' and 'civic' elements exist in every nationalism, only they are given different emphases. The mere idea of an 'ethnic-less' nationalism makes no sense. If there is no perception of being a distinct ethnic group, there can be no idea of the nation, and any political movement ceases to qualify for the label 'national'. So much, at this point, about the fomenting *factors* of political nationalism. In the sections to follow, what has been termed fomenting *actors* will be considered more closely.

Top-down vs. bottom-up processes

In his famous study *Nations and Nationalism* (1983) Ernest Gellner
tried to pinpoint the processes of and reasons behind nation-building. In
it, he focuses on the emergence of nineteenth-century nationalism as a
dominant force, and reaches the conclusion that both nations and
nationalisms are largely constructs designed by an economic, political
and cultural elite to create the coherence and social structures that were
at that point a necessary precondition of modernisation in the form of
industrialisation and capitalism. In an attempt to explain the form of
this process of nationalising the masses, Gellner introduces the concepts
of 'garden' (or high) cultures and 'wild' (or low) cultures. The wild
varieties 'are produced and reproduce themselves spontaneously', while
the garden varieties are 'most usually sustained by literacy and by
specialized personnel, and would perish if deprived of their distinctive
nourishment'.[25] The high culture existed independent from the low
cultures in pre-industrial societies, but when modernisation set in it
became normative, pervasive and universal in society. At this point it
'wants a state, and preferably its own'.[26] Thus the Age of Nationalism.
Gellner's account of the state of affairs from that point is summed up in
this statement: 'Nationalism is, essentially, the general imposition of a
high culture on society, where previously low cultures had taken up the
lives of the majority.'[27] But here a problem arises. As Tom Nairn has
argued, nationalism is not as much a question of telling a group of
people to embrace the idea of the nation, as of mobilising it. In fact,
Nairn informs us, 'the masses – the ultimate recipients of the new
message – . . . determine a lot of what the 'message' is'.[28] To become
normative and universal, a high culture needs the general acceptance
and support of the bulk of the people. The masses need to appreciate it
as natural and as theirs, and to ensure this, argues Gellner, parts of all
the local 'wild' cultures must be incorporated into the national high
culture – which is then filtered down through society by its elite
producers. He puts it like this: 'Nationalism uses the pre-existing,
historically inherited proliferation of cultures or cultural wealth, though
it uses them very selectively, and it most often transforms them radically
. . . Nationalism usually conquers in the name of a putative folk culture.
Its symbolism is drawn from the healthy, pristine, vigorous life of the
peasants, of the *Volk*.'[29] The people will from thence recognise familiar
elements and embrace the new national culture and make it their own,
thus contributing to the beneficial national coherence. Gellner's theory
corresponds well with the idea of national identity as hegemonic
discourse that runs through this book, but with respect to contributing

further to the understanding of modern nationalist movements, it has some drawbacks. Because Gellner is concerned with historical, largely nineteenth-century, nationalism and hence with societies with little or no democratic tradition, and whose level of communication was still at a minimum (the emergence of industrialisation is a focal point in his argumentation), his theory of national identity-building, rather abruptly, stops here.

Gellner's focus is not on liberal democracies, and therefore he should not be blamed for leaving a lot to be said about the participation of what has been referred to as the 'subaltern strata' in nation-building processes. When investigating national identities in contemporary societies, however, it is not satisfactory, as it may be for historians describing nineteenth-century identity-building processes, to look exclusively at top-down processes. Arguing along the lines of Ernest Renan – who, early in the history of nationalism studies, realised that 'the existence of a nation . . . is an everyday plebiscite'[30] – and Antonio Gramsci – who argued that renaissance man is no longer a possibility in the modern world, as still larger groups of people actively and directly take part in history[31] – people in enlightened liberal democracies are not easily manipulated by elites. They most often prefer to make up their own minds based on the subjective interpretation of their own experiences.[32] Although large segments of the subaltern strata sometimes choose not to participate in the politics of society, in terms of achieving popular acceptance, passive consensus is often just as essential to the success of a political project as is active consensus. National identities are negotiated and re-negotiated continually as people 'try on identities for size' and then, from a qualified point of view, reject any that appear not to fit. A similar argument is made by Anthony Giddens, who says national identities 'need to be sustained in an open and discursive way, in cognizance not only of their complexities but of the other loyalties with which they overlap. Implied is a more reflexive construction of national identity, a modernizing project *par excellence*.'[33] In other words, in modern liberal democracies, identities are negotiated. A set of values and elements of one collective social identity may eventually become the predominant one, but first this identity must be based on agreed, collective interpretations of existing structures and developments.

This would seem to imply that to investigate such a thing as national identity one must in fact analyse signs of self and other in *all* existing strata of society. This, however, need not be necessary. In his major study of images of self and other in three European countries, Hedetoft is aware that he might be criticised for investigating only the perceptions of a rather limited group of people, in terms of social class. In countering this potential critique, he touches upon what he describes as an 'obvious advantage'.[34]

> It is necessary for an investigation of the present type to have this stratum of society ['intellectuals'] well represented, both because they have always been harbingers of the future and *sensitive seismographs* of the present, and because in an important sense . . . they are the most genuine representatives of the nation, meaning: combine national identity, national interest, and internationalism in ways that are more expressive of the current *Zeitgeist* than the often far more romanticised notions of other people, and in ways that mix idealised attitude with social practice: they are, after all, very often the determining practitioners of the nation.[35]

In Hedetoft's study this may indeed amount to no more than an 'obvious advantage'. In this study, his observation becomes a valid argument for including in the investigation exactly this social group. National identity-building is indeed a bottom-up as well as a top-down process, but since one can not possibly investigate all strata of society exhaustively, the 'sensitive seismographs' are crucial in achieving an understanding of this process. In the following section this argument will be further developed, and other groups in society will be included in the final definition of what will be termed the 'nationalising domain'.

Phases and actors

Another theorist of nationalism, Miroslav Hroch, has introduced an interesting theory of national identity-building. He argues that it can be divided into three phases, each characterised by the actions of specific social strata. The first phase, phase A, can be likened to what has already been defined in chapter 1 as 'cultural nationalism': a period characterised by 'a passionate concern on the part of a group of individuals, usually intellectuals, for the study of the language, culture, the history of the oppressed nationality'.[36] Important to note is that, according to Hroch, the intellectuals release these energies 'without, on the whole, pressing specifically national demands to remedy deficits', and 'usually do not even attempt to mount a patriotic agitation'.[37] The second phase, B, is the one Hroch considers the really important phase. This is where active nationalist agitation occurs. The actors include a range of different powerful social groups which see an advantage in nationalising the masses. One recognises the actors of phase A in phase B too, as scholarly research is now becoming part of nationalist agitation. Phase C, the last phase of any successful national revival, is characterised by the coming into existence of a nationalist mass movement. Even if Hroch's theoretical model is not implausible, it is not entirely satisfactory either. As a theoretical model, Hroch's division of the national identity-building process into phases A, B and C can be utilised in the analysis of national identity-building processes in Scotland and Newfoundland, where either phase C has been extraordinarily belated or where a transition from phase A to phase B was followed by what appears to be a *return* to phase A.[38] Still, real-life nationalist movements are often too complex and differ too much to fit neatly into any such simple prefabricated models. The model needs modifications.

Hroch argues that the beginning of every national revival is marked by phase A, and indeed the initial stages of nationalism tend to be characterised by an elite intellectual movement. The wall that Hroch puts up between the actors of phases A and B, however, is probably less rigid and more porous in contemporary nation-building processes than is suggested by him. This is not a matter of arguing in favour of a Marxist theory of bourgeois (or other ruling class) domination of intellectual and academic life. The argument is rather that it is difficult to imagine intellectuals and academics in contemporary societies as completely detached from the political consequences of the celebration of the national ideal. This may have been true in certain historical national identity-building processes, but in arguing that this is the model that will fit nation-building processes *as such*, Hroch falls into the same trap as Gellner, whom he accuses of providing merely 'inductive descriptions'.[39]

It is equally difficult to agree with Hroch's point of view that nations precede nationalisms,[40] and that the intellectuals of phase A simply 'discover' the nation.[41] It is much easier to accept for instance Gellner's and Hobsbawm's argument that, on the contrary, nationalism precedes any concept of nation and the 'discovery' was in all cases the *invention* of an imagined national community. In one of his famous quotes Gellner phrases it this way: 'Nationalism is not the awakening of nations to self-consciousness: it invents nations where they do not exist.'[42] In practice, this part of Gellner's theory carries more weight. This is the basis for arguing that the actors in what Hroch refers to as phases A and B should not in contemporary liberal democracies be rigidly distinguished from each other. In any case, and regardless of whether the first ones to articulate the 'idea' of a particular nation see an advantage in terms of personal gains (as in Hobsbawm's instrumentalist approach) or gains for society as such (as in Gellner's functionalist approach), or do it in a Romantic spirit, the nation they celebrate remains an invention.

Groups of actors can be divided into different categories, but it is a futile exercise to attempt to apply rigid divisions based on function between them. Although assigning the traditional role of inventors to the intellectuals, in *Nationalism: Five Roads to Modernity* (1992) Liah Greenfeld believes that they have also historically taken up an activist function. She says: 'These are, in the first place, the people who came up with, articulated, and popularized the new concepts. This explains the central role played in the emergence of national identities by intellectuals – by definition, articulators and disseminators of ideas.'[43]

When trying to decide which are the important social groups in the analysis of national identity-building processes, it makes little sense to speak of two important strata with separate roles, roughly defined as the intellectuals and the political agitators. Rather, the reference should be to one nationalising domain consisting of some (but not necessarily all) academics, artists, political groupings, the media, educators (secular and ecclesiastical), etc., formulating and distributing discourses in constant negotiation about their content with other social strata.[44]

The nationalising domain

Importantly, Hroch's typology reveals that, although class interests are a relevant factor, participation in the movement is not conditioned by membership of a particular class. Nationalist movements arise from different historical situations and have different goals, and consequently the social compositions of such movements vary. The consequence of this reasoning must be a definition of the nationalising domain which is not based on class, but is based on roles in the national identity-building processes. Such a definition must also, then, be partly based on power relations in society. Often political and cultural power involves the power to influence and distribute images of the national self and its others. Here, and in the following, the nationalising domain is defined as the domain through which national discourse is mediated to other parts of society. The nationalising domain acts as the catalyst and dynamo through which all images of self and other pass to be constantly redefined, and in the process surface as manifest expressions.

Crudely outlined, this is how the dynamo of the nationalising domain works: initially images of self and other are either conceived or received from outside the nationalising domain, for them to be filtered out (rather than down) to other parts of society. When returned to the nationalising domain with society's comments and suggestions, the images of self and other can then be reinterpreted and redefined; and so the process continues. A very important point to make is that there is nothing deterministic in the existence of a nationalising domain. What is meant by 'nationalising' is that it is within this domain of society that the *potential* to nationalise or create a nationalist discourse lies. At points in the existence of a given society, one can easily imagine the nationalising domain being anti-autonomist, and even opposed to cultural nationalism.

Compared to a class-based stratification, potential roles in the nationalisation process are not as clearly defined, but more fluctuating. The nationalising domain is illustrated in Figure 2.1 below, not by the demarcation with a sharp horizontal dividing line in the cone that denotes society, but by a sphere. This is to emphasise the lack of congruence between any one class in society and the nationalising domain. It places itself in the upper part of society in terms of economic, political and cultural power, but nevertheless cuts across class borders and excludes as well as includes power holders within all areas.

The members of this domain are the carriers of a set of shared symbols and common perceptions of the nation and its others. Images created in the nationalising domain are interpreted by their recipients, but how do we know that they are interpreted the way they were intended? It is highly possible that the images and messages transmitted by actors in the nationalising domain are in general understood somewhat differently than intended. However, another important point to make is that *negotiation* takes place. If the time span investigated was short, there would be no guarantees that the transmitted images were understood in the way they were meant to be understood – that any widespread agreement existed. However, as image-building is not entirely a top-down process – the images mediated to society outside the nationalising domain are constantly being returned and adjusted, either to suit demands, or to

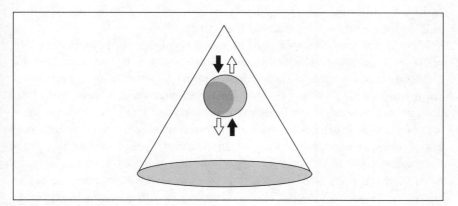

Figure 2.1: The nationalising domain

better persuade the recipients of the validity of formerly transmitted images – if the time span is long enough, such nonalignment will be significantly reduced. What is thus achieved over the long term is consensus or, in other words, the hegemony of discourses.

SPECIFIC GROUPS OF ACTORS

It would be foolish to argue that a conclusive definition of the nationalising domain, including a full account of the social actors who comprise it, can be given. Although many general characteristics are usually the same, different political nationalist movements have different points of departure, and follow different routes with emphases placed differently. This section includes a discussion of which actors can be seen as relevant in relation to the analysis of images of self and other in changing national discourses in Scotland and Newfoundland.

Intellectuals

The list of theorists who name intellectuals as one of the most influential groups in nation-building processes (be it in both phases A and B or only in phase A) is long.[45] Still, most of these theorists have not concerned themselves with the study of recent processes in stateless nations in liberal democracies. It can therefore with relevance be argued that the role of intellectuals in contemporary nationalist movements still needs to be established.

What is meant by 'intellectuals'? Many different meanings and definitions can be found or constructed, and it would serve no purpose to discuss various definitions at length. A useful definition of intellectuals would resemble Smith's. He defines them broadly as poets, musicians, painters, sculptors, novelists, historians and archaeologists, playwrights, philologists, anthropologists and folklorists.[46]

Øyvind Østerud suggests that the strong position of intellectuals in phase A of national identity-building processes may be explained by the fact that national mobilisation occurs mainly in times of social upheaval and identity crisis. He argues that the intellectuals are, almost by definition, placed with a leg in both the traditional and the modern worlds – in a perfect position from which to function as mediators of tradition.[47] The theory carries some weight. Intellectuals presumably, *qua* their professional interests, keep a finger on the pulse of folk or popular culture, while they also, *qua* their professional position, have access to avant-garde developments. This situation has not changed much from the age of classic nationalism until today. Being an ideological movement, nationalism needs intellectuals to formulate and propound the idea in a way which can garner widespread acceptance and support. Such a task takes a highly developed set of skills, which, generally speaking, intellectuals tend to possess. In relation to nationalism in modern and post-modern liberal democracies it must be questioned, though, whether intellectuals alone can be said to possess these skills. In a late study, Smith has wisely extended the group of actors able to exercise such skills: 'Intellectuals and *intelligentsia* know how to present the nationalist ideal of autoemancipation through citizenship so that all classes will, in principle, come to understand the benefits of solidarity and participation. Only they can provide the social and cultural links with other strata.'[48]

In his definition Smith includes some, but far from all, academics. Interestingly he decides to include historians, philologists, anthropologists and folklorists, while excluding sociologists and political scientists. This is not a wise exclusion, as these groups of academics often have direct influence on politicians and media because they function as 'experts' in conventions, think-tanks, news reports, etc. In short, they can be highly influential in determining which discourse should be hegemonic. In relation to Scotland and Newfoundland in particular, this would appear to be the case. Experts for local government commissions and advisory boards, for instance, are recruited mainly from within these disciplines. Experts interviewed by local television, and thus given a platform for expressing opinions exactly about issues of autonomy, political, economic and even cultural distinctness directly to the public, come largely from the same group. Historians seem to be well-represented in this category as well. Another sub-group within the larger group of intellectuals who reach out to a considerable number of people are novelists and, increasingly, certain categories of bloggers.

Political actors

Hroch rightly abstains from considering democratically elected politicians as actors in some of the classic processes of nation-building that he describes – for the simple reason that generally they did not exist. But in contemporary societies which are part of a liberal democratic tradition – such as Scotland and Newfoundland – they should be considered very important actors indeed. The scholar who has argued most strongly in favour of taking politics as the point of departure in researching any kind of nationalism is John Breuilly. In his *Nationalism and the State* (1995) he holds that nationalism should be understood as a form of politics, and that its development can only be understood by considering it as closely associated with the state.[49] With this as his principal argument, Breuilly dismisses the common assumption that 'nationalism arises ultimately from some sort of national identity or that it is the search for such an identity'.[50] This, however, does not mean that he also dismisses ethnicity – or culture, class, and social and economic issues for that matter – as irrelevant factors in particular nationalist movements. His argument is that all nationalist movements, or rather, nationalism as a generic concept, is 'above and beyond all else, about politics and that politics is about power'.[51] Since Breuilly sees power, in the modern world, as being principally a question of control of the state, his conclusion is that the objective of nationalists is to obtain and use state power. According to Breuilly, then, nationalism is nothing but an instrument by which to mobilise the masses and attain political power.

A natural consequence of emphasising the political aspects of nationalism is that a great deal of importance must be ascribed to those who exercise politics: the politicians. Defining the role of politicians in the process of mobilising the population for a political cause, Breuilly writes: 'One can identify various general changes which make it possible or necessary for politicians to forge links with large parts of the population . . . These processes I will call mobilisation . . . Nationalism is one way of coping politically with this mobilisation.'[52] He also argues that intellectuals and professionals, because of their position in society – they are more vulnerable to radical changes in the political power set-up – and their communicative and organisational skills, are those who are most likely to become political leaders.[53]

Political parties and pressure groups are in the business of persuading the voters, the media and other politicians that a certain view of the world is correct. In the process of doing this, images of every kind of self and other, including those which make up national identity, are constantly produced and put forward in an attempt to woo support. Moreover, political parties are able to set the agenda of debates which they find it worthwhile to discuss. This is what Calhoun suggests when he says: 'Political parties do act as identity formulators by defining issues and aligning with other parties.'[54]

To be sure, political parties are also splendid 'seismographs', indicating predominant moods outside the political sphere: if a certain policy is seen to fail to attract voters, a party manifesto can often be seen to change accordingly, in the hope of securing a larger share of the popular vote. As a part of the political game, politicians must, as Michael Billig points out in his *Banal Nationalism* (1995), claim to speak for the nation or the people, as well as to them.[55] Billig's study is concerned with nation-state nationalism only, but nothing indicates that the same would not apply in regard to stateless nations as well.

Billig too places much emphasis on the role of politicians, but, unlike Breuilly, also argues that although 'political discourse is important in the daily reproduction of nations', this is not because politicians are necessarily 'figures of great influence'.[56] Politicians are important, he argues, because they are familiar faces who, through the media, have the power to invoke national identity. Hence, politicians are powerful projectors of images of self and other: not necessarily through powerful nationalist rhetoric, which may risk alienating existing and potential popular support, but through the continued subtle stressing and naturalisation of new and older images. Billig makes the useful observation that 'unmemorable clichés and habits of political discourse are worth attention because of, not despite, their rhetorical dullness'.[57]

The only group allowed to appear as frequently as intellectuals in the media to express their opinion on the national state of affairs are politicians, and as Arthur Siegel has shown, media and politics are intertwined to a degree that what is emphasised in the one group is immediately reacted to in the other.[58] The following section will consider the importance of media in the production and dissemination of images of self and other, and thus in the analysis of national identity-building processes.

Media actors

Ernest Gellner writes of national high cultures, using an organic metaphor: 'Industrial man . . . lives in specially bounded and constructed units, a kind of giant aquarium or breathing chamber. But these chambers need to be erected and serviced . . . It requires a specialized plant. The name for this plant is a national educational and communications system.'[59] Smith agrees: 'Nations must have a measure of common culture and a civic ideology, a set of common understandings and aspirations, sentiments and ideas, that bind the population together in their homeland. The task of ensuring a common public, mass culture has been handed over to the agencies of popular socialization, notably the public system of education and the mass media.'[60]

Although such statements immediately ring true, it is important to keep in mind that influencing or maintaining attitudes is not a straightforward task, and certainly not entirely a top-down process, as these excerpts would seem to imply. Before simply accepting the immense impact and importance of media with respect to nationalism and national identity-building processes, it may be useful to consult research that has been done on the influence of media in socialisation processes as such.

The results of an extensive analysis of the 1984 Canadian federal election carried out by Wagenberg et al. concluded: 'Election campaigners have two not entirely distinct targets: the *public* is of course the ultimate target, but the *media* are the necessary and immediate one.'[61] The impact of media on long-term socialisation processes will be altogether more difficult to prove, but a few scholars have persuasively rendered it probable.

In 1976 Robin McCron, one of the pioneers in the field, concluded in his overview of the study of mass media and socialisation: 'There is, then, considerable evidence that the mass media can selectively fashion images of society which are at best partial . . . It is obvious that socialisation is a basic feature of social life . . . It is also clear that mass media have an important role to play in socialisation.'[62] The validity of these and similar theses soon became generally accepted, and in 1980 Stuart Hall in *Culture, Media, Language* explained the view of media that lay behind media studies at the Centre for Contemporary Cultural Studies in Birmingham thus: 'Our approach defined the media as a major cultural and ideological force, standing in a dominant position with respect to the way in which social relations and political problems were defined and the production and transformation of popular ideologies in the audience addressed.'[63] According to this argument, the media are in a position to shape the beliefs and values of its audiences. George Gerbner explains why this is so, when he points out that, even if socialisation involves an active selection of images, tastes and views by the individual, he/she is unlikely to select those which have not been made available to him/her.[64] The media are in a position to provide, and just as importantly, to *not* provide, a certain collection of images and values to choose from.

Although the audience are not *tabula rasa* – the media can not actually tell people what to think – the media are often successful in telling people what to think *about*. It is a long way from setting the agenda to thought control, but the power to influence what people should debate over the dinner table makes the media, taken as a whole, a very powerful national identity-building actor.

Gerbner also makes a useful interpretation of the importance of knowledge becoming *public* knowledge – and thus of the nature of mass communication with regard to identity formation. Touching upon elements which also lie behind Benedict Anderson's idea of the imagined community, he says: 'As a quality of information, the awareness that a certain item of knowledge is publicly held (i.e. not only known to many, but commonly known that it is known to many) makes collective thought and action possible. Such knowledge gives individuals their awareness of collective strength (or weakness), and a feeling of social identification or alienation . . . Publication is thus the instrument of community consciousness and of governance among large groups of people too numerous or too dispersed to interact face to face.'[65]

The political power of the media can thus be argued to stem from both agenda setting (because the media do not transmit all the news they collect, they in fact hold the power to decide what should be publicly known and debated), and their influence on political actors (politicians are very much aware of the power of the media, and act accordingly by, for example, nurturing a certain image and sending up 'test balloons' before making public statements). Still, although agenda setting and influence on politicians should be considered very real features of the relationship between the media and society as such, the power they exercise is by no means absolute. As contended by Gerbner, the analysis of media discourse can not substitute the study of policies and effects,[66] but it can function as an invaluable source of information not obtainable elsewhere.

Benedict Anderson argues convincingly in *Imagined Communities* (1983) that without the advent of modern media there could have been no idea of the nation nor of nationalism. Other important factors played a part, but the invention of the printing press – and the use made of it by capitalist entrepreneurs – provided the essential invention and spread of vernaculars without which the use of Latin, with all its impli-cations, would have remained dominant. This would have rendered it extremely difficult for future co-nationals to think of each other as belonging to the same ethnic or 'imagined' community.[67]

Strangely, Anderson never refers to Marshall McLuhan, the Canadian communications philosopher who, two decades before, had brought up many of the same ideas in his *Understanding Media* (1964). McLuhan too pointed to the changing apprehension of time and history and the ensuing secularisation of the world – both consequences of typography and thus the capability of reproducing books *en masse* – as the major preconditions of the emergence of nationalism.[68] He also noticed the same coalition between capitalism and printing that Anderson refers to as 'print-capitalism': 'In the Renaissance it was the speed of print and the ensuing market and commercial developments that made nation-alism . . . as natural as it was new.'[69] He even spoke, although in different words, about the 'print-languages', which Anderson sees as having laid the bases for the development of early national conscious-ness *qua* their fixedness, their place between Latin and the spoken vernacular, and in some cases their status as 'languages-of-power'.[70] McLuhan said: 'The psychic and social consequences of print included

an extension of its fissile and uniform character to the gradual homog-
enization of diverse regions with the resulting amplification of power,
energy, and aggression that we associate with new nationalisms . . .
Another significant aspect of the uniformity and repeatability of the
printed page was the pressure it exerted toward "correct" spelling,
syntax, and pronunciation . . . Nationalism was unknown to the
Western world until the Renaissance, when Gutenberg made it possible
to see the mother tongue in uniform dress.'[71]

Anderson is generally credited with this theory of print-capitalism as *the*
most significant precondition of the emergence of nationalism, but clearly
he was not the first to think along these lines. In any case, Anderson's and
McLuhan's theses are highly plausible, especially when one considers the
fact that most nation-building processes take place on a large scale.

If we accept that the media exert a high degree of influence on socialisation processes as such, can we then confidently assume correspon-
dence between the values and perceptions of the media and of the
people who make up the audience? Almost without exception the media
claim to serve public interest, to be the 'voice of the people' and often
also their 'champion': compare the major Scottish newspaper *The
Herald*'s claim to have 'served the people of Scotland for more than
200 years', the *Scottish Sun*'s slogan, 'Dedicated to the People of
Scotland', and the major Newfoundland newspaper *The Telegram*'s
view of itself as 'the people's newspaper'.[72] As a consequence, what is
expressed in certain media is often considered to be public opinion.

At times, however, the opinions transmitted are seen by a particular
paper or TV station as what *ought* to be public opinion, and the task of
the medium itself may therefore be to influence public opinion to become
what it should preferably be, rather than simply convey it. Hence, due to
editorial views, nationalists can not expect even 'national', i.e. local,
media to back up their claims *a priori*. The purpose of this book is not
merely to investigate cases where political nationalism has clearly been
developing, but also a case where it can be seen to have, at least momen-
tarily, disappeared. Therefore, other important processes will be those of
nation-state or union-state-building, which also take place in the media.
Competing national discourses exist, and some may stress the benefits
and superiority of Canadian or British national identity. According to
Siegel, 'mass media play a central role in Canada's struggle to build a
nation and to develop an identity of its own. To this end, they can be
vehicles for bonding the nation or instruments of fragmentation.'[73] This,
surely, would also be the case in the UK.

Limiting the analysis to the media which, in the period studied in this
book, reached most effectively into all parts of society, and thus can be

argued to have been most influential, the field immediately limits itself
to newspapers, television and radio.

In the investigated time span, radio was neither the generally preferred,
nor the most influential, medium – although it can certainly be said to
have been so in earlier periods of history.[74] A Canadian Radio-television
and Telecommunications Commission (CRTC) survey in 1975, for
instance, showed that only 25 per cent of Canadians relied on radio
for news, as opposed to the 36 per cent who preferred television and the
39 per cent preferring newspapers/magazines.[75] Television has changed
considerably from being largely a medium for entertainment to being
also a much relied-on source of news information. However, only one
medium can be said to have remained to the fore during the entire period
analysed here, providing in the case of both Scotland and Newfoundland
a more obvious actor for investigation. Although newspapers, with the
development of television, no longer reign supreme in the mass media,[76]
this does not change the fact that they still set the agenda. Whereas the
Canadian and British public rely mostly on the electronic media for their
news and information, the electronic media in their turn rely on the
press for their sources. As a result of the fact that they get most of their
information from the newspapers' news services, the broadcast media
are dependent on these as their major reference point as to what is
newsworthy. This is supported by the fact that the media always seem to
be in total consensus as to what constitutes newsworthy events. This may
be a situation which is rapidly changing with the new emphasis placed
on not only news reporting but also the newsgathering that major TV
news stations such as BBC World and CNN have introduced. It remains
the case, however, that in the period considered in this study, newspapers
remained the more important medium in terms of setting agendas and
providing information and views.

McLuhan acknowledges another important aspect of the newspaper–reader relationship, when in passing he mentions that the owners
of the media are in a sense the victims of the audience, and must be
constantly aware of what the public *wants*. The owners, he says, 'sense
that their power is in the *medium* and not in the *message* or the
program'.[77] MacInnes points out that 'as well as selling stories to
readers, newspapers sell readers to advertisers'.[78] To be sure, politicians
and the media alike exist only because they have an audience of voters,
listeners, viewers, readers, etc. The audience possesses the power of
economic and political support, which can be withheld in case of significant disagreement. Again it should be emphasised that socialisation and
the forming of public opinion should be seen both as a top-down and a
bottom-up process, and one reason is the power that a democratic free

market society bestows on the receiving public. Neither newspapers nor any other medium can decide public opinion, but this does not make the analysis of images of self and other in newspapers less interesting. Quite the contrary. It emphasises the fact that newspapers both make up perceptions and reflect them. The analysis of newspapers can therefore be seen as doubly important.

The press in Scotland and Newfoundland

Sevaldsen and Vadmand argue that, traditionally: 'British media is . . . the forum of analysis and criticism of contemporary society, following the ideals of the press as "the fourth estate".'[79] In the case of Scotland specifically, according to Maurice Smith, the major newspapers 'play a key role in shaping public opinion, as well as reflecting it'.[80] Smith illustrates his point by relating the story of the failed attempt by the Scottish Conservative Party to acquire the *Glasgow Herald* after the disastrous 1987 election. He says of the affair: 'If nothing else, that underlines the distinct powers enjoyed by the press in Scotland. . ., and how highly those powers are valued – possibly to the point of exaggeration – by the political establishment.'[81]

It must be considered important also that the Scots read more newspapers than do people in the rest of Britain. In 1990 Scots were thus 20.5 per cent more likely to pick up a daily newspaper than people in the rest of the UK.[82] When this is considered together with the fact that Britons rank number one in Europe with regard to the percentage of the population regularly engaged in reading newspapers, and the fact that the Scots read almost entirely Scottish newspapers,[83] this would seem to emphasise the relevance of including local newspapers in our analysis of the Scottish case.

Still, circulation numbers in themselves are not all-important. What is important is the real *influence* of the paper in shaping public opinion, which can not be measured simply by circulation. The most important fact to note with regard to Scottish papers is thus, argue Meech and Kilborn, the 'entrenched position of papers produced in Scotland, which owes much to the local loyalties and national consciousness of their readers'.[84] Siegel uses the Quebec (nationalist) newspaper *Le Devoir* with a 1981 circulation of only 42,482 as another fine example of this.[85] Many other examples of both newspapers with more influence than the size of their readership would seem to suggest can be procured. Such papers are often considered 'intellectual' and are read and referenced in influential social circles and often quoted by other media. Likewise, some newspapers in Scotland would seem to be important in setting agendas

2 National Identity-Building 35

and in influencing decision makers. An indication of this would be the strength with which the presiding officer of the re-established Scottish parliament, Sir David Steel, hit out at this particular part of the Scottish media after a period of 'bad press' for the parliament.[86] It serves to illustrate the immense importance that Scottish politicians still ascribe to newspapers.

Judging from circulation figures alone, Newfoundland newspapers with a circulation per household of almost half the Canadian average (38 copies as opposed to 67 per 100 households)[87] would seem to be of little importance in influencing publicly held images of self and other. Some parameters, however, modify this perception of the relevance of the Newfoundland press. Newfoundland newspapers are players on a very small media scene. Apart from newspapers, the local media in Newfoundland (in 2006) were made up of a few magazines – such as the *Downhomer* and the *Newfoundland Herald* – two quasi-local TV stations, and three radio stations – CBC Newfoundland and Labrador, VOCM ('Voice of the Common Man') and OZ-FM. Newspapers are therefore likely to be much more influential with regard to providing Newfoundlanders with information and views of both local and other events than circulation figures would seem to indicate. Consequently, the media situation in the province renders newspapers a highly relevant medium to local politicians when it comes to desseminating political messages, as well as to others who need to communicate their views to the public.

In a study of this kind one should take care to achieve an appropriate balance between papers influential in terms of being heeded by intellectuals, politicians and academics, and papers with a reasonably high popular appeal and impact on people outside what has been termed the nationalising domain. Also, the papers should have a certain measure of consistency and seriousness in their editorial line. In the case of Scotland, the two local dailies which, in the period studied here, can best be considered to fulfil these criteria were the *Scotsman* and the *(Glasgow) Herald*.[88] Although the two broadsheet papers circulated mostly in their respective regions, Edinburgh and Glasgow, they came closest to what in the case of Scotland can be described as 'national' and 'quality' at the same time. In combination they provided, argue Meech and Kilborn, 'the principal forum for serious debate of Scottish public affairs'.[89]

From the beginning of the period to the late 1970s, when Arnold Kemp took over as editor, the *Glasgow Herald* was reportedly a staunch supporter of the Conservative Party.[90] In the words of Arnold Kemp, the leader writers 'used to consult Tory central office to make sure they had the right line'.[91] The *Scotsman*, on the opposite political side, throughout this part of the period remained aligned with Labour.[92] From the late 1970s to 1994 (when the *Scotsman* was bought by the Barclay brothers, and Andrew Neil became editor), the two papers agreed in their commitment to anti-Thatcherism.

In the investigated period, Newfoundlanders too generally read Newfoundland newspapers, leaving the *Globe and Mail* – the only paper aspiring to become pan-Canadian – with a circulation in Newfoundland of only 1 per 100 households.[93] There existed in Newfoundland during the period only two newspapers that can be considered to match the criteria for selection. They were the *Evening Telegram* and the *Daily News*.[94] The nationalist weekly newspaper *The Independent*, with a circulation of 10,000 copies, would seem to be obviously relevant, but it was not founded until 2003. The *Evening Telegram* and the *Daily News*, however, were influential papers in terms of having the ear of politicians, intellectuals and other groups in the nationalising domain. The *Evening Telegram* has traditionally had the highest circulation figures of all Newfoundland papers by far,[95] but as the two have consistently taken up opposite positions on most issues, including political affiliation, the *Daily News* remained, at least until 1982, when it became a tabloid, an influential voice in Newfoundland public life.[96] Throughout the period analysed in this study, the *Evening Telegram*, published by Thomson Newspapers, would be considered supportive of the Progressive Conservative Party, both in provincial and federal terms. The *Daily News*, on the other side, self-owned during most of the period, was a supporter of the Liberal Party. When in 1984 the *Daily News* folded, the *Evening Telegram* became the only major daily printed source of information for Newfoundlanders; its influence grew – and so did its relevance with respect to this study.

TWO ACTORS NOT INCLUDED: THE EDUCATIONAL SYSTEM
AND THE CHURCH

Creating his famous link between education and nationalism, Eric J. Hobsbawm states: 'The progress of schools and universities measures that of nationalism.'[97] However, when Hobsbawm makes the close link between education and nationalism, he does this from a historical point of view (illustrating his point by the conflict between the universities of Kiel and Copenhagen in 1848 and 1864). To be sure, aspects such as keeping a language and a culture 'alive', and the memory of it vivid, are extremely important parameters in explaining the emergence of the idea of the nation and the early nationalisms. Whereas Hobsbawm's analysis is no doubt historically correct – certainly in regard to the development of Danish nationalism – nothing renders this close link a probable feature of contemporary nationalisms.

A look at the specific cases of Scotland and Newfoundland reveals that, as considerable autonomy is the unusual feature of education in both societies throughout the period investigated, education and the actors within the educational systems might indeed be seen to be important parameters to take into account in national identity-building processes here: Confederation in 1949 did not take away Newfoundland's denominational school system, and the Union of 1707 left the Scottish educational system intact. In the case of both, however, national – in the sense of Newfoundland and Scottish – material has been conspicuously absent from the curricula. The importance of educational systems in the two societies should probably be placed in the fact that, being largely autonomous, they have been serving as preservers of a distinct sense of identity; not so much through their curricula – which in most of the period investigated have been largely similar to those in the rest of Canada/the UK – but by their mere existence.

Still, applying the role of education to Hroch's model, stateless national identity-building processes in educational institutions would play an important part mainly in phase C. Focus here, however, is on phases A and B and the transition to phase C. Schools have a preserving, protecting and strengthening function mainly in relation to national identity, which makes them interesting with regard to state-maintenance discourse, but less so when it comes to autonomist discourse. In addition, the two societies do not have distinct vernaculars.[98] It follows that one of the most important functions of organised education in nation-building processes, as guardian of the indigenous language, is of minimal or no relevance in this study.

As Gopal Balakrishnan informs us, many contemporary theories stress the importance of myths and symbols in the make-up of the nation,[99] and the religious qualities of both nation and nationalism can not be denied. As Bruce Kapferer correctly says in the opening statement of his *Legends of People, Myths of State* (1988): 'Nationalism makes the political religious and places the nation above politics.'[100] But in a more specific sense, in many cases already established churches and religions have played a part in nation-building processes – as either resisting[101] or assisting them.

Elie Kedourie has described how a Western-educated Indian elite led by Pal, Ghandi and Nehru managed to utilise traditional religion in mobilising the many different ethnic groups in India in a mass nationalism.[102] The initial phases of nineteenth-century Irish nationalism took the shape of a reform movement against conservative Catholicism,[103] and included an attempt to redefine it to accommodate the new aspirations for modernisation and the revival of the culture of the *Gaeltacht*. The same can be said to have been the case in Quebec in the 1960s, where a similar confrontation between old and new values, *La Revolution Tranquille*, took place and indicated the birth of Quebec nationalism. Hans Hauge has illustrated how Danish nationalism owes a great deal to the Danish version of Protestantism for functioning as a midwife and later a vehicle – just as the Church in turn owes its survival to nationalism.[104] Indeed, history provides many examples of church- or religion-based nationalisms.

The particular case of Danish nationalism may serve as a fine illustration of how nationalism via a useful marriage achieves its status of pseudo- or *ersatz*-religion in classic nation-building processes. However, it must be questioned whether such an alliance is of importance in many contemporary political nationalist movements in liberal democracies – many of which appear to be characterised by an emphasis on rationality and a denouncement of the spiritual. In addition, it could be argued that, as is the case with the educational system, the Church only really becomes important when, after a successful nationalist struggle for independence or autonomy, it is turned into a national (people's) Church to nurture what Michael Billig has dubbed 'banal nationalism'.[105]

As regards the two specific case studies, Gordon Rothney has suggested that with respect to Newfoundland, 'because of the geographical distribution of the denominations, political regionalism has at times produced a superficial appearance of sectarianism. But party politics in Newfoundland have never really been concerned with matters of religious doctrine or morality.'[106] As will be illustrated further on, historically, religion has been an important identity-building factor in Newfoundland. Yet, at least since Confederation, this has not been the case. Ralph Matthews has argued that the 1971 provincial election was decided on religious grounds.[107] However, he never succeeds in explaining why religion then suddenly became of so little importance in the 1972 election, where a landslide victory gave the Conservatives 20 of the 28 traditionally Protestant seats. On the contrary, he ends up supporting what Rothney indicated when he declared that 'despite a return of the traditional religious division, "urbanism is now the main force in Newfoundland politics" '.[108] Also Sid Noel, who at one point singled out religion and the debate over Confederation as 'the two most ... potent factors in Newfoundland politics',[109] in his *Politics in Newfoundland* (1971), acknowledged 'the growing secularization of Newfoundland society generally'.[110]

Although historically of some importance, religion in Scotland did not become as contentious an issue as in Newfoundland. Harvie argues:

'Religion had never been the opium of the Scottish masses. The politics of the Kirk . . . were run by a male elite, and in the 1960s they were steadily losing their grip.'[111] The shift no doubt did occur, but the Church of Scotland has nevertheless remained a player on the political scene. Writes Graham Walker: 'The level of support accorded by the Church to home rule has underscored its importance as a symbol of Scottish national identity and its willingness to act as such.'[112] After the union in 1707 the Scottish Church remained intact and thus came to function as a reservoir for national identity, simply by being different from other British churches. However, as a reservoir for the production and utilisation of images of self and other, the Kirk has become a less important national identity-building player than many others in Scotland.

THREE

Scotland and Newfoundland
in Comparison

This chapter will explain the relevance of comparing Scottish and Newfoundland experiences with regard to the development of political nationalism by outlining important similarities and differences. Both societies are physically placed on the 'periphery' in the Western world, and share a great deal of social, cultural and geographical similarities. Yet, admittedly, the choice of case studies is not an obvious one.

It might be argued that whereas the Scottish case lends itself easily to a study of nationalism, the Newfoundland case is more dubious. Nevertheless, justifications for using Newfoundland as a case study of nationalism are numerous. It is tempting to consider Newfoundland simply as a province or a region, and any movement for increased recognition or power thus an expression of provincialism or regionalism. But as will be illustrated further on in the book, Newfoundlanders must indeed be considered to have developed a fully fledged sense of Newfoundland nationhood in the period leading up to 1949 and Confederation with Canada. It is nearly impossible to imagine such a powerful national identity having completely and suddenly evaporated in the post-Confederation period studied here. Newfoundland national identity developed parallel to, and quite differently from, that of other Canadian national identities. We should not deny Newfoundland its recent history of nationalism and national identity, and the proper interpretation of it, just because the former dominion became part of a large federal state little more than sixty years ago.

Another scholar studying national identity has considered Scotland and Newfoundland in comparison. Anthony P. Cohen has discussed how Scotland compares with Catalonia and Quebec – the preferred case studies in such comparative analyses. His conclusion goes: 'In formal terms, the similarities among the nationalist politics of these three societies are strictly limited. After all, Scotland was a sovereign nation until 1707. The language issue which looms so large in Quebec, and which underpins Catalan distinctiveness, is much less obvious in

Scotland. Both Spain and Canada have been less centralised states than Britain, and have long and now-established traditions of governmental devolution.'¹

Cohen thus correctly points out that both differences in language and constitutional experiences are aspects which constitute serious impediments to a direct comparative analysis of these societies – albeit they do not render comparisons impossible. Cohen, however, regards the similarities between Newfoundland and Scotland as more obvious: 'Formerly self-governing states, Newfoundland and Scotland are alike in having surrendered their sovereignty to larger powers . . . [B]oth are geographically peripheral to the states in which they now nest (and Newfoundland remains economically and politically peripheral to Canada) . . . [T]hey are alike in having retained a very strong sense of and commitment to their differences from their metropolitan neighbours.'²

Cohen's list of relevant similarities thus includes: constitutional history, various kinds of peripherality, and a strong sense of community identity. Although these similarities would seem to speak in favour of a direct comparison on most points, Cohen does not pretend that such a comparison can be made uncritically. Several differences exist, which must also be taken into account. He notes: 'Apart from the loss of statehood, the histories, cultures and social structures of Newfoundland and Scotland differ significantly.'³ Both societies find themselves in the same climate in the northern part of the Western Hemisphere and can be characterised, to use a very general term, as anglophone cultures. But Cohen is right: obvious differences also exist between Newfoundland and Scotland. Demographically, the population of Scotland (5.1 million) is ten times that of Newfoundland (510,000 in 2010) and although the world of nationalism is one where 'size doesn't matter',⁴ this complicates a direct comparison. In Scotland, for example, there are two major cities, each with more people than inhabit the entire province of Newfoundland and Labrador. Even though exposure to external economic influences and rapid industrialisation has resulted in altered social structures and large-scale urbanisation in Newfoundland, Scotland – having developed over the past two centuries from small-scale industry via heavy industry to high technology industry – remains a more industrialised and urbanised society. It is also important to keep in mind one of the arguments that Cohen introduced in explaining the lack of similarities between the situations in which Scotland and Quebec find themselves. He argued that Canada in some ways is a less centralised state than the UK. This, naturally, impacts on the comparative analysis of Scotland and Newfoundland too. Constitutionally, the major difference is the fact that until recently Scotland did not have its own parliament – and thus no devolved legislative or fiscal powers whatsoever. Newfoundland (as in the case of Quebec) has enjoyed limited powers in these respects throughout its history as a Canadian province. These and other differences should be taken into account when comparing the two societies.

There are, as Cohen points out, also many similarities which make the Newfoundland–Scotland comparison interesting and useful with respect to studying national identity and political nationalism. He unfortunately does not discuss these similarities at length, but his brief list has served as inspiration in the following more extensive investigation.

MARRIAGES OF CONVENIENCE, NOT OF LOVE:
CONSTITUTIONAL HISTORIES

Whereas nationalist movements are often fuelled by emotional demands for 'natural' self-determination, the reverse would seem to have been the case when Scotland and Newfoundland gave up sovereignty in 1707 and 1934/1949, respectively.[5] In both cases, surrendering independence was a pragmatic or, some would argue, necessary response to a critical social and economic situation; in other words, *Realpolitik*. Scotland was virtually bankrupt after losing about a quarter of the country's combined assets in an unfortunate attempt to establish a colony in what is today Panama, and the country was therefore in dire need of immediate financial injections. England wished mainly to secure its 'back door' from invasion and definitively put a stop to the traditional connection between Scotland and France – the so-called 'Auld Alliance'. Westminster therefore offered to assume Scottish debts and reopen both the English market and overseas markets to Scottish trade in return for union. It was an offer the Scottish parliament could, or would, not refuse, and it voted itself out of existence. The contractual nature of the union at this point is clear.

This early eighteenth-century situation resembles Newfoundland's situation in the early 1930s, when the Newfoundland Assembly, led by Prime Minister Alderdice, voted to suspend responsible government, surrender dominion status (enjoyed since 1907) and place Newfoundland under administration by a Commission of Government appointed by Westminster. It also, to a lesser extent, resembles the situation of Newfoundland in the early post-World War II period. In 1948, Ottawa offered, in return for Newfoundland joining the Federation, to assume Newfoundland's debts and provide the framework for future prosperity, both in the form of a greater market and the introduction of the welfare state. Gerald M. Sider believes the primary reasons for Newfoundland's support for Confederation with Canada were socio-economic: 'When Newfoundlanders voted to renounce independence and confederate with Canada, they were doing more than abandoning a country that had done little for them; they were voting for – as they were repeatedly promised by Joey Smallwood, and as the terms of union guaranteed – a variety of transfer payments from Canada to Newfoundland families: "baby bonuses", old-age pensions, the possibility of unemployment insurance for fishermen . . . and so forth.'[6] Both pro- and anti-confederate historians confirm that this was the perception among a majority of Newfoundlanders.[7] As was the case in Scotland, this was a question of a golden offer of union, and as many found it hard to resist, 'Newfoundland . . . joined Canada for pragmatic reasons'.[8]

Daniel Defoe, Westminster's secret agent in Edinburgh during the 1706–7 negotiations of the Act of Union, reported that most of the Scots were actually fiercely opposed to entering the United Kingdom of Great Britain, and one of the commissioners relayed how the articles had been carried 'contrary to the inclinations of at least three-fourths of the Kingdom'.[9] Without making any direct comparison, it must be questioned whether many of the 52 per cent who voted to join Canada in 1948 did so out of affection for the mainland. Rather, pro-confederate Newfoundlanders at the time would have been looking, pragmatically, to the immediate and long-term benefits which Confederation promised to deliver. Thus, it may well be argued that both acts of union were 'marriages of convenience',[10] not of love.

Differences also exist between the two acts of union in 1707 and 1949, most notably in terms of the level of democracy involved and the very different historical contexts in which they occurred.[11] It remains the case, nevertheless, that the 'loveless' circumstances under which Newfoundland and Scotland made their respective unions are important, not so much historically, as because they provide all the necessary arguments for proto-nationalists to further the development of a political nationalist movement. If the perception remains that the union of which one's nation is part was joined out of necessity or simply because it was beneficial at the time, there is little emotional incentive to remain within the union if the relative social and economic benefits of union are seen to have disappeared. Scottish nationalists today can agree with national poet Robert Burns, who wrote of the Act of Union:

> What force or guile could not subdue,
> Thro' many warlike ages,
> Is wrought now by a coward few,
> For hireling traitor's wages.

The English steel we could disdain,
Secure in valour's station;
But English gold has been our bane –
Such a parcel of rogues in a nation!
                    Robert Burns, 'Such a Parcel of
                                Rogues in a Nation'

Present-day nationalists are likely to find the thought equally uncomfortable, but nevertheless more useful than Burns did.

Before moving on to a discussion of socio-economic circumstances and histories, a difference of constitutional experience essential to this study should be considered. Newfoundland became a part of a newly born Confederation of provinces, each with a relatively high degree of autonomy. Scotland, on the other hand, was an old kingdom now being absorbed into the early British empire. Although Scotland for a period of almost one hundred years was left largely to govern itself, the country later became subject to very strong London-based governance, carried out mainly by English MPs with no intention of devolving powers to the smaller regions of the UK. This means there has been a great difference in terms of the democratic influence exercised by Scots and Newfoundlanders as a consequence of the constitutional set-ups of their respective states.

IN BED WITH ELEPHANTS: SOCIO-ECONOMICS AND POLITICS

As regards the socio-economic and political experiences of Scotland and Newfoundland within their respective unions, it would appear that here, too, the two societies share somewhat similar experiences. Historically, Scotland has reaped many benefits from being part of a British empire 'ruling the waves'.[12] Still, until recently, Scotland remained England's poor cousin. In the 1950s and 1960s, growing emigration and an increasing percentage of Scottish families living in council or state housing testified to this. Forty-two per cent of Scottish households in 1961 rented public authority housing, 51 per cent in 1971.[13] This was twice the proportion in England. In the 1960s and 1970s, the quality of housing remained a major problem in Scotland. The 1967 Cullingworth Report found that 'one in three persons lives in a house considered either substandard or unfit for human habitation'.[14] Primary and secondary sectors of Scottish industry (fisheries, steel production, mining, ship-building, textiles), which used to provide work and prosperity, were severely hit by long-term economic decline after World War II, culminating in the symbolic closing down of the Ravenscraig steelworks in 1992. Consequently, the 1970s and 1980s in particular were characterised by massive layoffs, urban decay and generally low standards of living, especially compared to the southernmost parts of the UK. In January 1979, the Scottish unemployment rate of 8.7 per cent was 2.7 per cent above the UK average; in 1983, the Scottish rate of 12.3 per cent was 1.8 per cent higher; and in 1989, although the Scottish rate had decreased considerably to 9.3 per cent, the gap had widened to 3.0 per cent.[15] As in the 1970s, the 1980s was a decade which 'economically, Scotland could have done without'.[16]

Although Scottish economy was, in historian Gordon Donaldson's words, 'heading for disaster',[17] the desperate socio-economic situation has been gradually changing in the last couple of decades. The oil industry is providing some activity in related areas; the production and export of whisky has been constantly increasing, as has the number of tourists contributing to an industry in explosive growth; and much hope is vested in the development of other secondary- and tertiary-sector businesses: electronic industries in 'Silicon Glen', banking, insurance and engineering. Since 1992, unemployment rates in Scotland have resembled the British average – even if certain parts of England can still boast unemployment rates which are 2 per cent below the Scottish rate – and the Scottish gross domestic product per capita is higher than anywhere else in the United Kingdom, except London and the eastern regions of England. In addition, the percentage of Scottish households renting from local or state authorities declined from 54 per cent in 1979 to 39 per cent in 1991.[18]

Nonetheless, the recollection of a not too distant past characterised by industrial decline and massive redundancy keeps the Scots focused along what can be termed 'post-Keynesian' lines: state involvement in social welfare and the creation of jobs are regarded as very important issues which ought to be prioritised. In spite of the fact that oil and gas have been discovered in the North Sea off the coast of Scotland, this part of the UK is still considered dependent on state subsidies. In the 1997–8 fiscal year, the block grant received by Scotland was £14 billion,[19] calculated on the basis of the 'Barnett' formula (a financial tool used by the British Treasury to allocate public expenditure in parts of Britain outside England, based on population figures), while the amount that Scotland itself contributed to the UK remained highly disputed.

The consequence of decades of existing as a socio-economic laggard is a deeply rooted distrust among many Scots towards the capability or willingness of Westminster politicians to deal properly with Scotland's economic and social problems. This is a feeling which was stressed during eighteen years of Conservative rule (from 1979 to 1997), under which Scottish heavy industry and mining became nearly extinct. As only administrative powers were devolved to Scotland before 1999, it has seemed to Scots that all important decisions directly affecting their lives have been made in Westminster, most often by politicians elected not in Scottish, but in English, constituencies. It is against this background that many Scots find that they have, particularly during the last few decades of the twentieth century, been 'in bed with an elephant'.[20] This is a feeling which is also recorded by Anthony P. Cohen and which, he argues, also characterises Newfoundland's perception of central government: 'One would have little difficulty in finding among Newfoundlanders and Scots a sense of their domination by an alien government which they are legally and constitutionally powerless to resist.'[21]

Cohen's assertion appears to be correct. For the past three or four decades there has existed among Newfoundlanders a widespread sense of mismanagement and indifference to the province's needs on the part of changing federal governments in Ottawa.[22] Jurisdiction in fisheries has remained the responsibility of the federal Department of Fisheries and Oceans (DFO), in spite of multiple attempts by Newfoundland governments to change this situation. When in 1992 obvious flaws in the management of fish quotas led to a moratorium on cod fisheries – Newfoundland's only stable source of income and jobs throughout much of its modern history – fishermen, media and politicians in Newfoundland immediately pointed their fingers at Ottawa.[23] A long-liner skipper captured the general attitude towards Ottawa when, in a CBC interview, he asked: 'Is the government intentionally starving us, or is it just stupidity?'[24]

After an extended economic boom in the decade from the early 1960s to the early 1970s, where Canada's economic growth remained positive and unemployment was at a mere 4–6 per cent,[25] a recession set in by the mid-1970s. For the first time since 1954, Canada's economic growth became negative in 1982. Anti-inflation measures were introduced to alter Canada's economic course, but the result was increasing unemployment, and the Canadian economy entered the 'Great Recession'. Part of this recession was the crisis in the federal economy. The federal government deficit rose from $3.8 billion in 1975 to $20.3 billion in 1982,[26] and the consequence of increasingly stretched budgets was 'retrenchment on the social-policy front'.[27] In other words, federal assistance was no longer available to solve local problems to the extent that it had previously been. As was the case in the UK, the welfare state was being rolled back, and Newfoundland – even more reliant on the welfare state than Scotland – found itself in a difficult situation.

Newfoundland's economy was and is more tied up with, and dependent on, the state budget than is Scotland's. Federal equalisation payments made up an estimated 42.3 per cent of a total revenue of $3.377 billion in the Newfoundland 1999–2000 budget,[28] but just as Scotland has been catching up with England's economy, Newfoundland may now also be moving up the socio-economic ladder, albeit slowly. In this case, unemployment figures may serve as an indication of the social and economic condition of Newfoundland relative to the rest of Canada. The unemployment rate of the province dropped to 17.5 per cent in 1997, but was back at 18.6 in May 2000.[29] In comparison, unemployment rates in other Canadian provinces were 11.9 (New Brunswick), 9.4 (Nova Scotia), 8.8 (Quebec), 5.8 (Ontario), and 5.0 (Alberta).[30] The province has been struggling with high levels of out-migration, the highest food costs and the highest provincial sales tax in Canada.

In October 1999, the *Globe and Mail*'s business magazine ranked Newfoundland first with regard to economic growth, referred to Newfoundland's economy as 'the hottest provincial economy in the country', and stated: 'The Rock's on a Roll'.[31] The main reasons for the fine ranking were, according to the magazine: offshore oil, higher newsprint production and an increase in fish processing. However, progress is relative, and although 'on a roll', the 'Rock' has clearly not caught up, socio-economically, with the rest of Canada. To be sure, there has been a windfall from the rising price of oil at the turn of the century, and the unemployment rate fell. However, Newfoundland continued to be marred by large-scale out-migration caused by low wages and cuts in income support. Having remained for five decades the rest of Canada's poor cousin – the 'have-not' province *par excellence* – this has resulted in a strong focus on the need to develop new industries and jobs, and a concern by large parts of the population about the declining quality of welfare state services.

After a period of recovery in the mid- to late 1980s, Canada entered another period of economic recession beginning in 1989. Again, economic growth was negative, and unemployment increased from 8.1 per cent in 1990 to 11.3 in 1992.[32] Newfoundland in the 1990s, highly dependent on Ottawa for economic development, again experienced a Liberal federal government trying to deal with a severe fiscal crisis by cutting money transfers to all provinces – in the case of Newfoundland the announced cuts would be from $410 million in 1996 to $239 million in 2001.[33] Furthermore, the Chrétien Liberal government was seen to be causing all sorts of social and economic problems by mismanaging fish quotas, regional assistance programmes, and the TAGS fisheries adjustment programme. Still, there was no 'doomsday scenario' to be found in the region: in the 1997 federal election, the Liberal Party won four of seven seats in Newfoundland. This was a decline from the seven seats the Liberals captured in the 1993 election, but 57 per cent of Newfoundland voters still supported the governing party.

In sum, during the last three decades of the twentieth century, a marked sense of *relative* decline existed in both Scotland and Newfoundland; a decline which in some cases may have taken the actual shape of improvement, but much less so than in other parts of the state. People were not blind to the benefits of Union/Confederation, especially those benefits that used to exist, but increasingly felt sidelined with regard to socio-economic development and access to political power necessary to influence that development.

SCOTCH AND THE ROCK: CULTURAL HERITAGE AND IDENTITY

History has provided Scotland and Newfoundland with cultural traits that can not be found elsewhere, and of which Scots and Newfoundlanders are very much aware. As neither British nor Canadian governments have pursued assimilationist policies, even the lack of clearly distinctive languages has not prevented the two societies from developing strong cultural identities. Historically, the harsh social and economic realities specific to each region have shaped the cultures to mirror the hard life of fishermen, foresters, shepherds and farmers. Much of traditional art and literature in Newfoundland and Scotland depicts the roaring sea swallowing up tiny fishing boats (or, in the case of E. J. Pratt, the world's greatest ocean liner), people scraping by on bare windswept mountainsides and in outports, or people being forced to leave the land from which they can not make a living. It is not coincidental that two of the most popular contemporary pop-rock bands are named 'Runrig' (Scotland) and 'Great Big Sea' (Newfoundland).[34]

Scotland has been inhabited for at least twenty-five centuries, but although Aboriginal peoples have called Newfoundland home even longer, permanent non-Aboriginal settlement in Newfoundland only really gathered momentum in the early nineteenth century. This is bound to have had an impact on the local sense of history and, as a consequence, also on the nature of national identity. The history of 'settling' and of a society carving out its place in the wilderness is still prevalent in Newfoundland, as are recent memories of extreme poverty and poor health conditions caused by pre-Confederation underdevelopment. In Scotland, an ancient kingdom with a separate history that includes such experiences as the Wars of Independence and the Jacobite

Rebellions, historic memory is necessarily of an altogether different kind. Still, what seems to be characteristic in the collective memory of both societies is the emphasis on a relatively small community surviving *in spite* of what is thrust upon it by outside forces – be these Nature or 'the English'.

Scotland

A pronounced sense of 'self' and 'other' based on national heritage remains in modern Scotland. The separate existence of distinctly Scottish institutions, and thus a high degree of *de facto* autonomy in Scotland since 1707, partly explains why this is so.[35] The 1707 Treaty of Union ensured that such important identity-building institutions as the Church, the school system and the legal system – all of an entirely different nature than their English counterparts – remained intact. The importance of this is summed up by James G. Kellas: 'While possessing neither a government nor a parliament of its own, [Scotland] has a strong constitutional identity and a large number of political and social institutions . . . [T]hese became the transmitters of Scottish national identity from one generation to the next.'[36]

The Union of 1707 was predominantly a political union, which left other spheres of Scottish life largely intact for future generations to build a uniquely Scottish identity upon. Scotland, for example, always issued separate Scottish banknotes, and kept a separate national football team. Most importantly, a separate Scottish press was allowed to develop, and was still in the 1990s largely independent in terms of editorial lines, albeit a significant part was foreign-owned. Meech and Kilborn have found that the semi-autonomy of the Scottish media has served to produce 'their own distinctive characteristics'. This means that they 'contribute, particularly in the case of the press, to Scotland's self-perception as a nation'.[37]

In addition to all this, or perhaps as a consequence, Scottish writers, painters, playwrights, etc. have continued to occupy themselves with Scottish themes. Such works as William McIlvanney's novel *Docherty* (1975; taking place in West Scotland), George MacKay Brown's poetry (deeply inspired by the history and atmosphere of the Orkneys), Alasdair Gray's novel *Lanark* (1981; set in future Glasgow), and Irvine Welsh's novel *Trainspotting* (1993; depicting the dark sides of Edinburgh) are all examples of how internationally recognised Scottish writers write from and about Scotland. All describe life in Scotland, but their work has another feature in common: a preoccupation with the presentation of the life of the working class, and those who are socially disadvantaged.

This leads to what is claimed by many to be another important thread running through the Scottish mentality: a preference for equality, as prominently expressed in Robert Burns' 1794 song 'For A' That and A' That'. It is a sense of egalitarianism which owes a lot to the perception of Scottish Presbyterianism as more democratic than other religious doctrines.[38] Cohen maintains that 'prominent in the self-identity of Scotland is an ethos of democracy . . . and of the possibility of rising through the social hierarchy',[39] and Jonathan Hearn reports 'a long-standing belief among Scots that their society has benefited historically from higher than usual levels of literacy . . . resulting from the reformed Kirk's policy of establishing a school in every parish'.[40] One of the key features of the Scottish education system is still seen to be a somewhat wider access. As the Scottish parish school system was based on Presbyterianism, Scottish education came to be seen as essentially more egalitarian than its English counterpart, not only by Scots. In 1868, D. F. Fearon wrote in his *Report for the English Schools Inquiry* (1868): 'The average middle Scotchman has more humanity and refinement than the average middle Englishman. Education has been more diffused; riches have been less rapidly and largely accumulated . . . The same social causes, combined with the existence of a better system of primary education than any we hitherto had in England, have prevented the opening of a gulf between the middle and labouring classes.'[41]

Writing on the same subject in 1980, James G. Kellas was not convinced that the comparison would still be so favourable to the Scots.[42] In a similar vein, David McCrone has shown how in terms of class structure Scotland is little different from the rest of the UK.[43] But as McCrone acknowledges, one thing is actual structure, another is the perception of it. He refers to the conviction that Scotland is a more egalitarian country than England as a strong myth which 'no amount of counter-evidence seems to be enough to banish'.[44] The reason, he argues, is that the myth is part of Scottish identity. Indeed, to question such a myth would be to tamper with the pseudo-religion of the nation. The national myth of Scottish egalitarianism is part of the legitimisation of cultural (and political) nationalism because it distinguishes 'us' from 'them' by attributing values to the Scots which the English in particular are not believed to posses. So a sense of Scotland as the more egalitarian society remains. Gordon Donaldson, for example, argues in his *Scotland: The Shaping of a Nation* (1993): 'It is true to this day that Scotland is a more egalitarian country than England.'[45]

Another sign of the power of the myth might be the particular version of the 'tall poppy' syndrome occasionally exercised in Scotland. The expression 'I kent his faither' may be heard, representing, as Hearn describes, a somewhat defensive world view, and a distrust in those who leave the small pond to attempt to make it in a larger pool;[46] a view which is also prevalent in Kailyard literature (see Chapter 4).

Other value differences between Scotland and England have been documented by Michael Keating who in his *Nations Against the State* (1996) writes: 'Notions of class and social solidarity remain stronger [in Scotland], as do expectations of the state.'[47] In support of Keating's conclusion speak the voting patterns in the two countries. Scotland can be said to be of a more leftist disposition than England and was considered a Labour stronghold in the last half of the twentieth century. Not since 1974 has the English Labour Party received a larger share of the vote than its Scottish counterpart, and since 1974, the Scottish Conservatives have received between 15.8 and 22.2 per cent less support than the Conservative Party in England.[48]

In some respects, comparisons with other parts of the UK than England would be relevant. In this myth, however, the mirror image which appears to be of most importance is that of 'the English'. Cohen has argued that 'England seems often to lurk behind Scottishness as the source of the significant and usually dominant other'.[49] In a less diplomatic way, and stressing the importance of that particular other, Tony Dickson contends: 'To be Scottish is, to some degree, to dislike or resent the English.'[50] There is a point to Dickson's claim, but it is a point which needs modification. In England, the areas known as the North, the North West and Yorkshire, and Humberside make up a region which resembles the southern parts of Scotland closely in terms of industrialisation, demographics and socio-economics, and therefore a different image than the one held of southern parts of England is applied to this region. This is an image characterised by the 'like-us' perception, belonging to what Hedetoft referred to as the 'gradualist mode'. As regards the Scotland–Wales relationship, and to a certain extent the Scotland–Northern Ireland relationship, the same can be argued to be the case. With this and previous analyses in mind, it is more correct to argue that Scottish national identity's most signifi-cant other is not 'England' but certain parts of England, most notably the South East/London, and often, more specifically, Westminster or Whitehall.

The fact that some parts of the UK are considered more commendable than others does not mean that Scots do not make a distinction between 'Scotland' and 'Britain'. Recent surveys confirm the existence of a strong Scottish *vis-à-vis* British identity. Since 1986, at regular intervals, Scots have been asked the so-called 'Moreno question': 'We are interested to know how people living in Scotland see themselves in terms of their nationality. Which of these best reflects how you regard yourself?' The results (see Table 3.1) show that although some change has occurred in terms of the percentage of respondents who agreed with the statements, the vast majority of the sampled Scots place themselves within the first three categories.

If the Moreno question had been asked in the first half of the century, it is likely that many more would have given greater emphasis to the 'British' aspect of their identity. The decline of the British empire in the wake of World War II, however, had an impact on the sense of Britishness in Scotland. This is likely to have occurred not only in Scotland but in other parts of the UK as well. After all, national identity does not as easily lend itself to decline as to greatness. The reason why the Scots after almost three centuries as a part of the United Kingdom have not yet become assimilated into a wider British identity must be found mainly in the fact that the union was in the first place – and has continued through the centuries to be seen by Scots as – a consequence of pragmatic, mainly socio-economic concerns, not emotional or ideological attachment to England or other parts of the UK. In addition, it is likely to be of some consequence that neither cultural, legal nor religious assimilation was ever practised as a policy by Westminster. The culturally unitary state was never the goal. As will become clear later, a similar perception and situation explains the lack of Canadian identity among Newfoundlanders.

Scots thus have developed a clear sense of the Scottish 'self', and judging from conclusions reached above, the most significant others remain the *Sassenachs* (the English), and, to a lesser extent, the more distant 'Britain'.

TABLE 3.1
Scottish Identity

	1986	1991	1992	1997	2000
1. Scottish not British	39	40	19	23	32
2. More Scottish than British	30	29	40	38	28
3. Equally Scottish and British	19	21	33	27	27
4. More British than Scottish	4	3	3	4	3
5. British not Scottish	6	4	3	4	9
6. None of these	2	3	1	4	1

Sources: Brown, McCrone and Paterson, *Politics and Society in Scotland*; McCrone, 'Opinion Polls in Scotland'.

A more elusive and ill-documented source of Scottish national identity is the projection of stereotypic images of Scots by non-Scots –
particularly popular images produced by Hollywood. Mel Gibson's epic
Braveheart is a recent example, but far from the first one. When Arthur
Freed, producer of another 'historical' film on Scotland, arrived there to
scout for places in which to shoot his musical *Brigadoon*, he was sorely
disappointed – 'I went to Scotland and found nothing there that looks
like Scotland'[51] – and ended up shooting the film in Hollywood studios,
complete with cosy thatched cottages, papier-mâché bridges and flown-
in Highland cattle.

Interviewed for a TV series, *The Divided Kingdom* (1988), Scottish
filmmaker Barbara Grigor said of Scottish self-perception: 'The Scots
also seem to think that they're in *Brigadoon*. It's rather like the notion
that you *become* like your birth sign, once you know what your birth
sign *is*.'[52] In other words, as long as foreigners expect a certain type of
Scottishness to meet them when they visit Scotland, when they watch
documentaries or when they read about the country, Scots will adopt
some of these images and start acting them. This, according to Barbara
Grigor, explains the power of the romantic myth of 'tartanry' in Scottish
culture (see Chapter 4), but it may also easily explain the stamina of
other myths, such as that of egalitarianism (cf. Fearon's report above).

Newfoundland

It is very unlikely that Newfoundlanders, as Calhoun suggested in 1970,
would identify with four communities: Newfoundland, Canada, the
United States and the UK.[53] The level of identification with both the US
and the UK are, and by 1970 would have been, insignificant. But fifty
years after Newfoundland joined Canada there is still a strong sense of a
distinct Newfoundland national identity as opposed to that of Canadian
citizenship. Important to note in this respect is that Newfoundland has a
long history of *de facto* independence. With eyes fixed firmly on the UK
in the east, Newfoundland declined the offer of Confederation made to it
in 1867 by the then existing colonies about to form the Canadian federation. In historian Kenneth McNaught's interpretation, 'Newfoundland,
with the greatest sense of separate identity, resisted union until 1949'.[54] In
fact, following the economic failure of Newfoundland's two major banks
in 1894, the colony asked for renewed negotiations on Confederation,
but now the Canadians had no overwhelming desire to embrace
Newfoundland as a province.

Newfoundland therefore remained outside Canada, first as a colony of
Britain and later, from 1907 until 1934 (in which year she was placed

under administration by a commission government) as a semi-self-governing dominion.[55] In a collection of essays, Malcolm MacLeod has illustrated how security and communication links were established between Newfoundland and Canada,[56] but political and economic links remained relatively weak until 1949, and this presumably constituted an important factor in the creation of a distinct Newfoundland identity. In spite of the tendency of many (mainland) sociological and political surveyors and pollsters to categorise New Brunswick (NB), Nova Scotia (NS), Prince Edward Island (PEI) and Newfoundland under one designation as the 'Atlantic Provinces', everything suggests that there is only a weak sense of a common Atlantic Canadian identity – as opposed to a Maritime (NB, NS, PEI) identity. Also, historically there has been little willingness on the part of Newfoundland to engage in Atlantic Canadian co-operation. To be sure, when regional integration and political and economic union has been discussed, no one has ever pretended that Newfoundland would seriously consider joining.[57] A sharp distinction between the Maritimes and Atlantic Canada is constantly maintained in a region defined mainly in geographical terms.[58]

As in Scotland, this sense of a separate identity has been reinforced by the existence of more or less independent Newfoundland media, reporting Newfoundland events and expressing a Newfoundland view on Canadian and international events. Calhoun's survey of six Canadian newspapers in April 1969 indicated a distinct emphasis on local content, ranking the two most widely circulated Newfoundland papers, the *Daily News* and the *Evening Telegram*, first and second of the six in terms of frequency and emphasis placed on provincial news. Conversely, the same two papers ranked fifth and sixth in terms of the amount of Canadian news stories they carried.[59]

The institutionally forged identity, which has been argued in the case of Scotland, exists only to a limited degree in Newfoundland. A distinctive feature which remained until 1998 was the separate denominational school system confirmed as a Newfoundland right in Term 17 of the 1949 Terms of Union. By the mid-1990s, however, mounting public criticism led to a referendum in which Newfoundlanders voted the denominational school system out of existence. In the years up to and around the 1948 referendum, religion used to be an important characteristic of Newfoundland public and private life, but today it cannot be said to differ markedly from other parts of Canada, and religion does not *per se* constitute a reservoir for a sense of unique identity. The closest Newfoundland comes to a 'national sports team' is the Maple Leafs hockey club, but as it functions as a talent pool for the 'real' Maple Leafs in Toronto, the effect is more likely to reinforce a sense of being Canadian.

In terms of cultural output, on the other hand, Scotland and Newfoundland resemble each other. Much Newfoundland literature from Harold Horwood's *Tomorrow will be Sunday* (1966) to Percy Janes' *Newfoundlanders* (1981) and Wayne Johnston's *The Colony of Unrequited Dreams* (1998) has focused on particular Newfoundland themes. This preoccupation with Newfoundland culture and society was specifically prevalent in the Newfoundland cultural revival of the 1960s and 1970s, and has contributed to a sense of Newfoundland identity.

In 1981 Robert Paine noticed how 'today, the self-ascribed identity tag "Newfoundlander" . . . carries ethnic voltage. It is commonly used in distinction from "Canadian", even while professing one's Canadian membership',[60] and six years later Harry H. Hiller argued: 'The intense loyalty Newfoundlanders feel to their homeland is without parallel among English-speaking people in Canada.'[61] Identity surveys confirm this still to have been the case in the period studied here, and they even suggest that one can include French-speaking Canada in Hiller's comparison as well. In 1990 and 1994, the popular magazine *Maclean's* asked Canadians across the country whether they thought of themselves mainly as Canadian or as a resident of a particular province or region.[62] A series of flaws exists in the data-collecting method used in these surveys, most notably the lack of alternative options, but since all respondents were asked the same question, the surveys can still be used comparatively. The results, reproduced in Table 3.2, reveal striking differences between the identity patterns of Ontarians and Newfoundlanders. In brief, Newfoundlanders would appear to have felt less Canadian than other citizens of Canada, and this identity gap seems to have been widening in the four-year period.

In his 1970 study, *The National Identity of Newfoundlanders*, Calhoun concluded that 'the younger Newfoundlander has acquired his life style since Newfoundland has been part of Canada, and he has more mobility, less religious identification, and more exposure to and acceptance of the North American mass culture. The younger Newfoundlander is not exposed to the cross pressures of old and new life style which causes ambiguous identity patterns among older Newfoundlanders . . . Younger Newfoundlanders have a high potential for identifying with Canada and a decreasing potential for identifying with Newfoundland.'[63] Although such a conclusion makes logical sense – at least the potential should under such circumstances increase – the figures presented in Table 3.2 clearly indicate a different outcome than Calhoun expected.

Previous surveys have showed similar indications of the existence of a strong Newfoundland identity. The 1979 'Report of a Special Survey of Newfoundlanders' Attitudes Towards Confederation with Canada' by the

TABLE 3.2
Newfoundland Identity

Percentage identifying mainly according to province:			Percentage identifying mainly as 'Canadian':		
	1990	1994		1990	1994
Quebec	55	49	Quebec	44	45
Newfoundland	53	57	Newfoundland	47	39
P.E.I.	43	44	P.E.I.	57	50
Nova Scotia	37	27	Nova Scotia	63	69
New Brunswick	25	26	New Brunswick	75	64
Alberta	24	16	Alberta	74	74
British Columbia	17	17	British Columbia	83	76
Saskatchewan	16	7	Saskatchewan	83	82
Manitoba	15	11	Manitoba	84	77
Ontario	9	9	Ontario	90	90

Sources: Mollins, 'An Uncertain Nation', 13; Laver, 'How We Differ', 11.

Data Laboratories showed that 64.9 per cent of those asked considered themselves Newfoundlanders first, 34.2 per cent saw themselves mainly as Canadian, and 0.8 per cent defined themselves as something else.[64] In The Newfoundland 1982 Election Study', in which respondents were offered a range of five options, corresponding to those in the 'Moreno Question' above, Mark Graesser found that only 8 per cent chose the 'A Newfoundlander only' option, 42 per cent chose the 'A Newfoundlander first, then a Canadian' option, and 43 per cent regarded themselves as 'A Newfoundlander and Canadian equally'.[65] The relevance of including the option of 'equally X and Y' in such surveys becomes obvious from the study of these results. Nevertheless, as the percentage of respondents who chose the 'A Canadian first, then a Newfoundlander' option remained low, at 7 per cent, this study also indicates a strong Newfoundland identity. A survey conducted by Corporate Research Associates for CBC in 1999 confirmed this picture of identities in contemporary Newfoundland. This survey showed that 67 per cent of respondents saw themselves as Newfoundlanders first, 29 per cent considered themselves Canadians first, and only 2 per cent chose the 'both equally' option.[66] These surveys do not reveal any regional variations, but according to sociologist J. D. House, 'Newfoundlanders . . . share an image of themselves as a distinct people, which is as strong for the businessman in St. John's as it is for the fisherman in Fogo'.[67] Surveys thus indicate the existence of a shared, unique Newfoundland identity, but a sense of distinctness on 'the Rock' is also illustrated by the fact that Newfoundlanders continue to refer to other Canadians as 'Mainlanders', and to outsiders in general as 'CFAs' (Come-From-Aways). In spite of Confederation, Newfoundland is still occasionally referred to as a 'nation' – although particularly with reference to its pre-Confederation history – and the idea of nation is closely linked to a sense of cultural uniqueness.[68]

In the discussion of Scottish national identity above, it was argued that the main reason for the non-existence of Scottish assimilation into a British national identity was the pragmatic perception of the nature of union. Also, it was argued, the absence of assimilationist policies on the part of changing Westminster governments played a part in this effect. Similar explanations seem to offer an understanding of why Newfoundlanders never, to the extent that Calhoun foresaw when he spoke of a Newfoundland national identity in transition, fully became Canadians. To many, if not actually a majority, of Newfoundlanders, Canada is still after fifty years of Confederation first and foremost a socio-economic partner. The fulfilment of what has been perceived as the obligation of Canada to increase the standard of living in Newfoundland considerably has not produced a highly developed sense of Canadian identity. Newfoundland has remained the all-important point of identification for a large majority of Newfoundlanders. Again, it must be questioned whether Newfoundlanders would have been able to resist a full-scale attempt at 'Canadianisation'. In any case, the lack of any such attempt has contributed to the present identity situation.

As for the more elusive idea of projected stereotypic images of the self, Newfoundland has its fair share. Two images have dominated Newfoundland mythology. One is positive and describes the Newfoundlander as brave, hardy, self-reliant and valiant. This image is referred to as that of the 'All 'Round Newfoundlander', taking its name from a poem by P. C. Mars, an immigrant Scot, who in his poem declared: 'I'll raise my old Scotch Bonnet and proudly grip the hand / Of the best all-round man on earth, the man from Newfoundland.'[69] The other is negative and portrays the Newfoundlander as 'a barely civilised half-brute who had been beaten into submission and stupefaction . . . by centuries of neglect, oppression, and ceaseless, grinding poverty'.[70] The similarities between the Newfoundland 'All 'Round Newfoundlander'/ half-brute myth and that of Scotland's tartanry are remarkable. Both myths are carriers of the romantic celebration of bravery and nobleness in spite of hardship, as well as the equally romanticised themes of defeat and misery. Although the origins of the myth can be traced back to descriptions produced as entertainment for a non-Newfoundland audience, the Newfoundland myth, argues folklorist Pat Byrne, has been embraced not only by the world outside Newfoundland, but by Newfoundlanders themselves[71] – just as has been the case with tartanry. This is another example, perhaps, of Barbara Grigor's birth-sign theory unfolding in praxis. Whereas many mainland Canadians see little harm in the ever-popular 'Newfie jokes' – and might even regularly exercise the stereotypic portrayal of Newfoundlanders as happily ignorant fishermen – these views are deeply resented by a large part of the Newfoundland population, and reinforce a sense of being different.

On the background of all the above, it is tempting to attribute to Canada the label of Newfoundland's significant other. However, Newfoundlanders are very much aware of being Canadians themselves, so the conclusion must be modified: Newfoundland's significant other is not Canada, but mainland Canada, or in certain circumstances different parts of it. Among all the 'others' which constitute the rest of Canada, the one which would appear to be the most significant is the central government in Ottawa – just as Westminster is often construed as Scotland's most significant other. In comparison with Scotland, the separate Newfoundland identity does not as clearly translate into a distinct voting pattern. Newfoundland voters in the period investigated seem to have been in agreement with the average Canadian voter – 1968 and 1988 being the only notable exceptions.[72]

To pull together the strands of the above analysis, this chapter has explained the relevance of comparing Scottish and Newfoundland experiences in the particular context of political nationalism. Important differences exist; most notably in terms of size of population, historical and cultural heritage, and the less centralised nature of the Canadian system of government compared to the British. Although such structural and cultural differences speak against a direct comparative analysis, they do not render comparisons impossible. Rather, since there are also a great number of similarities between the experiences of the two societies, these differences can provide vital clues as to the reasons why paths chosen in certain respects might differ.

The many similarities lending credibility and relevance to a comparative study of nationalism in Scotland and Newfoundland include the special circumstances under which these societies gave up sovereignty in order to achieve socio-economic development, the continued strength of a sense of distinct local collective values and identity, as well as the critical response to relative decline and restraints placed on the welfare system brought about by central governments fighting fiscal deficits.

FOUR Scottish National Identity
and Nationalism

Ralf Rönnquist has argued that in spite of the largely constant results of identity surveys indicating a strong sense of Scottish identity, and the equally constant support for Scottish self-government, it is not possible to make a direct link between the existence of a Scottish national consciousness and the success of political nationalism.[1] Rönnquist correctly points out that too often this link is uncritically assumed. As the Scottish case proves, it is quite possible in a nation to have a set self-perception, distinguishing it from other nations, without entertaining notions of independence or even developing political demands for less radical constitutional changes. The Scottish Covenant, a petition calling for Scottish home rule, was signed by almost two million people between 1949 and 1950. Organised by the Scottish Convention, the Covenant can rightly be seen as a political expression of popular national identity, but it remained outside the established political, partisan framework. The Scottish National Party (SNP), for example, did not gain any significant support until the late 1960s. Apart from the Covenant movement, for a long period during the twentieth century Scottish national identity expressed itself in a predominantly cultural form, in what was defined in chapter 1 as 'cultural nationalism'.

TARTANRY AND THE CABBAGE BED: CULTURAL NATIONALISM
IN SCOTLAND

When asked about his preferred whereabouts at the apocalypse, German poet Heinrich Heine allegedly replied: 'England, because every-thing happens a hundred years later there!' If applied to the case of political nationalism, the characterisation would fit Scotland nicely. In the place of the political nationalism that became characteristic of most Western European societies in the eighteenth, nineteenth and twentieth centuries, in Scotland one would find cultural nationalism thriving throughout most of that period. It was a nationalism which celebrated the cultural heritage and distinct history of the Scottish nation without ever jeopardising the political union and the socio-economically beneficial partnership with the rest of the UK. Sir Walter Scott was among the most convinced propagators of what has also been termed 'unionist nationalism'. There was no contradiction for him – as a patriotic Scot – in celebrating in poetry and prose of the failed Jacobite Rebellions and engaging in the struggle to maintain the note-issuing powers of Scottish banks, while at the same time – as a patriotic Briton – remaining a personal friend of George IV, and a staunch supporter of political and economic union with England, Wales and Ireland.[2]

Cultural nationalism had existed in Scotland before Scott, particularly among the intelligentsia of the Scottish Enlightenment, who would endorse James Macpherson's and Robert Burns' romantic re-writings of Scottish history, while consistently referring to themselves as 'North Britons'. It is tempting to misread the popularity of Burns' poetry among his contemporaries as a manifestation of dawning nationalism. After all, Burns would write emphatically and patriotically about the Wars of Independence and the Jacobite Rebellions. One of his most famous poems, written as if it is King Robert Bruce's address to his army before the Battle of Bannockburn, reads:

> By Oppression's woes and pains!
> By your sons in servile chains!
> We will drain our dearest veins,
> But they shall be free!
>
> Lay the proud Usurpers low!
> Tyrants fall in every foe!
> Liberty's in every blow! –
> Let us do or die!
> 　Robert Burns, 'Scots Wha Hae'

This is the kind of strong rhetoric utilised in classic nationalist movements on the European Continent, but just as Burns' radicalism was seen by the Scottish establishment more or less as an insignificant or even amusing aspect of his work, so were, to an even higher degree, the nationalist elements. Burns' romantic outbursts of sympathy for Scots fighting against oppressors were amalgamated into the emerging Scottish cultural nationalism, and never allowed to develop into political demands for constitutional change.

Scott and the emerging Scottish bourgeoisie, however, made this particular passive brand of nationalism, by critics often closely associated with tartanry, the hegemonic cultural and national discourse in Scotland for more than a century to come. Christopher Harvie speaks of it as 'the strategy of noisy inaction' and 'non-national nationalism'.[3] Cultural nationalism, although maintaining most of its basic elements, cannot be argued to have been a static phenomenon. Like all other myths, tartanry, the romantic historic myth of Highland bravery and Jacobite chivalry, had to adapt to fit changing social, economic and political circumstances. Tartanry did not confine itself to the ages of Burns and Scott. By the end of the eighteenth century, the infatuation among literati in Ireland and Scotland with Celtic/Gaelic history and culture remained strong; in fact it blossomed. This 'Celtic Twilight,' writes Roderick Watson, 'tended to be suffused with a melancholy sense of loss',[4] a characteristic making it akin to Burns' and Scott's romanticism. In the movement one finds the Scottish writer Fiona Macleod.[5] 'Her' longing for national identity was typical of the movement, but so was, for the Scottish part, her dismissal of 'the dream of an outward independence [as] a perilous illusion'.[6]

Another part of Scottish culture in the late nineteenth century served to hinder the development of political nationalism, but in a rather different manner. The new aspect was the 'Kailyard' literary tradition. Up until then, much Scottish fiction had been inspired by the historic novel in the tradition of Sir Walter Scott. Now a new literary style – emphasising not the dramatic or the heroic spirit of the Scots but quite the contrary, the parochial and insular character of Scottish Lowland small-town life – became popular.[7] Craig argues that Kailyard authors such as J. M. Barrie and S. R. Crockett had consciously committed themselves to English culture and to never describing any political or social conflict.[8] So when Kailyard writing became immensely popular and a source for identification by large parts of the Scottish population, particularly the working class, another harmless and politically conservative addition to Scottish national identity was the result.

Many, mainly literary, personalities have attempted to debunk the tartanry and Kailyard myths and put in their place what they considered a serious debate about Scottish identity. In the 1920s, many writers of the Scottish Literary Renaissance, led by Hugh MacDiarmid, argued strongly along nationalist lines for Scottish independence. In his autobiography, *Lucky Poet* (1943), MacDiarmid wrote of Walter Scott's books that they were 'the great source of the paralysing ideology of defeatism in Scotland, the spread of which is responsible . . . for the acceptance of the Union'.[9] The movement nevertheless remained mostly a literary and entirely elitist phenomenon with little popular support – what Christopher Harvie might have labelled, as he did in describing the Scottish Labour Party of the mid-1970s, 'an army of officers looking for a rank-and-file'.[10] Scottish national identity, dominated by the tartanry and Kailyard images of Scotland, appeared to be immune to attempts at politicisation.

The powerful influence of a tartanry- and Kailyard-dominated cultural nationalism on Scottish life is not confined to the nineteenth and early twentieth centuries. Attacks on the core of cultural nationalism, the tartanry and Kailyard images of Scotland, have been frequent in recent times as well. Scholars and literary critics such as Colin McArthur and Cairns Craig[11] have attempted to debunk what they considered parochial and false manifestations of Scottish identity. They were joining artists like Barbara and Murray Grigor,[12] and the most fierce critic of tartanry, Tom Nairn, who, in describing in *The Break-Up of Britain* (1977) the strength of 'cultural sub-nationalism' in twentieth-century Scotland, wrote: 'An anomalous historical situation could not engender a "normal" culture: Scotland could not simply be adapted to the new, basically nationalist, rules of cultural evolution. But since the country could not help being affected by this evolution, it produced something like a stunted, caricatural version of it.'[13]

It is difficult to imagine that an almost autonomous mythic beast (or 'tartan monster' in Nairn's words) should possess such enormous power over a defenceless collective Scottish mentality, and indeed Scottish culture in the twentieth century has included a great deal more than tartanry and Kailyard. The year 1947, for instance, marked the first, soon widely respected, Edinburgh International Festival, and large areas of literature and theatre – such as the 7:84 Theatre Company – have developed independently of the romantic historical ballast.

Still, in many ways the critics of Scottish cultural nationalism are right: the general attitude of political inaction was served wonderfully by cultural nationalism. It was accepted or embraced by what would 'normally' have been the nationalising domain and other strata alike, because it provided a safety valve for national pride that could not be otherwise expressed without endangering a partnership considered worth keeping. A high degree of administrative devolution existed via the Scottish Office in Edinburgh alongside a distinct Scottish national identity forged by particularly Scottish institutions, tartanry and Kailyard. For more than half a decade, only a small number of Scots found it worthwhile to jeopardise this situation for an increased say in Scottish affairs. The hegemony of cultural nationalism, however, would be seriously questioned from the 1960s onwards.

RESPONDING TO THE DECLINE OF BRITAIN: POLITICAL
NATIONALISM IN SCOTLAND, 1967–1979

In arguing fiercely against the regressive nature of cultural (sub-)nation-
alism, Nairn is really lamenting not so much the lack of a normal culture
as the lack of a normal – i.e., political – *nationalism*. Actually, when
Nairn declared its absence, political nationalism had already appeared
on the Scottish agenda, albeit still on a rather small scale. It can be
argued to have been an aspect of the home rule movement in the 1880s
and 1910s; several of the literati of the Literary Renaissance also had
serious political aspirations, and the National Party of Scotland, which
in 1934 merged with the Scottish Self-Government Party to become the
Scottish National Party (SNP), was a minor feature of Scottish political
life from 1928. Still, political nationalism only made its first serious
impact in the latter half of the 1960s. Although neither the popularity of
the SNP nor the popularity of the 'independence' or 'devolution' options
in opinion polls can be argued to be equivalent to the popularity of political nationalism, they may still be indicative of the *relative* rise in political nationalist sentiment. In 1967, the SNP won 200,000 votes and
69 seats in the local elections, as well as the previously safe Labour seat
of Hamilton in a by-election. In the elections and by-elections of the
decade following Hamilton, the nationalists enjoyed increasing, although
not constant, support: the SNP's share of the Scottish vote increased from
5 per cent in 1966 to 11.4 per cent in 1970, 21.9 per cent in February
1974, and 30.4 per cent in October 1974. The rise in the percentage
of Scots supporting options other than the status quo also indicates a
move towards political nationalism. In the first poll of its kind in 1945,
only 8 per cent of Scots claimed to be in favour Scottish independence;
53 per cent favoured devolution, and 39 per cent declared themselves
happy with the constitutional status quo. In the period 1965 to 1974,
those in favour of independence increased to 22 per cent, devolution was
now the preferred option of 63 per cent, and the proportion in favour of
keeping the status quo had declined to 15 per cent.[14]

The decline of Britain and the perception of mismanagement

In his contribution to *Scotland in the Twentieth Century* (1996), James
Mitchell argues that several new developments from the 1950s onwards
would come to be significant to the perception of Scotland's position in
the UK. Of the three developments that Mitchell stresses: the decline of
the British Empire; the rapid increase in Scottish unemployment rates;
and early European integration,[15] two can be singled out as having an

immediate impact on the perception of the Union in Scotland. European integration was not to become a significant factor in the debate until much later, and not until the mid-1980s was the European Community (EC) seen by a significant proportion of Scots as a serious alternative to central rule from London.[16] To be sure, in the 1975 EC referendum only 58.4 per cent of Scots voted for continued membership, compared to the UK average of 67.2 per cent. Michael Keating suggests that the dominant fear towards the EC among both ordinary Scots and politicians at the time was that membership would make Scotland even more peripheral in an even bigger market.[17]

Of much greater importance in the late 1960s was the decline of the British empire, industry and economy generally (the beginning of the so-called 'British Disease'); later, as part of that process, of the British welfare state also. Both of the Wilson governments and the Heath and Callaghan administrations found themselves in a series of economic crises with an obvious negative effect on the quality of life in British society. As the economic and social benefits of the British welfare state were gradually removed, being ruled by Westminster suddenly appeared much less of a bargain. Since the late 1940s, when the British welfare state was established, the philosophy of the Beveridge Report remained the basis for British welfare policy as well as a strong unifying force. This is a philosophy which Scots have always appreciated, not least because Scotland was often seen to be more in need of welfare benefits than other parts of the UK. Many saw changing governments as failing to deliver according to the social contract which had been 'signed' between state and people in the immediate post-war period. Says Harvie: 'The recession made radical ideology acceptable.'[18] It was not coincidental that Winifred Ewing's victory in the 1967 Hamilton by-election – which would prove to be a breakthrough for the SNP – appeared at a time when the British economy was at a severe low.

In this period of recession all parts of the UK were affected, so why should Scots react by increasing their support for political nationalism? In this respect, an interesting argument has been put forward: Scotland was being abused in the process. This may be a point of special relevance to the development of Scottish political nationalism. Certainly, there existed at the time a sense in Scotland of relative deprivation with regard not only to other small European societies, but also to (south-east) England.[19] Scotland was ridden with high unemployment rates and general socio-economic malaise, while other parts of the UK were seen to prosper in comparison. Andrew Marr attributes the relatively high unemployment rates in Scotland to the '*laissez-faire* attitude of Heath in London'.[20] Already in the early part of this period there was some discrepancy between voting patterns in Scotland and the rest of the UK. From 1959 onwards, Scotland was slowly becoming a Labour bastion, but only from 1964 to 1970 was Conservative rule at Westminster replaced by a Labour government. This is a situation far from the 'doomsday scenario' which would come to characterise Scottish representation in Westminster in the 1980s and 1990s, but it may nevertheless have been of some significance. However, in the late 1960s, Scots also felt neglected by the Labour government. Unemployment rose to new heights, but in spite of its promises, the Wilson government did not appear to be doing anything to ease Scotland's problems.

So far, incentives to the rise of political nationalism in Scotland as discussed above appear to have been of a negative kind. The protest vote is a negative vote, and it seems plausible that support for the SNP in the late 1960s may indeed be classified partly as a protest. Labour were no longer able, as they had been in the past, to translate Scottish discontent into Labour support. Scots in this part of the period saw Scotland not only harmed disproportionately by economic crisis – a situation which their preferred party, Labour, seemed incapable of altering – they were also experiencing a degree of democratic deficit and a sense of deliberate neglect from the ruling party in Westminster. It is not coincidental, however, that the choice of party became the SNP, and the cause chosen became the national one. A strong sense of Scotland as a separate entity already existed, and the success of the Scottish Covenant in the early 1950s testifies to some degree of sympathy for home rule among the Scots. Still, had not negative incentives occurred, along with other fomenting factors pertaining to both the SNP and other political actors, it is doubtful whether the SNP would have had the same amount of success in channelling this appreciation for the idea of home rule into support for the party in the late 1960s. The breakthrough in the Hamilton by-election and the rate of success of the SNP in this period must also be explained partly by the role played by relevant actors. Before turning to these, however, it is necessary first to consider another important feature which, from the earliest 1970s, should be added to the list of fomenting factors.

North Sea oil

Judging only by votes garnered by the SNP – it is less hazardous to do so at this point in history than later, when several other parties start subscribing to an autonomist agenda – the support for political nationalism rose constantly in the late 1960s and early 1970s. The SNP went from a 5.0 per cent share of the Scottish vote in 1966 to 30.4 per cent in 1974. A slightly different pattern is revealed, however, by the study of SNP membership figures. The number of members rose from 2,000 in 1962 to 42,000 in 1966, and (possibly) 120,000 in 1968; by 1971, however, it had shrunk to 70,000.[21] Also, the SNP share of votes in the 1969 local elections slumped from 30 per cent to 22 per cent. In the 1970 general election the SNP increased its share of the vote more than two-fold. Still, as the party was now running candidates in 65 of the 71 constituencies – as opposed to just 23 in 1966 – the number of votes cast per candidate fell. Although such decline in the light of a 128 per cent increase in overall electoral support does not warrant Harvie's surprise at the survival of the SNP in the 1970 general election, political nationalism certainly seemed to have lost some of its momentum. This might well have been the beginning of a weary journey for the Scottish political nationalist movement had not new additional fomenting factors appeared. Harvie argues that the rise of the SNP in the late 1960s was 'premature and might have evaporated' had not the more dynamic 'linkage in 1973 with the post-imperial phenomenon of the oil crisis and North Sea oil' become a possibility.[22] Two new incentives to support a nationalist agenda had appeared. First, there was a further decline of socio-economic conditions in the UK and in Scotland, and second – and most importantly – oil entered the nationalist equation.

It is widely agreed that a decisive factor in relation to the development of political nationalism in Scotland was the discovery of oil in the North Sea (the Forties Field) off the coast of Scotland in November 1970. It occurred at a time when Britain's severe socio-economic crisis was discernible to all, and it offered, in historian Michael Lynch's words, 'Scots the prospect of escape from their dependence on the new, lesser Britain'.[23] Forecasts rose quickly – from 12m tons to 158m tons by 1980 – and as oil prices were steadily rising, oil indeed promised to make Scotland a wealthy society. The SNP made good use of what looked remarkably like an alternative to economic dependence on the UK, and the new resource soon became a powerful weapon in the nationalist struggle. The SNP slogan of the 1960s, 'Put Scotland First', was replaced by the highly successful 'It's Scotland's Oil' (1972) and its follow-up: 'Rich Scots or Poor Britons' (1974).

The SNP's two 1974 General Election manifestos accentuated the oil discoveries and the consequential prospects for Scotland. The main idea presented was that 'the enormous wealth of the oil and gas fields off the Scottish coast, allied to our other vast resources, offers ever-improving living standards to the people of Scotland – *when they demand a Scottish Government*'.[24] The 1977 manifesto continued along the same lines:

'The choice for Scotland has become even more urgent. The discovery of massive oil-fields in the Scottish sector of the Continental Shelf has given us a unique opportunity.'[25] Still, although oil remains an important issue in the 1977 manifesto, it is less dominant compared to the 1974 manifestos. Both the November 1978 manifesto and the April/May 1979 supplementary manifesto continue to emphasise the necessity of oil ownership and development for a prosperous future for Scotland. Oil remained an important part of the SNP's proposed budgets for an independent Scotland, but the 1978 manifesto nevertheless takes a slightly less aggressive stance on ownership. It still maintains that '[t]he oil and gas reserves off the Scottish coast are Scottish', but it also produces the offer that 'the Scottish people would share the wealth with others'[26] – although the party retains the right for Scotland to decide with whom and by how much. The 1979 supplement of only two pages reveals little in terms of details, but argues that 'Scotland's resources and taxation has made England prosperous with little of that prosperity remaining in Scotland. This drain . . . continues apace with the drain of tax revenues from Scotland's oil.'[27] So oil remains an important part of the SNP platform throughout the period, albeit by the end of it, a less aggressive attitude towards the sharing of revenues can be detected.

With the discovery of oil and the SNP's utilisation of this new resource in its policies, the unionist argument that Scotland would never be able to make it alone lost a great deal of its appeal, and the SNP managed to reach out to a larger number of Scots than ever before; probably because many voters who had not previously prioritised national issues now had an economic incentive to do so. In the first of two 1974 general elections (in February), the SNP almost doubled its share of the vote – from 11.4 to 21.9 per cent – and in the October 1974 general election the party further increased its share to 30.4 per cent of the votes cast. Rönnquist points out that the fact that no SNP candidate lost his/her deposit indicates the geographically widespread support for the nationalist party.[28] There can be little doubt that the renewed impetus that political nationalism enjoyed through increased support for the SNP owed a great deal to the positive oil prospects of the day. Whereas oil was an important fomenting factor, the political players of the nationalising domain were very important actors in the development of political nationalism in this period; they will be the subject of the following sections.

The policies of the Scottish National Party

Although one can easily imagine a number of Labour MPs silently hoping for a return to the old Labour policy of home rule, and although the Liberals were in favour of devolution, at least in principle, it is fairly safe to argue that active political nationalists in the early part of this period should be found largely within the SNP. It is likely that the nationalists received the unprecedented amount of support simply because the major parties were late to react to Scottish problems. This can be interpreted as the nationalist vote lending itself to a voice of protest. Another plausible interpretation is that many Scots supporting political nationalism were abandoning the major parties to constructively search for a way to achieve what these parties appeared to be unable to achieve. Both interpretations ring true but, in the late 1960s, the former more so. The relative slump in support for the SNP in 1970 signals why this is the case. By then, the Conservatives had been pondering the possibility of a Scottish Assembly and were taking over from a weary crisis-ridden Labour government. It looks as if faith in at least one of the old parties had been temporarily restored and the services of the SNP protest vehicle might not be needed after all.

Another factor of some importance needs mentioning. As both Webb and Marr have pointed out, the SNP itself in this period became a better-structured modern party with an effective propaganda machine,[29] and this is bound to have had an effect as well. The Liberal Party had a history of supporting home rule but, like the two major parties, failed to woo the politically nationalist-minded Scottish voters. In addition, the lack of interest in any measure of devolution on the part of both major parties of the time had a serious impact, just as the eventual conversion of Labour to the devolution cause would.

In the October 1974 general election the SNP increased its share of the vote from 21.9 per cent to 30.4 per cent and the number of seats from seven to eleven. Labour had no doubt anticipated stemming the tide of radical political nationalism and support for the SNP by its new devolutionist line, but for various reasons this did not happen. A relevant question to ask at this point, then, would be whether nationalist support for the SNP's policies – as it did not translate into support for Labour devolution – had, after all, something to do with ethno-cultural views? The 1974 SNP manifestos seem to indicate that this was not the case. The two dominant and interrelated themes in the manifestos were socio-economic considerations and a lack of democracy/political influence. The February 1974 manifesto asked what it considered to be a straightforward question: 'Do you wish to be "Rich Scots" or "Poor British"?', and foresaw that 'the desirable Scotland will never be created by government from Westminster ... Successive Tory and Labour governments completely failed to create living conditions like those in S-E England.'[30] Only if people demanded a Scottish government, it was argued, could they make Scotland a place of which to be proud. This included a Scotland with full employment, fairly distributed wealth, opportunities for education, protection from exploitation, compassionate social services, and a share of international responsibilities. Generally there seems to have been little space reserved in SNP rhetoric in the 1970s for ethno-cultural issues. Analyses of the SNP's manifestos from the late 1970s support this perception.

Although the introduction to the 1977 manifesto states: 'The SNP has a deep commitment to democracy, to Scotland's distinctive history and culture and to the social and economic well-being of the Scottish people',[31] and thus can be seen to list the three priorities as democracy, ethno-cultural uniqueness and socio-economics, two are clearly emphasised. The ethno-cultural arguments are quickly forgotten, as the introduction moves on: 'Without political power Scotland can not control her own economy . . . Without political power there can be no hope of regenerating Scottish society. When the Scottish people have this vital power, it will be up to them to choose their own social and economic priorities.' Ethnicity remains implied in references, for instance, to the 'Scottish people', but specifically ethno-cultural matters, surfacing only sporadically, remain a supportive rather than a causal element in the SNP's struggle for Scottish independence. The real concerns of the SNP remain 'the centralism of the British Conservative and Labour Parties',[32] as well as '[u]nemployment, emigration . . . totally unsuitable economic policies . . . – the dismal legacy of London Government'.[33] Equally, the November 1978 manifesto speaks only of fairness in the distribution of wealth and democratic power. Not until page eleven is there a mention of Scotland's cultural heritage, which within another page leads to a discussion of Scotland's economic history and problems within the Union.[34] The April/May 1979 manifesto in a similar fashion lists the important issues as being the democratic deficit, emigration, economy/resources and social standards/unemployment.[35] Socio-economic deprivation, lack of political influence and the promises of oil wealth thus appear to have been the main instigating reasons for the SNP's popularity throughout most of the 1970s. At least that is the conclusion which must be drawn from analyses of the party's manifestos.

The policies of the Labour Party

The Labour Party had been in favour of home rule during periods of the first half of the century, but by the mid-1950s it had committed itself to unionism. Not until 1974 did either of the two major parties seriously commit itself to some sort of devolution. In the meantime the SNP, with its policy of independence, had plenty of space in which to manoeuvre. This is not to say that the major parties did not have other policies regarding Scotland's problems. As Keating reports, political invention steered a significant measure of state and private investments to Scotland, which also benefited from regional funds.[36] The Highlands and Islands Development Board was set up in 1965, and in 1966 the 'Plan for Scotland' published by the Labour government aimed to remove the high levels of emigration,[37] unemployment and low wages through more state grants and by directing more industry to Scotland. However, in the late 1960s, economic crisis set in. Although Keynesianism and the welfare state were not abandoned overnight, in the years that followed Labour governments were forced to slow down the pace of and eventually roll back state support and involvement – thereby expanding the vacuum in which nationalism could grow, not least because the regional development aid had the longer-term effect of creating a stronger sense of the Scottish nation as an economic unit with different needs and wishes than other regions of the UK.

As oil came to provide a viable economic alternative to the existing dependence on Westminster, and as the SNP kept increasing its vote in both local and general elections, other groups and parties started considering devolution as a necessary political move. In 1969 the Royal Committee on the Constitution, later to be headed by Lord Kilbrandon, had been set up to consider the pros and cons of different measures of constitutional reform. In October 1973 it published its report, which recommended that a Scottish Convention, elected by a proportional representation system and headed by a Scottish prime minister, be set up. In practice, this was a mild reform towards Scottish home rule. The recommendations of the commission were not unanimous, however, and two minority reports were published along with the majority report. Scotland's political parties and civil institutions were equally split in their support. The SNP, the Liberals, the Scottish Trade Union Congress (STUC), the Kirk and the Communists all supported the implementation of Kilbrandon's recommendations. In contrast, the Conservatives – who had just denounced devolution at their 1973 convention – and Labour – many party members still finding it difficult to merge socialist ideology with nationalist aspirations – were not persuaded by the report.[38] It is very likely that the then prime minister Harold Wilson's intentions of setting up the Royal Committee were contrary to the outcome. Obviously, he did not need a report advocating measures which were in opposition to existing Labour policy. There is much to speak in favour of interpreting the setting-up of the Commission in the first place as a policy of deliberate stalling: an opportunity to let a difficult issue linger quietly in a commission which would spend years taking minutes. The Commission was set up at a time when political nationalism had made some gains, and from a Labour point of view it needed to be checked, without associating the party with a cause which would mean 'a dramatic fall in living standards'.[39]

It took the February 1974 general election to seriously change the minds of the Labour leadership. Riding on a wave of oil and protest votes, the modernised SNP won 21.9 per cent of the Scottish vote. The Labour Party, seeing its very important and formerly safe Scottish seats threatened,[40] felt forced to reintroduce the old Labour policy of home rule to its manifesto. This happened contrary to the wishes of *Scottish* Labour. Keating argues that 'the breakthrough of the SNP in 1974 was an embarrassment to Labour, *forcing* it to revert to its historic policy of Scottish home rule'.[41] Indeed, Labour's U-turn on devolution can only be interpreted as a result of *Realpolitik*, a pragmatic choice made by Labour's leadership in London for tactical political reasons. Conveniently, the new policy – which could be legitimised as a return to the old Labour Home Rule creed – could now be introduced to the public within weeks of the October 1974 General Election.

Labour, far from convincing in their support for a Scottish Assembly – which was clearly and firstly a tactical move – lost 0.3 per cent of the Scottish votes received in the February 1974 election. Still, in contrast to the Conservatives, at least a majority in the Labour Party remained in support of devolution throughout the period. This has been a crucial aspect of the development of political nationalism in Scotland. First, political nationalism had now placed itself firmly on the political agenda – it could no longer be ascribed to a freak protest vote. Second, nationalist sentiment was from the mid-1970s no longer measurable only or even mainly by support for the SNP. Third, devolution became so closely associated with Labour policies that the success or failure of the party spelled the success or failure of Scottish autonomism. In November 1975 the Labour government produced its White Paper on devolution, *Our Changing Democracy*. The White Paper would eventually become the Scotland Bill, which would form the basis of the 1978 Scotland Act, to be laid out for a consultative referendum in 1979. The legislative and administrative powers of the proposed assembly would include some aspects of health, social welfare, education, housing, local government, transport, physical planning, agriculture and fisheries and the legal system. However, there were important exceptions, such as social security, the universities and railways, and the assembly would not be able to raise or lower taxes.

Labour was clearly trying to take the lead on the question of increasing Scottish autonomy, but the pragmatic acceptance rather than a full-hearted embrace of devolution, which had characterised Labour under Wilson, was continued under Callaghan's leadership. The new Labour prime minister was tempted to withdraw one of the first devolution bills altogether but decided against it, he wrote in his memoirs, because 'the Scottish National Party would have had an electoral field day: the demand for independence might begin to grow and even reach dangerous proportions if no effort was made to accommodate the middle ground'.[42]

The policies of the Conservative Party

In his May 1968 'Declaration of Perth' Edward Heath had shocked the Scottish Conservatives by announcing Conservative support for a Scottish Assembly, and had set up the Douglas-Home Commission to decide on its form. This Commission proposed in March 1970 that a Scottish Assembly of 125 members with merely advisory functions be set up. In power (1970 to 1974), the Conservatives, however, made no serious attempt at establishing such an assembly. At their 1973 conference, the largely unenthusiastic Conservatives voted not to speed up the process of establishing a Scottish Assembly, and the idea of devolution was in essence rejected in favour of a policy of local government reform. The reasons were many and varied, but an obvious explanation for the lack of Conservative enthusiasm in this respect would be the relative decline in the fortunes of the SNP around 1970. Nevertheless, sections in the Conservative Party did not abandon devolution altogether, and therefore the party in the mid-1970s found itself split over the issue into a pro-devolution wing and an anti-devolution (Thatcher) wing. Margaret Thatcher had initially endorsed devolution as a principle, but by the end of 1976 her U-turn had been accomplished.

Academics and the relationship between political and cultural nationalism, 1967–1979

In a different capacity, Scottish academics – mainly the left-wing section – also served as fomenters of a political nationalist agenda. The political message was more diffuse as regards political nationalism, but they introduced for the first time a focused debate about Scottish politics, national identity, nationalism and the constitutional set-up. Contributions to the debate included Ian Budge and Derek Urwin's *Scottish Political Behaviour* (1966), James G. Kellas' *Modern Scotland* (1968), Tom Nairn's *The Break-Up of Britain* (1977), Keith Webb's *The Growth of Nationalism in Scotland* (1978), Jack Brand's *The National Movement in Scotland* (1978), and the *Scottish Government Yearbook* (published from 1977 to 1992, when it became *Scottish Affairs*). Although this debate appears to have been less vigorous and extensive than that which would come to characterise the mid-1980s, it did effectively raise the awareness of political nationalism in Scotland.

In his *Growth of Nationalism* (1978) Keith Webb makes a distinction similar to the one made in this study between cultural and political nationalism: 'National feeling is a permanent feature of Scottish culture. It is not possible, therefore, to explain the rise of a nationalist movement by referring to a sudden spread of nationalist sentiment. What is needed is an explanation of why nationalist feelings already held by many Scots became politicized when they did.'[43] Writing in 1978, Webb is relating his findings to the period from the mid-1960s to the late 1970s, a period remarkable for its clear distinction between cultural nationalist celebration and political nationalist demands. John Breuilly characterises the Scottish autonomist movement as 'a rather tough-minded . . . nationalism which is very different from the anti-modernist, rather romantic nationalist movements . . . in many nineteenth-century European countries', and adds, 'the cultural appeals [are] weak'.[44] Indeed, political nationalism in Scotland in the first part of the period appears to have grown almost independently of the pre-existing cultural nationalism. In 1998, David McCrone saw political and cultural nationalism in Scotland 'developing apace'.[45] This, however, does not necessarily contradict his argument from 1992, when he stated that the cultural content of the Scottish variety of nationalism was 'relatively weak'.[46] As McCrone points out, the autonomist debate in Scotland in this period was characterised not by arguments pertaining to ethnicity, language or culture but by arguments about the balance of trade and the economic relationship between Scotland and London.[47] It would appear that although cultural and political nationalism may have developed 'apace', one never to any significant extent became the legitimisation of the other. No relationship of dependence was ever developed in this period; indeed, political nationalism often tried to distance itself from cultural nationalism, focusing instead on the control of natural resources, the right to self-determination and better, more effective, government. Unlike the early nationalist parties, the SNP had no cultural renaissance writers to provide cultural legitimisation for its cause. In fact, the SNP publicly denounced such support in the shape of the 1320 Club.[48]

The rise of political nationalism in Scotland in the 1960s and 1970s serves to illustrate the importance of external factors in the emergence of this particular kind of nationalism. A political nationalist movement does not arise in societies content with the existing constitutional set-up. If the general perception is that the society one lives in is getting a fair deal – that it generally benefits from being part of a larger whole, or has no better alternative – cultural nationalism (presupposing that one such exists) remains the only expression of national sentiment. It is when a positive situation deteriorates that alternatives are sought, and sometimes found.

David McCrone has argued that the rise of the SNP in the 1960s 'owed more to economic concerns over North Sea oil' than to the sense of being 'Scottish'.[49] As illustrated above, this was not entirely so. It is true that an ethno-cultural argument was practically non-existent in early Scottish political nationalism, but the idea of a common Scottish identity and of Scotland as a social and economic entity combined into a significant precondition. Ethnicity was thus often implied, while arguments based on culture were shunned. Also, North Sea oil did not in fact become a relevant factor until the early 1970s. At that point, however, it did take prominence.

THE 1979 REFERENDUM: HIGH EXPECTATIONS AND THE
FAILURE OF POLITICAL NATIONALISM

1979 saw a temporary culmination of political nationalism in Scotland. This was the year when, in a referendum, the Scots were asked their opinion about the possible establishment of a separate Scottish Assembly with devolved powers. All major Scottish newspapers, including the until recently unionist *Glasgow Herald*, along with most politicians from Scotland's major political parties, except the Conservatives, supported Scottish home rule in the spring of 1979. In spite of high expectations for the referendum, and as a big surprise to politicians and media alike, the seemingly unstoppable march of political nationalism in Scotland came to an abrupt halt on 1 March that year. What should have been a landmark in the history of political nationalism in Scotland, the establishment of a Scottish Assembly, failed to materialise as only 32.85 per cent of the electorate chose to endorse such a move. Although this constituted a majority of the vote,[50] this was far below the 40 per cent mark, which Labour backbenchers had successfully demanded be added as a separate clause, required for any change to take place.

Explaining the political nationalist decline

Ever since the failed referendum, politicians, scholars and others have discussed possible reasons for what appeared to be this sudden dwindling of support for an autonomist discourse in Scotland. It is likely that radical political nationalists considered the Scotland Act not far-reaching enough: most importantly, Westminster would retain the possibility of veto in all matters in which the Scottish Assembly would be able to legislate. Other groups, such as many voters in the Orkneys and Shetlands, probably had no wish to add another layer of bureaucracy in Edinburgh. A factor which many analysts credit with the major responsibility for the outcome of the 1979 referendum was the close association of the Scotland Act with the image of Labour government. It was the 'Winter of Discontent', with massive dissatisfaction and strikes in the public sector, and the failure of the Labour government that this represented was invariably associated with the devolution proposal it had developed. As a consequence of the economic and political crises, the Conservatives had increased their popularity in Scotland by the time of the referendum – to 35 per cent support according to one opinion poll – and as they were actively advocating a 'No', promising that they would introduce a better devolution bill later, this is likely to have persuaded a significant number of Scots to choose this option. Labour, on the other hand, was clearly losing its grip on power, and the devolution scheme could be seen as just another attempt at saving votes. To be sure, Labour was far from united on the issue, and thus its campaign was less than convincing. One wing of the party, which included Robin Cook, Tam Dalyell and George Cunningham, were directly hostile to the entire idea of devolution, and actively advocated a 'No'.

In fact, the entire 'Yes' side was divided. The SNP had agreed to support the assembly in 1975, but Labour refused to be part of the 'Yes' campaign along with them. Therefore, the umbrella 'Yes' campaign, 'Yes for Scotland', included 'the SNP, the rebel Scottish Labour Party, a string of prominent clergymen, trade unionists, writers and public figures',[51] while another, 'Labour Movement Yes', was run by the Labour Party alone. Confident that the outcome would be positive to their respective causes, the SNP and Labour engaged in hostile party politics, even during the campaign. The SNP itself was split internally between fundamentalists and gradualists, which is not likely to have contributed positively to the fortune of the 'Yes' campaign either.

The British economy was still staggering along but it had, by the time of the referendum, recovered slightly under IMF supervision. In addition, some oil-based industry had been directed to Scotland. These were not major improvements, but they constituted proof that Westminster was indeed taking serious measures to accommodate Scotland's material needs at a time when conditions were otherwise deteriorating – unemployment had risen from 3.6 per cent in 1974 to 7.6 per cent in 1978. The fact that Scotland could now be seen to be improving its economic position within the UK, at least relatively, might have persuaded some Scots that Westminster, rather than an inexperienced Edinburgh assembly, would be better equipped to get Scotland out of the socio-economic morass it found itself in. This certainly seems to have been the case for Scotland's business community, predominantly hostile to even modest constitutional change. But it was also true for large sections of the Scottish middle class. Stephen Maxwell argues that what he terms the 'historic compromise' was the cause of the hesitation on the part of the middle-class voters: they were historically the beneficiaries of the Union, which secured their positions within the 'protected markets' of the Church of Scotland, Scottish education, Scottish law and the Scottish Office.[52] In 1979 they had still not been persuaded to leave all these benefits behind in search of a brighter future based on oil revenues. As argued previously, the Scottish population was still highly critical of membership of the EC, which would therefore not have provided, in the minds of most Scots, a viable alternative to full membership of the UK. Neither would North Sea oil. The oil industry had started production, but it turned out to be not quite the bonanza that had been expected in the early part of the decade. It must have been difficult for Scottish voters not to associate economic dependence with political dependence, and perhaps even devolution with the slippery slope to independence.

These factors all combined into a lack of confidence in Scotland's ability to do better as a more autonomous entity within the UK. Britain was not exactly doing well, but neither were most countries in the world at this time, due mainly to the energy crisis. It was a frightening scenario to most Scots (those who voted 'No', and no doubt many of those who chose not to vote at all), one in which a 'Yes' would have demanded a high level of self-confidence. At this point, argue both Harvie and Marr, Scotland's humiliating defeats in the 1978 Football World Cup had already taken its toll on that particular resource.[53] It is a factor whose influence is very difficult to verify, but Harvie nevertheless insists that the ' "we were rubbish" hangover certainly contributed to the 1 March outcome'.[54]

The Scottish cringe

Cohen touches upon the negative self-image which he finds inherent in both the Scottish and the Newfoundland mentality: '[Newfoundlanders' and Scots'] perceptions of their potency and the perceptions others have of them are discrepant to an extent which may itself limit their power to tweaking the system at its edges, rather than grappling radically with its central structures and directions.'[55]

What Cohen's argument boils down to is a lack of national self-confidence in both societies. A theory of Scottish culture as inflicting upon Scottish psyche a sense of inferiority – a lack of personal and political confidence known as 'the Scottish Cringe' – has been forwarded as an explanation of not just the failure of the 1979 referendum, but the 'belatedness' of political nationalism in Scotland as such.[56] Tom Nairn has argued fiercely against the continued discursive hegemony of tartanry and Kailyard in the Scottish national identity, as these myths are seen to increase a sense of backwardness and inferiority, and thereby act as impediments to political change. However, the foremost advocates of a theory of the Scottish Cringe are Craig Beveridge and Ronald Turnbull. In their *The Eclipse of Scottish Culture* (1989) they apply Frantz Fanon's concept and theory of 'inferiorisation' to the Scottish case. They argue that Scottish culture has been deliberately corrupted by anglicised *évolués* – 'the academic establishment and the British media' and 'those natives who try to escape from their backwardness by desperate identification with the culture of the metropolis'. Because a native Scottish intellectual elite sustains a powerful discourse of Scottish inferiority, they effectively reinforce Scotland's political subordination and prevent 'cultural liberation and renewal'.[57] Tom Nairn, the nationalist thinker perhaps most critical of the 'intolerably vulgar . . . tartan monster',[58] also becomes subject to Beveridge and Turnbull's attacks on Scottish intellectuals who surrender to 'metropolitan ideology'.[59]

Along with most scholars, Beveridge and Turnbull acknowledge the culture-less nature of nationalism in Scotland in the early part of the investigated period. They say: 'The nationalist movement which shook Scotland out of its torpor in the sixties and seventies was overwhelmingly practical in character, a nationalism which lacked a substantial cultural and philosophical component . . . the SNP's advance at the electoral level was not matched by any corresponding intellectual achievement . . . Suspicious of concepts like 'tradition' and 'identity', many tough-minded left-wing nationalists were even prepared to abandon the cultural argument entirely.'[60]

Beveridge and Turnbull find the lack of a cultural component in Scottish political nationalism unfortunate. In fact, they argue, this lack explains why political nationalism experienced decline in the last part of the 1970s: 'Scottish nationalism's cultural-intellectual base was . . . altogether too narrow for the nationalist challenge to be sustained over any extended period.' Again, this lack of cultural elements is explained within the framework of Fanon's post-colonialist theory as a result of the successful effort to 'bring the colonised person to admit the inferiority of his culture'.[61] In this line of argument, Beveridge and Turnbull move on to explain in detail why 1979 spelled the temporary defeat of political nationalism in Scotland: 'Devolution, independence would be dangerous, since the Scots require the civilising hand of the southern neighbour (the English, within this mythology, being characterised by liberalism, tolerance, decency, etc).'[62] The theory of an anglophile Scottish elite always ready to dismiss Scottish culture as parochial, 'the internal anglicisers', is supported by P. H. Scott, who also agrees that 'Scotland looks like a textbook demonstration of the theory which Frantz Fanon advanced.'[63]

Apart from placing too much emphasis on the power of cultural myths, Beveridge and Turnbull's theory greatly over-simplifies matters. Their theory completely buys into Fanon's theory, developed for societies in altogether different situations, without regard to any of the factors included in the discussions of this chapter. By 1979 a certain sense of being inferior no doubt existed in the minds of many Scots, but it was not one which was determined by cultural myths alone. Socio-economically the Scots had been through some turbulent decades, and it had become clear that the alternatives to dependence on the UK were non-existent or at least underdeveloped. Just as the 'lack' of political nationalism at most junctures in Scottish history until the mid-1960s was motivated by pragmatic reasoning, so was the rise of political nationalism after that point. In the same way, the decline of political nationalism, symbolised by its defeat in the 1979 referendum, was a consequence of insecurity created not by cultural colonisation, but by the perception of changed political and socio-economic circumstances.

Against Beveridge and Turnbull's interpretation speaks also the fact that a large majority of Scottish intellectuals, academics and the media (the so-called '*évolués*') all supported devolution and a Scottish Assembly. The 'No' was not caused by fears among the Scottish elite that devolution 'would be dangerous, since the Scots require the civilising hand of their southern neighbour', but by fears among many Scots that they might be worse off socio-economically. In the light of the above discussion of the values and qualities seen to be inherent in Scottish national identity, the entire argument pertaining to the civilising hand of the English seems to fall through. Although Enlightenment thinkers might have felt Scotland to be inferior on most counts, both the elites and others in Scotland around 1979 had become conscious of the value of certain aspects of Scottish culture and mentality, and were able to think critically about them. This brings us to a contradiction in Beveridge and Turnbull's theory. In an attempt to show that tartanry is not the real problem, but that inferiorism is, Beveridge and Turnbull correctly state that 'the meanings are never passively consumed, but always subject to selection and adjustment to other discourses'.[64] This is a point of view which can be easily shared. However, it directly contradicts the theory that an anglicised elite should have been able to impose on the Scots a sense of inferiority – indeed that such a sense should have been uncritically adopted by Scots at some point. Beveridge and Turnbull thus fail to acknowledge the fact that Scots, like most people, in modern liberal democracies at least, are not merely empty vessels, waiting to be filled with a prefabricated identity. They are able to think critically about their position and their values, and to act accordingly.

Beveridge and Turnbull (as well as Nairn, McArthur and Craig, among others) do have a point, though: with Scottish national identity ridden with romantic and parochial images of a long-dead culture and of defeat, it was not particularly prone to politicisation by nationalists looking to build a 'classic nationalism' with an emphasis on cultural pride, historic heroism, etc. In fact it would have been difficult to circumvent it and its in-built defence against political nationalist action. However, the crucial element provided by any national identity – the sense of imagined community and a common destiny – was always there. By utilising only that sense of community, manoeuvring around and away from the tartanry and Kailyard images, the political nationalist movement in the early 1970s had been able to rise *in spite of* these images. The 1979 referendum was different from the early 1970s, when political nationalism could be expressed without as great a consequence. It can be argued that in terms of national identity, the same preconditions and possibilities were available, only now there was something more at stake. Nothing suggests that the lines of argument differed much from previous periods. Rational argumentation pertaining to the political and social spheres dominated the debate, as before.[65] So this was not a question of political nationalists turning to ethno-cultural arguments, and ending up paying the price. Certainly, tartanry and Kailyard were still slumbering away in the Scottish national identity, and although the political nationalist movement had previously successfully avoided the defeatism inherent in these images, they may have been invoked by other, more decisive, political and socio-economic circumstances in the hour of destiny, and therefore have become more difficult to avoid.

Although of some importance, the 'Scottish Cringe' is a factor whose power should not be overestimated. As illustrated above, the failure of the 1979 referendum was a combination of several factors: the 'Yes' side was divided at all levels, and carried the stigma of failed government, and for the first time in recent history Scotland had climbed a rung on the socio-economic ladder to become one of the relatively well-off parts of the UK, meaning there was no (better) alternative to economic dependence on the UK.

Another important reason for the outcome of the 1979 referendum on a Scottish Assembly has been suggested by Andrew Marr. Rather than being a fomenting factor in itself, this explanation includes some of the conclusions reached above with regard to various factors. The majority of the political leaders and the media, Marr argues, were caught by a sensation, but in their anxiousness they forgot to bring in 'the people'. He concludes: 'Devolution failed because it was imposed from above.'[66] Those who have been defined as the nationalising domain were largely in favour, while two thirds of those eligible to vote either declined the offer or stayed at home. However, a significant fact remains that while more than 50 per cent of the working class voted in favour of devolution in the 1979 referendum, only about 30 per cent of members of what are defined by sociologists and political scientists as social groups A and B (professionals, semi-professionals and managers) and about 45 per cent of members of social group C1 (skilled non-manual workers) did the same.[67] So this is not a question of a failure of getting the message 'down' to the people. The upper and middle classes, many members of which would themselves be defined as belonging to the nationalising domain, had in opinion polls indicated an increasing desire for home rule but in the referendum 'lost its collective nerve'.[68] In contrast, more than half of the working-class voter segment remained in favour of Scottish self-government. Politicians and media alike may have been deceived by opinion polls and the SNP's 1974 progress to believe that significant parts of all strata of Scottish society were truly in favour of constitutional change here and now (see Table 4.2), but such surveys do not consider the degree to which people wish for such fundamental change, nor the considerations they might otherwise take into account.

POPULAR POLITICAL NATIONALISM, 1980–1997

The 1979 experience, says Marr, left a long period of 'self-doubt and even self-disgust'.[69] Scott seconds this, detecting a 'mood of humiliation and resignation'.[70] As this has become the conventional interpretation, it is useful to keep in mind that this was probably true only for the one third of the population who voted 'Yes', as well as a part, presumably, of the one third who stayed at home on referendum day. However, a large part of the one third who made the conscious choice to vote 'No', along with many of those who did not vote, very likely did not share either self-disgust or a mood of humiliation. To be sure, Scottish political nationalism, not Scotland as such, found itself in a serious crisis. As regards the large part of the Scottish nationalising domain which had supported the establishment of a Scottish Assembly, the 1979

referendum did mark a traumatic turn in the fortune of political nationalism, from which it took some time to recover. After all, the 1979 referendum had revealed a discrepancy between what the Scots were ready
to participate in and what the dominant actors in the nationalising
domain believed to be best for the country. One can easily imagine how
many, on both sides, must have believed that this spelled the death of
political nationalism in Scotland. This, however, would turn out not to
be the case. Several factors combined to make the nature of autonomism
in the 1980s and 1990s even stronger than that which characterised the
1960s and 1970s.

Thatcherism and the 'Doomsday Scenario'

The initial outcome of the failed referendum, however, seemed to point
in a different direction. The Callaghan administration's decision to drop
devolution for Scotland deprived it of the parliamentary support of SNP
MPs, consequently leading to the government's defeat in a vote of no
confidence.

By the time the Conservative Thatcher government came to power,
the conditions of Scottish industry and the general socio-economic situation were severe. During the last two decades of the twentieth century,
dissatisfaction with this state of affairs fostered a growing sense in
Scotland of neglect by Westminster; of having become increasingly
peripheralised by indifferent Conservative regimes concerned only with
the interests of southern England. A 1993 poll for the *Herald* showed
that 70 per cent of the Scots agreed that Scotland had been 'worse
treated than other parts of the UK'.[71] An indication of Scottish anti-
Tory sentiment in this period is the history of the Conservative vote
in Scotland. As Table 4.1 shows, the relatively low share of the
Conservative vote, declining from 31.4 per cent in 1979 to 17.5 per cent
in 1997, stands in sharp contrast to the Conservative share of the vote
in England, illustrating a particular anti-Conservatism in Scotland.

Conservative rule from 1979 to 1997 did little to reassure Scots that
they would not be worse off socio-economically. Margaret Thatcher set

TABLE 4.1
The Conservative Vote (percentages) in Scotland and England, 1979–1997

	1979	1983	1987	1992	1997
Scotland	31.4	28.4	24.0	25.6	17.5
England	47.2	46.0	46.2	46.7	33.7

Source: Brown, McCrone and Paterson, *Politics and Society in Scotland.*

out to alter the British welfare state radically, and these alterations, affecting mainly health and education, combined with general policies of centralisation to quickly alienate most Scots. In addition to cuts in the welfare state, Scotland suffered the indignity of being used as a guinea-pig for Thatcher's 'poll tax' – opposed almost universally by everyone in Scotland except the Conservative Party.[72] It was felt that Thatcher had deliberately decided to disregard altogether that part of the British Isles called Scotland, and this galvanised support for political nationalism among an increasing number of Scots. According to Harvie, the Scots 'hated her with a venom scarcely seen since Edward [I]'s day'.[73] A 1987 poll found that 37 per cent of respondents in Scotland saw Margaret Thatcher as a good prime minister for the UK, while only 9 per cent rated her as good for Scotland.[74]

David McCrone quotes the results of a MORI poll conducted for the *Scotsman* in 1989. Of the Scots who were asked whether they thought the Westminster parliament worked for Scottish interests, only 11 per cent agreed or strongly agreed; 49 per cent disagreed or strongly disagreed. Asked if they thought decisions made by UK ministers worked in Scotland's interests, 12 per cent agreed or strongly agreed; 60 per cent disagreed or strongly disagreed.[75] An important explanatory factor with regard to such Scottish political cynicism was the increasing problem of the so-called 'Doomsday Scenario'. During the 1980s and the first part of the 1990s, the Conservative share of the vote in Scotland hovered around 25 per cent. All that time the Conservative Party formed the British government, leaving the Scots in effect with a ruling party that only about a quarter of them had voted for, and with which most were far from content.

Scottish institutions, such as the nationalised industries, the education system, local government and the churches, fell victim to many of Thatcher's policies, and as these institutions had come to be carriers of a distinctly Scottish identity, the Conservatives were seen as deliberately targeting Scotland. Conservative economic policies in Scotland meant that recession in the early 1980s hit Scotland particularly hard. The Strathclyde region, which holds about half the Scottish population, lost almost 20 per cent of jobs between 1979 and 1985. Scotland neverthe-less surfaced more quickly and in a better shape than most parts of the UK after the late 1980s' recession, which may, together with the fact that John Major replaced Margaret Thatcher as prime minister, account for the modest increase in the Scottish Conservative vote in the 1992 general election. But it would take much more to seriously change the electoral fortune of the Conservatives in Scotland.

Of crucial importance to the development of political nationalism at this stage was the decisive rejection of Conservative policies by the

Scottish middle class. The almost universal rejection by the Scots of Conservative neo-liberal values by 1992 moved David McCrone to declare: 'We're all nationalists now.'[76] His point is that there was a merging of political nationalism and party politics to the extent that Thatcher was seen as standing for everything which was not Scottish. Nairn remembers: 'From 1979 onwards . . . suddenly we began hearing so much about "community", and the humane anti-materialism of the Scots – "our way of doing things", so distinct from the vile egotism of the south-east.'[77] Marr tries to capture the prevalent feeling among Scots at the time: 'The state was far away; it was 'them down there'; it was, in some indefinable way, English . . . [A] cold-hearted regime too far away for imagination to reach or anger to affect.'[78] If this was indeed the dominant image of the Thatcher government – and much speaks in favour of Marr's interpretation – it is little wonder that in this period 'to be truly Scottish was to be anti-Thatcher'.[79] Michael Keating has argued how growing political nationalism in Scotland in the 1990s became closely tied to perceptions of class and Conservative neglect, rather than perceptions of ethno-cultural distinctness.[80] A certain sense of anti-Englishness did exist, he explains, but it was one which 'aimed at the structures of the British state rather than the English people as individuals or a race'.[81] The consequence was an almost universal Scottish rejection of Conservative policies found to be English in nature and *imposed* on Scotland in spite of the existence there of an entirely different set of values.

Scotland was in fact experiencing social and economic growth by the late 1980s and in the 1990s, and had even caught up with and over-taken most parts of the UK in terms of unemployment and GDP. Still, the Scots were as discontent with London government as ever. A plausible explanation seems to be that the Scots were nevertheless still retaining a sense of *relative* decline. Scotland was, in other words, seen to be doing well, but able, in other circumstances, to do more than well.

Here the question of the existence of alternatives to the constitutional, political and economic status quo becomes important. A range of alternatives, including more or less radical forms of autonomy, had always existed, but all options were not always viable from a rational political and economic point of view. As Table 4.2 shows, there was in the period from 1974 to 1997 an almost steady decline in support for constitutional status quo in favour of devolution or independence.

The fact that a certain number of people choose the 'independence' option in such surveys does not necessarily indicate a strong wish for constitutional change or political support for the SNP. What should to be taken into account is the fact that the issue of constitutional change

TABLE 4.2
Support for Constitutional Options, 1974–1997

Percentage in favour of	1974	1979	1984	1987	1989	1992	1997
Independence	21	7	25	32	34	23	26
Home rule	44	54	45	50	49	50	51
No change	34	26	27	15	15	24	17

Sources: Brown, McCrone and Paterson, *Politics and Society in Scotland; Scotsman*, 14 March 1987.

has been singled out for the purpose of the survey, which does not indicate to what extent the respondent agrees with a certain option. Home rule may be only the third or fourth priority to someone who finds social security, world peace or greenhouse gases to be the really important issues. Still, in relative terms, the figures may reveal interesting information about changes in attitude from one survey to the next.

The surveys reproduced above show an increase in support for the independence option from 1979 to 1989, indicating a radicalisation of political nationalism in Scotland in this period. However, a likely explanation is also to be found in the fact that independence in the 'old' sense – full sovereignty in all matters, political, cultural and economic – became in this period increasingly unrealistic. The sharp increase in the period 1979 –1984 may be accounted for as a reaction to Thatcherism, as should probably the 12 per cent decrease from 1984 to 1987 in support for constitutional status quo. The stable support in the rest of the period, however, is likely also to owe something to the idea of 'Independence in Europe', an option which entered the scene from the late 1980s.

Europe as an alternative to the UK: the SNP view

An increasingly positive incentive to political nationalism in the 1980s and 1990s was the EC/EU, which was providing economic assistance to troubled regional economies through its structural funds, and ready markets for export. Although this is now increasingly disputed,[82] in the late twentieth century the widely entertained myth was that there was a direct causal link between aid from Europe and the impressive Irish economic development that made Ireland the 'Celtic tiger' of the Western World. Scottish political nationalists, particularly the SNP, now looked to Ireland and imagined the success story repeating itself, with Scotland as the protagonist. During the 1975 EC referendum debate, the SNP had advocated a 'No' to EC membership 'On Anyone Else's Terms'. The two 1974 manifestos had indignantly referred to the European Community as 'the centralist empire', and had advocated leaving it on the grounds that 'within the Common Market, not only Scotland, but the UK, would find its quality and standards of living deteriorating'.[83] An important aspect of the SNP's opposition seems to have been the fact that Scotland was not represented in the European Community as a nation. This negative perception of the EC had not changed by 1979. The SNP manifesto from that year found that an 'essential . . . is to say to the EC: "Halt, either change to fair policies, in which nations are treated equally, or we get out." '[84]

In 1983, the same irreconcilable attitude to the EC prevailed: 'Whilst seeking co-operation with our European neighbours, we would not wish to join the Common Market (EC), since the EC has been extremely damaging to many of Scotland's interests and its centralist thinking from Brussels is as ill-suited for Scotland as that from London.'[85] Later, however, the party changed its strategy and embraced Europe with Winifred Ewing – '*Madame Ecosse*' – elected as SNP member of the European parliament. A change in attitude had occurred by 1987. Now the party recommended membership of the EC, provided that 'guarantees of protection for vital Scottish interests . . . can be obtained'. The main reason for this change of mind seems to have come from a belief that a 'Europe of Nations' could place 'greater investment in regional and social funds to ensure greater assistance to areas of relative deprivation and peripheral regions'.[86] As a remnant of previous policies of EC resistance, the manifesto maintains that the SNP will oppose moves for further centralisation of the European Community. By 1989 a complete U-turn on the question of EU membership had been accomplished. The SNP were now fully convinced of the benefits of the EC, and saw it as the springboard for a new kind of 'Independence in Europe'. The situation which was now portrayed placed the Scots between an old malfunctioning union and a new progressive one: 'Independence in Europe is an opportunity to achieve the economic and social objectives which the majority of Scots aim for . . . Within the present constitutional set up in the United Kingdom it is certain that living standards will decrease with little prospect of improvement . . . The choice is clearly between integration into Thatcher's England or Independence in Europe for Scotland.'[87]

The party maintained its objection to centralisation, but a more yielding attitude also characterised the manifesto, as it accepted that 'there will be a voluntary pooling of sovereignty by member states on specific issues'.[88] The change of heart was an indication of a more pragmatic line on Europe, compared with the party's British counterparts, and it reflected, as Mitchell pointed out, the fact that the SNP were 'beginning to sound relevant, modern and international'.[89] The conversion in the SNP to what may be termed 'international nationalism' certainly reveals an acknowledgement of the premises of a changing world in the era of globalisation. Rather than continuing its former anti-European line, an isolationist position which would no doubt have resulted in the party becoming increasingly isolated, the SNP chose to accept the given circumstances, and in the process managed to turn these circumstances to its own advantage. Many Scots who had previously felt reluctant to risk economic and political independence from the UK now had in the EU a real alternative, a safety-net which could guarantee that a greater measure of autonomy would not result in socio-economic misery. Independence in Europe remained the policy of the SNP throughout the remainder of the period investigated.

Europe, an alternative to Thatcherism: the Labour view

Like the SNP, the Scottish section of the Labour party had once been strongly opposed to British membership of the EC, but by the late 1980s it had changed its view of Europe from hostility, based on social concerns and industrial protectionism, to viewing it as a means for progress. A determining factor in Labour's change in attitude, explains Keating, was the 'ill-disguised hostility of Margaret Thatcher, identified with southern English conservatism, to the social and political dimensions of the European project ... Shut out of access to the British central state, they sought other means of influence, including local government, a renewed commitment to devolution, and the European Community.'[90]

In 1979, Labour was, much like the SNP, unimpressed with what the EC had to offer. In the 1979 manifesto for Scotland, the European Community is mentioned in one paragraph, beginning at page 24, which speaks of 'much-needed reform of the EC' and favours creating a 'wider and looser grouping of European states, thus reducing the dangers of an over-centralised and over-bureaucratic EC'.[91] By 1987, however, Labour's attitude had softened, and some benefits of membership were acknowledged: 'Labour's aim is to work constructively with our EC partners to promote expansion and combat unemployment.'[92]

The 1992 Labour manifesto for Scotland reveals an even more positive attitude to Europe, and it also outlines the relationship between Scotland and the EC that the Labour Party hoped to see: 'Scotland will have all the advantages of being part of a large member state, but will also have the opportunity to benefit from the new evolving power structures in Europe.'[93] Thus, instead of seeing the Common Market as an alternative to the UK, Labour proposes that Scotland would benefit from the EC *because* it is a member of the UK. The manifesto furthermore promises to increase the Scottish say in European affairs 'by seeking representation for Scotland in European institutions'.[94] The same idea of empowering Scotland in Europe by means of British 'muscle' is expressed in Labour's 1997 manifesto for Scotland: 'Britain . . . will be a leader in Europe. That leadership will mean Scotland's concerns will be heard at the heart of Europe as part of one of Europe's biggest players.' At this point, Labour is fully embracing EU membership as a consequence of the socio-economic benefits it will bring to the UK. Based on the perception of such benefits, the party even declares: 'Withdrawal would be disastrous for Scotland and Britain. It would put millions of jobs at risk. It would dry up inward investment. It would destroy our clout in international trade negotiations.'[95]

Although the Labour Party repeatedly accentuated the power of a united UK as the means to benefit from being part of the EC/EU, membership of the European Community – and the positive image of expected socio-economic benefits as a consequence of membership – can also be seen to have increased the incentive for many Scots to opt for devolution. Paterson ascribed the shift in attitude of the middle class towards constitutional change partly to Thatcherism and partly to 'a growing belief that Scotland could have a viable future as part of Europe'. Paterson continues: 'Europe symbolises economic opportunities, and a guarantee against isolation; both of these are especially alluring the more Britain sinks into parochialism and fundamental economic difficulties.'[96] Likewise, Maxwell argued in 1991 that European integration would likely foster, not only an increased middle class and business demand for a voice in Europe to minimise the disadvantages and maximise opportunities for Scotland, but also 'the incentive to change' while securing 'the opportunity for change without the perceived risks of "separation" '.[97]

This all rings true, but for the EU to be seen as a real alternative to the existing constitutional UK set-up, the perception of membership as beneficial to Scotland would have to be widespread. Therefore, it is important to note that Scotland became one of the most pro-European parts of the UK in the 1980s. A 1993 poll for the *Herald* thus reported 23 per cent of Scottish respondents as being against EU membership, with 46 per cent more or less in favour.[98] These figures, however, reveal a decrease of about 12 per cent in favour of membership compared with the 1975 referendum. What the figures fail to reveal is that, among the 46 per cent of the Scottish population who supported continued membership, many were likely also to feel that EU powers should be reduced. A 1992 survey reproduced by Brown, McCrone and Paterson shows that whereas 35 per cent of the Scottish respondents agreed that the powers of the EU should not be changed or should be increased, 52 per cent thought the UK should leave the European Union, or that its powers should be reduced.[99] Still, as the popularity of the EU had decreased significantly in the UK in general, the 52 per cent that were critical in Scotland should be compared to the 53 per cent in Wales, the 61 per cent in the north of England and the 64 per cent in the south of England.[100] In relative terms, Scotland therefore remained the most EU-positive part of the UK, with EU membership a factor to take into consideration with regard to the development of Scottish autonomism.

The diminishing role of oil as a viable economic alternative to the UK

It has often been argued that the importance of the North Sea oil issue had diminished by the 1980s. The analysis of SNP manifestos and budgets speak both in favour of and against such an argument. The 1983 manifesto still includes a fair deal of talk about 'Scotland's oil',[101] but it is correct that oil as an issue in SNP rhetoric, although it had not disappeared altogether, was stressed less in the manifestos from 1987 onwards. In the 1987 manifesto the first and only mention of oil is to be found on page 11, as an almost non-existent issue. This is in stark contrast not only to the oil rhetoric of the 1970s but also to the rela-tively prominent place the oil issue took in the 1983 manifesto. Similarly, the 1997 manifesto included a very brief mention of North Sea oil (on page 24) in a text otherwise extensively addressing a wide range of problems and prospects for Scotland. However, in the SNP's proposed budgets for an independent Scotland, oil maintained its importance. In the 1997 SNP general election budget, for instance, projected oil revenues made up the main part of the relative fiscal surplus with the UK, which the party counted on as by far the most important pillar of its budget for an independent Scotland.[102]

This discrepancy between the use of oil revenues to produce a convincing budget for an independent Scotland and the lack of an 'oil factor' in SNP rhetoric can be explained by the following: manifestos based on oil had failed to produce the desired middle-class and business community support in 1979; and the SNP share of the vote had continued to dwindle to a level of only 12 per cent in 1983. Clearly, oil was obviously not the vote-winner it was once thought to be. Also, from the mid-1980s there had been a collapse in oil prices. Although Labour acknowledged the positive prospects for the Scottish economy that

North Sea oil provided, that resource was always regarded by the Labour party as a British asset, and it never became an issue in Labour's devolution plans for Scotland.[103] Two major political and socio-economic incentives to political nationalism thus existed in Scotland in the 1980s and 1990s: a negative one – Thatcherism; and a positive one – the occurrence of a viable alternative to the existing constitutional situation in the shape of the EC/EU. However, more and equally powerful fomenting factors and actors combined to create the unprecedented rise of popular support for the autonomist agenda in this period.

Recovering and redefining: The SNP

In the May 1979 election, support for the SNP, which had invested all its prestige in a 'Yes' vote at the March referendum, dipped from 30.4 per cent to 17.3 per cent. The SNP had compromised its previously held conviction that Scotland deserved 'independence – nothing less', and this had placed the party in the same fold as Labour, the new autonomist player on Scotland's political scene. Labour, however, was the traditional choice of party for the Scots, and it had at this point many more strings to play on issues which were close to Scottish hearts. The field on which the SNP could now play had been severely diminished. Scottish business found denationalisations more appealing than decentralisation, and traditional Labour voters could now trust their own party to work for devolution. Thus, the advance of the SNP had been successfully stemmed both by Conservative free market policies and by the adaptation by Labour of a home rule policy. In addition, Labour had never played with the idea of separation, and it might thus have attracted some of the less convinced SNP voters. The same mechanisms – a sense of insecurity and a lack of socio-economic confidence – which prevented more than one third of the Scots from voting in favour of a Scottish Assembly, thus served to make many Scots turn once more to their old protector, the Labour Party. The Scots did not vote against the SNP in the 1979 general election because of the outcome of the referendum; everything indicates that the decline in support for the SNP was part of a general mood swing that had been under way for some time.

After 1979 the party was deeply divided between the fundamentalists and the devolutionists, the right wing and the left wing. As the 1980s went on, the SNP became gradually more leftist and more pro-EU. This new image was successful in spreading the appeal of the party to voters less radical in terms of constitutional change, and the party's share of the vote in general elections increased from 11.8 per cent in 1983 to 14.0 per cent in 1987, 21.5 per cent in 1992 and 22.1 per cent in 1997.

In 1991 the party even received, for the first time, the declared support of one of the Scottish newspapers, the tabloid *Scottish Sun*.[104]

The SNP kept nurturing an image of Scottish nationalism as pragmatic and rational – 'civic' rather than 'ethnic'. Paul Hamilton argues that 'the SNP's electoral advertising projects a modern, vibrant society and avoids appeals to kitsch and cultural caricatures'.[105] The 1983 manifesto contends that Scotland needs a government 'democratically accountable to the Scottish people, to reawaken our national identity and purpose'.[106] Interestingly, orthodox nationalist reasoning is here turned upside-down: national identity is not, according to this argument, the cause of political nationalism, but something which may be reawakened as a consequence of it. This was symptomatic of SNP policy in the 1970s, and it remained so in the 1980s and 1990s. The 1983 manifesto illustrates the low priority given to explicitly ethno-cultural rhetoric. Although stressed slightly more than in the manifestos of the 1970s – all of chapter 4, two pages, is now dedicated to the question of 'Safeguarding Scotland's Identity' – Scottish culture and its survival never becomes a dominant theme.[107] The really important issues to the SNP remain the achievement of self-determination, and freedom from what is considered 'the centralist and often undemocratic thinking of the British system'[108] and Scotland's socio-economic problems. The manifesto thus argues: 'The British system has failed Scotland. Under successive London Governments, we have seen the destruction of the Scottish economy. Industry has declined far more than in most other countries. Unemployment has soared . . . Emigration has drained away many of our most skilled people. But there is a better alternative. A Scottish Government, with the political will and control of Scotland's resources, could create more jobs and revive the economy.'[109] In this particular regard – the emphasis placed on the pragmatic arguments of democracy and improved socio-economic conditions rather than on ethnic arguments – little or nothing changes in the manifestos of the following years. The 1987 manifesto again speaks of 'decades of London mismanagement', 'Scotland's right to self-determination', 'the failure and injustice of the British system' and a 'dramatic rise in unemployment and the consequent decline in Scotland's economic and industrial base' as a consequence of this mismanagement.[110] Much emphasis is now placed on these issues and what is best described as social democratic policies of social welfare offering the basic services that the UK is no longer seen to be able to offer its citizens. Education and culture is once again confined to one minor chapter. The 1992 and 1997 manifestos are not much different in this respect – although they change with regard to the increased emphasis placed on social democratic policies of an increased level of social welfare provided by the state, and the role of the EC. The following quote sums up the 1992 manifesto's position on the familiar questions of democratic deficits and the impact on the socio-economic situation of many Scots: 'By rights, we should be a confident, open people, enjoying living in one of the wealthiest nations in Europe. Instead, we are forced to devote all our resources and energy to resisting the policies of a London government we neither voted for nor believe in.'[111] These points of view were echoed in the 1997 manifesto, which stated: 'Scotland's institutions . . . still have their distinctive national characteristics despite a constant erosion by the Westminster Parliament . . . For two hundred and ninety years Scotland has remained within a United Kingdom which has contributed less and less to our well being. Scotland has the potential to be a rich and vibrant economy yet we export our wealth south of the border. . . . Scotland has the skills and resources to be free, but it is denied its democratic right to self government.'[112] An element of ethnicity is obviously a part of such an argument; after all, this is a question of the Scottish people suffering and being in need of special care. An ethno-cultural argument, however, is hardly ever stated explicitly. There is some mention of Scottish culture and ethnic distinctiveness in the manifestos of the 1990s, but it amounts to very little, as is by now the custom in SNP manifestos. Of a total number of thirty-two pages, the 1997 manifesto thus devotes only about two pages (in chapter 7) to education and culture, including the vision of a multicultural Scotland.[113] Unless the signals transmitted by the SNP have been generally misunderstood by Scottish voters – and nothing indicates that they should have been – support for the SNP does not indicate support for 'ethnic nationalism'.

From the point at which Labour embraced home rule, the SNP was no longer the only carrier of political nationalism in Scotland. Indeed, argues McCrone, 'it was Labour rather than the SNP which inherited the nationalist mantle in the 1980s'.[114] Scottish autonomism, like so many movements of its kind, has an ill-defined goal. Most likely, Scots did not, in the period investigated, see constitutional change as an end in its own right. A comparison of the results of identity surveys (see Table 3.1) and surveys measuring support for independence and home rule (see Table 4.2) reveals a discrepancy between 'Scottishness' and the willingness to support independence at this time. This sociological mystery has been dealt with in detail by Ross Bond. His argument is too extensive to reproduce in full, but one must agree with Bond's conclusion: 'Even those with the clearest sense of their Scottishness are often reluctant to see Scotland's political future as lying outwith the UK, or to support the major Scottish political party which endorses and purports to work for this constitutional vision: the Scottish National Party.'[115] This serves to illustrate 1) that a strong Scottish national consciousness was not necessarily an indication of support for independence; and 2) that Scottish political nationalism was now indeed to be characterised as predominantly autonomist. Scottish nationalist sentiment placed itself far from the Gellnerian definition of classic nationalism. The goal of Scottish political nationalism had at this point ceased to be full congruence between the political and the national unit.

In addition, the SNP was drawing votes from Scots less than convinced about the party's separatist stance but who found its policies otherwise appealing. The Scottish Election Survey indicated that in 1997, 34 per cent of SNP supporters preferred either the status quo or home rule to independence.[116] Since the late 1980s the SNP – formerly known as the 'Tartan Tories' – had become a left-of-centre alternative to Labour. The success of the SNP in the late 1980s and 1990s is most likely closely linked to this fact. A great number of Scots, with their already mentioned preference for the welfare state, now associated its benefits (as was the case in both SNP and Labour rhetoric) with a measure of Scottish autonomy.

The new main standard-bearers: Labour

Since Labour converted to devolution, political nationalism in Scotland ceased to be measurable only by support for the SNP. A 1991 survey correlating identity with voting behaviour found that 44 per cent of Labour voters compared with 51 per cent of SNP voters, 27 per cent of Conservative voters and 21 per cent of Liberal Democrat voters defined themselves as 'Scottish, not British'.[117] Taking the difference in size of voting groups into consideration, more Labour voters than SNP voters chose this option. Although indicative of point of view on political nationalism, national consciousness does not necessarily prove a particular preference in this regard. Brown, McCrone and Paterson found that of the 23 per cent of respondents who in 1997 defined themselves only as Scottish, only 40 per cent preferred independence for Scotland, while 18 per cent chose the home rule option, and 12 per cent the status quo. Among the 38 per cent defining themselves as more Scottish than British, the percentage in favour of independence was the same, 40 per cent, with 43 per cent favouring home rule, and 23 per cent believing in maintaining the status quo.[118] A strong Scottish identity thus appears to be seen as perfectly compatible with Labour's policies of devolution as much as with SNP policies of independence in Europe.

Even though large segments of the content refer to the overall British policies of their parties, both Scottish Labour and Scottish Conservative manifestos with specific reference to Scottish problems and solutions were produced from 1979 onwards. In both cases, this is likely to have contributed to whatever sense existed of the parties' acknowledgement of a special Scottish dimension. The Labour Party was effectively shut out from political power from 1980 to 1997. Consequently, the party had to seek other means of political influence. Apart from local government and the EC, the answer was to attempt to reawaken the autonomist movement. By the late 1980s, Scottish Labour had made the conversion from unionist party in the early 1970s to convinced autonomist party.

As at all times, Labour manifestos in this period emphasised the importance of the quality of the welfare state, job creation and social security. This also, for a large part, became the incentive in Labour's devolution plans for Scotland. Manifestos point out Scotland's special situation and Scotland's particular sufferings – unemployment, high tax burdens, cuts, closures and charges – under Thatcher's rule[119] and speak of Scotland's particular need for the welfare state,[120] and of what is considered the fact that 'Scotland . . . benefits enormously from being a part of an integrated UK market'.[121] The Labour arguments ran thus: Scotland has overwhelming and unique socio-economic problems caused mainly by British Conservative governments and the lack of Scots' influence on decisions made by these governments; still, Scotland needs the UK to solve its problems. The pragmatic alternative to separation and complete integration, Labour found, was Scottish devolution.

With improvement in the Scottish socio-economic situation and the avoidance of constitutionally radical answers to Scotland's problems constituting the main instigators of Labour devolution policy, Labour's devolution plans were never a question of preserving or strengthening Scottish culture or ethnic identity. In the 1997 manifesto, the shadow secretary of state for Scotland, George Robertson, recognises that a distinct Scottish identity exists,[122] but the remaining parts of the manifesto all indicate that 'distinct identity' refers to Scotland's special political, legal, social and economic situation.

Rather than being preoccupied with a classic nationalist concern for the vitality of culture and heritage, Labour's devolution rhetoric in the 1980s and 1990s emphasised a more pragmatic focus on what could be done to change Scotland's democratic deficit and, as a result, Scotland's poor socio-economic state of affairs. The 1979 manifesto stated: 'We are deeply concerned to enlarge people's freedom. Our policy will be to tilt the balance of power back to the individual . . . and away from the bureaucrats of . . . Whitehall.'[123] One reason for this tilting of the balance is revealed at a later point: 'Circumstances in Scotland are not always the same as in the rest of the UK.'[124] In the last part of the manifesto, a sentence indicates another likely reason for the need to change the constitutional set-up of the UK, as the fear of the break-up of Britain at the hands of the SNP is expressed.[125] This element became more explicit in the manifestos of the following years. In the June 1987 manifesto, Donald Dewar, then shadow secretary of state for Scotland, spoke of 'plans for an Assembly which will give Scots a greater say over Scotland's affairs while retaining our essential links with the United Kingdom',[126] and the 1997 manifesto stressed, no less than three times, that the real strength of devolution was its ability to strengthen the union and provide an end to the threat of separatism.[127] Apart from the fear of a British break-up, Labour's 1987 manifesto, which gave devolution priority over all its other policies, also stated two other closely related reasons for the establishment of a Scottish Assembly: the democratic deficit and the socio-economic crisis caused by political neglect.

Similar arguments were put forward by Dewar in 1992: 'A Scottish Parliament is not an end in itself. It is a means to an end. It will give us the power to rebuild the Scottish economy, tackle poverty and invest in our people. Labour wants do [sic] more than give a democratic voice to the Scottish people. We want to renew Scotland as a community.'[128] The 1997 manifesto also pointed out the harm that neglect by previous governments had caused to Scotland's socio-economic condition: 'In Scotland, as elsewhere, people have been hit by . . . tax increases and economic mismanagement. Youth and long-term unemployment are wasting lives. Our health service is strangled by red tape.'[129]

In sum, the three main arguments expressed by Labour for Scottish devolution in this period were almost entirely non-ethno-cultural, focusing instead on the need for improved democratic representation, socio-economic recovery and the removal of the threat of separatism. Labour's policies, although not necessarily those pertaining to devolution alone, seem to have appealed to the Scots. Except for a brief rebuff in 1992, Labour support continued to climb from 1983, and by 1997 it had reached 45.6 per cent.[130]

Civil and political society meet: the Scottish Constitutional Convention

Many institutions in what can be defined loosely as civil society – the education system, trade unions, local government, the churches, etc. – felt threatened by Thatcherite neo-liberal policies and therefore, in the

1980s, moved into the autonomist camp. Scottish business, which had been opposed to the Scotland Act in 1978, was less hostile to devolution in the 1990s but was still the segment of Scottish society least convinced about the benefits of constitutional change. Consequently, Scottish business decided not to have representatives take part in the important Campaign for a Scottish Assembly (CSA) established in 1980. Its members, representatives from the political sphere (Labour, the Liberals, the SNP and the Communist Party), academics and representatives from STUC, for the first time sat down in plenary to discuss how best to achieve an increased measure of autonomy for Scotland. The goal of the CSA was to get home rule back on the political agenda, and it was believed that the only way to do this was to bring together all devolutionists and separatists in Scottish society and work towards a united claim.

Another significant move closely related to the CSA was the publication from the early 1980s of the magazine *Radical Scotland*. It was a forum for debate, mainly by the left and nationalist groupings in Scottish politics. Academics, literati and politicians of established and future prominence such as Stephen Maxwell, Christopher Harvie, Cairns Craig, Robin Cook, Alex Salmond, Tom Gallagher, Kevin Dunion, Andrew Marr, Isobel Lindsay, William McIlvanney, Bruce Lenman, Alice Brown, Bernard Crick, Iain Crichton Smith, David McCrone, Lindsay Paterson, Neal Ascherson and Alan Lawson contributed to the magazine. As the list of contributors indicates, this was a forum for all walks of Scottish non-Conservative life – a useful sparring ground somewhere between the SNP and the Labour Party. Also, it was a space where people outwith the political parties could voice their opinion and concerns in a forum where politicians would listen to them directly. The magazine was blatantly anti-Conservative, and pro-home rule. It led the fight against the Poll Tax and, significantly, strongly supported the initial idea for a constitutional convention.

In July 1988, after the 1987 general election had entrenched the power of the British Conservatives – still staunchly opposed to any measure of autonomy for Scotland – a constitutional steering committee within the CSA produced a report, 'A Claim of Right for Scotland', recommending that a constitutional convention, to include representatives both from the political parties and civil society, be set up with the purpose of assembling support for constitutional change. In spite of Conservative refusal to be part of the scheme, in 1989 the Scottish Constitutional Convention (SCC) sat for the first time, and included fifty-eight Scottish MPs from Labour and the Liberal Democrats, as well as representatives from the SNP, the Scottish Green Party, the Orkney and Shetland Movement, the Communists, most of the Scottish MEPs, almost all the local authorities, the STUC, the Scottish churches (Canon Kenyon Wright was made chair of the Executive), the Federation of Small Businesses, the Committee of University Principals, the Women's Forum Scotland, Ethnic Minorities Communities, the Law Society and *An Comunn Gaidhealach*.[131]

Although the Federation of Small Businesses was represented, along with observers from the Scottish Council of Development & Industry, one Chamber of Commerce, and the Forum of Private Businesses, the Scottish business community was largely absent; not least due to the fact that the Confederation of British Industry (Scotland) chose not to participate. Still, most of civil and political society in Scotland now joined hands to form the Scottish Constitutional Convention to try to bring about some kind of devolution of powers from Westminster. In Keating's opinion, this represented a 'sharp break in the British tradition of adversary politics'.[132] The break was not complete, though: in January 1989, before the convention's first real meeting, the SNP left it, arguing that Scotland needed 'Independence – nothing less'.[133] The withdrawal of the SNP was most likely a consequence of the arrival of a new charismatic leader, Alex Salmond, at a time when the party was doing increasingly well in opinion polls. In other words, the SNP considered itself in a position strong enough to walk alone. Consequently, Labour now found itself occupying an unchallenged position within the SCC, as the locomotive of the autonomist movement.

The media

In the period up to 1979, the *Scotsman* – enthusiastically – and the *Glasgow Herald* – reluctantly – had supported the establishment of a Scottish Assembly, while several other Scottish newspapers, particularly those on the right, opposed it. By the 1990s, however, the situation was altogether different. Smith writes in his *Paper Lions* (1994): 'Prior to each recent election, every major newspaper in Scotland has endorsed Home Rule, and especially the parties which support devolution but not independence.'[134] MacInnes has illustrated how by the early 1990s all Scottish-based newspapers, except for the *Sunday Post* and the *Dundee Courier*, opposed the continuation of Conservative government.[135] With the exceptions of the *Dundee Courier* and the *Press and Journal*, all Scottish papers supported a Scottish parliament. In Smith's words, 'to be pro-Home Rule was to be politically correct'.[136] One paper, the *Scottish Sun*, even went as far as endorsing Scottish independence. Such widespread support obviously gave credence to the autonomist cause.

As indicated previously, this is an immensely important factor, and it will be dealt with specifically in chapter 6 on political nationalism and changing images of self and other in the Scottish press.

Middle-class alienation and conversion to autonomism

In this period, the political parties working for autonomism were careful to include in their struggle 'the people' – particularly the middle class – in the form of representatives from various sectors of civil society. It was important, in order not to repeat the failure of 1979, to make sure that the demand for constitutional change was not merely the wish of the media and some political parties, but of a united nationalising domain and the bulk of ordinary people. Backing for the CSA, and later the SCC, clearly illustrated that an autonomist discourse enjoyed the support of a large majority of almost all strata of Scottish society. This had also been indicated by opinion polls. Based on such polls, in 1990 Lindsay Paterson could persuasively argue that the Scottish social groups A, B and C1 had finally 'gone native'.[137] He based this argument on a greater determination among members of these groups to opt for the 'independence' option than in the 1970s, and thus an expectation that middle-class people increasingly choosing this radical answer would be less prone to lose their 'collective nerve', as they had done in 1979.

The alienation by the Conservatives of what would under normal circumstances have been their core support group, middle-class Scots, thus becomes an extremely important fomenting factor. Tom Nairn considers that the alienation of the middle class, and the subsequent increase in support for political nationalism among its members, is the result of the inherent erosion of its power in Scottish society. The 'second-in-command class,' he writes, 'knew instinctively that they could never survive a drastic overhaul of the UK command structure.' This class, argues Nairn, realised that 'self-subordination is one thing; the dissolution of its whole social universe is quite another'.[138] The many decades of complacent cultural nationalism on the part of ruling Scottish elites were being replaced by political nationalism as the middle classes were increasingly being pushed to the periphery. Significantly, those hit hardest by Thatcher's economic and social policies were not only the public sector employees, but also the previously fiercely anti-devolution business community, now witnessing how Scottish companies were rapidly leaving Scottish hands. In 1991, Stephen Maxwell believed there to be 'some grounds for believing that the Scottish middle class will adopt a more radical political stance in the 1990s'.[139] The two reasons he stressed were 1) a changed perception among sections of the middle class of the social and economic benefits of the status quo; and 2) the strengthening of middle-class forums of debate outside the political establishment. The 1990s would prove him right.

Lindsay Paterson has provided a persuasive account of the processes of middle-class alienation and protest. His argument goes: Scotland had remained administratively autonomous up until the era of Thatcherism. It had maintained a high degree of *de facto* self-government via its separate institutions, the Scottish Office and informal political conventions and consensus, allowing it to control among other things the practical implementation of the welfare state.[140] When Conservative policies from 1979 set out to significantly alter this state of affairs through privatisations, the introduction of 'a more commercial style of management to the health service', reform of local government and the legal system, and general restrictions on the welfare state, the Scottish professional middle class realised that its local hegemony and opportunities were threatened and therefore rejected the Conservative Party.[141] As a consequence, by the late 1980s, there was a significantly lower level of support for the Conservative Party in the Scottish middle class (about one third of the votes) than in the English middle class (about two thirds of votes). Another consequence of Conservative alienation was a growth in middle-class support for Labour, the Liberals and political nationalism. The mounting support for Scottish self-government meant that, as socialism fell out of fashion, Labour could now enthusiastically engage in autonomism instead.

A *national claim denied: the* 1992 *disappointment*

In general, there was increasing support for independence in the 1980s, which was sustained in the 1990s (Table 4.2). Because of the widespread support in Scotland for constitutional change among the people, the media and the politicians, ahead of the 1992 elections there was a general expectation that Labour would form the new British government, and that they would therefore soon be able to deliver on their promise of devolution. In fact, the *Radical Scotland* editorial board were so convinced that the fate of Scottish politics had been radically altered that they chose to close the publication in July 1991.[142] All of the media were pushing the story, and with the political classes created 'the bubble that burst'.[143] The Conservative victory, based on English votes, was a major shock to the political parties and to Scots in general. In the 1992 general election, the two major SCC parties and the SNP received a large majority of the Scottish votes, 73.6 per cent, with the

Conservatives garnering only 25.6 per cent. The party manifestos were concerned with more than just constitutional questions, but since this was talked up as the 'devolution election' – or, in the mind of Alex Salmond, the 'independence election' – it can be argued that these percentages also illustrate the spread of autonomism vs. unionism in Scotland. This time, Scotland was, by and large, ready for change and voted for it. Still, it was the new Conservative leader, John Major, who held on to power.

In Labour's 1992 election manifesto, Donald Dewar found that the Scottish Constitutional Convention had been 'a real success'. For the first time, he argued, 'political parties and people from all walks of life came together to devise a scheme for the better government of Scotland', and he vowed to introduce legislation to establish a Scottish parliament 'firmly based on the proposals agreed in the Scottish Constitutional Convention'.[144] In the wake of the general election, however, party co-operation faltered, and the previously united autonomist movement began splitting up into factions. The SCC nevertheless finished its work and published its final document, *Scotland's Parliament. Scotland's Right* on St Andrew's Day, 30 November 1995.

It was when the SCC sat for the first time in March 1989 that Canon Kenyon Wright put forward his famous rhetorical question and answer: 'What if that other single voice we all know so well responds by saying, "We say no, and we are the state?" Well, we say yes – and we are the people.'[145] Canon Wright's remark is symptomatic of the spirit of the SCC, which is also present in its final document and for this reason worth quoting at length:

> The first and greatest reason for creating a Scottish parliament is that the people of Scotland want and deserve democracy. Their will is powerful and clear . . . and has strengthened rather than diminished with the passing of time . . . Scotland's legal system, its educational system, its social, cultural and religious traditions . . . are the very fabric of Scottish society, yet Scotland has come to lack democratic control over them. Their conduct is determined by a government for which few Scots voted . . . This is a democratic deficit which runs contrary to Scotland's distinct political identity and system. It is affecting relations with the rest of the United Kingdom in which most Scots wish to remain, and hampering Scotland's ability to make its voice heard in the world, particularly within a fast-developing European Union well attuned to such voices. . .
>
> Scotland's Parliament will be able to make a real difference to the prosperity of the people of Scotland, and to the quality of life they

lead . . . [T]he Scottish economy can be differentiated from those of other parts of the UK, both in its strengths and in its weaknesses . . . [Scotland] has a long-standing difficulty in creating new growth companies and lasting jobs. UK economic policy has, hardly surprisingly, failed to address these circumstances closely, systematically and effectively. Scotland's Parliament . . . will be able to do much better . . . Much the same applies to the field of social welfare – a broad phrase, but the one that best describes the wide range of concerns which have so sharply distinguished the political will of Scotland in recent years.[146]

These are the basic ideas in *Scotland's Parliament. Scotland's Right*, which became the basis for Labour's (as well as the Liberal Democrats') programme for devolution.

The 1992 general election may have split the autonomist movement, but it was not as severely wounded as in 1979. Autonomists were quick to bounce back in the face of defeat. Labour and the Liberal Democrats stayed committed to devolution, as did most parts of civil society, with the SNP as committed to some sort of independence as ever. With the background of the previous analysis of the defeats in 1979, it is easy to detect why. The autonomist movement swiftly recovered because, whereas in 1979 the people had been asked and had said 'No', in 1992 they said 'Yes', but were denied what they voted for. Rather than sending constitutional change back into the dark, this denial seems to have strengthened the resolution among Scots that a doomsday scenario should no longer be possible.

In 1994, the same year as Tony Blair became leader of 'New Labour', the Scottish branch of the party officially took the name the Scottish Labour Party, stressing its commitment to work for Scotland. The 1997 general election, in which the Scots did not return a single Conservative MP, saw the landslide victory of New Labour and, as a direct consequence, a change of government policy towards constitutional change in the UK. On 11 September 1997, referendums were held in both Wales and Scotland to decide whether there was popular support for the devolution of powers through the establishment of elected assemblies in these parts of the UK. Later, in 1998, a similar referendum was held in Northern Ireland. The implications of the kind of devolution proposed by the Labour government comprised Scottish control over a wide range of areas. The Scottish parliament would be able to legislate on the following subjects with regard to Scotland: health, education, training, local government, transport, social work, housing, economic development, the legal system, environment, agriculture, fisheries, forestry, sport, the arts – and would have the powers to regulate taxes by up to 3 pence in the pound (the 'Tartan Tax', so-called by its critics). The Westminster government would keep control of such areas as foreign and defence policy, social policy and the fiscal and economic system. The Scots would elect 129 members of the Scottish parliament (MSPs), and for a time still be represented in Westminster by the usual 72 Scottish MPs. The latter caused some debate, usually referred to as the 'West Lothian Question'.[147] The complaint concerns the fact that Scotland would still, through its 72 MPs, have a say in the making of the laws of all of the UK – including those pertaining only to England. However, with the Scottish parliament taking care of all Scottish matters, the English MPs would not have the same opportunity to influence Scottish laws. A reduction in the number of Scottish MPs was therefore suggested in the Scotland Act 1998, which re-established the Scottish parliament. As a consequence, the Boundary Commission for Scotland winnowed down the number of Scottish MPs from 72 to 58.[148] In the 11 September 1997 referendum, the Scots voted massively in favour of the re-establishment of the Scottish parliament; 74.3 per cent of the voters were in favour of devolution, while 63.5 per cent voted in favour of giving the parliament tax-varying powers. The Scottish parliament was re-established and re-convened on 1 July 1999.

The relationship between political and cultural nationalism, 1980–1997

In the period from 1967 to 1979, nationalism in Scotland can be seen as having been divided into two distinct branches: cultural nationalism and political nationalism. One was apolitical, harbouring no demands for constitutional change; the other set out to change Scotland's constitutional position within the UK, utilising rational argumentation pertaining to the political and socio-economic spheres. The two types of nationalism can be said to have followed parallel paths rather than a shared one. In contrast, the period from 1980 to 1997 was increasingly characterised by a significantly higher degree of confluence between cultural arguments and politically and socio-economically motivated demands.

Even if the 1979 referendum also spilled over into a period characterised by a cultural vacuum and introduced, for a brief spell, a sense of despair among writers and other intellectuals, the cultural sphere was the first to recover from the rebuff in the second major cultural revival of the century. Cairns Craig describes the dominant dark mood and the recovery from it: 'Many felt that 1979, and the failure of the Devolution Referendum, represented . . . a disaster: that the energetic culture of the

1960s and 1970s would wither into the silence of a political waste land in which Scotland would be no more than a barely distinguishable province of the United Kingdom. Instead, the 1980s proved to be one of the most productive and creative decades in Scotland this century.'[149]

In *The Scottish Novel Since the Seventies* (1993), Gavin Wallace records a similar perception of the experience: 'Objective, confident debate . . . about Scottish fiction has flourished as the laments which predominated the early 1980s for traditions immured in ignorance and neglect . . . have faded.'[150] Paradoxically, the bleak urban realism of James Kelman, William McIlvanney, Irvine Welsh and Ian Rankin, and, equally important, the international success of Alasdair Gray, Welsh and Rankin restored a positive image of the Scottish intellectual self, if not of Scottish society as such. All was not, after all, tartanry and Kailyard. Rankin recalls what prompted him to chose his settings and themes: 'I started writing about Edinburgh – and by extension Scotland – to make sense of my surroundings, but I also wanted to show tourists and outsiders that there is more to these places than short-bread and tartan, golf and whisky and castles. Scotland faces the same challenges as any other nation. We worry about crime. . . , employment and migration . . . Lacking confidence and battered by industrial decline, we've come to underestimate ourselves.'[151]

Some of these literati, like McIlvanney and Gray, were furthermore actively advocating Scottish self-government. The year 1992 saw the publication of the first edition of Gray's *Why Scots Should Rule Scotland*, which ardently advocated Scottish home rule, and in the same year McIlvanney wrote in an 'Election Essay', a supplement to the *Scotland on Sunday* on 8 March: 'This is the time for gathering the fuel for the rage of a country. That fuel can only come from a massive pro-Scottish and anti-Westminster vote. If we can, through the ballot-box, make Scotland almost exclusively represented by Labour, SNP and Liberal Democrat MPs, we will have made a mirror in which there will be a visible reflection of a nation's demand for Home Rule.'[152]

Previously, Scottish cultural nationalism, and culture as such, could be seen as a refuge or retreat from political and socio-economic realities. Now some of the literati were actively trying to change aspects of that reality by becoming involved in the debate, either directly or via their literary works. Cairns Craig speaks of the emergence of a new and vigorous debate 'about the nature of Scottish experience . . . and about the ways in which the Scottish situation related to that of other similar cultures throughout the world'.[153]

The writers of the cultural sphere thus 'crossed the border' to the political sphere and offered their assistance to political nationalism, and they were not alone in doing so. Popular rock bands and singers such as

Runrig, The Proclaimers and Fish were highly critical of what they gener-ally regarded as a malfunctioning established system, and proscribed Scottish pride and political nationalism as the cure for Scotland. In this part of the period, those in other spheres – politicians, administrators, academics, etc. – also crossed borders to enter the cultural realm. The 'Claim of Right for Scotland' – the document that led to the constitu-tional convention and eventually to a Scottish parliament – thus includes a regular ethno-cultural nationalist argument (among others of a more socio-economic and political nature): 'The Union has always been, and remains, a threat to the survival of a distinctive culture in Scotland.'[154]

It was about the same time (in the mid-1980s) that critical voices were heard, demanding that Scottish culture be reintroduced into Scottish curricula. Conservative governments provoked, according to Lindsay Paterson, 'that instinctive nationalism which runs right through the Scottish education system'.[155] One result was the report of the Review of Scottish Culture Group to the Scottish Consultative Committee on the Curriculum. The report proposed a restoration of the Scottish dimension to education in Scotland through the full inclusion of Scottish arts, languages, religion, geography and history in the curriculum. Part of the report reads: 'The Review Group strongly believes that the national education system should as a matter of policy cherish and promote Scottish culture and identity . . . Young people should be entitled to a curriculum which recognises the value of Scottish culture.'[156] A significant upgrading and repositioning of Scottish culture took place at university level also. Whereas previously Scottish literature was rarely taught in the Department of English Literature at the University of Edinburgh, in 1999 it had a four-year programme, a Scottish Literature degree and over 200 students specialising in Scottish literature.

An important outlet for writers of this cultural renaissance, as well as a forum for the debate about Scottish culture and identity, was the magazine *Cencrastus*, established like *Radical Scotland* in the wake of the 1979 devolution referendum in an attempt to 'rekindle flames'. In a 'Revalutation [sic]' in 1982, the editorial board explained their reasons for launching the magazine: 'The narrow terms in which the Devolution "debate" had been conducted highlighted how badly needed were alter-native forums.' The editorial continued: 'The creeping nationalism in the ranks of the Labour Party is . . . being mirrored by creeping socialism in the ranks of the SNP . . . It seems, therefore, that the issue of Devolution is about to be thrust to the forefront of Scottish politics again',[157] thus testifying to the political overtones always present in the magazine. Also political were the front page illustrations: one of the more famous ones shows a Hugh MacDiarmid-faced rampant Scottish lion clad in the Saltire, its tail an ink-dripping pen, trampling a frayed Union flag under foot.

Cencrastus was primarily a magazine for literary and cultural critique, but a great deal of the articles published in it dealt with Scotland's constitutional situation and with possible solutions to political problems, and several of the regular contributors were also published in *Radical Scotland*. Contributors to *Cencrastus* in this period included Ronald Turnbull and Craig Beveridge, James Kelman, Liz Lochhead, Stephen Maxwell, Cairns Craig, Iain Crichton Smith, Colin McArthur, Christopher Harvie, Lindsay Paterson, Michael Keating, Alasdair Gray, John Caughie, David McCrone, Angus Calder, Neal Ascherson, Tom Nairn, Tom Gallagher, Jim Sillars and Paul H. Scott – i.e., quite a few of the *Radical Scotland* group. Thus, sociologists, political scientists, literary critics, writers and filmmakers met in these forums and made the appearance of the cultural renaissance seem like a rebirth of more than the cultural sphere of society. Harvie traced 'a sustained intellectual and political revival, which led out of the Kailyard and into a critique of Scottish society as much as Westminster politics'.[158]

The new sense of flux led Michael Keating to proclaim: 'National identity in Scotland is nothing new but its political significance may have changed ... There is ... a cultural dimension to national life and a national dimension to cultural issues which was absent in the past.'[159] Scholars are not in agreement, however, about the degree to which this amalgamation has occurred. In his *Understanding Scotland* (1992), David McCrone maintains that, although a Scottish cultural renaissance has occurred, 'there is no direct connection between [this] and the waxing and waning of political nationalism'.[160] This is a point of view which Paul Hamilton also subscribes to. He regards Scottish nationalism as primarily civic. He contrasts it with Welsh nationalism, with its focus on language and culture, and says: 'Scottish nationalists manifest a much more subtle and elusive self-portrait based on an amalgam of distinct institutions and a shared sense of history.' He argues further that the SNP has avoided capitalising on ethnicity, and concludes: 'Such strenuous objections to exclusionary politics forms a fundamental element of civic nationalism.'[161]

Still, the bonds that now characterised the relationship between political and cultural nationalism in Scotland were certainly closer and stronger than had ever been the case before. The links were not, however, established overnight. Cultural nationalism can be said to have got a 'head-start', declaring cultural autonomy in the early 1980s, leaving the political sphere to gradually caught up.

The redefinition of Scottish identity and society had become the common ground on which actors from the political, socio-economic and cultural spheres could meet. Tellingly, dominant themes of *Cencrastus* articles in the 1980s were – apart from Scottish nationalism – internal colonialism, inferiorism, and the struggle to redefine Scottish stereo-types and mythology (tartanry and Kailyard). The discussion of how best to (re)define and utilise Scottish identity continued throughout the period and was much enhanced by the highly enlightening books in the 'Determinations' series, edited by Cairns Craig. In Scottish literature, new metropolitan writers working from a postmodernist stand (such as Alasdair Gray and Irvine Welsh) also gradually came to terms with the romanticised interpretations of Scottish heritage, and dealt with (some-times critically, sometimes affectionately) both tartanry and Kailyard images in their novels. The old romantic myths seem to have become radically reinterpreted at all levels in modern Scotland, not only in liter-ature. The entire set of symbols has been brought to signal something different from romanticism, primitivism, parochialism and defeat. In 1999, Cairns Craig explained: 'When you watch Scottish football fans or rugby fans, now they go in a dress which is a parody of all those versions of tartanry that we were complaining about in the early 1980s. Things which people thought were appalling have now become parodi-cally fashionable, as a kind of joke or statement of "I am different". Where, to my generation, all of these things were appalling because we associated them with this kind of stigmatized narrow culture, these have now become the signs of a difference which is quite confident – enough to say: "you can laugh at us, we can laugh at ourselves in relation to these things".'[162]

Craig continues his analysis by suggesting that what critical academics actually objected to when they criticised tartanry was that it was a small designated space left open within British identity for Scottish culture. In his view, Scots have now 'taken control of those things again . . . through parodying it'.[163] This is a convincing analysis, which suggests that in terms of the 'Scottish Cringe' detected by Beveridge and Turnbull, the cultural revival would seem to have done wonders for it. In light of such conclusions, it is easy to forget an important fact: in their original forms, tartanry and Kailyard also had an often-dismissed role to play. The myths most likely prevented the development of political nationalism by constantly invoking images of backwardness and defeat, but they were also, in this process, maintaining a sense of Scottish culture and history as distinct and different from English or 'British' culture.

Because the cultural sphere had not been particularly involved in the political nationalist battles fought in the 1970s, it was quicker to recover than the political sphere. The result was a novel kind of cultural nationalism, different from cultural nationalism in the old sense. The new cultural revival was of a much more political kind, and where political nationalism in the 1960s arose almost in spite of cultural nationalism, political nationalism and Scottish culture in the 1980s and 1990s met more often in fruitful exchanges. These have taken many forms, some of them critical and satirical, but most of them illustrating a renewed sense of pride in Scotland's unique qualities. This, however, does not indicate a full return to the romanticism and focus on ethno-cultural distinctness, which is characteristic of many classic nationalist movements. The claims of Scottish political nationalism focused on policies and accountability, which makes it one of the least romantic nationalist movements. Neither does this mean that the main fomenting factor of political nationalism in the period 1980 to 1997 was the added focus on Scottish culture and the higher degree of interchange between actors in the political and the cultural sphere. McCrone concludes: 'By and large, Scottish nationalism has eschewed a dependence on cultural issues. As a result, cultural concerns provide some raw material for nationalism, but rarely its *raison d'être*.'[164] The statement rings particularly true for the latter part of the period investigated here.

FIVE

Newfoundland National Identity
and Nationalism

NATIONS IN THE BOSOM: THE DEVELOPMENT OF
NEWFOUNDLAND ETHNICITY

In his 1839 *Report on the Affairs of British North America*, Lord
Durham wrote about the nature of the problems in Lower Canada: 'I
expected to find a contest between a government and a people: I found
two nations warring in the bosom of a single state: I found a struggle,
not of principles, but of races.'[1] Durham was referring to a division
between the francophone and anglophone cultures. As governor general
from 1838 he had been commissioned to investigate and prepare a
report on the causes of the 1837 rebellions in the Canadas.

Since then, the distinction between Canada's 'two founding nations' –
or 'Two Solitudes' as Hugh MacLennan had it – has often been the point
of departure for policies, visions or debates about Canada, Canadian
federalism, bilingualism and multiculturalism. Regular outbursts of
indignation and calls for basic rights, particularly in attempts to settle
Canada's problematic constitutional situation, indicate that also in
modern times this perception of two nations co-existing or confronting,
if not actually warring with each other, within Canada has far from lost
its influence.

With a theoretical point of departure in Louis Hartz's theory of fragmentation, this part of the book suggests that Newfoundland could
indeed be considered – at least historically – yet another such nation and
distinct society, since 1949 also in Canada's 'bosom'. In order to fully
appreciate the ways in which Newfoundland and Newfoundlanders have
reacted to and still react to central government and 'mainland Canada'
generally, it is necessary to understand the sense of Newfoundland
nationhood, which has existed and among some still exists. In other
words, it is necessary to track down the ethnic core of autonomism.

The idea of 'nations in the bosom' can be utilised on several levels.
Considering Newfoundland nationalism entirely generically would

disregard the importance of the sectarian division between Catholics and Protestants within the young colony/dominion itself. Hence, in the following, this schism will also be discussed.

It is not the purpose to establish here whether Newfoundland is a 'real' nation or not. This would be an impossible task; national identity remains a subjective matter and objective definitions of the nation cannot be made. The only thing that can be said with any certainty is that when a sense of ethnic identity, of 'peoplehood', exists, and a people decides to consider itself a nation and start thinking of itself as having certain features, rights and privileges because of its existence as a nation (regardless of whether that people chooses to exercise that right or not), it makes sense to talk about national identity and nationalism.

An important part of this study is the application of theories of nationalism and national identity-building to Newfoundland. Few people would question the application of these theories in the analysis of the development of Scottish nationalism. During research for the Newfoundland part of the analysis, however, it was often pointed out to me that one would have to view Newfoundland differently. After all, Newfoundland is a province within a federal state, and this calls for an entirely different set of 'tools' to be able to understand why political, intellectual and media actors act the way they do. There is an obvious point to the argument. Within a federal constitutional framework there are certain rules, traditions and mechanisms, which demand to be taken into consideration. The built-in brokering for power between the provincial and the federal governments must be considered in this context for one to fully appreciate the motivations, actions and goals of actors. Uncritically applying a pre-understanding based on how the struggle for power takes place between central government and sub-state units in countries with a different state form is not likely to result in reliable conclusions. However, at the level of imagination, when studying not so much *political practice* as the *collective social identity* on which it is based, in some cases – such as Newfoundland – adhering only to theories of the workings of federalism, regionalism or dependency theory, for instance, will not provide all the answers. Although in no way sufficient as a stand-alone explanatory theory, Louis Hartz's fragment thesis, forwarded in his *The Founding of New Societies* (1964), remains a useful starting point for the historical investigation of the perception of the Newfoundland self.

Hartz's fragment thesis

This is Hartz's fragment thesis in a nutshell: when groups of immigrants from European societies separated from the Old World to settle in the new they established themselves as 'fragments' of the old society and its predominant ideology at the time they left (or fled). These immigrants were often carriers of new and disputed ideologies: they were religious dissenters, liberals, radicals, etc.[2] However, state-sponsored plantations, such as Nouvelle France, meant the introduction of a fragment social order – in this case feudalism – to the new world. In the case of anglophone North America, bourgeois liberalism became the dominant fragment.

In the new world, the hegemonic fragment ideology was elevated to national identity: the once European ideology 'becomes a universal, sinking beneath the surface of thought to the level of an assumption. Then, almost instantly, it is reborn, transformed into a new nationalism ... Feudalism comes back at us as the French-Canadian Spirit, liberalism as the American Way of Life, radicalism as the Australian Legend.'[3] This transformation occurs as part of the more or less conscious process of recapturing a sense of wholeness and producing a version of the fragment ideology which is grander than that which it is a fragment of, and therefore valuable and independent.[4] According to Hartz, this process – the cultural part of which has been described as the invention of 'indigeneity'[5] – takes place over just a few generations. Besides making the fragment society conservative and self-protective with regard to its national identity, this process also allows the fragment to develop freely, without inhibition and ideological antagonism. New immigrants, not part of the original fragment, are expected to make the dominant ethic theirs.

Critical questions can be raised with regard to Hartz's thesis, most importantly what immediately appears to be its inherent determinism. Reading the thesis from a modern liberal democratic point of view, one must ask what happened to the will of the individual. Will times never be 'a-changing' because of the ideological baggage that early immigrants happened to be carrying with them?[6] What is of more relevance in this context, however, is the part of the thesis that deals with the origins of new nations.

Applying the fragment thesis to Newfoundland

Neither Hartz nor his co-writer on Canadian historical processes, Kenneth D. McRae, considered Newfoundland interesting enough to include in their study. Had they done so, however, they would have found a society which, according to the fragment thesis, would have been as ideologically, mentally and ethnically distinct as Upper and Lower Canada.

First, the emphasis placed by Hartz and McRae on the influx of Loyalists and 'American liberalism' to Canada after the American

Revolution[7] would indicate that Newfoundland – where Loyalists did not settle in large numbers – had a fragment creed which was significantly different from the rest of English Canada, at least until Confederation in 1949. The 'Tory streak' which, says Hartz, tempered American liberalism in English Canada[8] never arrived in Newfoundland (or at least did not arrive from the United States).

Second, McRae describes the nature of the English Canadian fragment as predominantly 'English' and, to a lesser degree, 'Protestant'.[9] This too would mark Newfoundland off as different from mainland English Canada. Newfoundland was mainly settled by the time of, and shortly after, the Napoleonic Wars.[10] Of those who arrived at this time to settle in Newfoundland, most were Irish Roman Catholics, and by the 1836 census, the Irish constituted half the population. Although this development preceded a similar one in the rest of anglophone British North America, this was not a pattern which remained particular to Newfoundland. By the middle of the nineteenth century about half of all immigrants from the British Isles were Irish. What makes Newfoundland special in this case is the fact that the founding fathers of the self-governing Newfoundland state – the reformers who came to define Newfoundland in the process of inventing its 'indigeneity' – were in fact, as will be illustrated later, largely to be found in this powerful Irish Roman Catholic group.

Third, Canada received a large wave of immigrants from non-British parts of Europe in the early years of the twentieth century. Although, according to the fragment thesis, these immigrants would have been absorbed into the hegemonic creed, the presence of such overwhelming numbers of culturally different peoples is bound to have made an impact on English-Canadian identity. Daniel Francis has argued convincingly how British heritage remained a very present, even dominant, part of Canadian culture through the uncritical celebration of Canada's place in the great empire[11] but, generally considered, anglophone Canada's sense of a British link was weakened by non-British immigration long before multiculturalism became official policy. In contrast, it has been the fate of 'the Rock' to become a stepping-stone for immigrants to Canada. Most of them have not remained in Newfoundland for very long before moving on into interior Canada.[12] This means that Newfoundland's ethnic composition has not been significantly altered since the early nineteenth century, and national identity is therefore not ethnically challenged.

Finally, the fact that Newfoundland stayed aloof from Canada until 1949 would, according to the fragment thesis, further accentuate the difference between mainland anglophone Canada and Newfoundland.

McCrae argues: 'Quebec is by no means the only province to uphold provincial rights jealously, but it has a compelling ethnic reason for doing so that is shared by no other province'; and he continues: 'it is possible that . . . insularity [as provided in a federal system] was an essential condition for the very survival of the [Quebec] minority fragment.'[13] According to this argument, Newfoundland's separate existence off the coast of Canada until 1949 would certainly cater for the perception of a rather unique ethnic identity here, in a largely intact fragment. The continued close association with the UK, and other cross-Atlantic links forged by fish exports, for instance, influenced the Newfoundland sense of self in a way that the anglophone Canadian sense of self – increasingly finding itself in the American political, economic and cultural orbit – was not.

One should be careful not to dismiss the similarities, of course. There are several and important common traits. For one, settler societies generally share a sense of equality; in the bush, the learned and cultivated would not survive long unless they too started digging and chopping – an experience which gentlefolk in Newfoundland would share with Susanna Moodie in central Canada. Also, the origins of a significant portion of the immigrant settlers, their time of arrival, and the continuous and growing contact between Canada and Newfoundland, as well as the increasingly important presence of the United States in the period leading up to Confederation, tell the story of fragments which on many points may have more in common than what separates them.

What is relevant, however, is the will to perceive national distinctness. The conclusion to this experiment of applying Hartz' fragment thesis to Newfoundland points to the fact that Newfoundland should indeed be considered a fragment of its own, most likely with its own metamorphosis of a fragment ideology into a sense of nationhood.

Over the years, many scholars have chosen to dismiss Hartz' thesis and McRae's analysis as altogether too simplistic, and it is certainly not suggested here that we should rely on this preliminary and highly theoretical analysis alone. Rather, a more thorough study of the society in question is likely to prove rewarding in revealing the nature of the ethnic core of Newfoundland autonomism; the core that makes it possible to speak of Newfoundland collective identity as 'national', and which would place Newfoundland in a category with Quebec, rather than with other English-speaking provinces.

The following analysis will further investigate Newfoundland identity as expressed in practise, and in particular the metamorphosis which took place from early immigrant 'old world' identity to Newfoundland national identity.

Founding moments in Newfoundland's nineteenth-century history

In the preface to his *Newfoundland in the North Atlantic World* (1988), Peter Neary says: 'Above all, perhaps, my work is a reminder that Newfoundland was a country before it became a province and that therefore its history is more than a mere record of those events . . . which led to Confederation.'[14] More than a simple expression of nostalgia or patriotism, Neary's words emphasise the historiographical demand to consider historical developments in their own right; not least because they have shaped societies and cultures and to a very large extent determined how and why people think and act the way they do today. Thus, we should not deny Newfoundland its history as a colony and a settler society, and the proper interpretation that we apply to other societies with a similar background, just because it is now part of a large federal state, i.e., Canada. Newfoundland national identity developed parallel to, and in many cases quite differently from, other Canadian national identities.

On what we might phrase continental Canada, the borders between different provincial selves and others are marked only on maps by 'dash-dot-dash' lines. In the case of Newfoundland there is a much more tangible physical barrier, literally a 'gulf': the Gulf of St Lawrence.[15] Significant to the development of a unique sense of Newfoundland-ness as this has been, founding moments in Newfoundland's history have been even more important. McRae is particularly concerned, and rightly so, with the gradual introduction of democracy and self-government in the Canadas (most notably the 1848 granting of responsible government) as defining moments for the anglophone fragment. In the search for founding or defining moments, it is rewarding to look at similar points in Newfoundland history.

What sets the founding moments of the Newfoundland nation apart from the nation-building processes in the Canadas of the nineteenth century is the different fragmental input that the different societies received. There can be little doubt that, in terms of ethnic composition, contemporary Newfoundland is quite unique in Canada. Newfoundland heritage remains predominantly that of immigrants from the British Isles. In most parts of the nineteenth century that was the case also for the other anglophone colonies and, from 1867, anglophone Canada, but what makes Newfoundland different are the alternative immigration and demographic patterns.

Early settlement in Newfoundland was predominantly English but only semi-permanent. Fishermen commuted to work on the Grand Banks only to return, in the case of most, to what remained their homes in

Devonshire. By the early nineteenth century, however, after a large wave of immigration following the Napoleonic Wars, the Irish section of the population had grown to close to fifty per cent.[16] As a consequence, the Irish Newfoundlanders came to dominate politically and thus became very important players with regard to forging a Newfoundland national identity. Contrary to elsewhere in North America, it was a different fragment from the English Protestant one that became dominant. In one of the most turbulent periods of Newfoundland's existence, from the end of the eighteenth century until the mid-nineteenth century, Newfoundland underwent drastic social and political changes. Massive immigration and fast socio-economic development (mainly due to expansion of the fisheries) created a situation in which a growing section of the Irish newcomers demanded fair representation to replace the oligarchic rule of a few English-Anglican fish merchants. For many, the reform movement in Newfoundland came to take the shape of a call for individual and religious rights against English and Anglican authority, much like the struggle in Ireland for Catholic emancipation that Irishmen led by Daniel O'Connell were engaged in at the same time.[17] An important exception, which to the Roman Catholics further accentuated the need for political reform, was that Newfoundland Catholics were denied the rights granted in 1829 to Irish Catholics with the Catholic Relief Act. Initial Catholic celebration in the streets of St John's was to be followed by shock, followed by 'sincere hurt and dismay that soon gave way to bitter anger',[18] when Governor Cochrane hesitated to introduce the act in Newfoundland. It was to be three years before the privileges attained by Catholics elsewhere in the empire would be introduced in Newfoundland.

The origins of the call for reform were more complicated than that, though. Historically, demands for an increased local say in local affairs were almost always initially voiced by the emerging urban middle class. This too was the case in Newfoundland. As argued by Kevin Major, it was the merchants on Water Street who first saw the relevance of attaining more direct control over Newfoundland politics and trade.[19] William Carson, a Scottish physician, and Patrick Morris, an Irish merchant, both recently arrived to settle in Newfoundland, became leaders of the reform movement which would eventually lead to the granting of representative government in 1832.[20] The date was not coincidental. The reformers tapped into the general strain of radicalism which characterised British politics at the time, winning support for Newfoundland representation from, among others, Joseph Hume.[21]

Carson made his goals for Newfoundland clear: 'We shall rise into a national existence, having a national character, a nation's feelings, assuming that rank among our neighbours which the political situation and the extend of our island demand.'²² Since after the second general election the new assembly came to be dominated by the Liberal reformers, Carson and others sharing his point of view now had the opportunity to work towards realising his vision. However, the predominantly English and Protestant upper class jealously guarded its power through the appointed institutions of government and remained an obstacle to radical reform. Support for the reform movement came predominantly from Roman Catholics of Irish descent. Support came also almost entirely from the Avalon Peninsula, where two thirds of the population lived, and where most Irish Catholic immigrants had found their home.

It was to be another twenty-three years – somewhat belated, compared to its sister colonies – before Newfoundland achieved home rule in the shape of responsible government,²³ but during this gradual winning of political power, the sense of a Newfoundland nation developed further. Political power provided the power to define the nation, and this was political power predominantly in the hands of Irish Roman Catholics. St John's was quickly becoming the centre of economic and political power, and it is no coincidence that the Catholic Basilica of St John the Baptist was the second largest in North America.

Roman Catholics supported the Liberal Reform Party, and therefore it was not coincidental either that the first premier of Newfoundland, Philip Francis Little, was Liberal, Catholic and Irish. Thus, from early on, the Newfoundland nation was forged in the image of the Irish. Naturally, this did not go down well with the English-Anglican fragment settled mainly in the outports. Few population groups willingly accept being without or with very little influence on the invention of their national identity.

Sectarianism and denomi(-)nationalism

In the early nineteenth century, before reform, the situation in Newfoundland spelled trouble. An equal number of English – bringing with them from the west country 'a heritage of puritanical Protestantism, social deference, and semi-feudal relationships' – and Irish – bringing along 'a heritage of poverty, Roman Catholicism, and hatred of their English oppressors'²⁴ – faced each other in a young, constitutionally and politically immature society. Furthermore, the almost entirely Protestant establishment was ruling the colony from St John's, the home of a much greater proportion of Catholics than Protestants.

Although five years after the Penal Laws were repealed in 1778, Newfoundlanders were granted 'full liberty of conscience',²⁵ the established church in Newfoundland was still the Church of England, leaving about half the population, the Irish, religiously afloat. Retaining a policy of not rocking the boat, Roman Catholic bishops had traditionally collaborated with the Protestant authorities, but with Bishop Michael Fleming this would change. From the 1830s, this champion of Catholic emancipation and Irish nationalism started backing Liberal Catholic candidates for the assembly.[26] Catholic priests were preaching politics from the pulpit, and Protestant newspapers, most notably the *Public Ledger*, engaged themselves in an anti-Catholic crusade. As a consequence, politics in Newfoundland became increasingly sectarian. Phillip McCann relates how, from 1837 to 1841, serious political fighting took place between the Liberal Catholic-dominated assembly and the Tory-Protestant council, resulting in the temporary suspension of self-government by the British in 1841. According to McCann, by this time a separate Irish-Newfoundland nationalism was developing: 'St. Patrick's Day festivals held under the auspices of the [Benevolent Irish] Society fused ethnicity and religion with militant nationalism for all but a minority of the Newfoundland Irish.'[27]

Pan-Newfoundland movements, such as the Natives' Society were founded around the same time. Although originally an anti-Irish, anti-Liberal club, the Natives' Society came to function as a bulwark dividing the sectarian waters, while at the same time providing a common ground on which to meet. It was soon realised by concerned British officials that the Society held the balance between Protestant Tories and Catholic Liberals, and with its creed of 'nativism, patriotism and a respect for social order'[28] it came to enjoy the support of the governor. An interesting aspect of the Society's creed was the fusion of Newfoundland 'nativism' or nationalism and British patriotism. It was possible to be a loyal British subject as well as a true Newfoundlander.

The invention of *shared* consciousness and destiny significantly altered the content of Newfoundland national identity. Where previously it would have been possible to detect an emerging Irish-Catholic Newfoundland national identity, perhaps even an English-Protestant one, now the creation of common antagonistic others opened up the opportunity for peaceful co-existence.[29] McCann describes the shift in attitudes: 'The cutting edge of nativist criticism was turned not against the mercantocracy or the administration, as was Liberal policy in the 1830s, but against "strangers".'[30] But religious and political reconciliation did not happen overnight. It took a long process to achieve it.

By the time responsible government was granted, William Carson and Patrick Morris had both passed away, and new leaders with a more Catholic and Irish outlook had taken over the reins of the Liberal Party. Liberal leader Francis Little was a devout Catholic and the son of a political refugee from Ireland, and although after being elected premier in 1855 he included two Protestants in his cabinet, Newfoundland politics was still marked by sectarianism. In the elections, every Roman Catholic constituency was won by the Liberals, and every Protestant constituency went to the Tories, who had campaigned on Protestant unity.

Political and religious strife continued, and widespread protest culminated in 1861, when a Tory election victory – achieved almost entirely through a sectarian campaign and Protestant votes – led to street fights in St John's. The predominantly Catholic and Liberal inhabitants of St John's found the election result dubious and rioted at the Colonial Building. During the riot three were killed and twenty wounded after troops opened fire.

Newfoundland was not, however, in Noel's words, 'to become simply a microcosm of Ireland'.[31] The reason can be described briefly as political pragmatism. Through the political system, Conservative merchant Protestants had now re-established themselves as the ruling elite, with economic and political power, and their interest was security and undisturbed conditions for economic development. In order to achieve this, the large Liberal Catholic section of the population – or at least its leaders – must be kept content. In 1865, Conservative premier Frederic B. T. Carter brought into his cabinet two Catholic Liberals, and he introduced a system whereby positions in the cabinet and in the civil service, patronage appointments and public works were distributed on a proportional basis between the major denominations.

The system, which came to be known as the 'denominational principle', was a progressive and successful sharing of power between religious groups for which Newfoundland has become famous. It was an approach which can be described with a technical term as 'consociation' – a political arrangement which has various groups, for example, ethnic or religious, agreeing to share power according to a commonly defined formula.[32] Major believes 'it is this agreement that is responsible more than anything for a cessation of sectarian turmoil'.[33] What might be considered a less fortunate consequence, however, was that in this 'pattern of elite accommodation',[34] liberal radicalism was curbed to the extent that the former Liberals quickly neared the Conservatives, only for the two parties eventually to switch names and sides on the political continuum. Liberal and Catholic leaders had received their share of the spoils and saw no need to destabilise the situation. In national identity-building terms, the dominance of the Irish Catholic fragment diminished, but due to the inclusion in public affairs guaranteed by the denominational principle, it still held much influence.

The fact that the Conservatives under Charles Fox Bennett, an Anglican and extreme Tory with estates in England, carried every Roman Catholic district in the 1869 election illustrates how sectarianism at that point had been marginalised in the political sphere. In fact, Bennett made a point of his anti-sectarian creed, and called upon Protestants to 'put down Orangeism with the same strong hand that you would Fenianism'.[35] Significantly, the rallying issues that replaced sectarianism were nationalism and anti-confederalism.

In the period that followed, the power of sectarianism declined. Still, while in partisan politics the value of sectarianism 'was symbolic rather than substantive',[36] relapses of public sectarian violence such as the 'Harbour Grace Affray' in 1883, in which Orangemen and Irish Catholics clashed and five men were killed, shows how the denominational principle was a top-down elitist project which did not immediately catch on among people of lower social rank, who had less immediate interest at stake. Nevertheless, over time, pragmatic concerns and a more pan-Newfoundland sense of self came to dominate in all social spheres. In what can seem a paradox, Newfoundland witnessed a very rare marriage of nationalism with consociationalism.

Common national identity-building

When Lord Durham reported back to Westminster in 1839, he recommended not only the union of Upper and Lower Canada. He also made it clear that to have Prince Edward Island and Newfoundland join a union of the British North American colonies was 'absolutely necessary, as the only means of securing proper attention to their interests'.[37] Still, Newfoundland was not among the colonies which joined to form Canada in 1867. There was a heated debate between Confederates and 'Antis', which culminated in the election of 1869 when the 'Antis' led by Charles Fox Bennett annihilated the opposition by winning twenty one seats to nine. Newfoundland patriotism along with the threat of increased taxation were the most important reasons why the pro-Confederate government under Frederick B.T. Carter was defeated.

After 1867, Canada was engaged in a special nation-building process which sought to accommodate different provinces within a federal framework as well as settling and developing the peripheries (at least up to a certain level) through the National Policy. Meanwhile, Newfoundland was engaged in its own nation-building process – one which more closely resembled that of most European countries at the same time. The 1860s saw the introduction of stamps with Newfoundland national symbols: codfish, seal, and later the Newfoundland dog. To commemorate the

400th anniversary of the re-discovery of Newfoundland by John Cabot, the powerful symbol of the Cabot Tower was built at the Narrows of St John's,[38] and by the turn of the century, Newfoundland got its own national anthem. Passports were introduced, as was a Newfoundland currency in 1834 in the wake of the introduction of representative government. In 1897, the Newfoundland railway was completed, and although it never became economically viable, the completion of this means of communication would have served to produce a sense of national cohesion.

The final settlement of the question of the French Shore also gave a boost to a sense of cohesion and independence. With the Treaty of Utrecht in 1713, France had retained the right to use the north-western parts of the island of Newfoundland and adjacent waters to catch and dry fish. This had been a constant thorn in the flesh of Newfoundlanders and changing governments, and although this in itself added to a sense of a hostile other, and thus to a stronger sense of a Newfoundland self,[39] it also undermined the colony's ability to exercise the power that was gradually ceded to it. Another important consequence of the French Shore situation is mentioned briefly by Noel. He notes that from the 1783 redefinition of borders, the French Shore was also that part of Newfoundland's coastline that faced the mainland continent. Consequently, Newfoundland tended to orient itself more towards the east and the United Kingdom, and less towards British North America and, eventually, Canada.[40] All this would change after 1904, however, with the Anglo-French *entente cordiale*, under which France gave up its fishing rights in Newfoundland in exchange for territory in West Africa. This made one of Newfoundland's most charismatic premiers, Sir Robert Bond, declare to the assembly that Newfoundland was now 'freed from . . . the blasting influence of foreign oppression', and that the island of Newfoundland was finally 'ours in entirety, solely ours'.[41] In its pre-Confederation history there are plenty of such patriotic references made to Newfoundland and its people, including expressions of xenophobia by, for example, prime minister Edward Morris, whose government argued that Newfoundland needed an immigration policy which might exclude those perceived as 'a menace in the national upbuilding [sic] of the country'.[42]

The tragic and traumatic near-annihilation of the Newfoundland Regiment at Beaumont-Hamel, further participation in the First World War and representation at the Versailles peace talks generally added further to a sense of Newfoundland distinctness and national maturity. Another important defining moment in the nation's history might well have been the 1931 Statute of Westminster which, if adopted by the Newfoundland legislature, would have made Newfoundland a fully sovereign state. But this was an opportunity for independence which arrived at a political and socio-economic low point for Newfoundland, and it was to be followed shortly by the Commission of Government, which in practice made Newfoundland a crown colony.[43]

Clearly, prior to 1949, Newfoundlanders' sense of the Newfoundland nation was well-developed. The forum that convened in September 1946, 'its job to recommend to the United Kingdom constitutional choices that might be put before the Newfoundland people in a referendum',[44] was thus called the 'National Convention', and it was during one of its debates that the leader of the anti-Confederate party, Major Peter Cashin, exclaimed: 'Our country must not allow itself and its nationhood to be absorbed by the Dominion to the west of us!'[45]

His opponent in the Confederation camp, Joseph (Joey) R. Smallwood, seems to have been less certain as regards the perception of Newfoundland as a nation. In his addresses to the National Convention of 27 October 1946 he would argue: 'We might manage, precariously, to maintain independent national status . . . Our danger, so it seems to me, is that of nursing delusions of grandeur. We are not a nation. We are a medium sized municipality.'[46]

Confederation: beggars can't be choosers

In 1949 Newfoundland became a province of Canada. In the second referendum on the constitutional future of Newfoundland, the population was divided 52 per cent to 48 per cent into a Confederation camp (78,323 votes) and an anti-Confederation camp (71,344 votes). The close race between Confederates and anti-Confederates serves to strengthen the argument that we should not deny Newfoundland its history as a nation simply because it is now part of Canada. Half a century ago, Confederation was far from a certainty.

The second 1948 referendum result reveals how regionally divided Newfoundland was. All districts outside the Avalon Peninsula voted to confederate. On the peninsula, seven of the nine districts voted for a return to responsible government. Only the two northernmost districts of Trinity South and Carbonear-Bay de Verde were in favour of a union with Canada, and the latter only by a small margin.[47] At first glance, there appears to be a remarkable correlation with the general settlement patterns of Irish Roman Catholics on the Avalon Peninsula and English Protestants in the outports, and it is tempting to try to explain the referendum results by sectarianism. As several scholars have documented, the second referendum campaign in particular had indeed been fought on sectarian issues, and the tone of the accusations had been belligerent.

The first referendum had revealed a split between the way most Roman Catholics and most Protestants voted; at least this is one obvious interpretation. Noel argues: 'This in itself would probably not have triggered off an outburst of religious sectarianism, but it did provide a situation conducive to its growth.'[48] And indeed it would seem the confederate side was not late to rekindle the long-standing religious antagonisms in Newfoundland for the political purpose of union with Canada. However, it is also important to note that Roman Catholic Archbishop Edward P. Roche was an ardent Newfoundland patriot, and 'an unrelenting enemy of confederation, which, he believed, would destroy the distinctive Newfoundland way of life'[49] – a position which would also come to be held by cultural nationalists and autonomists in the last half of the twentieth century.

In E. P. Roche and other responsible government supporters, the strong currents of Newfoundland nationalism and the continued quest for sovereignty and self-government met again. His vision of Newfoundland, according to Major, 'was of an innocent yet fiercely proud and independent nation, a legacy of the Irish patriotism that had propelled the first fight for self-government'.[50] In the Catholic *Monitor*, Roche and other Catholic community leaders advocated the responsible government option on the grounds that denominational education and a proper religious Newfoundland way of life would be respectively destroyed and corrupted by Confederation.[51] The confederate side also played the religious card in their campaign magazine, *The Confederate*, and elsewhere, to organise support from Orangemen and Protestants generally. In particular, this camp warned that Roman Catholics had been instructed to vote according to the wishes of the Church.

Many of the concerns of the Catholic Church and of the conservative forces advocating responsible government focused on Newfoundland culture, history and sovereignty, acknowledging that economic prosperity was not their primary argument, nor something which could be guaranteed under responsible government. In Noel's view, 'a vote for responsible government was also in effect for the maintenance of the old Atlantic-oriented Newfoundland, poorer than its North American neighbours but also different from them, holding to more conservative values, and preserving a culture historically rooted in the pre-industrial societies of Ireland and the west of England'.[52] In contrast, the Confederates made use of pragmatic reasoning and economic arguments, such as the promise of baby bonuses and family allowances. Again, Noel sums up the situation: 'A vote for confederation . . . was also in effect a vote to integrate Newfoundland into the more prosperous, dynamic and competitive system of North American industrial capitalism with its "consumer culture" and liberal values.'[53]

It would thus be to misinterpret the situation to argue that sectarianism was the main cause of the 1948 referendum outcome. A more likely explanation is one that takes regional differences and class into consideration. Neary notes that in the first referendum two of the pro-responsible government districts on the Avalon were predominantly Protestant, and two of the pro-Confederation districts off the Avalon had a Roman Catholic population.[54] Also, on the west coast prominent Roman Catholics led the Confederate movement. Socio-economic and more general cultural differences are likely to have been decisive. As Neary also documents, 'the Commission's assessment of the occupational basis of support was that Responsible Government had done best among the professional and commercial classes . . . Confederation had done best among lumbermen and fishermen.'[55] Newfoundland's political leaders, civil servants, business people, etc., almost all resident in St John's and on the Avalon Peninsula, are not likely to have shared many common views or interests with the fishermen in the outports – including the perception of the benefits of Confederation. This made pensions and family allowances Joey Smallwood's trump cards. Many different interests and needs played into this decision, wealth and social standing among them.

No simple explanation of the result is possible. In an attempt to square the circle, however, dominant issues during the campaigns can be singled out as being religion/education, Newfoundland's socio-economic situation and nationalism. An important point to make is that the deep cleavage between the Avalon Peninsula and the rest of Newfoundland is hardly an indication that 'Townies' were more patriotic than 'Baymen', or that Catholics were more patriotic than Protestants. The crux of the matter seems to be that certain social groups could better afford to harbour nationalist feelings than others. A large proportion of the voters, argues Blake, 'held little sentiment for a return to a "Newfoundland nation" that had treated them shabbily since the emergence in 1855 of responsible government controlled largely by the elites in St. John's'.[56] To the majority, the old saying 'beggars can't be choosers' made more sense than any feeling of national pride, however deeply felt. In other words, off the Avalon, socio-economic pragmatism won the day over cultural–emotional patriotism. Major describes the situation well: 'The people on the west and south coasts saw confederation as a chance of equality . . . No person who walked into a polling booth wanted anything more than a chance at building a workable nation, where independence was coupled with

equality of opportunity. But a majority of voters didn't see that as one
of the options before them . . . So they opted for the next best thing.
Canada.'[57] As Noel points out, under such circumstances the fact that
responsible government was still so close to carrying the day is an indication of 'the powerful hold which the idea of a separate national life
had upon the minds and hearts of Newfoundlanders'.[58]

But did Confederation mean that Newfoundlanders lost their
national identity overnight – specifically the night between 31 March
and 1 April 1949? On the surface, it may seem as if there was a total
surrender to Canadian nationhood along with the embrace of modern
society, and consequently a rejection of Newfoundland's own national
fragment identity in favour of a pragmatically chosen, materially better
life. If one accepts the existence of a collective national identity in
Newfoundland prior to Confederation, such an interpretation is difficult to adhere to, even if Newfoundlanders are indeed a pragmatic
people. A very large portion of pre-Confederation Newfoundlanders are
still alive, and it is difficult to believe that they simply replaced their
national identity with something else in 1949. As an indication of the
strength of the notion of nation, the problems which European integra-
tionists face because of strong national identities in certain EU member
states serve as illustration. Rather, large sections of Newfoundlanders,
including post-Confederation generations, have continued to think of
their community and their identity in ethnic and national terms – even
if for a long period after Confederation identity was expressed merely
culturally, in what has been referred to as cultural nationalism.

'NEWFCULT' AND RENAISSANCE: CULTURAL NATIONALISM IN
MODERN NEWFOUNDLAND

In both Scotland and Newfoundland there has existed, for extended
periods of time, a strong sense of national identity with no adjacent
political nationalism. Newfoundland identity has also asserted itself
strongly in surveys (Table 3.2) in periods characterised by a notable
absence of political demands for constitutional change. Although close
links exist between the celebration of Newfoundland culture and the
perception of Newfoundland as a nation, cultural nationalism, as in the
case of Scotland, predates autonomism.

Pat Byrne has illustrated how the idealised romantic images of
Newfoundland regional mythology were popularised beyond the colo-
nial/provincial borders by the collections of traditional songs published
by Gerald S. Doyle.[59] Similarly idealised images of traditional
Newfoundland life occupied the writers of what Byrne appropriately

labels Newfoundland's 'Romantic realism'. In the 1940s and 1950s, Scammell, Pollett and Russell all continued the development of the image of the 'hearty, handy, all 'round Newfoundlander' supposedly capitalising on situations of isolation and deprivation.[60] Patrick O'Flaherty had little doubt as to the cause of this literary activity: 'the cause of this renewal was the same as in the earlier period: nationalism'.[61] Importantly, however, O'Flaherty indicates the nature of this nationalism when he says of the mood which characterised the important literary magazine the *Atlantic Guardian, a Magazine of Newfoundland*, that it was 'the mood of indulgent, uncritical nationalism, born of a sense of exile from an embattled homeland'.[62]

Newfoundland cultural nationalism was mainly a post-Confederation phenomenon, most strongly manifested from the late 1960s with the major cultural revival which had been simmering since the 1950s. Hiller has illustrated how this cultural renaissance came about prior to the emergence of political nationalism and thus was not simply politically or economically determined.[63] That is, it was not a convenient invention of ethnicity merely created to function as part of the legitimisation of political nationalism; quite the contrary. The Newfoundland myth of the 'all 'Round Newfoundlander'/half-brute, with its powerful theme of poverty and defeat, came to function much as did tartanry in Scotland, almost to prevent the emergence of political nationalism. The Newfoundland cultural movement would later take up a different role and enter into a coalition with political nationalism, but initially the cultural revival was caused by other factors.

Characteristic of cultural nationalism, as of the cultural revival, is an emphasis on Newfoundland heritage – myths, traditions, folklore, dialects – and identity. Similar to Scottish cultural nationalism – with its predominant myth of tartanry – the myth of Newfoundland at this point made only selective use of Newfoundland culture. Certain elements were deemed worthy of preservation and celebration, while others were not. With its special attraction to folk culture – that is, the culture of rural or outport Newfoundland – the early movement is best described as anti-materialist and traditionalist. By the 1960s, the romantic idealised images created and developed by Doyle, Scammell, Pollett and Russell had been, argues Byrne, trivialised and transformed by the proponents of modernisation and materialism into a mockery of itself.[64] The prevailing image of Newfoundland, within as well as outside the province, was now one of happy poverty: Newfoundlanders were seen to be content with being poor and dependent, because they did not fully understand the gravity of their own situation. This was the image of the goofy Newfie, which would come to dominate the representation of Newfoundland in all kinds of mainland media. The equivalent of the tartan image of Scotland, which Tom Nairn found 'intolerably vulgar!'[65] would define a limited space for the Newfoundland experience within the Canadian whole.

If one considers the cultural revival in Newfoundland to have its early roots in the 1940s and 1950s, it began as a celebration of Newfoundland uniqueness and turned into a superficial parody. The lack of politicisation which characterises these earliest stages of what would become a full cultural revival makes it a near-perfect case of what was defined above as cultural nationalism. The constitutional set-up was, at this point, not an issue of the movement.[66] Pat O'Brien has argued that by the Centennial Year, 1967, Newfoundlanders' commitment to Canada was largely based upon 'practical – almost dollars and cents – considerations'. Therefore, continues O'Brien, Newfoundlanders remained in favour of the constitutional status quo.[67] Progress was indeed tangible, if considered entirely in such terms. The 2003 Royal Commission on Renewing and Strengthening Our Place in Canada found that personal income per capita in Newfoundland had climbed steadily from 48 per cent of the Canadian national average in 1950 to 79 per cent of the Canadian average by 2001.[68]

A strong Newfoundland identity *vis-à-vis* a sense of Canadian-ness remained, and no strong emotional link with the rest of Canada had been forged. Economic dependence, however, had increased considerably, and the reliance on federal funds for the continued expansion of public services and welfare further contributed to a reluctance to rock the constitutional boat. The union had been joined primarily for pragmatic reasons, and the substantial social and economic benefits – the Newfoundland budget increased from $30 million in the first years of union to more than $300 million in 1969 – made an autonomist discourse an unnecessary and undesirable option to most. Cultural nationalism based on a vivid sense of community thrived and was celebrated beyond the borders of the province,[69] without concerning itself with constitutional questions and the federal–provincial relationship as such. Not until a decade later, in the mid- and late 1970s, would cultural nationalism come to provide a firm basis for political nationalism when Progressive Conservative (PC) governments made both cultural preservation/revival and political autonomy integral parts of their agenda. However, the cultural renaissance came to carry political overtones prior to that.

From the early 1970s, the movement was, for a large part, a reaction to the political regime of Joey Smallwood and his modernist 'develop or perish' agenda.[70] This second wave of the cultural revival in Newfoundland was largely the design of the new intelligentsia – the members of which were mainly graduates from Memorial University of

Newfoundland, themselves a product of modernisation and urbanisation.[71] More critical elements now came to characterise, and soon dominate, the Newfoundland cultural revival. Just as Scottish cultural nationalism had its devoted critics in anti-tartanry academics such as McArthur, Craig and Nairn, certain aspects of cultural nationalism in Newfoundland have been heavily criticised. Byrne writes: 'At that point [the early 1970s] the battle lines were drawn, and the battle still rages as to which image, if either, represents Newfoundland culture, or if, in fact, the concept of a distinctive Newfoundland culture *per se* is anything more than an idealized mental construct based on a particular reading of the evolved regional mythology.'[72]

A new group of writers of a more critical outlook than had previously been the case were entering the scene, intent on replacing 'facile depictions and stereotypical superficialities'[73] with more realistic images of the Newfoundland reality. This was not simply a quest to abandon the traditional Newfoundland way of life for a modernisation paradigm: partly continuing along the lines of 'romantic realism', partly attempting to go back beyond it in the search for 'real' traditional culture, most writers of this more powerful wave of the Newfoundland cultural revival opposed modernisation fascination – most notably uncritical industrialisation and urban centralisation – as well as a false, overly nostalgic perception of the past. Evoking traditional Newfoundland life in drama (including the revival of the old Newfoundland tradition of 'mummering'), fiction and poetry, they made the collision between the new and the old ways their preferred theme. This is illustrated in the writings of, among others, Farley Mowat, Franklin Russell and Percy Janes.[74] Ray Guy, the daily columnist at the *Evening Telegram*, was another of many literary opponents of the Smallwood modernisation agenda, and he wrote passionately about the qualities of outport life.[75] The anti-modernisation persuasion came to be shared (in his later work) by another great Newfoundland writer, Harold Horwood, who, after having been highly critical of many aspects of the traditional Newfoundland way of life, along with Farley Mowat would engage himself fiercely in the preservation of Newfoundland cultural heritage.[76]

Late twentieth-century Newfoundland literature remained positive towards traditional Newfoundland culture, but its writers heavily criticised the false mythic image of Newfoundland as backward, parochial and, most importantly, powerless. An inferiority complex prevented, in their view, the development of a more realistic image of a resourceful and strong province. One such critic was F. L. Jackson, who in his *Surviving Confederation* (1986) waged war on the 'Newfcult' or 'culture vultures',

the folklorists, anthropologists and politicians who, with their concern
for the preservation of Newfoundland outport culture, 'promote primitivism [and] cultural nostalgia'.[77] Like Tom Nairn, he made the distinction between a useful and a harmful kind of nationalism, 'authentic'
and 'inauthentic', or 'pop-', nationalism.[78] Joan Strong explains how
contemporary Newfoundland writers Wayne Johnston, William Rowe
and Gordon Pinsent in their novels address the self-mockery of
Newfoundlanders, and how they set out to debunk this as something
more serious and more dangerous than comic relief in a life of hardship.
She writes: 'The characters of their novels . . . very often destroy themselves in their inextricability from the past and the self-effacing humour
and perception which is tied to the past.'[79] An important aspect of this
problem remains the familiar Newfoundland theme of collision between
the new and the old. In her analysis of Johnston's *The Time of Their
Lives* (1987), Strong argues that self-loathing is an integral part of the
Newfoundland image projected by Johnston, and that it manifests itself
in both 'the impetus towards fanatical independence . . . and apathetic
dependency'. She continues: 'Johnston's understanding of this duality at
the foundation of the Newfoundlander's construct of self . . . reveals the
difficulties which arise when the values established . . . must be questioned in a search for alternative ways of living. . . . The rigidity of
culture maintained by those who adhere only to tradition creates a kind
of cultural schizophrenia that rings throughout Johnston's text.'[80] The
parallels with the 'Scottish Cringe' are striking.

The second wave of the Newfoundland cultural revival did not
confine itself to literature. It was a revival which was and is making
itself felt in Newfoundland society in general. An important consequence of the revival has been the development of a Newfoundland
publishing industry, including among others Breakwater Books and
Harry Cuff Publications. The establishment at Memorial University of
Newfoundland of the Institute of Social and Economic Research in
1961, the Centre for Newfoundland Studies in 1965 with the mandate
to collect and preserve all materials relating to Newfoundland and
Labrador, and the Department of Folklore from 1968 should also be
counted as results of the cultural revival. So should a more recent invention, the scholarly journal *Newfoundland and Labrador Studies*,
founded in 1985 as *Newfoundland Studies*. Aspects of pop/rock music
in Newfoundland (by, for example, Figgy Duff, Great Big Sea and Kelly
Russell and the Plancks), the arts (in the work, for example, of Gerry
Squires, Christopher Pratt and Ron Pelley), as well as theatre (by such
groups as Codco and the Mummers Troupe) represented the confluence
of the traditional and the modern.

THE DOG THAT SNARLED: AUTONOMISM IN
NEWFOUNDLAND, 1979–1989

Based merely on a superficial reading of Newfoundland political history, it would seem that post-Confederation political nationalism in the province is the Newfoundland dog that never barked. Such a conclusion might be based on the fact that a Newfoundland separatist movement never made the news in any significant way. However, a closer study of the period from the late 1970s to the late 1980s reveals that, although there has been no serious threat of separatism in Newfoundland since Confederation in 1949, political nationalism has been very much alive. In fact, there was for a period a fair bit of snarling. Cultural and political nationalism, as in Scotland, would seem at times to have lived almost separate lives for certain periods since 1949.[81] However, for a short period from the late 1970s to the late 1980s they firmly joined hands as Brian Peckford's Progressive Conservatives heralded an entirely new style of government in Newfoundland. Political nationalism was a key aspect of Newfoundland politics in the 1980s, but a certain extent of political nationalist rhetoric was also part of the agenda of both the Smallwood government's battles in 1959 with the Diefenbaker government over Term 29 of Newfoundland's Terms of Union, and the first post-Confederation PC government's struggle for control over local resources, most notably Churchill Falls hydropower.[82]

*Early political nationalism of the Smallwood and
Moores governments*

In *Canadians at Last*, Raymond B. Blake argues that Confederation was both necessary and beneficial to Newfoundland. In his words, 'to a society where poverty, hardship, and deprivation were the norm, social welfare programs from Ottawa came like manna from heaven'.[83] The dominant perception of the federal–provincial relationship during the Smallwood years certainly seems to have been one of gratefulness towards Canada for giving Newfoundland the opportunity to prosper. This is illustrated in the November 1966 Throne Speech. According to custom, the lieutenant governor read the following on behalf of the Smallwood administration: 'As we are about to start the eighteenth year of our history as a Province of Canada, . . . Newfoundland is entering upon a great new phase in her notable march of progress of these recent years . . . Canada enters upon her centennial year, and Newfoundland, although she has shared for so few years in the precious privilege of Canadian citizenship, will join with her sister Provinces in joyous celebration of this birthday . . . [W]e are indeed fortunate . . . that we are part of the great nation of Canada.'[84]

Hence, in the view of Newfoundland's governing Liberal Party, being part of the 'great nation of Canada' was seen at this point to be of indisputable benefit to Newfoundland, and Canada was regarded almost as family (note the reference to 'sister Provinces'). There seemed to exist, in other words, both a pragmatic and an emotional link. The positive image of Canada and of Newfoundland's part in it remained strong in the following years, and a 1969 Throne Speech was convinced that it would be with 'heart-felt feelings of gratitude and gladness' that the people of Newfoundland would mark the twentieth anniversary of Newfoundland's confederation with Canada. The Throne Speech maintained that 'there is health and strength in Newfoundland as a Province of Canada that was never known before', but also that regional economic disparity still existed and should be addressed, as it formed the 'greatest single obstacle still standing in the way of Canadian national unity'.[85] All Throne Speeches in the mid- to late 1960s concerned themselves with regional development and prospects of socio-economic benefits of membership of Canada, but none mentioned Canada with as much affection as the 1966 speech. The impression remains that the wellbeing of Newfoundland was the priority, and Ottawa was mainly a convenient source of economic assistance. In a 1970 Throne Speech, for instance, the Newfoundland government appreciated the 'generous, imaginative and indispensable help of the Government of Canada [and the] friendly and intimate collaboration with the Department of Regional Economic Expansion',[86] but nevertheless also informed the assembly that '[Liberal] Ministers, notwithstanding the opinion of the Supreme Court of Canada . . . continue to believe in the soundness of our Province's claim to mineral rights lying off the shores of our Province. They have therefore engaged the services of distinguished Canadian constitutional and legal authority to advise them on this matter.'[87]

The dominant perception of the Smallwood era in contemporary Newfoundland is that it was characterised by assimilationist unionism and an almost uncritical belief in Canada. Although the Smallwood governments can certainly be seen as having been pro-Canadian and willingly dependent on Ottawa for economic assistance, the quote above shows that the discourse was not characterised by a dogmatic desire for assimilation. Rather, the pragmatic line which had been introduced when Newfoundland joined Canada in 1949 had been followed to the extent that whatever policy was socio-economically best for Newfoundland was to be exercised. This explains why the seeds of oil-based political nationalism were sown already during Liberal government in 1970. What

happened when a more radical critical stand towards Ottawa was introduced should therefore not be reduced to a simple change of focus away
from Canadian patriotism towards Newfoundland patriotism.

Smallwood and his Liberal ministers no doubt had the wellbeing of
Newfoundlanders as close to their hearts as later PC governments had.
The desire to help Newfoundlanders to a better life and the province to
prosperity must be characterised as an expression of nationalism – even
a form of political nationalism. But it was a different kind of political
nationalism from the one Smallwood's political opponents would be
champions of. What changed was the perception of the means through
which to reach the goal of Newfoundland prosperity. Whereas
Smallwood had confined himself to symbolic protest by declaring,
during the Term 29 dispute, a three-day mourning period in which flags
were to be flown at half mast, future PC governments were to apply
tougher measures in the struggle to achieve better deals for the province.

Frank Moores, Newfoundland's next premier, at one point pondered
the possibility of Newfoundland separation from Canada. In an interview
in 1977, he considered commissioning a study to find 'what the cost of
Confederation is compared to what the cost would be getting out of it'.
The reason, he argued, was that Newfoundlanders were getting 'damn
well fed up with some of the attitudes in Ottawa'.[88] Still, as Throne
Speeches testify, this was not a policy symptomatic of PC government in
this period. In the first Throne Speech of the Moores government there
was a firm commitment to keeping the benefits of natural resource development in Newfoundland to create a higher level of self-sufficiency in the
province: 'My Government is very strong in its belief that the natural
resources of this Province and the benefits to be derived therefrom are the
birthright of my people,' it ran, but the speech also appreciates the value
of Confederation: 'It has been nearly twenty-three years since our
Province became part of the great Confederation of Canada and it is
fitting that we pay tribute to those who brought this about and to those
who have been responsible for the progress that we have made since
then.'[89] The new PC administration also, however, found it necessary to
make Newfoundland less dependent on Ottawa: 'My Government real-
izes that it must capitalize on our assets, it must minimize our liabilities.'[90]
It was made clear in this and other Throne Speeches that 'our assets'
meant Newfoundland's natural resources – mainly oil, hydropower, fish
and forests.[91] The Moores government signalled a new era and a lower
level of willingness to put up with what was considered poor government
from Ottawa in the name of economic assistance to Newfoundland.
Above all, it aimed to rid Newfoundland of dependence on Ottawa. At
the same time, the Moores government also stage-managed the grand

six-month celebration of Newfoundland's twenty-fifth anniversary as a Canadian province, and on this occasion Moores exclaimed: 'We are first proud to be Newfoundlanders and second, no less strongly, proud to be Canadians.'[92] In many respects the Moores government can thus be seen to have marked a transition period. The budding political nationalism of the Moores administration had at its source mainly what Robert Paine refers to as a 'new cadre of . . . policy-makers'.[93] The foremost figures in this 'new cadre' were Leo Barry, minister of the Department of Mines and Energy, Cabot Martin, his legal adviser, and Brian Peckford. The importance of the presence of these talented and zealous actors – the right people at the right time – should be stressed. At this point they were clearly working along autonomist lines, but it was not until Brian Peckford became premier in 1979 that political nationalism in Newfoundland seriously gathered momentum.

Progressive Conservative government and the autonomist agenda

From 1979, successive PC governments led by Premier Brian Peckford maintained an aggressive political nationalist agenda. James Overton explains how the autonomist movement in Newfoundland – based partly on a theory of exploitation and dependence on the Newfoundland periphery by central Canada, and partly on romantic notions of authentic Newfoundland society – focused on '(1) control of resources and economic and political decision-making; and (2) what [was] identified as the "Newfoundland way of life" '.[94] As the most significant actors in that movement, the PCs emphasised the disappearance of 'real' Newfoundland culture as an important concern of theirs.[95] This was a policy which struck a chord with many Newfoundlanders. In the 1979 *Survey of Newfoundlanders' Attitude Towards Confederation With Canada*, 56.1 per cent of the respondents found that since Confederation, Newfoundland had suffered 'severe losses' or 'some losses' in terms of cultural traditions.[96]

As was the case with the policies of the Moores government, the Peckford vision was clearly to free Newfoundland from economic dependence on Ottawa by use of the province's natural resources. Only Peckford was prepared to take the fight over control of these resources several steps further. It is important here to underline that Peckford's agenda was always an increased measure of autonomy for Newfoundland, never secession. Talk was always of decentralisation and the transfer of certain powers while retaining Canadian unity. At points when Peckford's rhetoric was interpreted as separatist, he always vigorously opposed the thought of Newfoundland secession from

Canada.[97] The July 1979 Throne Speech stated: 'My Government's basic position will be first, that the unity of the Nation must be preserved', and spoke of 'the need to ensure that . . . decentralization be accomplished without impairing national unity or affecting the level of social services in a so-called "have-not" Province'.[98] The argument thus seems to be that Canadian unity is to be endorsed, not so much as a principle as because it is the best means for providing the necessary economic assistance to Newfoundland. The emphasis placed on national unity remained an aspect of PC policy. One 1985 Throne Speech, for instance, expressed its confidence that 'the recent period of acrimony in our national life is now behind us and that all Canadians in all provinces are once again committed to internal cooperation and prosperity so that Canada can take its rightful place on the world stage'.[99] A policy of autonomism was seen by most Newfoundlanders as viable. A policy of separatism would very likely have been rejected. In a 1979 survey, 90.2 per cent of Newfoundland respondents said they would vote for Confederation with Canada had Newfoundland not already joined. Equally, 90.9 per cent replied that they would not vote for separation from Canada if a referendum was held on the issue.[100]

The trademark of the policies of PC governments became the link between cultural and socio-economic argumentation. One of the very first passages of the 12 July 1979 Throne Speech illustrated this link:

> While it is clear that our entry into Confederation can not be questioned, there is a growing realization that the present structure of Confederation does not allow this Province to realize the full economic benefits of its own resources or to adequately promote the enhancement of our unique cultural heritage.
>
> . . . Our people are, I am sure, ready, yes, even anxious, to complete the task of securing to themselves the means by which they, as a people, can assure their future as a distinct society. This objective can only be achieved if we, once again, have adequate control over our own marine resources – fisheries and offshore oil and gas.[101]

The preservation of Newfoundland culture thus became an important part of the legitimisation of the demand for the transfer of powers from Ottawa, and although the first priority of the Peckford regime remained provincial control of natural resources, concerns about cultural preservation and socio-economic disparity were merged together in the autonomist struggle. Harry H. Hiller suggests that 'the traditional cultural nationalism of the "baymen" [was] linked with the more economic nationalism of the "townies" '.[102] This distinction, however, overlooks the fact that Newfoundland autonomism was very much a project designed by middle-class urbanites. In fact, paraphrasing Hiller, Newfoundland ethno-cultural distinctness was politicised. Still, this was not only a question of politicians utilising an already existing cultural revival. There was a degree of confluence of movements already politicised and 'culturalised', as it were. As an example, the Mummers Troupe's political satire involving critical assessments of Newfoundland values and the province's place within Canada testify to this. Political and cultural nationalism can thus be said to have joined hands at this point in Newfoundland history. As illustrated, the roots of cultural nationalism were old; but the autonomist agenda owes its advent more to a variety of new factors, which were not cultural in nature.

Autonomism as a reaction to discontent with federal mismanagement

The perception among most Newfoundlanders at the time of the first Peckford administration was that the province was not getting an entirely fair deal from the federal government – nor from other Canadian official authorities. Bruce G. Pollard found that the dominant images of self and other centred around the perception of Newfoundland uniqueness and the lack of federal appreciation of this uniqueness. Including in his description of Newfoundland national identity relevant aspects of many different spheres apart from the cultural, he argues: 'Newfoundlanders feel . . . their history, their culture, their social fabric, and even the nature of their economy is unique. Moreover, they believe their distinctiveness is neither appreciated nor understood in the rest of Canada, including the national capital.'[103] There is much evidence in support of Pollard's argument. Mark Graesser's 1982 election study found that as many as 52 per cent of respondents believed 'the government in Ottawa is more interested in what they can get out of our province than in how to help us develop'. Forty-six per cent thought Newfoundland would 'not receive a fair hearing in the Supreme Court of Canada on ownership of the offshore'. Interestingly, 55 per cent of respondents also found that, even at this high point of hopes for oil prosperity, 'Newfoundland's hope for a better future depends mainly on getting more assistance from the Federal government in Ottawa'.[104] In contrast to this acknowledgement of dependency, and paralleling the decline of the welfare state in the UK, federal Canada in this period went from economic largesse to cutbacks necessitated by general economic recession. Newfoundland had for some time been investing heavily in social welfare, education, transportation, trade and industry, while remaining heavily dependent on transfer money from Ottawa.[105] Up till then, federal Canada had been the guarantor of the welfare system that many Newfoundlanders regarded as the real asset of Confederation. At the same time, the economic crisis resulted in rapidly increasing unemployment rates, and the fact that Newfoundland was hit harder than other parts of Canada contributed to a general feeling of unease and speculation about the effectiveness of federal government in the province. Newfoundlanders in 1982 suddenly found themselves between the Rock and a hard place: on the one hand, federal support was still largely regarded as an important solution to Newfoundland's socio-economic problems. On the other, Newfoundlanders also believed that the province had plenty of reason not to be content with the present provincial–federal relationship.

Under such circumstances, autonomism would have seemed a favourable discourse to many: the perception would be that Newfoundland should receive a larger share of the cake, and control that share itself. Still, radical solutions such as independence would be out of the question for socio-economic reasons. As indicated above, the negative image of federal authorities was shared by the Peckford government. Pollard writes in the 1985 version of *Canada: The State of the Federation*: 'The Newfoundland government has tended to be defiant and to blame Ottawa for its economic woes. [It] argues that its interests are too often in conflict with or irrelevant to those of central Canada, such that they are ignored in federal policy-making.'[106] Thus, of much relevance in the search for possible reasons for the rise of political nationalism at this point in Newfoundland history is the co-existence of the Liberal Trudeau government in Ottawa and the PC Peckford government in St John's. Previously, the Smallwood government and changing federal governments had provided 'unexcelled virtuoso performances of power brokerage between province and Ottawa',[107] but as the 1968 federal election saw both the revolutionary return of six PC Newfoundland MPs and the Liberal Pierre Elliott Trudeau solidly fixed in the prime minister's office, things changed considerably, and a political culture of confrontation emerged. The exception were the few months of federal PC government in 1979–1980, which occurred simultaneously with the election of the first Peckford government in Newfoundland, promising a good atmosphere in future negotiations between the two governments. Had the Clark administration stayed on longer, the autonomist movement in Newfoundland might not have developed as it did, but Clark's minority government was defeated in 1980, and this made possible the reintroduction of Trudeau's hard-line centralist agenda.

Confrontation culminated in Trudeau's second government from 1980 to 1984, which coincided with the first period of Peckford administration. The two new governments pursued opposing policies based on irreconcilable discourses: the Trudeau Liberal administration emphasised centralisation and a strong federal government that could 'speak for Canada'; the Newfoundland PCs stressed decentralisation and strong provincial government. Keeping in mind the perception of the federal government in Ottawa among Newfoundlanders, one can easily imagine the loyalties of Newfoundlanders being cast in favour of Peckford's cultural patriotic rhetoric rather than in favour of Trudeau's uncompromising conform-and-assimilate style. The overwhelming support that the PCs enjoyed in the 1982 provincial election no doubt came about partly as a consequence of this.[108]

Autonomism as a civil society reaction to discontent with provincial government mismanagement

Trudeau's centralisation policies did much to harden Newfoundlanders' perception of Ottawa, but internal factors have been equally significant with regard to the emergence of political nationalism. A factor rarely mentioned by theories of nationalism became a decisive factor in Newfoundland: general discontent with the existing *local* regime. The Liberals, headed by Joey Smallwood, won six consecutive provincial elections from 1949 to 1966, but by 1971 the 'Burn Your Boats'[109] modernisation paradigm of the Smallwood era seemed decreasingly effective in changing Newfoundland's position as Canada's poorest province. The resettlement schemes[110] – which were judged by critics to have been traumatic for those affected – and the many failed attempts at creating large-scale industrialisation in Newfoundland combined with a dislike for Smallwood's patriarchal style of leadership to create a strong sense of disillusionment with the visions of the existing government. Perceived resource giveaways came to be seen as too high a price to pay for modest economic development, and benefits from Smallwood's 'cap-in-hand' approach to federal Canada appeared to many to be lessening. In 1973, personal income per capita in Newfoundland still remained the lowest of the federation at 52 per cent of the Canadian average. The view that the old regime had not provided the optimal outcome for Newfoundland was reflected in the 1982 election study, when 75 per cent of respondents agreed with the following statement: 'Most of Newfoundland's present problems are the result of bad decisions by provincial leaders over the years.' The popularity of the Peckford government at the time of the survey suggests that respondents associated this statement with Smallwood and/or Moores: a total of 85 per cent of respondents also rated Peckford an 'excellent' (18 per cent), 'very good' (35 per cent) or 'fairly good' (32 per cent) premier.[111] Also, by the late 1960s, internal cracks were beginning to show in the Liberal Party: Joey Smallwood would alienate many previously loyal supporters by announcing his retirement as leader, then shortly after refusing to give up power. He would eventually be forced out of the Liberal Party and go on to form the rival, ill-fated, Reform Liberal Party.

The Newfoundland provincial and federal voting patterns largely resembled each other in the first twenty years of Confederation. The first indication of a change of political preference came in the 1968 federal election: departing completely from conventional voting behaviour, the Newfoundlanders ousted the Liberals and chose to have six PCs of the province's seven MPs represent them in Ottawa. 'The Father of Confederation', the Liberal premier Joey Smallwood, was clearly disappointed about the behaviour of his fellow Newfoundlanders. His comments on this occasion may serve to illustrate why certain strata in a democratically maturing society like Newfoundland were tiring of the Smallwood regime: 'It seems to me it is a sad sorrowful thing the Newfoundland people have done . . . But they have exercised the sovereign right and they have a right to be wrong.'[112]

General fatigue with oft-repeated but inefficient modernisation mantras produced a strong reaction among a new middle-class elite of professionals and civil servants. This young, educated, urban middle class – which largely owed its existence to the modernisation of Newfoundland that had actually occurred during the Smallwood years – grew increasingly discontent with the old regime, and they eventually revolted against it to become the carriers of the political nationalist agenda. Hiller describes the autonomist movement in Newfoundland as a wide and unlikely coalition consisting of the new middle class of well-educated people, the romantic cultural traditionalists, parts of the business community and anti-Confederate forces.[113] Jim Overton's definition of the coalition is largely similar. He defines it as consisting of the business community and people employed in education, the civil service, the media, the arts and the social services.[114] There is not, however, complete agreement about the social anatomy of the Newfoundland autonomist movement. Doug House questions whether the movement can be characterised as a new middle-class ideology, and correctly states that Peckford's political nationalism received much support from rural Newfoundland.[115] Certainly, it was partly legitimised by the desire to preserve rural communities, and thus can not be said to have been confined to the new St John's middle class. However, the movement was not born in rural Newfoundland, and as a consequence of being the product of urban intellectuals' and politicians' imagination, it became the carrier of middle-class values and wishes.

Newfoundland's natural resources, an alternative to economic dependence

Brian Peckford and the other young men of the 'cadre' – Barry returned as minister of Mines and Energy, Martin in the Premier's Office – all belonged to this class and generation, and PC policies combined the celebration of the 'Newfoundland way of life' and legally and economically reasoned demands for the devolution of political power. In his *The Past in the Present* (first published in 1983), Peckford offered his view on the relation between cultural/social issues and political/economic issues, and thus provided an example of the political rhetoric that made most sections of Newfoundland civil society support the PC autonomist agenda: 'Ottawa's promises of revenues and 'spinoffs' do not take into account our determination to use this non-renewable resource to build a distinct and vibrant society rooted in our renewable resources of fish and timber . . . Are we to be denied that opportunity because we came late to Canada; or because we did not discover our resource potential before Mr. Trudeau grew tired of negotiating with provincial governments? . . . It is not so much the oil and gas in itself that is important as what it can do to provide the wherewithal to revitalize the fishery and forestry industries on which the very survival of rural Newfoundland depends.'[116] With the PCs in power, 'small is beautiful' became a mantra applied to both the outport cultures and Newfoundland's struggle with Ottawa for an increased measure of autonomy.

A very important fomenting factor of political nationalism in Scotland was the discovery of North Sea oil in the early 1970s. In Newfoundland also the development of natural resources promised future prosperity. In 1979, Richard Simeon and David J. Elkins were guessing that 'little beyond fiscal benefits ties Newfoundland to Canada', and as a consequence it was foreseen that the 'discovery of oil off its shores would powerfully reinforce autonomist tendencies'.[117] Simeon and Elkins reached this conclusion partly by studying the 1979 Newfoundland Throne Speech, which stated: 'The Province will, by force of its regulations, have first call for industrial purposes on all oil and gas produced. To accomplish this, our ownership of and control over our offshore oil and gas resources must be put beyond question . . . The great question today is whether we in this Province are ready to break away from a paternalistic centralized federalism. Are we ready to trust more in our own abilities as a society than in Federal transfer payments?'[118]

Control and development of the province's natural resources – hydropower, fisheries, oil and gas – remained a central issue for changing Peckford administrations throughout the period. After winning a renewed mandate on the oil issue in the 1982 provincial election, in the 10 May 1982 Throne Speech, the Newfoundland government acknowledged that in Newfoundland virtually all aspects of the province's economy were suffering as a consequence of international recession. One way out of recession, suggested the document, would be greater local control over fisheries management – devolved from the 'cold economic perspective' apparently exercised by federal government managers. Another would be increased control over the development of Newfoundland's 'birthright': offshore oil and gas. Finally, the way out of Newfoundland's economic malaise should be through obtaining a fair share of the revenues of the Upper Churchill hydropower scheme, based on a renegotiation of the contract made with Hydro-Québec, and the development of Lower Churchill hydropower.[119] In 1985, the same concerns about the severe consequences of recession produced a similar emphasis on development and local management of the province's resources, now including mineral production.[120] The idea that ran through much of the PC government's argumentation with regard to control of natural resources within the province was that Newfoundland should not be treated differently from other provinces of Canada. In the early parts of the century, other provinces were granted ownership of and rights over natural resources, and Newfoundland's PC governments felt the province should be treated similarly. Referring to Newfoundland's Terms of Union from 1949, the Peckford government's May 1982 Throne Speech argued that they were made to 'ensure that Newfoundland had equality with the other Provinces who also maintain ownership and control of their resources'.[121] A similar policy was a dominant part of the PC government's political agenda in 1984, when minister of Energy William Marshall maintained that Newfoundland should have the 'same right to the use of [its] resources – whether hydro, oil or fish – as other provinces enjoy'.[122]

The Hibernia oil field had been discovered in February 1979 at a point when oil prices were rapidly increasing, and following the Canadian declaration of the 200-mile zone, fisheries landings were up again after a slump. The prospects of development of hydropower – and not least the perspective of renegotiating the Upper Churchill contract with Hydro-Québec – provided yet another reason for economic optimism. It was in these areas in particular that the Peckford governments argued for increased Newfoundland autonomy. Combined, all the positive resource prospects promised to bring Newfoundland out of 'have-not' status and into the good company of the 'have' provinces. At least that was what the PC Party promised with its 1982 slogan: 'Have Not Will Be No More'.

Resource development, more than any other factor, provided Newfoundlanders with an incentive to support Peckford's aggressive policies towards Ottawa. According to the Peckford movement, Newfoundland's overarching problem was dependence on Ottawa and multinational companies, both exploiting the province's rich resources. The first 1982 Throne Speech, for example, argues: 'The Federal Government has unilaterally declared that it has the right to control our offshore resources . . . Their position is nothing less than an unprecedented and unconscionable attempt to seize the resources of this Province.'[123]

The general perception among Newfoundlanders at this time seems to have been that control of oil revenues would mean greater economic autonomy and control of the province's future, including the power to revitalise the Newfoundland 'way of life' as observed in rural communities. The force of the positive prospects in nurturing political nationalism were no doubt added to by negative ones, when the Trudeau government decided to embark on a policy of centralising control over oil and gas development in Canada. Other factors were significant too, but had Newfoundlanders, and in particular the new middle class, not perceived any real alternative to the current state of affairs, dissatisfaction with the constitutional status quo and a general weariness of Smallwood's modernisation paradigm might not alone have moved them to enter the path of political nationalism. With the prospect of a resource boom, this path now became a viable alternative to the present state of affairs. The struggle for jurisdiction over offshore oil (claimed by Ottawa to be legally under federal jurisdiction) thus became *the* symbol of political nationalism in Newfoundland.

Renewed self-confidence

Closely associated with this perceived resource-based alternative to Newfoundland's 'have-not' status appears to have been a new sense of confidence in the Peckford government and not least in the Newfoundland 'self'. The analysis of the development of Scottish political nationalism revealed the existence of this, more elusive, explanatory factor. In Scotland, oil and political rhetoric combined in the early 1970s to produce a sense of confidence in Scotland's ability to succeed, and a similar collective self-confidence can be recorded in Newfoundland society at this point. Hiller refers to 'a new mood . . . of local pride unhappiness with underdevelopment',[124] and Brown to 'a renewed confidence in the ability of Newfoundlanders to manage [their] resources'.[125] Paine notes a 'new mood in the province',[126] and Jackson records a 'new delight in life in Newfoundland' and 'a new optimism'.[127] Bill Lawton speaks of a 'slowly emerging optimism'.[128] They are all describing the same increasing sense of self-confidence, produced to a large extent by the positive resource development prospects and the existence of a 'home-grown' educated middle class willing to engage in a struggle with Ottawa to make the most of these prospects for Newfoundland. In 1981, Brian Peckford captured the rising feeling of self-confidence when in the *Globe and Mail* he declared: 'We have fish that are valuable to the world and we have people who are valuable to the world and we have energy, and we know we were wrong to feel inferior; and the psyche, the collective consciousness of Newfoundland knows it was wrong.'[129]

The previous year a new official provincial flag, designed by Christopher Pratt, to replace the Union flag had been approved. This was yet another sign of the decisive break with past practices, symbolised by Joey Smallwood, who during the 1964 Canadian flag debate stated: 'Newfoundland will continue to fly the Union Jack if we are the last place on earth to do so.'[130] The popularity of the new provincial flag, combined with the widespread use of VOCM bumper stickers bearing the text 'I believe in Newfoundland and Labrador', proved that the new-found self-confidence was not merely a feeling confined to a small group of politicians and artists. As in the case of Scotland in the 1980s and 1990s, in Newfoundland the new self-confidence would owe a great deal to the already flourishing cultural revival and its critical reassessment and re-alignment of cultural and national identity.

Other actors: the Liberal Party, PIN and the media

The Liberal Party in Newfoundland did not join the autonomist movement. It had sprung from the Confederate camp after 1949, and throughout the 1970s and 1980s the Liberals stuck to their traditional values. Drawing parallels between the development of nationalism in Quebec and Newfoundland, they saw the political nationalism of the PCs as outright dangerous and as a threat to Canadian unity. In 1983, Ed Roberts, an influential Liberal member of the Newfoundland House of Assembly, acknowledged that Peckford might not be a separatist himself, but he warned that the next generation of PCs would be. He also sketched out what he saw as the future dividing lines in Newfoundland politics between, 'those who believe that Newfoundland's future lies within and as a part of Canada and those who believe that Newfoundland should once again strike on her own, beginning, presumably, where we left off in 1934 when we gave up selfgovernment'.[131]

On the essential PC policy of Newfoundland control of offshore resources, the Liberals again took the opposite stand, and their 1989 manifesto argued that 'Hibernia would be in the process of development . . . if the PC Administration had accepted the 1982 proposal offered by the Federal Government'.[132] Judging by the Liberal vote in provincial elections (see Table 5.1), support for the anti-autonomist or centralist discourse declined from 1979 to 1982, stayed at a low until 1985, then made a full recovery by the 1989 provincial election.

As the Scottish case illustrates, it is not always possible accurately to determine the extent of political nationalism simply by the number of votes cast for political parties. Still, in Newfoundland in this period, the policies of the PCs were so closely reflecting an autonomist persuasion while those of the Liberals were reflecting a centralist persuasion, that it still makes sense to use such a method at least as an indication of the fortune of political nationalism.

No account of political nationalism in Newfoundland would be complete without a mention of the ill-fated Party for an Independent Newfoundland (PIN). The goal of the party was to have Newfoundland secede from Canada after a referendum, to become an independent nation-state supporting itself on oil and gas revenues. Today the party may seem a curious blink in the debate, but although PIN did not receive any significant amount of support in Newfoundland and eventually collapsed as a

TABLE 5.1
Number of Seats and Support in Provincial Elections as Percentage of All Votes

Date of Election	Liberal Seats and %		Progr. Cons. Seats and %	
June 18, 1979	18	40.7	34	50.6
April 6, 1982	8	34.9	44	61.2
April 2, 1985	15	36.7	36	48.6
April 20, 1989	32	47.2	20	47.6
May 3, 1993	35	49.1	16	42.1

Source: Government of Newfoundland and Labrador, *Historical Statistics of Newfoundland and Labrador*.

consequence, it received much publicity in the Newfoundland media.[133] This testifies to the seriousness with which political nationalism was treated in Newfoundland, particularly in the early 1980s.

A cardinal factor in both the Scottish and the Newfoundland cases was access to and the support of the media. One can easily imagine the difficulties Newfoundland autonomism would have encountered creating a voice for itself if the *Evening Telegram*, the only major broadsheet during the 1980s, and, to a lesser extent, CBC Newfoundland and Labrador, the only major TV station, had rejected it altogether. Pat O'Brien concludes that 'drift, indecision and a "let events overtake us" disposition' marked the attitude of Newfoundlanders towards constitutional change by the end of the 1970s, and that this attitude was expressed by Newfoundland newspapers too.[134] In fact, the two most important newspapers had already chosen sides in the autonomist–centralist battle. By the 1970s, the *Daily News* remained a staunch supporter of the Liberal centralist discourse, while the *Evening Telegram* leaned towards the PC autonomist discourse. The fact that the *Daily News* and not the *Evening Telegram* was the newspaper which, in the early 1980s, turned into a tabloid and later folded is thus likely to have had an important impact on the course of political nationalism in Newfoundland. The images of self and other held and put forward by both of Newfoundland's major papers will be analysed in chapter 7.

HIBERNATION, 1989–2003

During the ten years of PC governments, the confrontational rhetoric of the Throne Speeches accelerated from 1979 to 1984 but then gradually turned more complacent. In 1979, the Throne Speech spoke of a need for 'constitutional change and a new attitude in Ottawa towards the role that this Province . . . is to play within our confederation' and of placing Newfoundland's 'ownership of and control over our offshore oil and gas resources . . . beyond question'.[135] By 1982, the firm but negotiating tone of 1979 had been replaced by a much more strident attitude:

Newfoundlanders and Labradorians know that the resources of this Province belong to them by right . . . Government has had to take action to confirm ownership and control of Newfoundland's resources to protect the rights of our people . . . We had faith in the integrity of the British North America Act and in the Terms of Union. The Federal Government of today, however, has either lost sight of those sacred covenants or consciously chooses to ignore them . . . [M]y Government . . . could not, and would not, and will not surrender the birthright of our people. If Ottawa persists in its present course, the Supreme Court of Newfoundland will have to decide who owns the minerals off our Continental Shelf . . . Our case is strong and cause is just . . . To accept the agreement proposed by the Federal Government would be tantamount to sacrificing our offshore heritage to a serfdom of the Federal Government.[136]

Such rhetoric marks the high point of autonomism in Newfoundland. Already by the mid-1980s the rhetoric had become less confrontational and the policies less bold. As the Canadian High Court rejected Newfoundland's cases for ownership of both offshore oil and gas and hydropower, and as the Liberal Trudeau government was replaced by the Progressive Conservative Mulroney government, a new period of dialogue was introduced. In the 12 March 1984 Throne Speech, the Newfoundland government was clearly attempting a different approach to federal government. Talk was now of 'an offshore agreement which recognizes the legitimate rights of both the Federal and Provincial Governments', and with most other alternatives having failed, emphasis was now, as originally, placed on negotiation.[137] In his last Throne Speech as the newly elected head of a PC government in 1985, Peckford was therefore pleased to be able to announce the signing of the Atlantic Accord with the Mulroney government. There was a crass mention of the 'years of trust betrayed, acrimonious debate and eventually, court action' as Trudeau and Peckford confronted each other, but also clearly a sigh of relief at the mention of the new PC federal administration 'with a mandate to renew the co-operative and consultative aspects of our national life'.[138] Peckford might have been less pleased with the federal regime change, had he known that what waited in the wings was a period marked by considerable cuts in federal transfers to the provinces, and Federal Fisheries minister John Crosbie's declaration in 1992 of a complete moratorium on cod fishing – a decision that would put tens of thousands of Newfoundlanders out of work.

Changing discourses: Liberal policies

In spite of a much improved federal–provincial relationship and the signing of the Atlantic Accord, a milder form of autonomism remained on the agenda in Newfoundland throughout the 1980s, but it seems to have become increasingly diminished and had all but disappeared by the end of the decade. The highly diverging approaches of different Newfoundland governments to the Meech Lake Accord serve to illustrate a change of policies. Whereas Brian Peckford was an ardent supporter of the accord, which would have transferred more political power to the provinces, Clyde Wells, the new Liberal premier, refused to ratify it because it would jeopardise the kind of strong centralised federal government that the Liberals believed Newfoundland was in need of.[139] Wells, like Smallwood, was still using political means to further Newfoundland's interests *vis-à-vis* the interests of mainland Canada, and his rejection of the idea of Quebec as a distinct society was based on a claim that Newfoundland was just as distinct. Wells too, then, came to be seen as a champion of Newfoundland interests. Both the Manitoba and Newfoundland legislatures failed to ratify the accord before the deadline expired on 30 June 1990. The Liberal Party did not actually get a chance to vote down the accord in the Newfoundland legislature, but there can be little doubt that it would have. Later, in a 1992 national referendum, Newfoundlanders supported the likewise defeated Charlottetown Accord.

The change in attitude towards Ottawa and to federal–provincial relations was also clearly illustrated in the first Throne Speech of the Wells government. Although concerned about the fact that Newfoundland after four decades as a Canadian province had still not closed the gap with the rest of Canada in terms of public services, quality of life and economic opportunities, and concerned about recent cuts in federal government transfers, it declared that the anniversary was a cause for celebration. There was a return to the perception of Confederation as almost organic, with the rest of Canada referred to as 'our sister provinces'.[140]

Newfoundland was still at this point struggling with the familiar problems of socio-economic disparity and out-migration, exacerbated by redundancies in the wake of the cod moratorium, and the Wells government was thus forced to concern itself with the same issues as previous governments: increasing the level of productivity and the quality of the general welfare, mainly with regard to education and health care, while decreasing the level of economic dependence on Ottawa. In general terms, the problems and goals thus remained the same, but whereas the Peckford governments believed solutions were to be found in decentralisation and increased autonomy for Newfoundland to deal with its own problems and administer its own resources, the Wells government made no bones about its reliance on Ottawa for assistance – and the majority of voters chose to believe in that strategy.

The gravest concern of the new provincial government was thus the nature of the proposed Meech Lake Accord, which 'would reduce still further the powers of the Federal Government'.[141] To end poverty and dependency, the Liberal government was prepared to continue to vest powers with Ottawa. This was illustrated by the suggestion in the Throne Speech of a joint Canada–Newfoundland Fisheries Board (CNFB) to allow the province a say in the decision-making processes.[142] The Newfoundland voice was to be entirely advisory, and the argument revealed the main differences between PC government and Liberal government in this period: 'This [the CNFB] would provide effective provincial participation in the management of our basic resource without giving us the additional financial burden that would result from having legislative jurisdiction *even if it could be achieved.*'[143]

With the change of governments in 1989, Newfoundland voters no doubt reacted to Peckford's increasing opposition to organised labour demands, and the freezing of civil servant wages, as well as internal divisions within the Progressive Conservative Party – as a consequence of which Leo Barry, Peckford's old brother in arms, defected to become leader of the Liberal opposition. They would also, however, appear to have chosen to abandon Peckford's visions and his 'it's the squeaky wheel that gets the grease' policy, opting instead for the more traditional 'cap-in-hand' policy. The Wells government, however, did not abandon the aggressive approach to Ottawa. The Throne Speech was filled with references to 'federal responsibility', 'federal constitutional obligation' and Newfoundland's 'rightful position'.[144] The call for federal assistance took the form of demands rather than pleas. Wells' stance on the Meech Lake Accord and the frequent clashes with Mulroney's federal Progressive Conservative government also testified to this. From involving positions of federal political and economic assimilationism vs. provincial autonomism in the 1980s, the St John's–Ottawa dispute was now one involving positions of a federal wish for political and economic decentralisation vs. provincial economic integrationism.

Wells's successor, Brian Tobin (Lib) must, like Wells, be described as a centralist. This was illustrated in the press release issued by the Newfoundland government when Tobin left the Premier's Office on 16 October 2000. Alluding to the Liberals' major opponent in the upcoming federal election, Tobin said: 'Canada needs a strong national government to be a good effective working partner with strong provincial governments. There are those in this country today who believe that the national government must be weakened . . . There are those who believe that Canada should be governed as 10 principalities, with 10 regional and three territorial barons holding the reigns of power. I don't believe that and I know Jean Chrétien doesn't believe that. I don't believe that Canadians want that kind of country. Canada is more than a monopoly board and the Canadian experience is more than a winner take all game of survivor.'[145]

However, just as Wells' policy was not one of grovelling before Ottawa, neither was Tobin's. In the same press release Tobin's long-established policy of opposition to the clawback system was presented, and it was argued that the development of natural resources had been made difficult by the equalisation formula: 'The current claw back provisions in particular, slow the pace at which equalization receiving provinces can catch up to the Canadian average standard of living.' Speaking for the entire Atlantic region, Tobin said: 'We want to put the structural changes in place that will allow Atlantic Canada to contribute to the strength of the national economy and government, not to be dependent upon it.'[146] 'Captain Canada' – a nickname Tobin earned after, as federal minister of Fisheries, he stood up to Spain in the 'Turbot War', and also for staging a unity rally in Montreal immediately before the 1995 Quebec referendum – was still a Newfoundlander first and Canadian a close second, continuing the fight for Newfoundland economic, if not political, independence.

It is safe to say that the late 1970s and early 1980s represent a high point of autonomist thinking, but recent developments illustrate that some of the old political nationalist sentiments are still around in Newfoundland, and still have significant popular support. In the early years of the twenty-first century, there has been a gradual re-emergence of an autonomist agenda in Newfoundland. A renewed historical debate about the circumstances of Confederation thus followed in the wake of the fiftieth anniversary of Newfoundland's entry into Canada, and it resulted in the Liberal provincial government setting up the Royal Commission on Renewing and Strengthening Our Place in Canada.[147] Also, the new PC provincial government since 2003, with Premier Danny Williams at the helm, was elected on a platform of nationalist rhetoric reminiscent of the Peckford era, and October 2003 saw the launch of a new nationalist weekly newspaper, the *Sunday Independent*.

As contemporary Newfoundland is again experiencing political nationalism on a Peckfordian scale, recent developments seem to 'sandwich' the period between the present and the Peckford years, and illustrate the decline of autonomist policies from the mid-1980s to the early 2000s. An indication of the near-complete abandonment of an autonomist agenda in this period is the limited support that the Reform Party/Canadian Alliance Party candidates drew in Newfoundland. Its policy of less federal involvement in provincial affairs resembled the policies of the Mulroney and Peckford governments in the 1980s, but during the last decade of the twentieth century, very few people in Newfoundland seemed to be willing to stake the future of the province on such a policy.

Explaining the hibernation period of Newfoundland autonomism

Considering first the precondition, the possibility of summoning cultural heritage and identity in the service of the autonomist movement, little seemed to have changed during the Peckford years. Anyone who spent time in Newfoundland in the 1990s will recognise the frequent use of 'Proud to be a Newfoundlander' licence plates, the flying of the 'pink-white-and-green' and, more frequently, Pratt's red-white-blue-yellow provincial flag (also often to be seen on licence plates). The lively arts community, and the very active folk/rock music scene with the Ship Inn as its fulcrum, also testified to the continuing celebration of Newfoundland identity and heritage. Newfoundland's social and economic conditions still differed significantly from those of other Canadian provinces, and nothing indicates that Newfoundlanders should have become less aware of this fact. This is something which also contributed to a sense of Newfoundland as a separate entity with a unique identity. Equally, the Corporate Research Associates/CBC and *Maclean's* surveys indicated the existence of a strong Newfoundland national consciousness which would have been available to provide an important ideological legitimisation of political nationalism by the end of the 1980s and in the 1990s. In other words, political nationalism in Newfoundland did not die out because of a weakening of a sense of Newfoundland distinctness. The answers must be sought elsewhere.

In the beginning, the uncompromising form that characterised the Trudeau 'restoration period' probably did more to inflame political nationalist sentiment than to quell it – in Newfoundland as in Quebec. However, the fact that Peckford, for much of his time as premier, was up against the hard-line centralist Liberal Trudeau government, also explains the lack of success in obtaining increased autonomy for Newfoundland, and it is equally probable that this lack of success alienated many of Peckford's supporters in the long run. In contrast, the two PC leaders, Brian Peckford and Brian Mulroney, fully agreed on a policy of decentralisation. The field in which the former Liberal federal government had appeared most interventionist was oil, and the ideology of the PCs promised to reverse this trend. The Atlantic Accord, which was signed by the Mulroney government on 11 February 1985 and granted Newfoundland greater revenues from and increased control over offshore oil and gas, testifies to this. Mulroney embraced, argues Fossum, 'the view . . . that Ottawa had been the main culprit'.[148]

However, by the time the accord finally became reality, the autonomist balloon was rapidly deflating, and the signing of the agreement did little to stop this process. Part of the explanation is likely to have been declining international oil prices, threatening to diminish profits from Hibernia. According to Summers, Newfoundlanders had become 'very cynical about the potential of Hibernia to contribute to Newfoundland's development'.[149] In general, the positive resource prospects on which the Peckford governments had based their nationalist agenda in the early 1980s had been greatly reduced by 1989. Caused by a severe decline in fish stocks and the ensuing moratorium on fishing, Newfoundland's fishing industry was in the middle of a new crisis. Hibernia was still undeveloped due to declining international oil prices from 1985, the many attempts at renegotiating the Upper Churchill contract with Hydro-Québec had been unsuccessful, and Lower Churchill remained undeveloped. In all of the three important resource areas the province turned out to be severely restricted in producing legislation that would benefit Newfoundland. The Newfoundland House of Assembly simply did not have jurisdiction over these resources, and numerous legal battles with Ottawa in the Supreme Court of Canada did not alter this situation. Of the results promised in the confident five-year plan, which the first Peckford administration had announced in its Throne Speech in 1979, intending to secure within its span 'this Province's economic foundations and provide both employment and the tax base upon which our public services . . . can be supported',[150] few had materialised.

It can be argued that the Newfoundland economy had grown slightly stronger under PC government – in spite of general international recession in the 1980s – but unemployment figures remained stubbornly high at 20 per cent. By the late 1980s, after a decade of autonomist policies, Newfoundland was still fiscally dependent on Ottawa; and had in fact become even *more* dependent on federal transfers and equalisation payments. This paints a picture of Newfoundland by the end of the Peckford era as solidly placed on what Peckford in 1983 had himself described as 'the bottom rung of Confederation's ladder'.[151] The Liberal opposition had little difficulty in proving that the PCs had been largely unsuccessful in creating prosperity and jobs and in providing alternatives to out-migration. The Sprung Greenhouse fiasco, a government-sponsored project designed to make Newfoundland self-sufficient in cucumbers, reminded Newfoundlanders only too well of the many failed attempts at industrialisation which had taken place under Smallwood. In addition, Peckford had alienated large parts of the labour movement. The even longer-term results might have rendered Peckford's autonomist policies socio-economically viable, but in the shorter term the majority of Newfoundlanders lost faith. Rather than struggling in vain, and in the process risk alienating Ottawa, they seem to have preferred a policy of political and economic integration and of reaping the fruits of co-operation, however meagre. At this point, under these conditions, the collective self-confidence which had fuelled political nationalism in the early 1980s was at a low.

A lack of alternatives and the return of the inferiority complex

House noticed how already in 1985 the 'new energy, new confidence and new hope', which the Peckford movement had injected into Newfoundland society in the early 1980s, had been 'beset by a number of contradictory pressures that have taken the gilt off the edge of the initial optimism'.[152] Cohen's analysis of Newfoundland's negative self-perception as curtailing the power of the society to 'grapple radically' with the structures of the system, may at this point have become reality. Indeed, the declining level of self-confidence would, according to the writers of a late wave of the Newfoundland cultural renaissance, such as F. L. Jackson and Wayne Johnston, owe a great deal to the defeatist myth inherent in Newfoundland culture. Obvious parallels exist between Beveridge and Turnbull's/Nairn's critique of Scottish culture as conferring upon Scottish mentality a defeatist element, resulting in a large-scale inferiority complex. As in the case of Scotland, however, such a factor cannot alone explain the disappearing support for political nationalism. In the Newfoundland case, an element of pragmatic reasoning based on the lack of real alternatives to the status quo must be taken into account. A large share of Newfoundland self-confidence had been vested in the ability of Peckford and the PCs to make a new beginning for the province. It was when they were seen to have failed that Newfoundlanders realised there was little sense in keeping their hopes high. The Peckford regime lost support because of its failure to deliver an end to economic disparity and the preservation of the Newfoundland way of life through increased control of Newfoundland resources. These were promises which, in spite of the somewhat successful struggle for joint ownership of oil, it was seen as unable to fulfil. There can be little doubt that preconceived notions of the historic powerlessness of the Newfoundland nation to seriously alter its destiny and its harsh socio-economic realities have had an effect on the collective abandoning of autonomism, but the emphasis on this factor should not be overestimated: had oil flowed, had renegotiations with Quebec resulted in a larger share of the revenues from Churchill Falls hydropower, and had fish been in abundance, this factor is likely to have been irrelevant.

There may well have been, as House argues, a contradiction between the Peckford regime's rhetoric on cultural preservation and the fact that

bbotsford. Here, in his Baronial-style home, Sir Walter Scott produced the Waverley novels and ther works that added a tartan twist to the image of Scottishness, in Scotland and abroad, and fed e cultural nationalism that was predominant in Scotland before the 1960s.

utport. In Newfoundland, the romantic image of the traditional, non-urban, way of life in the utports became a significant element not only in the cultural nationalism of the first half of the ventieth century, but also in the political nationalism that was characteristic of the Peckford era. ʰhoto copyright World of Stock/Jane Cox)

The old Royal High School of Edinburgh where the 1978 Scotland Act assembly would have met. In the 1979 referendum, however, only one third of those eligible to vote endorsed the proposed assembly.

The Scottish Parliament Building, Holyrood, Edinburgh. In the 1997 referendum, a large majority of Scots were ready to vote in favour of the re-establishment of the Scottish parliament.

Above. Ethno-cultural traits have remained an important part of present-day Newfoundland autonomism, and in St John's Harbour, the Pink-White-Green flag and (in the background) the Cabot Tower for many continue to symbolise Newfoundland distinctness amidst symbols of a modern, globalised world.

Left. Media nationalism. Autonomist throughout the period studied here, the *Scotsman* became one of the strongest supporters of devolution in the 1990s.

Below. Van in Corner Brook. A sense of distinctness and separate Newfoundland identity remains. Since 1980, the new flag of Newfoundland and Labrador has become a symbol of it.

Right. In Scotland, the 1990s saw the emergence of cultural and political consensus, as well as confidence among the Scots in their ability to manage their own affairs. Tom Church tried to capture the new spirit in his *Braveheart*-inspired William Wallace sculpture in Stirling (removed in 2008).

Below. Nationalist graffiti in downtown St John's. After a period of 'hibernation', Newfoundland nationalism is on the rise again in the early twenty-first century. Contrary to what the graffiti seems to advocate, however, it takes the form of autonomism rather than separatism.

its economic policies favoured mainly the urban areas on the Avalon Peninsula.[153] Still, the PC Party seems to have maintained its support in Newfoundland's rural districts. Graesser's 1989 provincial election study shows how the major changes in terms of voter loyalty occurred in the urban areas, where the new middle class used to guarantee PC victory.[154] Apparently, Peckford's lack of success on almost all his major issues had alienated large parts of the urban middle class, including the business community. It is unlikely that people belonging to this group simply abandoned their patriotic sentiments. Rather, they realised that the means would have to change. Cultural nationalism lived on; political nationalism was sacrificed.

In the analysis of the development of Scottish nationalism, it became clear that although in serious crisis around the time of the 1979 referendum, Scottish political nationalism returned with a vengeance after a short period of adaptation and redefinition, not least because of the positive incentive provided by the EU alternative to the UK. There seemed to be no such alternative for Newfoundland autonomists to anticipate. A free trade agreement between Canada and the United States – from 1994 the North American Free Trade Agreement (NAFTA) – did not take effect until 1989, and in any case, NAFTA and its secretariat make up an altogether different organisation from the EU. Although an important factor to take into consideration for any Canadian autonomist movement, it does not provide the kind of political and economic alternative to dependence on central government that the EU does. NAFTA therefore never became an important positive incentive to autonomism. Nor can central government in Canada at the time of the weakening of Newfoundland autonomism be considered a negative incentive to autonomism. From 1982 to 1988 Canada did increasingly well in economic terms. GDP grew at respectable rates, and unemployment declined from its 1983 level of 11.8 per cent to 7.5 per cent in 1989. The Progressive Conservative Mulroney government, contrary to the Conservative Thatcher government in the UK, was in favour of decentralisation of political and economic powers, and thus did not provide political nationalism with the necessary obstacle and hostile image to confront.

Danny Williams and the resurgence of Newfoundland autonomism

It is outside the scope of this study to carry out an extensive analysis of the resurgence of autonomism in Newfoundland in the early twenty-first century, but it is pertinent to briefly describe some highly relevant developments.

Danny Williams led the Progressive Conservatives to victory in the 2003 provincial election, and since becoming Newfoundland premier he has enjoyed a popularity on a par with Peckford's twenty-five years earlier. His popularity was achieved partly by turning a giant provincial deficit into a modest surplus, partly through championing the Newfoundland offshore case against Ottawa. With large-scale migration from Newfoundland to other parts of Canada threatening the provincial economy and social structures, the PCs argued for Newfoundland's special status under the equalisation formula to ensure that this great opportunity for Newfoundland to move from 'have-not' to 'have' status was not destroyed by federal diminution of equalisation transfers in reverse proportion to increases in Newfoundland oil and gas revenues (so-called 'clawback' measures).

In December 2004, during a dispute with the Liberal prime minister Paul Martin over the balance between revenues and equalisation, Williams took up the symbolic tradition handed down by previous Newfoundland premiers and ordered all Canadian flags removed from provincial buildings.[155] When, a few weeks later, Ottawa and St John's renegotiated the Atlantic Accord and reached a deal expected to earn the province short-term gains of $2.6 billion, his approval ratings soared. According to one poll, 86 per cent of Newfoundlanders were satisfied with the performance of the Williams administration.

The level of public support remained high in the following years, boosted by another fierce stand against Ottawa, as the Liberal federal government gave way to a Conservative government headed by Prime Minister Stephen Harper. The new federal government allegedly reneged on a campaign pledge by reintroducing non-renewable resource royalties into the equalisation formula, and thereby earned the wrath of Williams and the great majority of Newfoundlanders (as well as Nova Scotians and Saskatchewanians). Soon after, an aggressive Newfoundland government-sponsored ad campaign across Canada warned Canadians not to trust the prime minister to keep his promises. Furthermore, the advertisements included the image of the Canadian maple leaf, with the text: 'Is this what Canada stands for now?'

Much like in previous decades, the autonomist discourse revolved around more than just narrowly economic considerations, and the rhetoric was reminiscent of the Peckford era; at a May 2007 rally Williams exclaimed: 'We know that we're proud, we know that we're hard-working, we know that we're industrious . . . But we also deserve dignity and respect, and it's about time we got it.'[156] Also mirroring the Peckford government, the Williams administration placed much importance on hydropower development, this time in the form of the Lower Churchill River project. Williams was adamant that this time

Newfoundland should be the real beneficiary: 'We're going to own it and we're going to develop it, as opposed to what we've done before – just kind of hand it off.'[157]

With a charismatic, devoted PC premier at the helm, unafraid of (even actively seeking) conflict with the federal government, and a provincial government whose priorities are decreasing Newfoundland dependency through development of and control over revenues from local natural resources, autonomism is clearly back on the political agenda in Newfoundland. Yet it has still (2010) to be seen to what extent the PC government is willing to play the national/ethnic card, and to what extent Williams is willing to carry through controversial policies in the face of firm opposition from a non-minority federal government.

SIX   Images of Self and Other in Scottish Newspapers

A previous chapter illustrated the high degree of influence exerted by mass media on socialisation processes generally and on national identity-building processes specifically. It was also argued that the printed media in particular are carriers of important images of self and other that feed into and to a large extent determine the content of such processes. Consequently, with a continued focus on autonomism, this chapter and the next set out to establish the nature and extent of images of self and other communicated by Scotland's and Newfoundland's most important newspapers from 1967 to 1990.[1]

IMAGES OF SELF AND OTHER IN THE *SCOTSMAN*, 1967–1979

In the period 1967 to 1979, the self portrayed in the *Scotsman* remains predominantly, and not surprisingly, Scotland and the Scots. The newspaper considers itself very much a Scottish voice expressing the opinion of at least a majority of Scots. The point of view from which events and situations are reported and assessed is distinctly Scottish, as their impact on Scotland is always considered, as are the best ways to either shield the Scots or secure them maximum benefits. On many occasions, statements such as 'the majority of Scottish people do not want complete separation from England'[2] illustrate how the *Scotsman* regards itself as being in a position to speak on behalf of not only its own readers but Scots in general.

The most significant others in this period are the major political parties/Westminster, and the British government. The *Scotsman* as readily attacks the party in power as the opposition for being weak – and particularly for being opposed to devolution. In other words, political affiliation is not made manifest, while opposition to the workings of British politics and Westminster in general is clear. It is easy to imagine the existence of images based on national conflict, in which case the English/England would make up a powerful image of other.

This, however, is not the case. There is some mention of England and 'the English', but these terms almost always function as pseudonyms for central power in London. There is little mention of additional others such as the EC, Commonwealth states or other parts of Britain (Wales and Northern Ireland). In general, the *Scotsman* in this period places little emphasis on internationally defined others, including images of England as such. Rather, images of the affluent south and the old dominant Westminster parties take prominence. From 1972 there seems to be an emerging perception of a Scotland–Britain dichotomy. Again, this is closely connected with the perception of a Westminster-situated other.

Images of self and other in the cultural sphere

In all the *Scotsman* editorials concerned with nationalism and devolution in this period, emphasis is divided equally between political, social and economic aspects. Only very rarely does the paper devote editorial space to Scottish cultural issues. One editorial, however, takes the form of a critique of a familiar aspect: 'Our music-hall tartan, the "Wha's like us" conceit behind many of the songs with which B.B.C. Scotland . . . are apt to affront Sasunnach ears, are not endearing to the outsider. There really may be some Scots . . . who believe that they live in a land of kilts, a hundred pipers and a' and a'. This is very far from reality, and an insult to the true spirit of the people.'[3] The editorial also laments the ill-informed ways in which English media portray Scotland and Scottish culture, and thus places Scots and English in opposition (the use of 'Sasunnach' for English), but still chooses to place the larger part of the blame on the Scots themselves. Culture seldom becomes an issue of importance in the *Scotsman* editorials with a focus on Scotland's relationship with the rest of Britain. The paper occasionally declares that autonomy in cultural matters will not be enough to satisfy the Scots, and essentially it does not acknowledge the importance of cultural matters to the home rule debate. It is clear that the paper does not see cultural difference as an argument for devolution in itself.

Except for a few occasions, such as the 1979 referendum editorial, the paper tries hard to avoid referring to Scotland as a nation in any ethno-cultural sense. In a 1973 editorial on the Kilbrandon Report, the paper thus declares its support for a federal UK constitutional set-up, although it is not quite prepared to disassociate itself from the idea of a Scottish nation: 'The Kilbrandon . . . minority . . . are not deterred by lack of [English] demand . . . They would put Scotland and Wales on the same footing as five English regions, having no regard for national sentiment . . . [T]heir plan . . . is remarkable.'4

Still, editorials resort to traditional cultural nationalist rhetoric at points when it is felt that emotions need to be stirred. Hence, in an editorial, 'Predictable Reactions', attacking the London media and politicians for their reaction to the recently published Kilbrandon Report, the *Scotsman* informs the reader: 'there were the usual cynical and facetious remarks, which English MPs seem to consider the appropriate reaction to anything about the "Celtic fringes" ', and continues: 'There are various good reasons for devolution, but the frank indifference of English back-benchers to the tribal business of the Scots and Welsh is one of the most persuasive.'5 In all the *Scotsman* data collected for this period, this is one of only two arguments regarding devolution that is remotely cultural in nature. The editorial does not continue along a cultural line of argument, but turns to a discussion of political and socio-economic pros and cons of devolution.

Only at one other point does the paper make use of culturally founded arguments, this time to appeal to Scottish voters immediately before the 1979 referendum on a Scottish Assembly. The mood and the language in this front page editorial is quite different from the usual standard of editorials in the paper. In its use of cultural arguments it also stands out as unique for this period: 'A Yes vote . . . will restore the self-confidence which dependence has sapped and exorcise the defeatism which possesses the No camp. It will preserve a sense of national identity, encourage a constructive kind of patriotism and revive faith in our culture and traditions . . . A No success would complete the process of assimilation, of reducing Scotland to a mere geographical expression. Scotland's survival as a nation, a worthy partner in the UK, depends on an emphatic and decisive Yes.'6 Although phrases such as 'faith in our culture and traditions' and 'Scotland's survival as a nation' place this as an example of classic nationalist, *Volksgeist* rhetoric, these are arguments which are not otherwise sported by the *Scotsman* editorialists in the entire period. The general impression of the point of view expressed in the *Scotsman* editorials is that cultural uniqueness can only be a small additive in a battle for autonomy which has other, much more important, components. There is no indication that London or any other external actor is ascribed with cultural imperialist intentions.

Images of self and other in the socio-economic sphere

The significant others in the socio-economic sphere in this period are not so much national others as others defined in terms of region and access to power. Multiple areas of dissatisfaction with the behaviour of significant others exist, and they are directly linked to images of Scotland's socio-economic situation. The perception throughout this period is that a time of relative prosperity in the early 1960s has now been followed by stagnation and decline, and the overall theme in the *Scotsman* editorials is that within a poor British economy, ill-managed by changing governments, 'Scotland is not getting a fair deal'.7

In terms of the state of the British economy and the economic policies of British governments, the *Scotsman* seldom has a positive critique to offer. The following excerpts are illustrative of the pessimistic mood characteristic of the entire period: 'Labour are adhering rigidly to a course which is failing to give assurance of consistent and speedy progress . . . why should our [Britain's] share of world trade in manufactures continue to decline?'; 'The UK can not continue for long with a trade deficit of the dimensions of the past few months.'8

In 1968, the Wilson government (1964–1970) received a no-confidence vote from the *Scotsman*: 'We ended 1967 with a bigger trade deficit than in the crisis year of 1964. What confidence can be placed in Mr. Wilson's diagnosis now? . . . [T]he Government, instead of lessening, will aggravate Britain's difficulties.'9 Based on the multitude of Labour-critical editorials, the paper may easily, but wrongly, be seen as right-wing. Criticism does not seem to be motivated by a right-wing ideology. When it comes to the economic policies of the Conservative government under Edward Heath (1970–4), the *Scotsman* does not pull its punches. In 1974, a conflict with the miners' union forced Heath to call an election, and discussing references to industrial relations in the Tory manifesto for the upcoming election, a *Scotsman* editorial titled 'Wrong Approach' asks: 'Are they living in a world of make believe? . . . [T]he losses to the nation are likely to outweigh by far any resulting gains.'10 The paper continues to warn the electorate: 'A nation that gives them a renewed mandate on this basis is taking a grave risk.'

In fact, the two major parties, Labour and the Conservatives, receive an equal share of criticism, even when not in government. Editorials in this period illustrate a general lack of trust in the ability of *either* of the major political parties to change Britain's socio-economic situation.

The second important aspect of the overall perception of self and other in the economic sphere is the sense of neglect of the Scottish economy. In a 1967 editorial, confronting Labour with the recent upsurge in nationalist sentiment demonstrated by SNP's by-electoral success, the paper argues: 'The Hamilton by-election is an unmistakable judgement on the claims of both the large parties to have promoted Scottish interests . . . [T]he presence of Welsh and Scottish Nationalist M.P.s in Westminster will be an effective reminder that these countries expect more from them than the stream of assurances and pledges about what they are pleased to describe as regional development.'[11] As with the British economy, there is a distinct lack of trust in the ability of either of the major parties to change Scotland's socio-economic situation. Argues a 1972 editorial: 'Since regional development policies of successive Governments have not been conspicuously successful . . . it is hard to feel confident that they will solve long-standing problems in the future.'[12]

Not only are Labour and the Conservatives seen to be incapable of improving Scotland's situation, government policies are even – although mostly in the early part of the period – seen as hurting Scotland specifically. In a 1968 editorial on unemployment trends, it is argued that the figures 'do not bear out the Government's declared intention of shielding Scotland from the adverse impact of their policies'.[13] In other editorials from the same year, government incentives are argued to have caused specific problems in Scotland, and of a particular economic policy referred to as 'stop-go', it is said: 'While [it] has harmed the English economy, it has harmed the Scottish economy much more.'[14]

In attempts to come to grips with the lack of success of various policies of successive governments in changing Scotland's socio-economic situation, explanations range from lack of interest, through a lack of understanding, to deliberate exploitation of Scottish resources to benefit other projects, including supporting less needy parts of Britain. The perception of lack of interest and ignorance on the part of governments and major parties is evenly spread from 1967 to 1979, while explanations focusing on ill will occur more frequently towards the end of the period. An editorial from 1968 discussing the Labour government's latest budget is symptomatic of the perception of indifference on the part of Westminster and the major parties to Scotland's problems: 'The Chancellor has been no more careful of Scottish interests than has been customary from London Governments . . . [T]here are dangers inherent in the Budget. These threaten to undo some of the good achieved since the early 1960s. It is worth pointing out that such a threat was no doubt totally absent from the Chancellor's mind when he made his choice of deflationary measures. But it has been the unthinking blows to Scotland which have hurt most in recent years.'[15]

In 1974, a similar point of view is expressed. In an editorial titled 'State Oil', prime minister Harold Wilson is accused of being only marginally interested in providing Scotland with a fair share of oil revenues – in spite of promises to use oil money to develop deprived areas – and of being 'out of touch with Scottish feeling'.[16]

On occasion, the major parties and governments receive modest (but reluctant) praise for certain initiatives. In a 1968 editorial the paper contends: 'Credit must be given to the Government for the efforts they have made . . . to attract new industries to Scotland.'[17] However, this sort of praise is never allowed to stand unmodified. The excerpt above, for example, is to be found in an editorial calling for much more to be done to reduce the Scottish unemployment rate to the British average, and right below another claiming that 'the unfortunate taxpayers . . . have every excuse for feeling no confidence in the Government, political parties and Britain's future'.[18]

In terms of mismanagement taking place within the socio-economic sphere, according to the *Scotsman* this also stems from another, more malevolent source. The first suspicion in this period of a deliberate policy of neglect of Scotland, in order to benefit other parts of Britain, appears in a 1968 editorial, 'Tory Illusions'. Here it is argued: 'Under conditions tantamount to laissez-faire, . . . it is not surprising that Scotland should be starved of new industrial development in comparison with the London area and the English Midlands.'[19] The editorialist more than indicates that Scotland's poor economic state at the time may be caused by a Westminster decision to assist English regions at the expense of Scotland. This stricture stands alone, however, in the first part of the period; later they become more frequent. In 1973 the allegation is made explicit: "In the affluent South-east it may be hard to understand why the natives in less favoured areas are restless . . . Higher unemployment, emigration, lower earnings, switches in economic policy that harm Scotland in order to relieve overheating elsewhere – all is forgotten in the glowing picture by anti-devolutionists of the rewards of dependence.'[20]

The perception held by the *Scotsman* is that the combination of these attitudes (of disinterest, indifference and exploitation) has hardened a Scottish lack of confidence in both Labour and the Conservatives to deal properly with Scottish economic affairs. The two major parties are the victims of most of the attacks by the *Scotsman* editorialists, but underlying all the accusations and criticisms, however, is also a general blame for Scotland's socio-economic state of affairs attributed to the nature of the entire political system. It is not so much the ignorance, lack of interest or even the opportune exploitation of Scotland by changing governments and old established parties, but it is rather the system, which allows these attitudes to influence economic policy for Scotland, that needs mending. Therefore, the solutions proposed by the paper include devolution.

In this regard, a recurring theme – and a constant source of irritation to the *Scotsman* – is what the paper considers a lack of trust in the ability of Scots to manage Scotland – and thus in Scottish devolution. Both Labour and the Conservatives, and other 'Unionists', are reported to hold this view. The *Scotsman*, however, is never in doubt, and increasingly positive reports of oil development off the coast of Scotland seem to enhance the perception that more autonomy in the economic area would benefit Scotland immensely.

A gloomy view of the state of Scottish economy persists throughout the period, but from 1972 it is mixed with more optimistic – at times almost ecstatic – forecasts based on future oil riches. On 16 March 1972, the editorial 'Golden Opportunity' rejoices: 'The ever-widening prospects are so immense that it is hard to grasp their potentialities for the Scottish economy, but it is certain that there will be opportunities for industry that could replace the current depression by several decades of bustling activity.'[21]

From 1972, oil becomes a powerful argument in the critique of the Westminster 'other'. This is a period in which the *Scotsman* is generally preoccupied with refuting the claim that Scotland is economically dependent on England/Britain. The paper argues repeatedly throughout the period that such dependence is non-existent, and that Scotland would in fact be better off socio-economically in a set-up allowing it to control its own domestic affairs, independent of policies designed to fit English and British economies. In one 1968 editorial, 'Rigidity of Mind', it is made clear that the devolution debate in Scotland is 'largely about economic control', while in another, 'Tory Illusions', the focus is on alternatives to economic ties with England: 'Labour spokesmen seem to be at one with the Conservatives in emphasising the point that if Scotland were on her own she would lose the benefit of existing entice-ments to attract English firms to Scotland. Even if that were the case . . . it by no means follows that American firms would cease to prefer Scottish sites . . . and if we joined the Common Market development of her deep waterways could give Scotland an advantage.'[22] This is the first time, at least in the period investigated, that the *Scotsman* seriously considers alternatives to the status quo of close economic ties with the rest of the UK. Economic autonomy for Scotland had been proposed multiple times, but without considering the practicalities of such a move. The brief mention of European and American ties can hardly be described as a thorough structural-economic analysis either, and indicates that the paper is not entirely certain as to how Scotland would fare with a higher degree of economic independence. When oil is struck, all such doubts seem to vanish. From 1972, oil is seen to provide a much more viable alternative to British economic union than both the Common Market and the US. An editorial from 1973 even purports that a fully independent Scotland would not be a poorer Scotland, 'particularly owing to the oil discoveries'.[23]

The new sense of optimism facilitated by the positive economic perspectives even leads the paper to predict that, with the assembly proposed by the Kilbrandon Report, Scotland would be in danger of being tied down by the rest of Britain. The optimistic mood based on prospects of oil development, however, does not last long. Already in 1974 it seems to have dawned on the *Scotsman* that Scotland was not going to be given control of either oil and gas development or revenues. The Labour Party, likely to form the next government, is in favour of the nationalisation of oil, not allocation by companies, and the paper realises that 'Scotland's share in its oil resources . . . is only of marginal interest to Mr Wilson', and '[t]he Tories see [North Sea oil] as Britain's great hope of salvation after existing for a few lean years on borrowing'.[24] The only parties which the paper sees as having purposeful ideas on the exploitation of Scottish oil are the Liberal Party and, to a lesser extent, the SNP. However, neither party is anywhere near political power, and thus hopes for a Scottish oil bonanza seem much less bright at this point. The *Scotsman*'s tone of bitter disappointment is expressed in an ironic and interesting statement on different types of nationalism: 'Mr Wilson's nationalism is . . . British and so above reproach. The SNP's nationalism, which would give Scotland the maximum benefits from the oil resources in her waters, is somehow selfish and absurd, according to both Tory and Labour Parties, who have no intention of letting the oil bonanza interfere with Westminster's policy of treating Scotland as a region, incapable of looking after its economic affairs.'

The 1975 EC referendum coverage provides information about the *Scotsman*'s perception of the European Community. Although not entirely happy about the prospect of a referendum, the paper's referendum comment, 'On with the Job',[25] happily welcomes the 'Yes' result as common sense, and necessary for Britain to cope with economic crisis.

In the heated debate leading up to the next referendum, in 1979, there is little mention of socio-economic aspects generally, and both oil-based wealth and the European market are rarely considered as alternatives to economic union with the rest of Britain. As regards devolution, from the first plea for Scottish autonomy in the socio-economic sphere in 1968 to the end of this period, in 1979, there is little difference. The 1979 referendum editorial informs the Scottish voter that 'A Yes vote . . . is an opportunity of attending to neglected areas of legal and social life. It means regaining responsibility for matters which a mature people ordinarily decide for themselves, whilst co-operating with our neighbours in common concerns.'[26]

In essence, the prevailing images in the socio-economic sphere in the period 1967–79 are characterised by a pragmatic attitude to social and economic problems, their possible solutions, and those outside forces perceived to cause them. The paper is never separatist, and it spends considerable time and space assuring its readers of this. It takes its most radical stand on Scottish autonomy when the negative incentives of the first part of the period (overall British decline, growing Scottish unemployment rates, etc.) are joined by positive incentives (oil development in particular). When the positive incentive to economic autonomy disappears, so do the radical aspects of the *Scotsman*'s discourse.

Images of self and other in the political sphere

Images of self and other in the political sphere are closely tied to images in the socio-economic sphere. The social and economic malaise that industrial decline, unemployment and a general lack of economic development was causing in Scotland in this period is mainly blamed on the lack of understanding or carelessness regarding Scottish affairs that Westminster politicians, including governments, are seen to harbour. Some images and perceptions, however, also place themselves entirely within the political sphere, and are associated mostly with what can be described as a sense of democratic deficit.

Not surprisingly, the most significant political others are the British government (regardless of which party is in power), Labour, the Conservatives and Westminster as an institution. Focus in this period is mainly on the political other, as opposed to the political self, a natural consequence of there being so little of Scottish politics actually decided in Scotland. When both are considered, the two are often seen to be in negative opposition to each other. In a celebratory editorial commenting on Winifred Ewing's by-election victory in Hamilton in 1967, the *Scotsman* holds: 'Mrs Winifred Ewing's election for Hamilton is a splendid victory for herself, for the Scottish National Party and for Scotland . . . [I]t is a crushing defeat for the Government.'[27] A similar point of view lies behind that day's front page coverage of the same event. The title of the main front page story reads: 'SCOTLAND DEALS BITTER BLOW TO MR WILSON.'[28] On this occasion, success for the SNP is interpreted as success for Scotland. In the years to come, however, there is little identification on the part of the *Scotsman* with either the SNP or what is considered its radical goal of independence.

Main themes in the political sphere can be divided into four. First, there is the perception of Britain as a state in decline, incapable of providing the benefits which a state is supposed to provide. Second, there is the perception of changing British governments as incompetent and indifferent to Scottish needs. Third, most of this is ascribed to an outdated political system, and finally, the only alternative to the unacceptable political and constitutional status quo is seen to be a healthy measure of decentralisation of powers.

On several occasions, the entire political system is attacked as unfair and outmoded. The *Scotsman* is particularly outraged after the October 1974 election, in which the Labour Party won 41 of 71 Scottish seats (57.8 per cent), while receiving only 36.3 per cent of the Scottish vote. The editorial's critique of the electoral system is fierce: 'Any public opinion poll which distorted public opinion to the extent that the electoral system does would deserve not only to go out of business but also to be prosecuted for fraud . . . How can a nation's political institutions be respected when they are founded on the same ethical basis as bingo halls and gambling dens?'[29] Similarly, by the end of the period – in the wake of the failed referendum in March 1979, and in expectation of the 1979 election – an editorial speaks of a 'breakdown of confidence in Britain's traditional political and constitutional arrangements'.[30]

Although a recurring feature, this point of disillusion is not as prominent as the one involving the incompetence and indifference of British politicians. Labour and Conservative politicians are generally seen to be out of touch with Scottish feelings and wishes. Labour and the Conservatives would do well, explains the paper in a 1968 editorial entitled 'Unmistakable Warning',[31] not to ignore the serious threat of nationalism and instead acknowledge that there is 'strong dissatisfaction with the present system of governing Scotland'. The general lack of coverage of the role played by Scottish MPs in raising awareness of Scotland's problems indicates that the *Scotsman* considers them either an integral part of the establishment or without powers to change the situation. Otherwise, the Labour party and its leaders (particularly Harold Wilson) are seen as rigid-minded and inflexible in their blind faith in the traditional support from Scottish voters, while the Conservatives remain, according to the paper, deliberately vague on the important question of increased political autonomy for Scotland. In the political sphere, as in the socio-economic sphere, the *Scotsman* does not trust either party to rule Britain, or to take care of Scotland's special needs.

One reason for Scotland's lack of influence over its own affairs is seen to be the great difference between Scottish and, principally, English preferences. In the 1974 election, England voted predominantly Conservative while Scotland voted Labour in what can be described as a forerunner of the future 'doomsday scenario'. The same situation in 1979 causes an editorial captioned 'Scottish Loyalties' to say: 'While the English kicked Labour out, the Scots clung closer than ever to their trusted patrons and protectors . . . [D]ifference is vigorously alive.'[32]

Neglect of Scotland caused by deliberate political exploitation remains the most common accusation. In fact, goes the argument, were it not for the votes Scotland provides, Westminster politicians could not care less. There is seen to be little incentive on the part of Labour (or the Conservatives) to make the political system fairèr; only public demand and the consequent allocation of votes will make an impact. A 1967 front page story, 'HAMILTON SET-BACK SPURS TORY DEVOLUTION MOVE', authored by 'our political correspondent', is clearly of the view that the Conservative Party would have made no move on devolution had it not been forced to do so by the SNP by-election victory. It muses: 'The shock of the lost deposit at Hamilton should concentrate the minds of its members wonderfully.'[33] The same perception is prevalent in a 1968 editorial, 'A Constitutional Extra',[34] discussing a Tory proposition for a Scottish Assembly. It says: 'However elevated the tone of Mr. Heath's aspirations for Scotland's welfare, there can be little doubt that it was another aspect of the Conservatism which produced Saturday's speech – namely the party's ability to change with the mood of the country. The phrase "panic measure" is pejorative in implication.'

Between the two elections of the hectic election year 1974, Labour suddenly changed its policy on devolution. Scotland is now to have some sort of political autonomy – provided Labour is restored to power. This, however, does not impress the *Scotsman* or make it embrace the 'new' Labour. On the day the news of Labour's U-turn is reported, the paper's editorial is titled 'Warning to Labour'. A cautious mood characterises the editorial, which reads: 'Mr. Harold Wilson and Mr. William Ross . . . lead an extremely precarious Government, and their previous record in avoiding devolutionary commitments hardly aspires hope.'[35] The *Scotsman* acknowledges that Labour's 'long-standing conservatism and unionism may indeed be mellowing,' but is critical of the reasons: 'While the SNP's share of the vote doubled . . . Labour's share declined . . . It is not, therefore, peculiar that a report should emanate from the very centre of centralist Labour thinking, proposing a devolutionary move . . . Would it have appeared at all if the SNP's support had declined or remained static?'[36]

The *Scotsman* thus proposes that both Labour and the Conservatives are simply exercising *Realpolitik* without truly caring about Scotland. Still, as long as the end-goal is a satisfactory measure of devolution, it is willing to accept this state of affairs. When this end-goal is seen to be moving beyond reach, the paper is less indulgent. After Labour's election victory in October 1974, the paper complains about the electoral system, which so favours Labour, and is concerned about Labour's 'position of selfish expediency'[37] which, now that the party is safely back in power, might see the government deliver an amputated version of devolution, or not deliver at all.

In 1979, the paper foresees Labour's demise as the party in power, but does not take much comfort in what will be the new ruling party's pledges on devolution: 'Scotland will watch with interest to see if the various Tory promises amount to more than devious hypocrisy. If the Nationalists fare ill at the election, then the pressure will be off, and the temptation to send devolution back to that dusty realm from which it emerged will be strong.'[38]

Ill-will and opportunism on the part of the political parties are thus seen as the immediate cause for Scotland's inappropriate lack of political influence in Scottish affairs. However, the real problem is not so much seen to be the attitude of the parties, but the fact that the system of government allows such attitudes to become decisive. The entire constitutional–political system is seen to be in need of revision.

Nowhere is the system so strongly opposed as in the editorials immediately before and after the 1979 referendum. The referendum editorial argues that the system of government represented by the Westminster set-up was never democratically agreed to by Scots, who will now have the first chance to choose a system themselves. It furthermore disavows any benefits of the present set-up and muses: 'It is surprising that so little was heard [from the 'No' campaigners] of the merits of government from Westminster; there was no pretence that it satisfies Scotland's needs.'[39] With the outcome of the referendum confirmed, the paper sighs: 'Westminster . . . may now return to its dreary, wasteful habits, hopeful that devolution, which would have triggered renewal and change, will go away.'[40]

The *Scotsman* remains in favour of decentralising powers throughout the period,[41] but often disassociates itself from separatism and claims that the majority of Scots do so too. A 1974 editorial says: 'There is surely huge support among Scottish voters, . . . for seizing, not independence, but the political and economic opportunities which are available to revitalise our nation.'[42] The emphasis is on making government for Scotland more efficient and Scotland-tailored, not on independence.

The paper laments the reluctance of the major parties to introduce even less radical changes, and when in 1979 the referendum draws near, it engages fully in the 'Yes' campaign, committing itself totally to the establishment of a Scottish Assembly as outlined in the Scotland Act of 1978. On 1 March 1979 – the day of the vote – a pro-devolution editorial, 'Moment of Decision', takes up almost the entire upper half of the front page of the *Scotsman*. The tone of the editorial is uncommonly emotional, and strikes the reader as an almost desperate plea for a 'Yes' vote. It is strategically placed next to a narrow left-hand corner article with a large-font title: 'Appeal to Scots for Courage in Voting', thus linking courage with support for a Scottish Assembly. As illustrated above, the main editorial argues that a 'Yes' vote will not threaten the existence of the Union, but rather have a range of positive consequences.

As it becomes clear that a Scottish Assembly will not materialise, the *Scotsman* finds it hard to come to terms with the fact that its case has been lost, and when defeat can no longer be denied, the paper is quick to point to the guilty party. In warlike rhetoric, the gloves come off in the first editorial to comment on the result: 'It will take a little time for the smoke to clear from the battlefield but the blood-spattered figure of the Scotland Act can be dimly discerned . . . What almost killed the Assembly stone-dead . . . was the politicisation of the devolution issue . . . The vote in yesterday's referendum may have been as much an expression of dissatisfaction with the Labour Government as about the question with which it was overtly concerned.'[43] Labour is accused of designing the act to fit a cause which was Labour's more than Scotland's, thus associating the entire referendum with the survival of the government, and the ills of central administration.

The failure to achieve home rule for Scotland, and what would appear to be an obvious misinterpretation of public opinion on the part of the paper, thus does not facilitate serious self-scrutiny. The arguments are similar to those displayed by the paper since 1967: those who are to blame for Scotland's misfortune are to be found in London. A couple of days later, however, the paper is forced to admit, for the first time, that although '[t]he idea of a measure of Home Rule has always been popular among Scots, . . . they rarely put it at the top of their list of political priorities'.[44]

IMAGES OF SELF AND OTHER IN THE *SCOTSMAN*, 1980–1990

Analysis of editorials from the *Scotsman* from 1980 to 1990 indicates that a pattern largely similar to the one described for the previous period dominates. What would appear to have been a move towards a more ethno-cultural kind of argumentation in the 1979 referendum editorial is not sustained. From 1980 to 1990, the *Scotsman* coverage and editorials contain no evidence of such a shift in attitude. The pragmatic, democratically and socio-economically motivated arguments for Scottish devolution prevail in this period also. A set of images more or less similar to those revealed during 1967–79 thus appears to characterise the *Scotsman* editorials in this period. Two notable exceptions remain, however: an evolving perception of autonomism as the will of the Scottish people, and an increasingly negative image of the Conservative Thatcher government gradually come to dominate.

Autonomy

From 1980 to 1990 the *Scotsman*'s feelings about devolution become stronger, but along lines similar to those followed in the earlier period. That is, the paper does not turn to a more radical stance with regard to the necessary steps to take for Scotland, but it does find the steps more urgent in the face of Conservative policies, and it voices its arguments more often and with more vigour. Independence is never considered a useful or desirable option for Scotland. As in the previous period, an important reason for the *Scotsman* to opt for devolution is that it is a viable alternative to independence. In a 1989 editorial, 'Power Only to Some People',[45] the *Scotsman* foresees Prime Minister Margaret Thatcher's counter-argument to the Scottish demand for devolution as being based on fears that it would fracture the UK. It refutes this belief as it explains: 'Because the Union is seen by many to be failing, the contrary is the case; devolution is perhaps the only way to repair and strengthen it.'

Although acknowledging in the early part of the period that the establishment of a Scottish Assembly in 1979 would not have altered Scotland's socio-economic situation immediately, the paper continues to believe the debate should be resumed, and that a form of devolution should be established, not least because such a move would in the long term improve Scotland's economic prospects. Therefore, the paper receives the 1988 'A Claim of Right for Scotland' report by the Campaign for a Scottish Assembly very positively: 'First the report is as clear and cogent an articulation of the constitutional position Scotland finds itself in as has been published . . . Secondly, it expresses the central problem facing Scotland today, which is . . . the state of Scotland within the Union at a time when the Scottish people have voiced their dissatisfaction at the polls with the present Government and its policies.'[46]

The paper agrees heartily with the cross-sectional nature of the Scottish Constitutional Convention (SCC), provides good coverage of the meetings of forum, and continues to express its general endorsement of it – as, for example, in this editorial: 'This is a people's cause, not one of party politics. The convention has set out on a great enterprise which, successfully completed, will restore to Scots their political identity and return their distinctive values to the political stage.'[47]

One might expect that an increasing amount of material on the EC and other European issues would characterise editorials from this period dealing with devolution and Scottish national identity. However, apart from a grand 1988 four-page survey assessing 'Scotland in Europe 1992',[48] there is little in the data set to suggest the paper's views on European integration and the relationship between Scotland and Continental European states.

Thatcherism

The most important reason for the *Scotsman* to actively advocate an increased measure of autonomy for Scotland is not the threat of Britain falling apart. It is the increasing lack of democracy coupled with stubborn unwillingness to accept the fact that Scotland is different, which it perceives Scotland to be the victim of. The all-dominant hostile other in this period is the Conservative government or, rather, Margaret Thatcher. An indication of this is the fact that although some pride is exhibited in the British victory in the Falklands War, the paper reserves no credit explicitly for the British government.

In the early 1980s, the paper restricts itself to criticising the Conservatives for having 'contracted out of the devolution race' in spite of 'former interests and pledges',[49] but by the mid-1980s a more unforgiving tone is assumed, and a new image of the Tories, as too un-Scottish to be able to understand the needs and wishes of the Scots, is developing. The paper finds it necessary to draw the attention of the Scottish Conservatives to opinion polls documenting the fact that 'a great majority of Scots do not like either the Conservative government or the system of governing Scotland via a Parliament situated in London'.[50]

A 1986 editorial blames the Tories directly, as well as the apathy of other political parties in Scotland indirectly, for the miserable state of the mid-1980s Scottish economy. There is, it says, 'a lack of people, from all political parties in Scotland, actually *doing* something, in co-operation with each other, to improve the situation. And even if this miracle . . . were to come about, it would be far too late to rectify so much damage that has already been done to the national economy . . . by the seven years of Tory Thatcher reformationist and centralist rule.'[51] 'National' in this editorial refers to Scotland, and thus pits the bad government of a foreign centralised administration against the Scottish nation. The images of Conservative London rule and the prime minister turn increasingly implacable as the 1980s progress. The paper subtly promotes the poll tax non-payment campaign, and places Malcolm Rifkind, the Scottish Secretary, and his government in an unfavourable opposition to the popular move for devolution as expressed by the SCC. Explaining Jim Sillars' surprising win in the 1988 Govan by-election, the paper takes the view that 'Mrs. Thatcher's misunderstandings of Scotland and Mr. Rifkind's unreceptiveness to Scottish feeling were among the most important factors that drove Govan to register its protest'.[52] Utilising an interesting piece of imagery, the paper explains what it finds to be wrong with the manner in which the Conservatives rule Scotland: 'Claims that Scots were Thatcherites before the term was invented and that Scotland only blossomed under the impact of the union are Government missives designed for the wrong target. They betray how badly it has misinterpreted not only Scotland's history but also its present discontents. None of this will help change the colour of Scotland's electoral map. Nor will repeated applications of policies devised to fit conditions in the comfortable South-east. As these travel north they become more ill-suited; when they finally cross the Tweed they have been translated into threats to the Scottish ethos, a means of Englishing Scotland's institutions and way of life.'

It is thus contended that failing to understand Scotland's premises on its own terms – terms which are implied to be of a more rough nature than those of the 'comfortable South-east' – the Conservatives simply impose policies and values on the Scots which have little or no place there. As previously, the paper does not oppose English, or even London, values per se, but, instead, the fact that these are forced upon the Scottish people in the shape of ill-fitting policies. In the *Scotsman*'s opinion, the UK has become an 'authoritarian and restricted society', and the 'freedoms Mrs. Thatcher has removed' can only be restored by the decentralisation of 'the power she has pulled to the centre'.[53]

IMAGES OF SELF AND OTHER IN THE *GLASGOW HERALD*, 1967–1979

There is a marked difference between the kinds of emphasis placed on images in the *Scotsman* and *Glasgow Herald* editorials in this period; the distinction between self and other is in many respects more subtle in the *Glasgow Herald*. From 1973, the paper adds to its front page mast-head the self-proclaimed 'Scotland's Newspaper'. Thus, one must assume the identification of the paper with the people of Scotland – or at least the wish to appear as such. Characteristic of the *Glasgow Herald* in this period, however, is a position of distancing itself some-what from the idea of the Scottish 'nation'. In the 1974 and 1979 elec-tion editorials, for example, the *Glasgow Herald* positions itself as a British newspaper, and takes it upon itself to advise all British citizens, not just the Scots, on how to vote. Another example is 'The Claim of Britain',[54] a critical response to a nationalist publication, which concludes: 'We are still, most of us, at least as much British as Scottish.'

Images of self and other in the cultural sphere

The analysis of the *Scotsman* articles revealed an emphasis with regard to autonomism on both the socio-economic and political spheres, whereas arguments pertaining to the cultural sphere were largely disregarded. The *Glasgow Herald* includes both less cultural and socio-economic considerations, finding the debate about political nationalism to belong predominantly to the political sphere. One notable exception, in which the paper makes use of ethno-cultural arguments to pit continent against nation against nation, is a small 1972 editorial (the third of three that day), entitled 'National Teams'.[55] Here the paper fiercely opposes the merging of British national football teams into one. These 'Continental suggestions' and 'foreign ideas' are prompted, argues the paper, not by 'concern for the blushes of the English rose' but by the cunning thought that such a team would be weaker due to 'inter-British frictions'. Being on the warpath, the Glasgow paper decides to deal the English a few blows as well; the paper does not find the positive response to the suggestion among the English surprising, as 'the abolition of the four separate teams would save the English the regular embarrassment of explaining away defeats at the hands of smaller nations'. However, most terrible of all, 'insult would be added to injury by the tactless Continentals who would insist on referring to the all-British team . . . as "England".'

The powerful images and strong language in this editorial might leave the impression that the *Glasgow Herald* is heavily and generally engaged in an ethno-cultural nationalist struggle in favour of its beloved Scotland. This however, is far from the case. In the only other two editorials partly pertaining to the cultural sphere in this period, the UK and British union are passionately defended against exactly nationalist demands for autonomy. In an editorial headed 'Nationality', the *Glasgow Herald* declares: 'To be anti-Scottish Nationalist, . . . and even (as we are) pro-English, and (even more so) pro-British, is by no means the same as to maintain that Scotland is merely a region of Great Britain without any tradition, culture, or characteristics of its own . . . Unlike nationalism (the desire for political independence or domination) nationality is an instinctive quality.'[56] Quoting J. D. Mackie, the editorial then moves on to agree that 'internationalism "does not involve the destruction of nationality" '.

Similar points of view pervade the editorial 'The Claim of Britain'. Here, the argument goes: Scottish nationality, which 'certainly goes far deeper than haggis and tartan and bagpipes, or than most of the English imagine' should be valued for its qualities and 'for the greater contribution it can make . . . to the spiritual and economic wellbeing of these islands'.[57] Hence there is an image of the English as different and as failing to appreciate the unique qualities possessed by the Scots, but also a commitment to let those qualities benefit the UK rather than let them work for Scotland only.

Images of self and other in the socio-economic sphere

The *Glasgow Herald* acknowledges that the UK's former leading economic position in the world is no more. In the paper's 1973 assessment of the state of the State, 'New Era Dawns',[58] the dominant image is one of Britain still mired in serious social and economic problems, although minor positive developments, such as increasing employment figures, have occurred. The overall problem, argues the editorial, has been the failure of the UK to adjust to the changed circumstances following WWII. The year 1973, however, also marked the entry of the UK into the EC, and in the eyes of the *Glasgow Herald* editorialist(s), this offered sustained hope for future recovery. At the time of the 1975 EC referendum, the paper leaves no doubt about its pro-European persuasion. The referendum front page editorial reads: 'This newspaper, mindful of the interests of both Scotland and the United Kingdom, has been a consistent advocate of British membership of the European Community . . . British interests will be most effectively served through a partnership with our European neighbours . . . [T]he climate of the world economy is far more hostile than that of the Community, whose members in any case have good reason to ensure that no partner slips into permanent economic decline . . . A 'yes' vote will . . . mean that we can tackle our serious and recently neglected economic crisis in a climate of relative certainty . . . A 'no' vote, for whatever reason, would . . . precipitate an immediate and damaging political and economic crisis.'[59]

By 1979, the *Glasgow Herald*'s cautious optimism has waned: 'What can be done to halt Britain's long economic decline?'[60] the paper asks desperately in the election editorial of that year. A small upturn in the UK's economic performance is dismissed as being the result of short-term income, such as North Sea oil and IMF loans. In fact, it is argued, the UK's credit is running out, and the paper is worried about the future quality of social services in the UK. The prescribed cure no longer features the EC, but a radical shift of emphasis from the public to the private sector, and thus support for Conservative rather than Labour policies.

The perception of British economic decline in the late 1960s is joined by one of Scotland in an equally serious socio-economic condition. A 1967 editorial thus speaks of Scotland's 'perennial problems of high unemployment, low wages, and heavy emigration'.[61] Scotland's 'perennial problems' are still seen to exist in the early 1970s. A 1972 editorial acknowledges that, in spite of general worries about Scotland's economy since WWII, Scotland actually did relatively well in the 1960s compared to other parts of the UK. The decline, however, with peaking levels of unemployment, is argued to have set in again during the Wilson government. Now the *Glasgow Herald* also fears that Scotland's socially and economically important steel industry will soon be run down. A 1971 editorial, 'Oil Strike',[62] believes that 'the economic climate in Scotland has not been so bleak since before the Second World War.' However, the hopes for socio-economic recovery are now sustained by the discovery of oil in the North Sea, 'which spells wealth for Scotland; which, surely, we can not fail to exploit'. In an equally optimistic mood, the paper contends in the following year: 'The North Sea oil boom is still more dream than fact, but increasingly it is a dream with substance . . . For one thing is certain – the oil will not go away.'[63] The 1973 editorial heralding a 'new era' as Britain joins the EC also credits North Sea oil with Scotland's recent economic recovery in some areas and maintains hope, as 'Scotland has a Texas off her North-East shore'.[64] Although the *Glasgow Herald* doubts that North Sea oil will ever make Scotland economically independent of the UK, in the mid-1970s hopes for socio-economic recovery are still vested in oil development, and Labour attempts at checking the powers of the multinational oil companies are opposed as obstructive, and dangerous to a Scottish economy in desperate need of the economic injection.

By 1979, the Scottish economy is still regarded as being in a critical state. The *Glasgow Herald* holds that antiquated, nationalised Scottish industry has special problems, causing a disproportionate amount of closings and redundancies. The paper is worried about serious social consequences, but maintains that 'modernisation is essential'.[65] In the latter part of the period, there is little mention of natural offshore resources, the main positive element of the early and mid-1970s. As a sense of oil realism creeps in, the 1979 election editorial acknowledges that North Sea oil will run out. Although there are some references to the Common Market, editorials from the late 1970s addressing the economic problems of the UK and possible solutions to them seldom mention the EC. The best promise of a way out of 'the present economic impasse', it is suggested, is a Conservative government with a policy of privatisation, emphasising the free market.[66]

In the period from 1967 to 1979 the *Glasgow Herald* frequently blames the British government in London for Scotland's social and economic problems. The underdeveloped British infrastructure is also blamed in this respect. Still, the overall perception of the economic relationship between Scotland and the rest of the UK is positive. In response to separatist demands, in 1972 the paper asks rhetorically:

'How are we disadvantaged now? Any one who sees economic answers in altering the political location of power must be able to produce evidence first that our economic problems are caused by the fact that the Government meets in London and, presumably because we are a minority, neglects our interests.'[67] Commenting on the conclusions of the Kilbrandon Report, another editorial reaches a similar conclusion. It speaks of the 'advantages the present system has demonstrably given to Scotland',[68] and holds that Scotland, 'has done well out of the United Kingdom and that her privileged position could not continue if she were given a greater say in her own affairs'. Scotland's 'long lead . . . in public spending per head', it warns, would discontinue if the Kilbrandon scheme were implemented.

Even though the *Glasgow Herald* acknowledges that a vote for the Conservatives in the 1979 general election may be a gamble, considering the danger of relentless market policies to Scotland's special needs, it still believes that Conservative policies will do more than Labour policies to create jobs and get Scotland out of the socio-economic difficulties she finds herself in. After the Conservative victory, the *Glasgow Herald* editorialist realises that the Scots have been less than enthusiastic about Thatcher's economic vision, and warns the new government that Scotland still needs special treatment. If it does not receive it, foresees the editorialist, 'the tide of nationalism could once again turn'.[69]

Images of self and other in the political sphere

The most significant others in this sphere in the 1967–79 period are the two major political parties and the SNP. Westminster as an institution is much less criticised and seen as less of an opponent than in the *Scotsman* during this time. Still, although the paper argues in its second 1974 election editorial that 'as a nation we are generally well served by politicians',[70] this period is not characterised by a general appreciation of British politicians, or of the British political system. As does the *Scotsman*, the *Glasgow Herald* warns London politicians of the danger of a growing sense of alienation in Scotland, coupled with a strong sense of national identity. A 1967 editorial for example speaks of a Scottish sense of nationality, which neither the Conservatives or Labour, with a lack of vision, should 'try to laugh away', and which 'the professional politician at Westminster ignores at his peril'.[71] Disenchantment with an 'over-centralised, impersonal, and often inefficient State machine', argues the paper, is shared by nationalists and 'the rest of us' alike. Yet, although the paper advocates new policies and mild reform in the area of local government to cope with Scotland's special social and economic problems, there is no whole-hearted *Scotsman*-like rejection of Westminster rule in principle.

A pro-Conservative stand is expressed throughout the period. After the SNP Hamilton by-election victory in 1967, the paper believes that only a Conservative government will be able to solve Scotland's problems and thus effectively nip the independence and home rule movements in the bud. Occasional slaps on the wrist, however, indicate that present *Herald* editor Arnold Kemp may not be quite right when he claims that until the mid-1970s 'the leader writers used to consult Tory central office to make sure they had the right line'.[72]

The *Glasgow Herald*'s point of view diverges most notably from Conservative policies on the issue of a Scottish assembly, an idea with which the party flirted from 1968 to 1973. With a sigh of relief, the *Glasgow Herald* thus greets the Labour plan for devolution in 1973 as a 'hotch-potch' with the virtue of avoiding the dangers of the Conservative plans for an assembly by rejecting 'dangerous and unworkable solutions to which others, who should know better, have succumbed'.[73] The paper regrets that Douglas-Home's Constitutional Committee kept the issue alive at a time when it should have been forgotten, and the expressed wish of the paper is that the party move on to 'matters more relevant to present-day Scotland'.[74]

In both of the 1974 general elections the *Glasgow Herald* supports the Conservative party, fully agreeing with their policies of lower taxes, denationalisations and keeping Britain as one political entity.

By the end of this period, however, even the *Glasgow Herald* detects potential danger for Scotland as the neo-liberal Thatcher government takes power. Nonetheless, the overall impression during this time is one of continued support for Conservative policies, except for the interlude of Conservative autonomism, from 1968 to 1973. In contrast, the policies of the other main party, Labour, are often targeted and found to be harmful to Scotland. As is the case in the *Scotsman* – although to a lesser degree – there is a belief that Labour's failure to address Scottish problems in the late 1960s is the main cause for the success of political nationalism. The 1967 Hamilton by-election editorial thus claims that the SNP victory should be interpreted as a 'resounding blow of no confidence'[75] caused by the 'widespread disillusionment with the Government's handling of Scottish affairs'.

When Labour considers reintroducing Scottish home rule to its 1974 manifesto in the aftermath of the February general election, the *Glasgow Herald*, keeping to its pro-status quo views, regrets this and says: 'The Scottish Trades Union Congress . . . have played an important part in changing Mr William Ross' originally sound inclinations.'[76]

For the main part of the period investigated, the *Glasgow Herald* remains strongly unionist and anti-SNP. At an early juncture, the paper warns that protesting via the SNP, as in the Hamilton election, could develop into support for home rule or even worse: independence. The prevailing point of view, which the paper believes it shares with the majority of Scots, is summed up in an editorial addressing 'Nationality'.[77] The editorial declares: 'As for this newspaper it remains, politically, anti-Scottish Nationalist . . . The Scots . . . are a people with a strong and enduring sense of nationality which transcends all political boundaries; . . . [but] we also have a vivid streak of internationalism in our make-up . . . That surely, is why . . . the great majority of us desire – and have the confidence – to remain patriotic subjects of Great Britain without seceding in any way.' The pragmatic distinction between cultural nationalism (to be lauded) and political nationalism (to be shunned) is clear. Scotland is best served, politically and economically, by the constitutional status quo, which also allows Scottish nationality to flourish. Separation is thus out of the question as far as the *Glasgow Herald* is concerned, but what about a lighter measure of autonomy? Although the paper warns about support for home rule, it does not appear to be altogether opposed to minor alterations, as long as they occur within the framework of the UK.

In an editorial from January 1968, the paper detects not only a strong dissatisfaction with the handling of Scottish issues, but also 'a general aspiration for some much greater Scottish control over Scottish affairs'.[78] Less than two months later, in March, the same kind of desire for devolution within the UK is displayed: 'Scottish nationality is something to be valued for its own sake and for the greater contribution it can make, given a measure of devolution, to the spiritual and economic wellbeing of these islands.'[79] The *Glasgow Herald*, however, does not allow itself to wander along this line of thinking for long. In the same editorial it reasserts its unionist self and reminds its readers that 'any change in our political structure must give priority to the claim of Britain as a whole'.[80] Also, the support for devolution detected in this period remains support for a small measure of decentralisation only. The paper holds that the popular solution to the problem of centralisation would be reform of local government rather than separate administrations for Scotland and Wales.

Having expected the worst, the paper can therefore greet the cautious 1973 Labour proposal for devolution as an 'interesting, perhaps even harmless, constitutional innovation'.[81] The *Glasgow Herald* is less lenient the following month, November, when it comments on the newly released Kilbrandon Report. The devolution measures suggested by the report are rejected as too radical, and 'Scotland's Newspaper' accuses the Kilbrandon Committee of having manipulated the evidence.[82] The paper detects no 'firm and mature desire for devolution in Scotland.'[83] To illustrate what it sees as the inherent danger of home rule, at this point the *Glasgow Herald* makes use of a well-known idiomatic expression, which would become almost a Unionist catch phrase: 'Half-baked plans for home rule, born of panic in London and Edinburgh. . ., will be the *first step on the slippery slope* leading to the dismemberment of the United Kingdom.'[84]

With such evidence of anti-home rule sentiment, it is hardly surprising that the SNP falls victim to most of the hostile images which the *Glasgow Herald* projects in the entire period from 1967 to 1979. Prior to the February general election, the paper ridiculed the SNP's proposed policies in an editorial called 'Manifesto of Dreams'.[85] The manifesto, it argues, 'floats on oil' and builds on 'rash promises based on financial nonsense'. The interpretation of the SNP electoral success as more than a protest vote is interesting because it is inconsistent with the editorial perception which has been dominant in the *Glasgow Herald* so far. After the SNP victory in the first 1974 election, the *Glasgow Herald* finds it necessary to warn SNP voters – of whom only a small minority are believed to be seriously in favour of the SNP policy of Scottish independence – about the consequences of support for the SNP: 'The SNP are an uncompromising group . . . What national politicians might regard as a meaningful concession to Scottish opinion could easily turn out to be the thin end of the wedge.'[86] Other warnings are issued in the days leading up to the October election. The paper tries to make voters understand that 'the Union . . . remains a tribute to almost every identifiable political virtue from tolerance to common sense', and that by voting SNP they are voting for a party seriously intent on destroying all these virtues.[87]

The belief in the strength of supranational unions extends to British and Scottish membership of the EC: 'British interests will be most effectively served through a partnership with our European neighbours. At present the common market is essentially an organisation for economic co-operation, but it provides a framework within which a mutually beneficial political union can be developed at a pace controlled by the member states . . . [C]ontinuing Market membership will involve some transfer of power to Brussels, but the extent of that transfer is surely not so contentious as to outweigh the advantages of being part of the Nine.'[88]

Although the pro-EC paper regrets the low level of support for membership in Scotland compared to other parts of the UK, it claims to know the reason for it, and argues it to be an 'understandable concern in Scotland that we might suffer from being on the periphery of the Community'.[89] The reaction to the outcome of the 1975 referendum, a vote in favour of continued membership of the EC, is – not surprisingly – positive. Under the heading 'YES!', the referendum comment welcomes the determined collective decision of the British people. The political impact of the decision at the height of the Cold War is stressed more than the economic advantages in this post-referendum editorial: 'Britain's decision will consolidate the power of the Western world at a time when its authority and unity has been seen to waver.'

At this point the *Glasgow Herald* is strongly opposed to any kind of radical political nationalist goal, as well as even a mild measure of devolution. The editorial reaction to the great success of the SNP in the October 1974 election, however, comes to mark a decisive break with the previous persuasions of the paper in this regard. The *Glasgow Herald* is clearly shaken not only by the Conservative loss of power, but equally by the pro-SNP election results for Scotland. In this state of desperation, the paper commits a U-turn and launches a new policy of reluctant support for devolution. The editorial regards devolution as a necessary move, the absence of which 'will merely fan the fires of nationalism'.[90]

In the time leading up to the 1979 referendum, the paper finds the 'Yes' campaign and Labour badly organised. The 'No' campaign is seen to be better organised and better financed and, as a consequence, believes one editorial, 'fewer people may be inclined to say "Yes" to an assembly simply as an unconsidered "patriotic" reflex'.[91] However, rather than regretting the consequences of this for the chance of establishing a Scottish Assembly, the paper stresses the Labour Party's opportune adoption of devolution to stem the rise in support for the SNP. The 'Yes' camp *is* told to shape up, but the reason provided does not reveal any deep attachment to the idea of a Scottish Assembly as much as it expresses concern about the democratic process as such: 'The assembly, after all, is widely regarded as a great democratic experiment, and it would be ironic if the referendum itself were to fall below standard in this respect.'[92]

The referendum editorial, 'Scotland Must Give Decisive Answer Today',[93] is an altogether different 'Yes' editorial than the *Scotsman*'s. As is the case with the Edinburgh paper, the *Glasgow Herald* places the editorial on the front page, but in contrast to the *Scotsman* this appears to be much less the consequence of a desire to propagate a message to which the paper itself is devoted. The editorial is characterised by a lack of complete confidence in the 'Yes' that it is nevertheless reluctantly advocating. It informs its readers that the Scots 'face a historic and complex decision', thus indicating the difficulties the paper has itself had in forming its opinion. The editorial furthermore expresses, once again, the paper's belief that a majority of Scots remain in favour of a future for Scotland within the UK, and that the real value of devolution is that it has the power to diminish the threat of separatism. But even this strategy, admits the paper, may fail, and the advice it offers is that 'those who are not inclined to accept these risks or who are fundamentally opposed to any radical change in the Government of the United Kingdom should vote "No" '. Finally, the *Glasgow Herald* reveals that it believes a 'Yes' vote would be best for Scotland. However, the arguments emphasised in this part of the editorial pertain to 'control within Scotland over those areas of life which are either distinctly Scottish or which could be improved by a more responsive Government' and the extension of democracy.

The main characteristic of images and perceptions in the political sphere (as in the socio-economic sphere) in the period 1967–79 is pragmatism. With regard to issues pertaining to Scotland's relationship with the UK, the EC or other issues involving the consideration of the political or constitutional set-up, it is always a matter of what will benefit Scotland, then the UK, most in political and socio-economic terms. Emotional needs and ethno-cultural reasoning are rarely deemed to be of any significance.

IMAGES OF SELF AND OTHER IN THE *GLASGOW HERALD*, 1980–1990

Autonomy and European integration

A distinctive feature of the *Glasgow Herald* of the early 1980s is its continued anti-SNP stance. The Glasgow paper was the more reluctant devolutionist of the two Scottish papers by the turn of the decade, and it remains opposed to any radical ideas concerning Scottish autonomy. As the SNP moves back towards a separatist agenda, the *Glasgow Herald* is further alienated, and coverage of the views and fortunes of the party turns more critical. For example, one front page headline from 1980 trumpets 'Another blow for the Nationalists'.[94] The reference is to an opinion poll which set back the SNP by 3 per cent compared to the May 1979 general election. There is little mention of the fact that support for the Conservatives, according to the same poll, was down by 11 per cent.

In response to the outcome of the 1980 SNP conference, the paper says: 'Old-style fundamentalism ... may excite the faithful, but it is unlikely ever to provide the basis from which the SNP can make that decisive surge ... In tactical terms those who argue for a more gradualist and pragmatic form of nationalism are right.'[95]

In the 1980s, the *Glasgow Herald* remains, like the *Scotsman*, in favour of reopening the debate about Scottish devolution. Along with the Edinburgh paper, it applauds the setting up of the SCC, mainly because it transcends party political lines. More than the usual argument for devolution as the only alternative to a worse scenario of a shattered UK, however, the *Glasgow Herald*'s autonomist views now seem to stem also from a perception of Scottish national uniqueness: 'Scotland is suffering a crisis of identity . . . Scotland is considered a region of the United Kingdom, if it is lucky, or, more usually, an appendage or even a part of England . . . [T]he Scots must live with powerful neighbours and make their way in the world. The problem for Scotland is that it does this from a constitutional position which is tending to blur and even eradicate its own national identity. The case for a Scottish Assembly is much more emotional and cultural than it is economic.'[96] The paper thus holds that socio-economic arguments have become less relevant with regard to devolution, yet contends that 'in the Europe of the nineties, the idea of an isolated and isolationist Scotland seems less and less real. Whatever form of government is eventually adopted, Scotland will want to play its full part in the economy of the UK and Europe.' The EC, in other words, has become the safety net which ensures that no matter what happens constitutionally, Scotland will not suffer socio-economically. Also, it now finds that political decisions with regard to Scotland should be made in Scotland: 'What Scotland needs . . . is some platform for her own national voice . . . To that task Westminster has proved itself unequal.'

From its former position of being cautiously pro-devolution as a consequence of its fear of the terrible alternative, the *Glasgow Herald* has now moved to one of more convinced autonomism, supported by the viable alternative to the UK which European integration offers. The long-term socio-economic security of EC membership has proved more persuasive than the short-term benefits of oil and gas exploration.

At this time, even the paper's opposition to the SNP is reconsidered. The editorial commenting on Jim Sillars' Govan by-election victory welcomes him back to Westminster, and interprets his election as a message from the Scottish people to the UK government. Still, the radical rhetoric and anti-English sentiments of sections within the party are rejected as 'the politics of the gutter',[97] and the paper calls for more substance in SNP policies in accordance with what slogans promise.

In the early part of the period, the paper thinks little of the Labour opposition and its stance on devolution. It accuses it of a 'Leftward lurch' and of lacking fresh thinking and popular appeal.[98] As for Labour's commitment to devolution, it was always, claims one editorial, 'suspect'[99] – thus maintaining its perception of political opportunism as the driving force behind Labour policies on Scottish autonomy. As Labour in 1982 renews its pledge to secure devolution for Scotland, the *Glasgow Herald* still remains sceptical of the sincerity of the party,[100] but by 1989 it has finally come to trust the only party likely to succeed in procuring constitutional change. 'Outbreak of Harmony'[101] welcomes the SCC and cross-party co-operation as a voice for mainstream Scottish opinion: 'The Convention can genuinely claim to represent a consensus of Scots in favour of an Assembly. Labour's commitment, long somewhat suspect, is now copper-bottomed.'

Thatcherism

In the early 1980s, the anti-Toryism of Edinburgh's *Scotsman* is not mirrored in Glasgow's *Herald*. Although the paper would like to see the Conservative government 'pursue a more flexible economic policy',[102] it remains supportive of it and takes it upon itself to explain the unpopularity of the administration: 'In the depths of the recession the Tories could hardly expect to be other than unpopular.' During the South Atlantic war with Argentina over the Falkland Islands, the coverage is patriotic, in favour not only of the British military operation but also of the Conservative government's handling of the conflict. By the mid-1980s, however, the paper has turned sceptical with regard to the policies of the Conservative government in Scotland. It detects continued 'popular resentment at economic policies which have seemed inappropriate north of the border despite Scottish Office exercises in damage limitation'.[103] The SNP victory in Govan is seen as a reaction to the reluctance of the Conservative government to seriously consider Scotland as a unique entity with special needs: 'At the General Election [in 1987] Scotland expressed its point of view at the ballot box. It threw no bombs, threatened no violence. The upshot was that it was totally ignored. Worse, it was told that it did not know what was good for it.'[104] The *Glasgow Herald* is sensing a democratic deficit, and this makes it join the popular wave of anti-Tory sentiment. Having once been a staunch supporter of Conservative free market policies, the always pragmatic paper now also considers these to be little more than practised dogmatism, and certainly of little use to Scotland. Government policies are seen to further regional imbalance in the British economy to the effect of increasing the north–south divide. Also, Thatcher's strong opposition to anything but a deregulated EC collides with the *Glasgow Herald*'s ideal of economic and political integration in Europe.

Having thus established the nature and extent of images of self and other in the *Scotsman* and the *Glasgow Herald*, we will move on to consider many of the same issues with regard to autonomism and similar kinds of images in the two major newspapers in Newfoundland in the period 1967 to 1990.

SEVEN

Images of Self and Other in
Newfoundland Newspapers

Also with a focus on autonomism, this final chapter of analysis explores
the nature and extent of images of self and other manifested by
Newfoundland's two most important newspapers from 1967 to 1990.[1]

IMAGES OF SELF AND OTHER IN THE *DAILY NEWS*, 1967–1984

The analysis of *Daily News* opinion covers only the period 1967 to
1984, when the paper folded. The paper turned into a tabloid in 1982,
but remained one of only two major newspapers in Newfoundland.
Paradoxically, as the paper itself turned tabloid in nature, its editorials
became lengthier and more detailed, more directly addressing problems
that the paper found to exist.

The *Daily News* pretends to speak on behalf not of that limited group
of Newfoundlanders that make up its readership, but on behalf of all
Newfoundlanders as such. Throughout the period analysed, editorials
for instance refer to Newfoundland as 'this province'. Newfoundlanders
are on several occasions referred to as 'a people', clearly distinct from
other peoples of Canada. It is clear, however, where the *Daily News*
believes Newfoundland's future and loyalty should be. Editorials continually speak of Newfoundlanders as 'new Canadians', and emotional, at
times organic, ties are also considered to exist within the Canadian
nation. For example, Canada is occasionally referred to as a 'family'.

Of the two major parties, the provincial Progressive Conservatives
(PC) are over-represented both in terms of attention and in the role of
other. As a rule, provincial Liberal policies are only mentioned secon-
darily. A federal other is prominent throughout the period, both in the
form of government and bureaucracy.

Images of self and other in the cultural sphere

Very few editorials contain elements which can reasonably be classified
as belonging in the cultural sphere. Even the editorials which deal with

cultural issues with regard to political nationalism do so almost entirely
against a background of socio-economic and political concerns. In the
early and late parts of the period, the questions of national unity and
Quebec separatism are at the core of editorialists' discussion of cultural
issues. The dominant feeling throughout the period is that unique
cultural output – mainly that of French-speaking Canadians, but also
that which makes other provinces view themselves as different from the
rest – has a positive local identity-building value and should in principle
be endorsed. The twenty-fifth Confederation anniversary editorial, for
example, portrays Newfoundlanders as a 'people that proudly preserves
the best traditions of a storied past'.[2] The infatuation of the paper with
local cultures, however, has its limits. It acknowledges their right to and
the benefit of their existence to the whole, but sharply attacks the notion
that they should also be politicised. The *Daily News* is deeply concerned
about the lack of a common Canadian national identity, and an editorial
addressing the centennial anniversary of Canada issues a warning: '[T]he
forces that have made for cohesion in the United States do not appear to
have been established in Canada.'[3] One of the forces that the paper is
worried might threaten the existence of Canada is revealed in a later
editorial, 'Appeal to Separatists'. In this address to Quebec nationalists,
a basic conviction of the paper is revealed: 'A higher standard of living
[is] only to be obtained by a united effort by all Canadians . . . when all
is said and done, this is a materialistic society in which individual wellbeing is the common goal.'[4] In connection with the 1980 Quebec referendum, the cultural vs. political nationalism debate again enters the
Daily News editorials. In 'Vive Quebec!', which celebrates the outcome
of the referendum, the editorialist rejoices: 'They are Canadians, after
all,' and then significantly adds: '. . .just as much as they are Quebecers.'[5]
The *Daily News* thus conveys the same message in 1980 as in 1967: local
cultural identity and Canadian nationhood are perfectly compatible, and
one should not be allowed to jeopardise the other.

A similar view is applied when Newfoundland culture and its constitutional position is considered. Much cultural pride is exhibited when
the talk is of Newfoundland distinctiveness and unique qualities, as
exhibited in the 1980 provincial flag debate. In an editorial called 'Our
New Flag' the *Daily News* fiercely opposes the new design approved by
the provincial PC government, and argues for a replacement of 'the
meaningless flag' with the 'meaningful pink, white and green'. The
paper therefore patiently awaits 'the opportunity that will come with
the next provincial election, to get rid of it'.[6] The editorial is unmistak-
ably a political statement aimed at the government, and much of its
resentment towards the new flag seems to stem from the association of

it with PC policies in general. By proposing the historical pink, white and green flag – which carries numerous connotations pertaining to historical nation-building in Newfoundland – the paper partakes in the celebration of Newfoundland cultural heritage.

Deep indignation results when Newfoundland's particularities are referred to by mainlanders wrongfully or in a derogatory fashion. A 1972 editorial gloats explicitly as it reports the federal election draw between Liberals and Conservatives, because it finds that, recently, the same situation in Newfoundland had Canadians across the country considering it 'some kind of Newfoundland curiosity – crudely put; a Newfie joke'.[7] The paper generally resents stereotypical representations of Newfoundland by other Canadians, and another editorial from 1980 boils over in indignation at the suggestion that the high unemployment rates in the province can be explained by Newfoundlanders' unwillingness to work. The paper dismisses the idea as a false myth, and argues: 'The myth was part of the Canadian "Newfy" jokes that have tormented the patient people of this province for far too long . . . There was nothing easy about life in Newfoundland and Labrador from day one, and few Newfoundlanders ever complained about that . . . It's galling to a bitter degree to think that smug mainlanders are sitting up there in Toronto and Ottawa and other parts of Canada and blaming high unemployment in this province on the laziness of Newfoundlanders.'[8] There is clearly a sense of pride in the Newfoundland community, distinct from and misunderstood by the mainland. Still, the *Daily News* maintains that this sense of distinctness should never be allowed to justify political nationalism. At the time of Newfoundland's twenty-fifth anniversary as a part of Canada, the paper stresses in two consecutive editorials that Confederation has been and is of great benefit to Newfoundland, and therefore is not to be jeopardised by ethno-cultural claims and nationalism. One editorial, 'Twenty-Five Years Ago', directly addresses Newfoundland nationalism, as it proposes that, to those who are Canadian citizens by birth, 'it is impossible . . . to understand the emotionalism of the time and the strength of nationalism although that particular characteristic still exists in a modified form'.[9] The editorial discards it as useless in present-day Newfoundland, because Confederation, it argues, 'was a union of mutual advantage'. Immediately thereafter, the editorial makes an unambiguous statement, instructing Newfoundlanders to vest their political loyalty in the Canadian nation, and thus leave Newfoundland's ethnic identity unpoliticised: 'But the nation is bigger than the parts and Newfoundlanders accept Canadian nationality with pride and look forward to an increasing role in their participation in the shaping of Canada's destiny.'

Images of self and other in the socio-economic sphere

In the period analysed, the perception of Newfoundland's socio-economic situation gradually changes from almost ecstatic optimism through scepticism to gloomy pessimism. In 1967, an editorial takes stock of the previous fiscal year and concludes that it has been an '*annus mirabilis*',[10] which even promises to be merely a springboard for the future. It lists recent epic moments in Newfoundland's economic and structural development: completion of the trans-insular highway, developments in hydropower at Churchill Falls, modern fisheries and education, the introduction of new industries – and it expects 'explosive change in the provincial economy' to result from these developments. Another 1967 editorial speaks of explosive growth and argues along a similar line: 'Urbanization of the population is increasing but modern communications and higher incomes have brought a measure of sophistication to the smallest rural communities. Security has been established for all in one form or another. A new generation have advantages that were beyond the wildest dreams of their fathers.'[11]

In the *Daily News* assessment of the first twenty years of Confederation in 1969, however, the first mention appears of a problem that is going to become a serious concern of the paper. The editorial notes that 'as the working force has increased, the opportunities for employment have failed to keep pace'.[12] On a similar note, a 1971 editorial reminds its readers that the 'eternal quest for rewarding jobs for all' continues, and finds it necessary to explain the gravity of the situation: 'To underwrite the standard of living that people have learned to demand. . ., we must find means of producing new wealth.' The *Daily News* finds one potential source of such wealth to be 'the discovery of vast resources of oil and natural gas on the continental shelf'.[13] Oil thus arrives at a point when economic crisis has changed optimism to scepticism. Still, as regards the *Daily News*, the effect of oil is less profound than was the case with the Scottish newspapers. In spite of new hopes of oil wealth, conceivably 'the magic solvent', the editorial ends by emphasising the new situation that Newfoundland finds herself in, following a sustained boom: '[W]e have come to a new crisis in our affairs at the end of a period of galloping progress.' This new mood of what may be termed socio-economic realism is expressed throughout the 1970s. While a glint of hope is maintained, the general image is turning gloomy. As far as the *Daily News* is concerned, the major curse of Newfoundland remains a chronic lack of jobs, and as it realises that Newfoundlanders will not find the needed jobs in the oil and gas business either, this leaves the impression of a paper far from confident in the socio-economic future of the province. The forecasts of the paper, however, are about to change their tone into one which is even gloomier, almost desperate. March of 1984 found the paper in a particularly pessimistic mood, which serves to illustrate the general change in perception and tone. One editorial, 'Pins and Needles', portrays Newfoundland as suffering from, among other things, 'cutbacks and layoffs and deficits and all the other things that still tag us as the poorhouse of Canada'. A week later, another editorial, 'It Will Get Worse', after once again defining the major problem of the province to be the lack of jobs, concludes: 'It can hardly get any worse . . . but it will.' If one is to believe the *Daily News*, a week later Newfoundland has finally hit rock bottom with the bank rate topping ten per cent: 'For sure, Newfoundland couldn't be any worse off . . . We are in a terrible bind. It's a year in which we can't even stand still.'[14]

Yet, the perception of the Newfoundland–Canada economic relationship is also characterised throughout the period by a never-diminishing belief in mutually beneficial progress and opportunities for growth. A grateful tone pervades most editorials on this subject from the beginning to the end of the period. An early editorial finds it impossible to imagine how Newfoundland would have fared had it not united with Canada in 1949, but it nevertheless attempts a prediction: 'We had stood alone, accepting the sub-standard services of a limited economy, and measuring our progress only by our own yardstick. Whether we could have equipped ourselves to meet the challenges of the new age is doubtful.'[15]

The continued belief is that Newfoundland is not only a receiver of, but also a contributor to, overall Canadian socio-economic progress. This is accentuated in one twenty-fifth Confederation anniversary editorial, which states: 'It was . . . a union of mutual advantage. Canada could never have felt totally secure as long as Newfoundland was independent and perhaps likely to have her policies influenced by the United States. And Newfoundland's resources have contributed substantially and will add more to the wealth of the nation.'[16]

Significantly, the twentieth anniversary editorial, 'Twenty Years After', is dedicated entirely to socio-economics. It maintains that Newfoundlanders have been lucky to be able to move from poverty to relative prosperity. 'We have bought our way out of isolation and into the enjoyment of substantially improved social services with special emphasis on education and health,'[17] it argues. The use of the word 'bought' is interesting, as it indicates that a price was paid for social and economic prosperity. That price is obviously political independence; it is less certain whether the *Daily News* also considers a loss of ethnic or cultural distinctness to have been the result of Confederation. The twentieth anniversary editorial lists the three sources necessary for Newfoundland to reach the average Canadian level of prosperity: additional federal grants, industrial expansion, and federal policies for ending regional disparity. As the *Daily News* editorialist would have been well aware, previous attempts at industrial expansion had been largely funded by federal transfer money. In other words, the editorial defines not three but one source of future Newfoundland socio-economic development: federal assistance.

Economic inequality among Canada's provinces is seen to be a major threat to national unity. It is acknowledged that Newfoundland has reached a stage of relative affluence as a direct result of becoming a part of Canada, but that Newfoundlanders remain an underprivileged minority, with a clear notion of having not fully reached the new socio-economic level their status as Canadians entitles them to. Newfoundland shares with the Maritimes, it is contended, a series of disadvantages which warrant special treatment. Certain structural disadvantages are regarded as existing in the economic system, and central Canada is seen to benefit from this state of affairs. A 1969 editorial speaks of the Atlantic economies as being 'outside the focal point of Canadian economic growth, victims of the east-west direction of the economy and serving largely as captive markets for the nation's industrial heat and as sources of manpower for the major growth centres'.[18]

On top of the structural disadvantages, it is argued, the decisions of previous governments have placed Newfoundland in an unfavourable and unfair situation. The hydropower deal signed between Hydro-Québec and the Smallwood government in 1969 turned out to be extremely favourable to Quebec as the price of oil (and thus of other sources of energy) rose dramatically in the 1980s. Hydro-Québec is seen to have reaped huge profits from reselling power from Churchill Falls, and in the last half of the period studied, the *Daily News* repeatedly appeals for a renegotiation of the contract, arguing that Quebec, 'a sister province', is in fact stealing revenues from 'poor old Newfoundland'.[19]

Although the *Daily News* finds that economic inequality exists in Canada, and that Newfoundland suffers from it, this does not entice the paper to advocate increased provincial powers. In an editorial from 1968, 'The Crowning Touch', the *Daily News* places itself in strong opposition to the idea of strengthening provincial powers. The paper argues: 'The trouble is that it would be achieved at the expense of limiting the ability of the central government to spread the nation's wealth and achieve for all Canadians a minimum acceptable standard of economic and social opportunity.'[20] So what the centralisation–decentralisation debate boils down to, according to the *Daily News*, are socio-economic advantages and disadvantages. This view is upheld throughout the period. Editorials also frequently speak of the need to remedy economic regionalism and resolve internal squabbles so that they will not endanger national unity. Parochialism must be overcome, it is maintained, and the larger provinces – such as the greedy West[21] – must learn to accept that Ottawa should have the power to redistribute wealth through the equalisation scheme.

The *Daily News* is concerned about the possible impact of Quebec separatism, and one editorial, 'The Two Nations', makes the *Daily News*' point of view perfectly clear: 'In the case of the Quebec Government . . . the demand is for total control over provincial revenues and economic and social policies . . . This would clearly under-mine national unity. The trouble is that with Quebec nationalists who seek more autonomy while paying lip-service to a united Canada, the appetite must grow with feeding . . . When Ottawa loses the fiscal capacity to make and direct national economic and social policy, the federal structure will break down.'[22]

The tone of editorials that direct criticism towards the federal govern-ment is seldom harsh, and such editorials usually also take the form of offering advice. A 1969 invitation to federal Fisheries minister Jack Davis to visit Newfoundland to get a better idea of what the real problems are, for instance, is part of an editorial which also includes an appraisal of the Fisheries minister for being 'one federal minister who is clearly trying to do his job well'.[23] One exception is a 1977 editorial, 'Second Class Canadians', which directly attacks Ottawa and federal government economic policies towards Newfoundland. By concentrating solely on socio-economic problems in Central Canada, federal government is seen to disregard equally severe problems in Newfoundland completely: 'While we hold that the Newfoundland government is not entirely blameless in its attitude and the way it has approached economic matters affecting this province, there is sound reason for believing that Newfoundlanders are indeed regarded as second class Canadians and are severely retarded economically as a result.' The editorial concludes with a warning that such mismanagement could easily result in the most regrettable scenario imaginable: separatism.[24] As a 1980 editorial illus-trates, the aggressive attitude does not last. The editorial titled 'It Wasn't Bad' applauds a federal budget, produced at an economically difficult time, as 'a budget that faces up to the reality of the times but keeps in mind what governments often tend to forget – that there are little people at the end of the line who in the end have to pay for it all.'[25]

The attitude towards the economic policies of provincial government clearly hardens as administrations change and policies become increasingly incompatible with the views of the *Daily News*. In the late 1960s, explosive socio-economic progress is attributed not only to Confederation but also to the man who became the last living Father of Confederation, Joey Smallwood, and his Liberal Party. For instance, by the time of the twenty-fifth anniversary of Newfoundland's joining Canada, in the mid-1970s, the paper lauds Smallwood for building 'better than he may have dreamed',[26] causing progress for both Canada and Newfoundland.

As economic recession set in by the mid-1970s, the perception of both the PC administration, whose policies had so far been cautiously accepted, and its opposition changed. In 1977, an editorial made it clear that the *Daily News* could not agree less with the PC government's last move in an attempt to improve Newfoundland's socio-economic conditions. Premier Moores was at this point considering the political and socio-economic pros and cons of Newfoundland independence, mainly in an attempt to put pressure on the federal government. The response of the *Daily News* is pragmatic, socio-economically founded and utterly pro-Confederation: 'The one thing more than anything else that we learned as a result of union with Canada is that it is better to be an integral part of a large and wealthy country than to try to go it alone.' The very thought of leaving Canada for wealth that has not yet materialised horrifies the paper: 'What are known quantities are the contributions of the federal government to provincial revenues . . . To even contemplate giving these up for the uncertain benefits that could be derived from petroleum discoveries could even be the matching of substance against shadow.'[27]

By the end of the 1970s, the paper is fed up with PC economic policies, and prescribes the return of the Liberals to power as the only cure for Newfoundland's socio-economic illnesses. Albeit generally in favour of Liberal policies, this is a rare expression of political affiliation by the *Daily News*. The scene is set for an almost unbroken string of critical assessments of PC policies in the 1980s. The Peckford government receives full support from the *Daily News* in its attempt to reopen negotiations with Hydro-Québec about the Upper Churchill deal, but this is the only part of PC economic policies that is acknowledged as useful. Otherwise, the paper considers the government greedy, incompetent and stubborn.[28] The victims of autonomism, maintain the editorials, can only be the people of Newfoundland. The 1984 editorials conclude that Peckford's aggressive attitude to Ottawa, particularly on the oil ownership issue, has done nothing but harm Newfoundland socio-economically. Contrary to the autonomist arguments, the *Daily News* now holds that there is nothing wrong with the set-up of the system as such, that federal–provincial negotiation is the only way forward and that the federal government is both honest and fair. The real danger, explains one editorial, is that in the process of maintaining stubborn provincialism, the Newfoundland government may risk alienating federal government to the extent that it 'may have no choice but to go ahead with offshore development without any reference at all to Newfoundland'.[29] The paper ascribes all the major socio-economic problems of the province to Peckford's misguided insistence on making oil and gas the livelihood of all Newfoundlanders, and deems the federal–provincial dispute regarding that resource sufficiently important to make it the subject of its last editorial ever. Captioned 'Let's Face It', it states: 'We believe that out of all the frenzy will come a settlement, or at least an agreed truce, of Newfoundland's offshore dispute with Ottawa . . . What we ask [the federal Liberals] to do, and Mr. Peckford to do, and everybody else to do, is to do all they can to remove this stumbling block from Newfoundland's economic recovery. It's a psychological barrier to anything moving in this province . . . All because this dispute remains a frestering [sic] sore.'[30]

Images of self and other in the political sphere

What are naturally seen to be of much importance in terms of Newfoundland's and Canada's future are regional differences within Canada and the struggle for national unity. Centennial editorials from 1967 sketch out what is to be the point of view of the paper with regard to the unity question throughout the period: 'Newfoundlanders were little aware, before they became citizens of a Canadian province, of the many regional and emotional differences to be found in their new country [including] the constitutional conflict between the provincial autonomists and centralists . . . [I]n Canada, provincial rights seem to have priority and national policy is too often the sport of party politics . . . If this birthday year should pass without a serious effort to analyze the obstacles to unity and to achieve a total sense of national identity, its commemoration will end with few useful consequences . . . That is a result to be avoided at all costs.'[31]

The *Daily News* remains a convinced believer in Canadian unity as editorials repeatedly stress loyalty to the nation and the dream of creating 'one Canada in spirit, as well as geography'.[32] The conviction to keep Canada united and strong manifests itself in expressions of Canadian nationalism. The paper celebrates the patriation of the Canadian constitution in 1982 thus: 'All Canadians know that something good and wonderful happened in Ottawa on Saturday . . . [W]e came of age as a nation . . . It was a sweet day, even for newest Canadians here in Newfoundland and Labrador . . . [O]ne of the great strengths of Canada [is] that we can quarrel and squabble and come out of it all stronger than ever . . . We . . . have the best nation on earth.'[33] It is an interesting attitude to entertain for a paper servicing a province which until only three decades earlier was, symbolically if not legally, an independent nation-state.

What is seen to pose the most serious threat to national unity is Quebec separatism and, increasingly from the early 1980s, Western alienation. In terms of the latter, the difference in political preference revealed by the voting pattern of the 1980 federal election concerns the *Daily News* a great deal: 'The majority Liberal Party hardly represents that whole vast territory west of the Ontario-Manitoba border . . . How to bind the country together? For national unity – not only in respect of Quebec, but equally of the West – is the compelling issue.' In a similar fashion, another editorial from 1980 warns that 'the West, led by Alberta, is now at war with Ottawa, a war that could endanger the very fabric of Confederation'.[34]

On several occasions, the *Daily News* laments what is perceived as the regressive and unreasonable nature of separatism in Quebec. The 1967 'Appeal to Separatists' thus speaks of how 'an articulate, activist and aggressive few can thwart progress and even set back the hands of the clock'. These few are likely, argues the paper, to 'be little inclined to listen to the voice of reason', and a realistic and pragmatic approach is recommended. The paper fails to understand why Quebec or any other province would wish to place itself outside 'the mild restraints of the present federal constitution'.[35] This, however, does not mean that the paper does not appreciate the need to accommodate provincial differences. It is in fact open to minor adjustments in the federal structure, such as the recognition of special rights for Quebec within certain limitations, to counteract more dangerous developments.

What the *Daily News* advocates throughout the period is co-operation and administrative, rather than political and economic, decentralisation. The analysis of images of self and other in the political sphere thus contributes to the impression of the *Daily News* as fervently unionist, but it is also highly in favour of strong central government, and as such it can be seen to support the policies of the federal Liberal government under Trudeau (1968–79 and 1980–4). Although this does not mean that the paper uncritically accepts all of the workings of federal government, whereas the entire set-up of the Westminster system caused the *Scotsman* to turn autonomist, neither the basic structure of the Canadian federation nor the workings of parliament as such are targeted to any similar degree by the *Daily News*. When government institutions are criticised, the criticism aims more at practices and bureaucracy than at fundamental structures. One example would be the 1970 editorial 'They are

Planets Apart', which calls for a more personal attitude by politicians and civil servants to the problems they are trusted to solve: 'Even when Ottawa assumes a more liberal attitude towards the obvious needs of the poorer provinces, the suspicions and rigidities of the bureaucracy are often obstacles to progress.'[36] Other editorials criticise the inert bureaucracy in Ottawa for not knowing enough about Newfoundland's special problems and for failing to live up to its responsibilities and take proper action.

At points, the paper appears irritated by the lack of understanding not only by bureaucrats but also by federal ministers, as is the case in two 1971 editorials. One calls for a regulation of offshore fisheries in Newfoundland waters and for Canada to 'show her muscle if it hasn't become too flabby for want of exercise'.[37] The other, 'The Politics of Expansion', targets the Regional Expansion minister Jean Marchand: 'Marchand sometimes exhibits an excessive degree of petulance when the DREE [Department of Regional Economic Expansion] programme is attacked . . . [S]ince the DREE programme is generous in financial terms, the Minister feels that the beneficiaries should show more gratitude.'[38] The *Daily News* clearly disagrees with such an attitude, but dissatisfaction never results in the paper considering a fundamentally altered relationship between Newfoundland and Ottawa. When federal government, i.e. Liberal, policies and actions are addressed directly, the *Daily News* usually compliments measures which favour centralised government and Canadian unity, and on occasion reassigns responsibility for failed ventures or projects to place it with provincial politicians.

However, there does seem to have been a less lenient attitude to federal government in the early years of the Moores government. One editorial, 'Hope for a Joint Hard Stand',[39] for the first time goes directly against Ottawa in a matter concerning economic powers. It describes the application to Atlantic Canada of a Supreme Court ruling concerning British Columbia's offshore resources as 'dubious', and in an unprecedented move places itself in what may be considered an economic regionalist camp, fully supporting Moores' confrontational stand: 'Moores . . . hoped for a joint, hard stand on the issue, as this would be in the best interest of Eastern Canada. Amen to that! Nothing would comfort the Ottawa resource grabbers more than disunity among the five, likely allowing them to be picked off one by one.' Here, the *Daily News* exhibits an attitude to federal government which is quite uncommon. It occurs at a point when there is no noticeable change in attitude towards national unity or confederation as such. Nevertheless, faith in the idea of strong central government seems to be temporarily weakened. In another editorial from 1975 entitled 'Our Existence at

Stake',⁴⁰ a dissatisfied and aggressive attitude to Ottawa is displayed once again. Only this time, it is to a degree which practically places the *Daily News* in the autonomist camp: 'Cabot Martin['s] impatience with Ottawa's obvious reluctance to take unilateral action in declaring a 200-mile fishery zone shows through very clearly . . . [H]e appears to give a good plausible explanation of why Ottawa is reluctant to take unilateral action even though it is a matter of life and death for Newfoundland . . . [H]e claims the federal government is influenced by the fact that the issue really does not affect the economic or social structure of the two great forces in central Canada – Ontario and Quebec . . . Does he exaggerate? . . . We don't think he does.'

It is worth noting that the character of the fomenting factor in this period of what might be termed the *Daily News'* autonomist flirtation is a socio-economic one. The aggressive stand is triggered by what the paper sees as the fact that Newfoundland is suffering on account of deliberate federal government neglect. In other words, Newfoundland is not receiving its fair share of the windfall it is a partner in producing. This, however, is a rather short-lived stance which survives in a weaker form only until the end of 1977.

The *Daily News* remains largely party neutral with regard to provincial politics in the first part of the period, with a slight preference for the Conservatives because it sees the party as a vehicle for change. By 1977, however, Moores – and his 'cadre' of young Newfoundland patriots – start considering Newfoundland independence as an alternative to Canada, and rather than serving to harden the paper's attitude to Ottawa it seems to scare it off the autonomist path. An additional plausible explanation for the rejection of both early-stage autonomism and of the Conservative government as such is the fallout between the Moores administration and the *Daily News* as a consequence of the trawlermen's strike in 1975. During the strike, the government withdrew all public advertising from the paper, claiming it to be politically biased. The dramatic change which takes place is illustrated in the 1979 provincial election campaign, where the paper finally takes a definite stand in provincial politics. The *Daily News* denounces the Conservatives in general and their leader, Brian Peckford, in particular: 'The issues . . . have rarely been so clearly defined. Top amongst them is leadership. Do Newfoundlanders want Mr. Peckford, who has been utterly unable, since his election in March to head the PCs, to make up his mind on anything; or do they want Mr. Jamieson, who has a reputation for decisiveness? And more – do they want the politics of promises made and broken over and over? Or do they want political realism, and frankness, and telling it like it is? . . . The PCs came to power on the claim the Smallwoodites had

got us in a mess. What they did about it was to make it infinitely worse
. . . [I]f anyone can straighten out our affairs Don Jamieson is that
person.'[41] Peckford is thus denied support, not on account of the autonomist agenda that he had campaigned on, but because of his lack of abilities as a leader and the lack of results produced by previous
Conservative governments. At least so it seems. The real reason seems to
be revealed in the paper's post-election editorial, 'We wish them luck!',[42]
which does not mention leadership abilities with a single word, but
sarcastically wishes the Peckford government luck with its autonomist
project, defined by the paper as the perception 'that the province could
have its Confederation cake and eat it too – a sort of Newfoundland
version of Quebec's nationalistic sovereignty association idea'.

In sharp contrast to the condemnatory post-election editorial, a mid-
July editorial, 'Not Bad',[43] praises Brian Peckford's government for
doing 'very well indeed'. In fact, the editorial admits, 'Mr. Peckford
obviously has dreams and visions of what Newfoundland can be, just as
Mr. Smallwood did, and this is good, for if a people lack vision they are
in danger of perishing.' This is one amongst very few *Daily News* editorials to lend support to Peckford. Significantly, these rare examples all
appear in the early period of Peckford government, and apart from these,
the *Daily News* generally distances itself from the dominant confrontational approach of the Peckford autonomist discourse. It repeatedly
argues that negotiation, not confrontation, is the way forward, and
warns that the only conceivable result of continued strife between
St John's and Ottawa over ownership of natural resources is to 'harm us
all in the long run [and] endanger our place in the Canadian family
of provinces'.[44] Hence, the aggressive autonomist stand is blamed
directly for the lack of regional development agreements between the
federal government and Newfoundland, and as one Supreme Court
ruling after the other goes against Newfoundland control and ownership,
Peckford is increasingly condemned as the stubborn Don Quixote of
Newfoundland, 'tilting uselessly and futilely against the ownership
windmill'.[45]

As illustrated above, in the 1980s the previously optimistic mood
which characterised the socio-economic forecasts of *Daily News* editorials rapidly deteriorated. A similar decline in confidence in the political
future of the province is characteristic. In a rare 1980 reference to the
Liberals, the *Daily News* laments their toothless opposition, and finds
that the PCs have nothing at all to worry about on that front. It is a
shame, argues the paper, that a powerful opponent does not exist
in Newfoundland politics, and it urges the Liberals to shape up. At the
end of the period, all hope for Newfoundland politics and for future

prosperity in Newfoundland has disappeared as an editorial asks: 'Where is the use, the good, the justification for the House of Assembly session that has just opened in Newfoundland? What relation does it have with the major problem facing this province. . .? The answer is no use, no good, no justification and no relation.'[46] The paper now strips the premier of the only praise it could ever bring itself to bestow on him – that he was visionary – and ends the editorial on a bleak note, revisiting its own 1979 words of wisdom: 'People without vision are in dire danger of perishing.'

IMAGES OF SELF AND OTHER IN THE *EVENING TELEGRAM*, 1967–1979

During the 1960s and 1970s, the *Evening Telegram* is quite explicit about the Newfoundland self in its editorials, especially compared to the *Daily News*, but also compared to similar discussions in the *Scotsman* and the *Glasgow Herald*. When the *Evening Telegram*'s self is clearly defined, this often coincides with the definition of a Newfoundland self. The effect in these cases is to create a sense of interconnectedness, a synthesis of the two selves; the voice of the paper and that of Newfoundland(ers) become difficult to distinguish, and at points they become one, merging completely, for instance, with the use of an ill-defined 'we' or 'our'.

While the predominant self is Newfoundland and its people, a frequently defined other is federal government, closely followed by mainland Canada, defined chiefly as the have-provinces. Provincial governments in Newfoundland are as frequently addressed and made the objects of attention, as are federal governments in Ottawa.

Images of self and other in the cultural sphere

Cultural distinctness can be an important feature of autonomism, as it produces a sense of uniqueness and purpose, but in *Evening Telegram* editorials, in the day-to-day struggle for or against political and economic autonomy, it is seen to be of little relevance. Still, the importance attributed to Newfoundland cultural heritage is greater in *Evening Telegram* editorials during this period than in *Daily News* editorials. Throughout the 1967 to 1979 period, the masthead of *Evening Telegram* editorials sports the Union Jack – Newfoundland's provincial flag from 1949 to 1980 – bearing witness to the celebration of Newfoundland history and culture. Editorials containing images belonging to the cultural sphere take immense pride in Newfoundland's heritage, and express a wish to have it acknowledged and preserved. Anniversaries are points of self-reflection, and this is mostly where one finds editorials that concern themselves with Newfoundland culture and history. At the time of Canada's Centennial celebrations, editorials direct the attention of the reader to the fact that Newfoundland has a long history of independence and distinctness, which 'Canadians' – from whom Newfoundlanders are in these instances clearly distinguished – generally fail to acknowledge. 'Lest We Forget!'[47] is a reminder to those on the mainland engaged in 1 July celebrations that Newfoundland has events of her own, of a less joyful character, to remember on this day. The reference is to Memorial Day, commemorating the heavy losses of the Newfoundland Regiment at Beaumont Hamel in the First World War. Canadians, it says, may celebrate 'their nation's birthday', but the people of Newfoundland have a long and proud history pre-dating Confederation. Another Centennial editorial speaks of how Newfoundland's 'own unique personality . . . did not disintegrate in 1949', and how, therefore, Newfoundlanders and Labradorians can continue to contribute 'color and dimension to the Canadian character',[48] and it is hoped that Canadians may some day learn to appreciate this.

Six years later, the paper expresses concern about the survival of this valuable cultural heritage. Still stressing the 'distinct Newfoundland way of life',[49] a 1973 editorial warns that 'too many people are trying to impose on us other cultures which do not suit our personality and character'. It is the 'real' Newfoundland self which is seen to be in danger of disappearing. The paper, however, is ambivalent as to the impact of modernisation on Newfoundland culture. The editorial acknowledges that a major reason for the 'new kind of growth, the artistic and cultural expression of a talented people'[50] is the opportunity provided by socio-economic progress brought about after Confederation. Still, it also maintains that the particular Newfoundland way of life needs protection from heedless modernisation: 'We have to dedicate ourselves to preserving this . . . and not fall into the snare of progress and change for their own sake.'

The only other issue of an obviously cultural nature that is discussed in editorials in this period is that of cultural rights of French Canadians. The paper agrees that in terms of language and cultural equality, Quebec has a good case. Cultural concessions, however, should not be allowed to translate into demands for further concessions in terms of political or economic powers. This is a point of view which informs the paper's attitude to the federal–provincial relationship for some time. Although this will later change somewhat, support for an autonomist policy is never, in the period from 1967 to 1979, directly linked with and legitimised by ethno-cultural arguments.

Images of self and other in the socio-economic sphere

In the early parts of this period, the *Evening Telegram* shares with the *Daily News* the optimistic economic forecasts for the province. Editorials from 1967 speak of Canada's 'great potential', and of Newfoundland's 'fabulous progress' since becoming part of it.[51] The value of the federation is clearly seen to be material. By the twenty-fifth anniversary of Newfoundland's entry into Canada, the *Evening Telegram* can still acknowledge that Confederation has been to the socio-economic benefit of the province, but it does not engage in the kind of appraisal seen in the *Daily News* editorials celebrating the event.

After the late 1960s and the early 1970s, when cautious optimism was prevalent, the outlook for Newfoundland is seen as becoming darker. A 1977 editorial, 'Is There a Policy?',[52] addresses the serious unemployment problem of the province. That same year, however, the development of a new resource enters the debate about Newfoundland's economy, and in late 1970s editorials, the *Evening Telegram* finds itself in an optimistic mood, based on the belief that oil could positively alter many of the economic prospects for the province. By the end of 1979, the paper no longer hides its enthusiasm and great hopes for the development of the petroleum resources of the province. An editorial titled 'Preparing for the Oil Boom'[53] makes a premature start at calculating the revenues: 'The Hibernia oil well . . . has now given indications that there's lots more black gold in the Banks of Newfoundland . . . That may seem like very good news, now that the price of Canadian domestic crude is going up . . . [B]y the time our anticipated "oil boom" begins, the price per barrel may well be as much as $40 or more.'

From the beginning to the end of the period under investigation in this section, the *Evening Telegram* expresses its discontent with what it considers the most important deficiency of Confederation: regional disparity. The paper opposes any development which will make the province further dependent on handouts, and instead argues in favour of equal opportunity for economic development. That, according to the paper, is the real value of Canada. In fact, one editorial argues, only if such equality of opportunity is achieved across the country will Canada cease to be an 'Unjust Society' and 'learn how to be a nation'.[54] In 1973, the paper opposes the initial autonomist moves of the Moores government on the same grounds as the *Daily News*: only a strong central government will have the power to transfer money from 'have' to 'have-not' areas.

A general distrust in federal authorities means that the paper most often finds inequality to be the result of neglect and incompetence on

Ottawa's part. For the same reason, the paper finds it necessary throughout the period to call unceasingly for Newfoundland's fair share of the federal budget, and for more involvement in and understanding of the problems of the province on the part of federal authorities. The specific issues change, but the pressure remains. One period of intensive 'fed-bashing' is the early 1970s, when the paper is worried about over-fishing by foreign fishing fleets, and Ottawa's seemingly sluggish reaction. The editorial 'Words without Action'[55] is not so much angry with the foreigners as it is about what it considers Ottawa's double talk and inaction. It accuses the federal government of being timid, and argues that a national fishing zone should be established. Again, the value of Confederation and Newfoundland's fair share in it are questioned: 'When the very existence of a country is threatened it does not mess about with multilateral agreements; it takes unilateral action . . . It is a strange twist of fate that if Newfoundland had remained an independent country she could have imposed her own 12, 50 or 100 mile limit and would probably have had it observed by fishing nations. But with Canada doing the negotiating on our behalf we don't get action, we get external affairs double talk, meaningless diplomatic phrases and little hope of anything other than more words more talks and multilateral agreements that seem to lose more than they gain.'

A 1973 editorial titled 'Come and See Us, Sometime'[56] regrets Ottawa's most recent health programme and speaks of the 'remote bureaucracy we have to endure'. The problem with federal bureaucracy, explains the paper, is that it fails to distinguish between 'have' and 'have-not' provinces, thus placing unbearable burdens on the latter. In the last part of this period, the dominant issue in this respect changes to become the Quebec–Newfoundland dispute over hydropower. In 1976, the *Evening Telegram* all but gives up hope of fair treatment by the National Energy Board, which is seen to be unshakeably in favour of Quebec, and in 1979, the paper again addresses the unfairness of 'Quebec getting the power from us dirt cheap'.[57] It acknowledges that for a resolution the parties have to look to Ottawa. However, it maintains, 'there isn't much hope in that direction'.

During most of the 1967–79 period, the image of the provincial government is almost as negative as that of the federal government. A recurring theme is the lack of trust in the ability of local politicians to initiate policies which can seriously alter the troubled socio-economic situation in which Newfoundland finds itself. One example is an editorial which concerns itself with regional disparity and Newfoundlanders' status as 'second-class Canadians'. It concludes: 'It can not have escaped financial advisers in Ottawa that for a province so woefully short of

money there seems to be an amazing ability to spend it rather reck-
lessly.'⁵⁸

The 'reckless' spending of money (seen as a direct cause of increased
dependence on federal transfers) is mostly seen to manifest itself in
over-expensive public services and unsuccessful industrialisation
schemes launched by changing provincial governments without regard
for the impact on traditional industries. Positive reviews of provincial
government socio-economic policies are rare in the years 1967–79, but
by the very end of the period this changes, as the economic prospects
seem also to change. The *Evening Telegram* places much hope in the
potential prosperity brought to Newfoundland by the development of
oil, gas and other natural resources, and therefore applauds any move
to keep the future wealth within the province. From the beginning, the
paper is supportive of minister of Mines and Energy Brian Peckford's
aggressive stand on the ownership issue. An early 1979 editorial thus
refers to the gas and oil prospects as 'a combination of commendable
[provincial] government policy and fortuitous circumstances', and two
days later another editorial on the offshore ownership dispute credits
Peckford for the vision and decisiveness of his oil regulations policy.⁵⁹

In terms of centralism and autonomism, a similar change is
detectable. For most of the period, the point of view on strong federal
government and the benefits of it for Newfoundland are basically
similar to those put forward by the *Daily News*. By the late 1970s,
however, Newfoundland's major broadsheet adopts an altogether more
aggressive attitude to the federal–provincial relationship – and the main
reason for this is the discovery of oil. The first mention of this new
potential source of wealth appears in the *Evening Telegram* in 1977,
and immediately the old issue of federal negligence and ignorance is
invoked and correlated with the development and ownership of the
natural resource. The first of a series of autonomist attacks on Ottawa,
'The Federal Joker', from 1977, confronts federal government head on
about the issue of control, as it asks: 'Is it a desire for making mischief
that prompts federal Energy Minister Alastair Gillespie to go on
needling the Newfoundland Government over its oil exploration regulations? . . . Certainly, whatever Gillespie has in mind it is not the best
interests of the people of Newfoundland.'⁶⁰ In the last part of the editorial, the *Evening Telegram* gives its full support to the autonomist policies advocated by Brian Peckford; the language used indicates the nature
of what is developing into a federal–provincial battle: 'Peckford is doing
right by sticking to his guns. If we handle this right the oil will still be
of value to us long after Mr. Gillespie has disappeared.' This editorial
marks the beginning of a new era of aggressive autonomism on the part

of the *Evening Telegram* and its declared support for the PC provincial government's policy of 'Newfoundland first'. The likely alienation of Ottawa thus seems to be a calculated risk, dwarfed by the positive prospects of oil wealth.

Although the value of Confederation is often questioned, and the idea of Newfoundland independence is sometimes almost implied, nothing indicates that a separatist position was ever seriously entertained by the paper. Still, the hard line on federal government and its ownership claims remains a feature from 1977. By 1979, it has, as far as the *Evening Telegram* is concerned, become a battle between federal Canada and the people of Newfoundland over the latter's inherited and rightful owner-ship of the offshore resources. This is illustrated in an editorial refuting Trudeau's claim to be a Newfoundland 'b'y'. Making a sharp distinction between the Newfoundland self and two others, Ottawa and Canada, the editorial says: 'There is a touch of sham about Prime Minister Trudeau singing "I's the b'y" for a Newfoundland audience when all the time he knows his government is trying to take away from us our rightful share of the continental shelf, never surrendered to Canada. He would be much more of a "b'y" if he were to say now that Ottawa will give up its attempts to cheat us out of our offshore territory.'[61]

Although still regarding Confederation as socio-economically benefi-cial – and therefore still advocating national unity, by Newfoundland's thirtieth anniversary as part of Canada, the paper sees little purpose in strong centralised Ottawa rule. On the contrary, what will benefit Newfoundland most in the current situation, and what the paper is becoming a convinced champion of, is a larger measure of autonomy.

Images of self and other in the political sphere

Throughout the 1967–79 period, an important concern of the paper is separatism. The paper is generally opposed to any kind of separatism in Canada, and places itself in opposition not only to Quebec and Acadian separatists, but also the 'socalled Western separatists who are not really sure what they're talking about when they growl about their shabby treatment from Ottawa'.[62] Significantly, at about the same time as the *Evening Telegram* starts voicing its own autonomist sympathies it refutes a separatist argument, not just for Newfoundland, but generally.

The *Evening Telegram*'s anti-separatist point of view is mirrored in its preference for national unity. In 1968, the first editorial to comment on the election of the Liberal Trudeau government prescribes: 'What is needed . . . is firm central control and a recognition and understanding of provincial problems . . . [Otherwise] the country will begin to break into minority factions demanding increasing power and attention.' By the end of the period, however, the paper regards the future of the nation as being in serious doubt. One editorial provides its own brief interpretation of Newfoundland's history as a Canadian province: 'Twenty years ago the euphoria of being a province of Canada was still with us; by mid-1960s there were many signs of disillusion; the twentieth anniversary was marked by growing concern about separatism; and, in the last decade the disillusion and concern have turned into alarm all across the country.'[63] Although the *Evening Telegram* has seen things go from good to bad to worse, and now questions the value of Confederation, it still refuses to reject the idea of a united Canada altogether: 'This, then, is no time to trumpet ad nauseam the blessings and wonders of Confederation, about which a lot of persons, the younger as well as the older generation, are beginning to have some second thoughts. It is rather a time to pledge ourselves to a renewed effort to reach a better understanding and a new determination to keep Canada together and united.' The second thoughts which Newfoundland's major broadsheet is having with regard to the benefits of being Canadian seem not to be based on a lack of belief in the principles of Confederation. Rather, what causes the paper to worry and protest is a feeling of mental as well as physical remoteness from the administration in Ottawa. A 1973 editorial invites not the mandarins but the 'Ottawa breed of civil servants' to 'Come and see us, sometime,'[64] to get a real understanding of the causes of Newfoundland's special socio-economic problems. As it is, the paper argues, 'decisions made by a remote and badly informed bureaucracy have been the curse of this province since 1949. We can only go on hoping that some day a ray of light will penetrate the dark recesses of the Ottawa mentality ... If that day ever comes we will know that at last Canada is beginning to learn how to be a nation.'

The vision of the early Trudeau government with regard to national unity corresponds well with the views of the *Evening Telegram*. In its post-election editorial from 1968, the paper indicates that it finds Pierre Trudeau's belief in a 'strong federal system with the central government being supreme in its own fields' agreeable.[65] However, the Liberal government of the 1974–9 term receives hostile treatment by the *Evening Telegram*. Suggesting the incompetence of the federal government, as well as its causes, a 1977 editorial, taking up the issue of oil exploration regulations, wonders whether the energy minister is 'one of the federal bullies who like to kick around the smaller provinces while being scared stiff of saying anything to a province like Quebec. Or, and this is a lot more sinister, it is possible that he is running interference for oil companies and, on their behalf, trying to clear an easy path for them.'[66] The post-1979 federal election editorial is not overtly in favour of the victorious Progressive Conservatives, but finds the change of government a cause for celebration, mainly because it removed Trudeau's Liberal Party from power.[67]

Many editorials in the data set have Joey Smallwood and the provincial Liberals as their subjects. Usually, the paper is highly critical of both, but Smallwood in particular receives much criticism, both prior to and after his 1972 election defeat. A 1967 editorial complains about the Liberal government's constant repetition of the great benefits of Confederation.[68] By this time, the *Evening Telegram* is becoming fed up with the Smallwood regime, and is longing for political change. Two years later, an editorial considering Smallwood's contribution to an Ottawa unity conference finds Smallwood's performance to be a humiliating, grovelling appreciation of federal government and of Premier Trudeau: '[Smallwood's] fawning references to Mr. Trudeau's speech, to the effect that he never really understood what the constitution meant until now, makes one wonder what he's been doing all these years.'[69] In an editorial discussing the result of the 1971 provincial election, PC leader Moores' 'drive and energy' is contrasted with Smallwood's 'financial profligacy'.[70] Significantly, the paper finds that the PCs, due to years of responsible leadership under Gerald Ottenheimer and Frank Moores, now make up the first 'really formidable opposition [and] credible alternative to the incumbent government in many years'. Yet, when Premier Moores decides to resign in 1979, the paper applauds the move, and contends that Moores never made any whole-hearted attempt to bring either of his early autonomist plans to fruition. Taking over from Moores is a young man, less 'nice', and his tougher attitude in federal–provincial relations pleases the *Evening Telegram* editorialist(s). Already from 1977, the focus in editorials is more often on the provincial minister of Energy Brian Peckford than on Premier Moores and, contrary to most other Newfoundland politicians, he receives plenty of praise for his policies.

As he takes Moores' seat in the Premier's Office in 1979, the paper keeps its positive view of Peckford and his policies. An editorial entitled 'The New Premier' congratulates Peckford on winning the party leadership, describing him as 'a young, intelligent man, with lots of drive, a capacity for work and with more than a bit of steel in him, something that differentiates him from his more easy-going, hail-fellow-well-met predecessor'. By endorsing the election of a more radically autonomist politician to premier of Newfoundland, the paper now places itself firmly in the autonomist camp. A week later, the paper again praises Peckford's qualities, and, importantly, stresses his patriotism. He possesses, it is argued, 'tenacity, a capacity for hard work, sound knowledge of government operations, and a reputation for putting Newfoundland first.'[71]

IMAGES OF SELF AND OTHER IN THE *EVENING TELEGRAM*, 1979–1990

When the *Daily News* folded in 1984, the only other major broadsheet in St John's and Newfoundland, the *Evening Telegram*, strengthened its position considerably as an opinion-shaper. With just a single major source of printed daily provincial news remaining, Newfoundlanders outside Corner Brook, where the local *Western Star* held out, were compelled to look either to the broadcast media or to the *Telegram*, not only for information about local events and politics but also, implicitly, for opinions on political, economic and cultural issues. As the paper's near-monopoly on printed local news coincided with the high tide and the eventual low ebb of Newfoundland autonomism, the analysis of images of self and other in the *Evening Telegram* becomes particularly important.

As regards the relationship between Newfoundland and Canadian selves, the distinction is as pronounced in this period as in the previous one. 'Canada' remains an infrequently occurring self, compared to 'Newfoundland(ers)'. With previous analysis in mind, it is of little surprise that the most significant other is the federal government, followed by central Canada.

Images of self and other in the cultural sphere

Previous analyses have illustrated how both the Scottish papers as well as the *Daily News* and the *Evening Telegram* in the period 1967–79 all attributed relatively little significance to cultural issues as part of the debate about political nationalism and autonomy. The analysis of *Evening Telegram* editorials from the period 1979–90 reveals that this pattern became even more pronounced. One front page story, 'Newfoundland Flies New Flag',[72] reports the 1980 replacement of the Union Jack by the new provincial flag designed by Christopher Pratt. The article, which does not give any information about its author, includes a photo of the first flying of the flag, captioned: 'Our very own flag'. The text itself takes care to note the nature of the musical accompaniment: 'The Ode to Newfoundland was played while the flag was being raised . . . O Canada was not played.' Much symbolism is part of both text and image, but no specific connection is made to any political issue. The story remains entirely cultural nationalist.

An editorial which makes the, for this part of the period, rare merging of political and cultural issues is 'Question of "Sacred Rights" ' from

1981.[73] The *Evening Telegram* is commenting on the worries of the Peckford administration regarding the effect of the Constitution Act 1981 on the clauses in Newfoundland's Terms of Union. The provincial government refers, according to the paper, mainly to Newfoundland's unique denominational school system and the Labrador–Quebec boundary as 'sacred rights'. Whereas the *Daily News* sneers at the very proposition that such 'sacred rights' be allowed to jeopardise the relationship with mainland Canada, and makes an effort to distance itself from the political-cultural argument,[74] the *Evening Telegram* shares the premier's concerns: 'The ruling of the Court of Appeal does reveal that the Newfoundland government was right in being concerned. . ., and that they were fully justified, and are vindicated in taking these issues to court.' Still, in terms of importance with regard to Newfoundland's position in Canada, cultural issues remain a distant, perfunctorily mentioned third, after socio-economic and politico-democratic matters.

Images of self and other in the socio-economic sphere

At the beginning of the 1979–90 period, there is continued dissatisfaction with the socio-economic condition of the province, and not much hope for a brighter future. Says one editorial from 1979: 'The people of this province have waited through one regime after the other to be led into the lush valley that was promised them so often.'[75] The despairing mood, however, is replaced by an increasingly optimistic one during the latter half of 1979 and in 1980, with a change of federal government, and as positive oil and gas forecasts are released. At this point, the *Evening Telegram* has much faith in the future of oil exploration in the province, but it does not completely alter its overall view of the province's economic problems. One 1980 editorial speaks of 'all the rosy prospects for offshore oil',[76] but then adds: 'It's well to remember that . . . transfer amounts from Ottawa . . . add up to almost half our total revenues.' An editorial titled 'That Oil Bonanza?'[77] later questions whether Newfoundland will in fact receive any significant spin-off from Hibernia. The paper warns about expecting ' "prosperity" . . . to come to Newfoundland', and foresees Ottawa and the oil companies taking the lion's share of revenues.

In 1985, with the Atlantic Accord signed, it appeared as though oil and gas would actually provide the much needed boost to the provincial economy. The paper's first impression of the deal is highly positive, and it speaks of 'the beginning of a new era for this province', and continues: 'We have always been the poor cousin in Confederation continuously

going to Ottawa with cap in hand looking for handouts. The Atlantic
Accord could be the catalyst in turning this around.'[78] The optimism is
short-lived, however. As the oil bonanza, on which the *Evening Telegram*
hinged almost all its hopes for Newfoundland's future economic
recovery, fails to materialise, the overall view of the province's socio-
economic prospects deteriorates further. By the end of the 1980s, the
paper shares outgoing Premier Peckford's bleak view of Newfoundland's
socio-economic future. The fortieth Confederation anniversary editorial
gloomily sums up the province's situation: 'The population is stagnant, if
not actually in decline. Problems of low productivity, unemployment,
high taxes, high debt charges, and dependency handouts seem permanent
fixtures of the local economy.'[79]

Often expressed points of regret are the high degree of dependency on
federal transfers, which has been the province's lot since Confederation,
and the lack of control granted to Newfoundland over its natural
resources. Whereas some editorials confine themselves to lamenting the
problem of dependency, others, such as 'ECC Report: A Shocker',[80]
goes further to explain why this is so. This particular editorial makes
use of an ECC study, hammering home the paper's own point of view
by emphasising the latter part of one particular sentence: 'The province
has become dangerously dependent on transfers from the rest of Canada
*while at the same time transferring elsewhere huge sums of money in the
form of lost revenue on natural resources* [Emphasis is ours]. So what
else is new?' Dependency, in other words, is seen to have been forced
upon Newfoundland against the will of the people of the province to
enrich other parts of Canada.

The perception that all natural resources in the province should be
managed by the province itself, in order to secure a proper spin-off for
Newfoundland, carries through the entire 1979–90 period. In 1979, the
basic argument is outlined in an editorial stating Newfoundland's special
case in this matter: 'The prime minister . . . declared that the province of
Nova Scotia was in the same . . . position as Newfoundland . . . This is
preposterous. The whole issue and point of Newfoundland's long-
standing claim is based on facts assembled to prove that ours is a special
case. Unlike any of the other areas of Canada which were either territories, colonies or provinces when they entered the Canadian Confederation
in 1867 and subsequently, Newfoundland was a separate, independent
country.'[81] A strong dichotomy between the Newfoundland self and the
rest-of-Canada other is created, and former independence thus becomes
the main claim to special status. The paper never abandons this persuasion, and throughout the remaining parts of the period demands for a fair
share of what is rightfully belonging to Newfoundland are frequently

voiced. The perceived differing treatment of provinces particularly infuri-
ates the *Evening Telegram*: 'This is unlike Alberta, which was once a have
not province like Newfoundland. During the 30s the government of the
day granted that province ownership of its mineral resources . . . Today
Alberta is probably the most wealthy province in Canada, thanks to that
ruling. Why Newfoundland should be treated any differently today is a
question which can only be answered by Mr. Trudeau and his
colleagues.'[82] An essential value of Confederation is seen to be economic
fairness and equality between various parts of Canada. In fact, the
Evening Telegram considers this form of economic equality a fundamental *raison d'être* of the Canadian state.

As illustrated previously, actions and reactions with regard to the
Meech Lake Accord are useful in trying to establish the dominant
images of self and other, as well as positions towards autonomism held
by different actors. Unfortunately, the *Daily News* did not live to have
an opinion on the Accord, but much is revealed about the *Evening
Telegram*'s points of view as it engages in the debate. At the time of the
Meech Lake Accord debate in 1990, it holds that the fact Canada is
ridden with, among other problems, 'regional disparity . . . and other
inequalities'[83] makes it increasingly difficult to govern. A major issue is
seen to be the unfair political dominance exercised by central Canada.
Political power provides economic prosperity, it is argued, and thus
socio-economic equality can only be achieved by a fair sharing of this
power: 'With political power, as everyone knows, comes economic
advantage. The time has come – indeed, is long overdue – for the power
to be shared, with Newfoundland, the Maritimes, the western
provinces, the Territories, to end their second-class citizenship.'[84]

However, the view of the paper is no longer that this should be
achieved through decentralisation. The *Evening Telegram* is a staunch
opponent of the Meech Lake Accord on the grounds that it is believed
to cement the disproportionate power of central Canadian provinces –
as opposed to the central government in Ottawa – over other provinces.
This is an interesting development from a decade before, when the
paper warned of a too-powerful federal government which would be
able to diminish Newfoundland's offshore revenues 'should it decide
that it needs the money'.[85]

Other highly useful events for 'collecting images' are anniversaries. At
the fortieth anniversary of Newfoundland's entry into Canada, one
editorial provides a very useful assessment of Confederation in terms of
what the *Evening Telegram* considers to have been its positive and negative consequences. Significantly titled 'Gains and Losses', the editorial
considers these almost entirely in socio-economic terms: 'There was a

time when the gains could be readily listed, as if the whole picture were a rosy one: politicians and others would rattle off the money handed to us in federal transfers, the roads built, jobs created, baby bonus, old age pensions, MCP [The Newfoundland Medical Care Plan], DREE, and the other familiar Ottawa acronyms. And there has indeed been a security net spread under us since 1949. But confederation has not been a total success. It is doubtful whether, in the four decades we have spent linked with Canada, there has ever been a genuine economic partnership forged between this province and Ottawa.'[86] The editorial moves on to consider the fortune of Newfoundland had it remained outside Canada: 'We could have been a small North Atlantic fishing nation, like Iceland; instead we chose to be the tenth province of a middle-ranking country. We chose to be poor relations in a family with many problems of its own. It is too painful to dwell on what we could have had in 1989 as an independent country, but it should be briefly stated for the record. We would now own the fish and undersea resources off our coasts. We would be players albeit minor ones, on the international scene . . . We would not have to endure the Churchill Falls rip-off. We could be masters in our own house, not caring a fig what the Supreme Court of Canada or the National Energy Board decided. On March 31, many among us find reason to rejoice. But isn't there ample reason to grieve too?' According to the paper, Newfoundland has obviously never become a full member of the Canadian family, and it still thinks of Newfoundland as possessing its 'own house' – albeit not one in which Newfoundlanders make the decisions.

In this period, the image of federal government in the socio-economic sphere is marked by distrust and the belief that officials making decisions for Newfoundland have little knowledge about the province. When the Liberals and Trudeau are returned to office in 1980 in particular, the attitude towards federal government hardens. The old accusations of ignorance with regard to knowledge about Newfoundland are brought forward, and the same budget that the *Daily News* finds 'masterful' the *Evening Telegram* finds 'politically slick'.[87]

Although its perception of federal government definitely sours in this period, a certain respect for the power the Ottawa government holds over Newfoundland is also prevalent: 'It's well to remember that . . . transfer amounts from Ottawa . . . add up to almost half our total revenues. So let's not get carried away by our new mood of standing up to Ottawa – a bird in the hand is worth two in the bush.'[88] The paper thus finds itself in the ambivalent position of endorsing both action against federal government and exhibiting caution with regard to the same. In Scottish terms, it finds itself engaged in a head vs. heart battle.

In the early 1980s, the heart dominates; aggression is frequent and caution rare. Later, as oil and gas resources are definitively ruled by the Supreme Court of Canada as belonging to the federal state, the head comes out the winner. Shortly after the decision is made, the paper sees no other way out of Newfoundland's socio-economic problems but for its government to offer an olive branch to Ottawa and start negotiations.

When the Peckford provincial government takes over from the previous PC government, the *Evening Telegram* has had enough of administrations that fail to produce the much-anticipated socio-economic breakthrough for Newfoundland. In contrast to the *Daily News*, the *Evening Telegram* is not impressed by the Peckford administration's first Throne Speech. It fails to see innovation in PC policies, and finds the speech both lofty and idealistic to a degree which will find the new government struggling to stand up to the 'hard realism of politics and economics'.[89] There is little at this point to suggest that the worried paper will later offer its full support to this government. It takes the revelation of potential oil and gas revenues in 1980 to produce a shift in attitude, but when it comes, it causes a full U-turn.

From this time onwards, the paper finds the aggressive attitude towards Ottawa displayed in PC policies increasingly agreeable – even to the point where it transcends these to become more radical than the PC government itself. The *Evening Telegram*'s appreciation of, and involvement in, the autonomist struggle seems to accelerate in the short time span from the beginning of 1980 to early 1984, and by the time of the 1981 budget speech it finds itself lambasting the provincial government for being too lenient in its dealings with the federal government. It even finishes with a statement that must be counted among the most radical of Newfoundland editorials with regard to political nationalism: 'The government . . . are somewhat naive in expressing a "sincere wish" that the Ottawa regime will "cease its unilateral and restrictive approach to federal-provincial relations" . . . We don't feel that the Ottawa establishment has much toleration or sympathy for the feisty and independent administration of Newfoundland and Labrador. If the government of this province have to go on from day to day and year to year, uncertain of where they stand with regard to the essential revenues it needs and now has within its grasp, then the groundswell of frustration and anger among the people is bound to grow to the detriment of all concerned, even the bonds of Confederation.'[90]

A new, highly aggressive tone has been set. If expecting to receive a warm welcome from the local media, Prime Minister Trudeau could not have chosen a worse time to visit Newfoundland. In May 1981 he arrived in St John's, where he called on the provincial government to negotiate an offshore resource agreement with Ottawa. The *Evening Telegram*, however, was in no mood to welcome negotiation at the height of its autonomist conviction. In its coverage, it compares the federal government to a greedy beast, desperate to secure the offshore wealth for itself, while portraying the Peckford administration as the knights in shining armour, defending Newfoundland from that beast: 'The prime minister . . . harped on the "anti-Canadian" and "anti-federalist. . ." stance of the Newfoundland Government, which is a cruel distortion of the facts. The Peckford administration is anything but anti-Canadian and anti-federalist; it is pro-Newfoundland, in that it's determined that the greedy maw of Ottawa won't swallow the lion's share of that wealth.'[91] In this metaphor, the Newfoundland self and the Ottawa other could hardly be more polarised.

Similarly emotional and autonomist editorials occur in the subsequent period, among them the celebration of the re-election of the Peckford government in April 1982, 'A Great Victory'.[92] In the exultant rhetoric of this editorial, the provincial government, the people of Newfoundland and the *Evening Telegram* become one, with shared feelings, wishes and goals. The other, on the contrary, is easily detected as the federal government: 'The people of the province have . . . sent a message to the federal government in Ottawa that will have to be taken seriously no matter what some arrogant ministers . . . may say . . . It was, as this paper has maintained, a time for all to stand united for their province, its present situation as well as its future prospects; and the electorate [has] fought through its government to recover and retain control over its vital resources.'

After a period of sharp anti-federal rhetoric and autonomist points of view, a drastic change takes place in *Evening Telegram* editorials in 1984 as a result of the Supreme Court ruling. The very first editorial after Newfoundland's right to control the offshore development has been rejected is entitled 'Start Talks Now'.[93] It strongly advocates what has previously been fiercely rejected: negotiation. The paper concludes that, as the province's unemployment rate has hit the 20 per cent mark, and as the public purse is running low, times are desperate and the call is for new measures. Although Peckford 'was right in his stand against Mr. Trudeau and his government', he must now 'sit down, without delay, and negotiate the best deal possible'.

From a stage of high-pitched autonomism, the *Evening Telegram* has now turned to almost desperate pleading for peaceful settlement. Therefore it seems paradoxical that by the time of the signing of the Atlantic Accord, an editorial reads – as if the 1984 interlude of disillusion had never occurred: 'The signing of the offshore agreement . . . has vindicated Brian Peckford's decade-long struggle . . . When the Supreme Court handed down its unanimous decision . . . Mr. Peckford was dumped on from all quarters to retreat and accept the Trudeau offer. Mr. Peckford will always have his detractors, those who will insist that Newfoundlanders will always regret the lost opportunities, the lost jobs, the cutback in services and the hardship of not coming to an early agreement with the federal Liberals. Those people are in the minority. That would have been the easy way out, but as we said on other occasions it would have been disastrous.'[94]

As the paper's appreciation of Peckford and his government's struggle to ensure natural resource control for Newfoundland is maintained, it manages – in a fit of convenient amnesia – to exclude itself from the unhappy 'minority'. Although fervently autonomist at one point, the threat of further socio-economic decline convinced it to leave this persuasion, in spite of its continuous dissatisfaction with the federal–provincial relationship. Then, as the threat of socio-economic misery and political dispute was apparently removed, the paper once again found it safe to praise the autonomist policies of the provincial government.

Editorials from the latter part of the period were written in a very different political climate, with a 'compliant' federal government under Prime Minister Mulroney restored in Ottawa; they continue to voice the paper's appreciation of the effort Peckford put in as premier, but also question whether much was actually achieved. Although the eventual Hibernia deal is regarded as a disappointment, and 'the biggest gamble' in the history of the province,[95] Peckford is commended for working and struggling in the 'wearying task of trying to pull Newfoundlanders up by her bootstraps'. By the time he resigns, an editorial, 'Peckford Bows Out,'[96] produces a largely positive assessment of his time as premier, and thus of the autonomist era in Newfoundland, although it is noted that his accomplishments have been modest: 'His years as premier appear, in retrospect, to have been a kind of crusade. . ., warring with Ottawa and . . . Quebec bureaucrats and politicians . . . That he was not a clear winner in any of [his major] struggles should not lead us to brand him a failure. He showed no failure of will or nerve.'

The, by then, only remaining broadsheet in St John's has at this point outlived its autonomist tendencies and finds itself capable of supporting other policies, including ones diametrically opposed to those of the Peckford government. Where the *Evening Telegram* of the early 1980s agitated for revolution, the *Evening Telegram* of 1989 preaches reform. Tellingly, the paper welcomes the new Liberal government in much the same fashion as it welcomed the Peckford government a decade earlier:

by acknowledging the value of the noble projects it will attempt to realise, but warning it of the restraining power of the financial situation in which Newfoundland finds itself.

Images of self and other in the political sphere

From the beginning to the end of this period, the paper believes in the idea of Canada as a united political unit. The paper rejoices in the patriation of the constitution in 1982, which it finds both as marking 'a new era of the growth of Canadian nationhood',97 and making Canadians 'masters in their own house, and in charge of their own destiny'. By the time of the Meech Lake Accord, the *Evening Telegram* assures the doubtful that 'few citizens of this wonderful country' want to 'say . . . no to Canada'.98 At points, however, the paper appears almost to have lost faith in the great project. Numerous editorials deal with the lack of understanding, on the part of other groups and provinces, of the workings of a federal state. Apart from the federal government, Quebec in particular is to be found in the spoiler role, as the paper wonders how much more politicians of that province can reasonably demand. What the paper calls for is in essence a Canadian sense of community, but it is a goal which it finds that too few Canadians share. Ontario and Quebec, for instance, are seen to have 'their own axe to grind',99 which means the other provinces must be careful not to bestow too much power on central Canada.

The fact that the *Evening Telegram* recommends that Canada remains a united country, and finds the federal system feasible as a principle, does not mean that it is happy with Newfoundland's place in the federation. Throughout the period, it finds that Newfoundland's basic rights, as well as those of other provinces, are being neglected, and continuously calls for redress of the workings of the federal system. The paper advocates that the Meech Lake Accord should not pass. 'To rescind the Meech Lake Accord is a very serious step,'100 the first of many editorials, 'Thoughts on Rescission', admits, and the unprecedented amount of coverage underlines the seriousness with which the paper considers the constitutional question. The main objection to the accord, which the paper shares with the provincial Wells government, is that the inequality that is perceived to exist under Confederation will be cemented if the accord passes. Although more power will be bestowed on provinces generally, the larger provinces – particularly Quebec – will benefit more from, for instance, the right to veto at the expense of the federal and minor provincial governments. The position of the paper is thus comparable to the one it took in 1973 when it went against the proto-autonomist policies of the Moores government, claiming that the existence of a strong federal government would be in Newfoundland's interest, as only it would be able to distribute wealth equally across the country.[101]

Opposing the Meech Lake Accord is therefore not a move on the part of the *Evening Telegram* to maintain the constitutional status quo; quite the opposite. It is necessary, it argues, to fundamentally reconsider the set-up of the federal system, and change it for the better. In the heated debate about the Newfoundland legislature's decision to ratify or rescind the accord, the paper stands firm on its points of view in spite of the pressure it perceives Quebec and the federal government in particular are placing on it. The self–other dichotomy is stressed, along with Newfoundland's claim to equal partnership: 'Never mind the snide and insulting references of the arrogant Robert Bourassa and the superior musings of the Globe and Mail. . ., and others that Newfoundland is too small, too poor, too illiterate, too newly arrived in Confederation to have a right to make that decision. The only province to choose by a free vote to become part of Canada has as much right as any of the others in a union in which all are supposed to be fundamentally equal.'[102]

In the immediate aftermath of the Meech Lake failure, the paper is not favourably disposed towards the PC federal government, which is accused of having exercised unfair and unsuitable pressure on Newfoundland. The paper speaks of 'attempted manipulation at the hands of the men in Ottawa for whom brinksmanship is a substitute for statesmanship . . . Premier Clyde Wells did the only thing he could: cause the vote to be deferred . . . Our judgement is that it was an honest decision, honestly and openly arrived at – more than can be said for the machinations of Mr. Mulroney and the Ottawa PCs, at whose door must be laid the failure of Meech and the consequences flowing from it.'[103]

In general terms, the entire political and bureaucratic system in Ottawa is seen to be remote and ill-informed, and thus ill-fitted to make decisions with regard to Newfoundland. The federal political establishment as such is also suspected of not always having the best interest of Newfoundland in mind when it makes decisions affecting the province. A 1989 editorial, for example, argues: 'Quebec is just too powerful and too important to the federal parties to step on its toes in favor of little Newfoundland.'[104]

During the paper's most autonomist period, in the early 1980s, it worries about what it considers Ottawa's 'grab for power'.[105] The paper interprets the Trudeau government's stand on the control of offshore oil and gas exploration as part of a larger scheme to further pool power in Ottawa at the expense of the provinces: 'They hope to reap vast revenues from it that will help them to keep consolidating the power of

the central government and further weakening the provincial authorities
. . . [T]he federal authority would be able to 'abolish' the provinces and
create a unitary state.' Against the background of such an image of the
Liberal government, it is hardly surprising that the *Evening Telegram*
welcomes the succeeding PC government warmly. Until the Meech Lake
dispute, the period of Mulroney PC government is characterised by
considerably less critical editorials and coverage.

Following the election of Peckford and his PC government in 1979, the
Evening Telegram warns that distinctly new policies will have to be
produced, and as the paper is gradually convinced by the performance of
the new administration, the quality of the Peckford government that the
paper comes to appreciate most is that it is 'pro-Newfoundland'.[106] The
paper's appreciation of the government culminates in the 1982 provincial
election comment which celebrates 'A Great Victory'.[107] Again the
'Newfoundland first' tune is trumpeted, as the paper finds it to be 'a time
for all to stand united for their province'. In 1983, the enchantment is
temporarily broken when Premier Peckford makes his notorious
'Newfoundlanders-are-lepers' remarks. Likening Newfoundlanders to
lepers who are forced to do business with other lepers – the Soviets –
because the federal government treats them unfairly, Peckford incurs the
reproach of the *Evening Telegram*: 'As could only be expected after
insulting Soviets, Newfoundlanders, mainland Canadians and lepers,
there was an outcry.' The paper advises the premier to 'think about it!'
before making similar remarks in the future.[108] Still, this does not herald
the beginning of a period of a general lack of faith in the visions or policies of the provincial government.

However, infatuation with the PC autonomist agenda is slowly
wearing off, and a new element of discontent occurs, which turns out
to last throughout the government term to 1989. The paper believes
the PC government is deliberately considering the interest of pro-PC
districts over pro-opposition districts. Of constant concern to the paper
throughout the entire period has been the lack of democracy inherent in
the policies of long-lasting political regimes, and the paper is clearly
alienated from its previously preferred party by this practice. The bond
forged in the 'mind' of the *Evening Telegram* between the people of the
province, its government and the newspaper is breaking, and the paper
chooses to come down on the side of the people, as their champion: 'Are
certain people to be penalized for the way they vote, or will all
Newfoundlanders be treated equally? An analogy could be made in the
way, as Peckford has said for years, that Ottawa treats Newfoundland.'
Although no decisive break is made between the *Evening Telegram*
and the PCs, the disappointment at the return of the PCs to old policies

of the early post-Confederation era seems to last, and as the paper welcomes the new Wells government in 1989, it is only too happy to be rid of the 'disgusting practice' of ignoring the needs of Liberal districts.[109]

Images of provincial political parties in the late 1980s are complex. The *Evening Telegram* can be said to use, more than usual, a palette of colours, rather than just black and white to portray the government and its opposition. When Peckford steps down in 1989, the paper still honours him with a predominantly positive editorial. Still, the 1989 provincial election editorial speaks of 'the blunders of Tory government for the past number of years',[110] and thus in retrospect distances the paper from the Peckford governments' policies. Superlatives are mostly reserved for the Liberal leader, Clyde Wells. He is described as both 'outspoken and courageous' and 'impeccable'. This appears to be the *Evening Telegram*'s decisive break with the provincial Progressive Conservative Party, and thus with what little remains of an autonomist vision in its manifesto. In turn, the paper quickly develops a great deal of respect for the new Liberal, centralist premier. Although the May Throne Speech is received with some reservations, by the time of the Meech Lake dispute, editorials express the paper's positive impression of Wells' firmness and political skills.

This concludes the chapter on images of self and other related to autonomism in the Newfoundland press. The following chapter will conclude the book by weaving together the many threads collected in preceding chapters into more coherent pictures of the nature of autonomism in Scotland and Newfoundland.

EIGHT

The Nature of Autonomism in
Scotland and Newfoundland

Definitions of nationalism, unless very general, are notoriously difficult
to make. Different nationalist movements are reactions to different
circumstances in different societies, which means their *raisons d'être*,
contents and goals often differ. In other words, nationalisms, although
agreeing about the idea of the nation as the point of departure, are as
diverse as the societies in which they occur. As has been illustrated in the
cases of Scotland and Newfoundland, contemporary political nationalist
movements in liberal democracies focus on other aspects and factors
than do more classic nationalist movements, which is why some are
appropriately referred to as autonomist movements. Theories developed
on the basis of classic nationalist processes, therefore, do not necessarily
apply to these. This book has sought to shed light on the nature of
autonomism in stateless nations, and although this investigation is not
meant to produce a generally applicable theory for the study of neo-
nationalist movements, it may be considered one step in that direction.

National identity can be defined as the sum of all images of self and
other pertaining to the perception of the nation in all society's spheres. As
such, national identity comprises national images in the political and socio-
economic, as well as the cultural, spheres. Since actions and reactions are
determined by the perception of reality in all of these spheres, a study like
this one must necessarily take national identity and all the images which it
contains as a point of departure for answering its main question: What
causes the rise and demise of political nationalism in stateless nations?

There can be no image of self without contrasting images of others,
and it is when the perception of the relationship between the self and its
significant other(s) changes that a reaction, sometimes in the shape of
political nationalism, may result. Perception thus remains a key word.
Rather than 'reality', it is the socially constructed reality to which
people or groups of people react. To understand why a specific reaction
such as political nationalism occurs (or indeed ceases to exist) it is necessary to attempt not to read events 'as they really are', but to understand

how they are portrayed and interpreted. That is why national identity should be seen as discourse, and the negotiation of images of self and other as a struggle of discourses for hegemony. Because national identity legitimises political nationalism, investigating these struggles caused by various factors and engaged in by various actors will bring the observer closer to understanding why political nationalism develops and why it takes a particular form. What are these fomenting factors; which images, based on them, are projected – and by whom? Why do some of the images become hegemonic? These are the questions the book has tried to answer with respect to Scotland and Newfoundland.

ETHNIC DISTINCTNESS AND NATIONAL IDENTITY

Differences as well as similarities make a comparative study of these two societies particularly relevant to the understanding of modern political nationalism in stateless nations. Because Scotland and Newfoundland share so many experiences and characteristics *and* also differ in some crucial respects (including the form and fate of autonomism), the close study of the two in combination helps us understand the nature of their political nationalisms better. Previous chapters have shown that, with regard to national identity, Newfoundland and Scotland have never been fully assimilated into the political unions they are part of. Cultural assimilation was never attempted by the union-states, and partly as a result of this there is not only a persistent but an increasing perception of being different from other parts of the state in both Scotland and Newfoundland. There is a widespread apprehension of differing culturally as well as socially, economically and politically; of being special, and thus of having special needs.

What becomes clear through the analysis of images of self and other is that Newfoundland media, intellectuals and politicians appear to be as devoted to giving the welfare of Newfoundland priority over anything else as Scots are to put Scotland first. The notion of the nation in Newfoundland, however, is perhaps best described as 'functional'. Nationhood is seen as something which can be officially transferred to the union-state without necessarily weakening a sense of ethnic community. The utilisation and continued development of a sense of community and common destiny is without doubt a crucial parameter in explaining the development of political nationalism in both Scotland and Newfoundland. However, two important and related notes should be made. First, in both cases the conception of ethnic distinctness is more a legitimising precondition than a direct cause of political nationalism. Second, actors of a centralist persuasion, such as the Liberal Party of Newfoundland and the pre-1974 *Glasgow Herald*, also acknowledge national distinctness, without making it an argument for political or constitutional change. Cultural nationalism, for example, as expressed by the *Daily News*, is a celebration of ethno-cultural uniqueness.

CULTURAL NATIONALISM AND ETHNO-CULTURAL ARGUMENTS

Cultural nationalism thrived in Scotland until the beginning of the period investigated in this study. Romantic and sentimental notions of historic Gaelic Scotland and parochial village life dominated the national myths and prevented, it was argued by many Scottish cultural critics, the development of a real Scottish national identity. Early attempts at redefining the tartanry and Kailyard myths about the Scottish experience failed, and largely as a consequence of this, traditional cultural images were barred from the first political attempts at changing Scotland's position within the UK. Ethno-cultural arguments were thus prevented from being incorporated into Scottish political nationalist rhetoric, and cannot be argued to have seriously entered the political debate about Scottish autonomy until the 1980s with the second Scottish cultural renaissance. Still, the perception of ethno-cultural distinctness was never allowed to dominate in the debate, and when it became part of it, it was not the old tartanry and Kailyard images that prevailed, but the critical reassessment of 'real' Scottish cultural identity. Not until the 1990s were the meanings of old images sufficiently reinvented to be allowed to become representations of modern Scottish national identity.

Compared to Scotland, the marriage between cultural elements and political nationalism in the late twentieth-century hegemony of the autonomist discourse in Newfoundland was much more pronounced. The policies of changing PC governments stressed Newfoundland culture significantly more than was the case, for example, with the SNP. This is a development which is mirrored in the form and emphases of the second wave of the Newfoundland cultural revival. Whereas the critics of tartanry and Kailyard denounced large parts of Scottish history and mythology as completely useless, and made the deliberate choice to turn their thinking towards the present and the future, Newfoundland folk tradition and outport cultural heritage remained an essential part of Newfoundland national identity as defined by intellectuals and artists of the cultural sphere. Part of the explanation may well be that tartanry and Kailyard had been allowed, over long periods of Scottish history, to manifest themselves negatively in the Scottish psyche, so that actors in the Scottish nationalising domain saw no alternative but to bring about a decisive break with the myths to escape the images they projected.

Although ethno-cultural arguments were from the outset a more integral part of Newfoundland autonomism than was the case in Scotland, political nationalism here is not to be characterised as classically 'ethnic'. Much as in Scotland, this was a question of achieving effective policy-making and obtaining political power to alter unfavourable socio-economic conditions. Also, it involved, to some extent, the struggle to debunk and redefine old national myths. In this respect, the second wave of Newfoundland's cultural revival, from the 1970s, resembles that of Scotland in the 1980s. Both became important, albeit far from all-important, carriers of political nationalism. It remains the case that the second wave of the Newfoundland cultural renaissance tended towards the less realistic, more towards Newfoundland life as seen in the traditional outports. Although the last wave is in some ways more directly comparable to the Scottish cultural renaissance of the 1980s, with its confluence of the traditional and the modern, the common stressing of national uniqueness, and a preoccupation with the more or less imagined inferiority complex, there are also important differences. Whereas Newfoundland cultural nationalism retained its core while developing a more modern outlook, Scottish cultural nationalism completely reinvented itself: from self-mockery and celebration of a romantic past of heroic but necessary defeat, it came to base itself almost entirely on the contemporary expressions of modern and postmodern Scotland. Therefore, Scottish cultural nationalism could more easily become a vehicle for an autonomist voice concerned not with the past but with the future. In contrast, even modernised Newfoundland cultural nationalism has kept its focus on outports and folk tradition, making it a less obvious 'partner' of political nationalism in a twenty-first century stateless nation.

It is easy to over-emphasise the importance of cultural elements in these autonomist movements, however. The close ties between the destiny of the Peckford administration and the destiny of autonomism in Newfoundland serve to show that autonomism was not so much an ethno-cultural phenomenon stirring up emotional feelings for 'the Rock' as much as it was the expression of belief in the ability, through an aggressive stance towards Ottawa, to facilitate a higher degree of democratic influence and socio-economic prosperity in the province. Although the study shows how most of the important fomenting actors considered questions pertaining to the constitutional and political situation with affection and loyalty placed firmly with Scotland or Newfoundland, ethno-cultural arguments, considering the *Volksgeist* of the communities to be endangered, were rare. Exceptions would seem to be the protectionist position of the *Evening Telegram* and the

Newfoundland PC government in the early 1980s towards the traditional outport way of life but, as illustrated, this issue was never among the most important legitimising arguments. In Scotland, no actors can be seen even remotely to consider cultural uniqueness a valid argument for political nationalism or constitutional change in itself. What is characteristic of all the newspapers analysed is how ethno-cultural arguments are emphasised only in isolated cases. The wording is usually strong so as to leave no doubt about the 'national' nature and loyalty of the paper, but such arguments are only put forward when it is otherwise considered safe to do so. That is, ethno-cultural issues are hardly ever coupled with political or economic issues; and are, in fact, generally regarded as irrelevant to them.

Ethnicity, defined broadly as all that which makes Scotland and Newfoundland special with regard also to political traditions, socio-economic structures and needs, remains a fundamental precondition of the political nationalist discourse in both societies. The strong sense of uniqueness, and an often clear-cut perception of the dichotomy between 'us' and the central government or other dominant others in the union, are crucial to the success of political nationalist discourse. Ethnicity, or the perception of it, in itself, however, is clearly not what causes political nationalism to rise in Newfoundland and Scotland, just as the decline of Newfoundland autonomism during the mid-1980s cannot in any way be ascribed to lack of a sense of national identity or ethnic distinctness.

This brings us to a range of negative incentives producing over time much national discontent. These fomenting factors are not individually determinant, but they have all to some degree added to the image of a distant other, wittingly or unwittingly inflicting harm upon the national self, and the perception of a situation in which Scots and Newfoundlanders are not acknowledged in ways that they believe they deserve and have a right to be.

SOCIO-ECONOMIC DECLINE, DEPENDENCY AND INEQUALITY

Such a powerful fomenting factor in Scotland was the perception of the political and socio-economic decline of the UK, and of the British empire as such. The image of a union-state struggling to maintain some of its political power as a player on the world scene was accompanied by the apprehension of a poorly sustained social contract between the UK and Scotland; the formerly beneficial economic partnership between Scotland and other parts of the UK, as well as the welfare state, were seen to crumble. The same perception of state decline surfaced only sporadically in the perception of Canada among Newfoundland actors.

Even if the fate of Newfoundland political nationalism varied almost inversely with that of the Canadian economy,[1] among intellectuals, politicians and the media alike, there was a widespread feeling that Canada would maintain its position amongst the wealthiest countries in the world, even at times of recession. This marks an important difference between the two societies, which could be seen partly to explain the lack of political nationalism in Newfoundland in the first part of the period were it not for the fact that a generally positive perception of the state of Canada's economic health persists throughout the entire period. However, it is very likely an explanatory factor with regard to understanding why political nationalism in Newfoundland took an autonomist rather than a separatist form. If the union is generally seen to *be able to* provide the demanded socio-economic benefits – even if *currently* it does not – the step towards separatism is likely to become more difficult to take. The initial separatist stance of the SNP received some support, most likely because this hope in the future prosperity of the British state had been temporarily removed.

A more important fomenting factor in both Scotland and Newfoundland, however, has been the perception of dependency as the greatest obstacle to positive socio-economic development and a cause of political impotence. Except for the *Glasgow Herald*, all actors seem to find this problem of immense importance. When alternatives to the present state of affairs occur, they gain force as positive incentives to political nationalism because they are seen to offer a way out of the paralysing dependency which handicaps not only Newfoundlanders' and Scots' abilities to make their societies prosper directly, but also their ability to make political and socio-economic decisions for themselves. The analysis shows, however, that the image of dependency can be both a fomenting and a preventive factor with regard to the development of political nationalism. Although generally in agreement as to the existence of economic dependency and its deplorable consequences, actors react differently. Some argue that the dependency yoke can only be thrown off through the political struggle for a greater say in the way policies with regard to one's society are conducted; others that dependency is precisely what makes such a step unfeasible.

The issue of dependency is closely linked with what must be considered one of the most important fomenting factors: the perception of socio-economic inequality. This is mainly a question of a sense of relative socio-economic deprivation; of Scotland/Newfoundland suffering disproportionately compared to other parts of the UK/Canada.

In Scotland, only the Conservatives (periodically) and the pre-1979 *Glasgow Herald* do not acknowledge this aspect of the relationship.

Here, the question of inequality develops from one concerned with the relatively higher degree of decline in Scotland, in a UK in general socio-economic decline, to one of Scotland suffering less from unequal socio-economic development than from the inequality of opportunity to develop to a stage *above* that of other parts of the UK. In Newfoundland, all dominant actors – including the Smallwood government and the *Daily News* – perceive socio-economic inequality to exist between Newfoundland and most other parts of Canada throughout the period studied.[2] Here, as in Scotland, this produces a sense of failure of union. All Newfoundland actors express, at some point, the view that the real purpose of Confederation and national unity is to produce socio-economic equality between the provinces. Dominant here is also the complaint pertaining not to the lack of material wealth but to the lack of opportunity to create it. Dependency and socio-economic inequality are thus considered by almost all actors in both societies – centralists and autonomists alike – to be the most pressing of Scotland's or Newfoundland's problems. A similarly high level of agreement exists with regard to the perception of the causes of these problems.

STATELESS NATIONS: CENTRAL GOVERNMENT NEGLECT AND
A MALFUNCTIONING CONSTITUTIONAL SET-UP

A strong sense of being not only culturally but also politically and socio-economically distinct exists in both societies during the entire period. This results in demands for special treatment and for policies designed with regard to the special circumstances in Scotland and Newfoundland, rather than the application of general policies. The poor, or relatively poor, socio-economic situation the two societies find themselves in is seen by most actors to be the consequence of a lack of appreciation on the part of the central governments in Ottawa and London of the need for specially-designed policies. Central government neglect is thus considered the main obstacle to ridding Scotland and Newfoundland of socio-economic inequality and the lamentable state of dependency. Only on rare occasions do local actors – such as the post-1979 *Daily News* and the early 1970s' *Glasgow Herald* – consider the central government to be doing its best to alter this state of affairs. At times, some actors – particularly the *Evening Telegram*, the Peckford PCs, the *Scotsman* and the SNP – go as far as to accuse central government political parties of deliberate and conscious neglect in order to enrich central government or other parts of the union closer to the political centre, but the most common interpretation of central government neglect is that it is caused by ignorance; an ignorance of the real nature of needs and demands in

Scotland and Newfoundland, which is seen as a natural consequence of remoteness, unresponsiveness and lack of local influence on prefabricated policies. The dichotomy in this respect between Scottish and Newfoundland actors and central government is most clearly expressed during the centralist Thatcher and Trudeau administrations.

The perception of Ottawa and Westminster neglect and lack of democratic influence causes, although in unevenly spread waves, most actors to consider the constitutional set-up to have failed, because it allows such mismanagement to take place. Hence, the sense of being a stateless nation is accentuated. Although parallels can be drawn between the conflicts between Newfoundland political nationalist actors and the federal Liberals in the early 1980s, and those between Scottish political nationalists and the Conservative administration beginning also in the early 1980s, there is a marked difference between the two scenarios. The sense of a malfunctioning constitutional set-up is dramatically sustained in Scotland during the years of Conservative government as increasingly few Scots vote for the Tories but nevertheless keep getting Tory governments. The resulting sense of a democratic deficit, which becomes a major fomenting factor in Scotland, does not exist to the same degree in Newfoundland. An important parameter to take into consideration when comparing Newfoundland and Scotland in this respect is the fact that since Confederation, the former has enjoyed a higher degree of both official and de facto autonomy than the latter. Neither a distinctly Newfoundland voting pattern nor a widespread sense of a 'doomsday scenario' can be detected. Although federalism is seen by political nationalist actors to have major flaws, allowing for the more or less conscious neglect of Newfoundland's special needs, the perception of a democratic deficit is a much larger fomenting factor in Scotland.

Federalism, in the form of the existence of a local assembly in Newfoundland, has both motivated and worked to prevent the further development of a political nationalist discourse. This is illustrated by, in this context, a uniquely Newfoundland fomenting factor: what can be termed 'local government fatigue' – weariness with a governing party which fails to renew itself and, most importantly, to follow up on powerful rhetoric with tangible results. With the level of government provided by the Newfoundland House of Assembly, the question of autonomy and prosperity in Confederation is not, to the same extent as in Scotland, a question simply of the relationship between the central government and the people. This means that it has been less clear for Newfoundlanders whom to blame when policies are deemed inadequate to provide the required economic development and material welfare. It also means that a political nationalist agenda might have been supported, not only as a reaction to federal policies or the constitutional set-up, but as a reaction to politics as conducted by the provincial government. In the period studied, Newfoundland had in practice a two-party system. Consequently, local government fatigue, as exhibited in the early 1970s towards the Smallwood government, automatically resulted in increased support for the opposition party. The PC governments' autonomist policies thus not only represented a change from the old, increasingly inefficient, Liberal policies, but also the only alternative. The same applies to the Liberal centralist agenda in the late 1980s. As a consequence, it is possible that the popular affiliation with autonomism and centralism is not as strong in Newfoundland as is the case in Scotland, where local political issues have not to the same extent 'blurred' the images of self and other, and where particularly the SNP provide an alternative to the two old parties. The image of the abilities of local politicians to run Scotland, however, has also played an important part in the development of Scottish political nationalism. The 'No' in the 1979 referendum can thus be explained partly by the lack of confidence in Scottish, not British, politicians, caused by the failure of these to co-operate and present the devolution case convincingly. Importantly, the presence of provincial government in Newfoundland also created a platform of powerful political actors in the nationalising domain; a platform which did not exist in Scotland between 1707 and 1999. Already, it is becoming evident that the re-established Scottish parliament provides a similarly powerful platform for Scottish political nationalists – but also that it, like provincial assemblies in Canada, functions as a 'buffer': a forum on which to blame current ills, which lies between the voters and the central government.

ALTERNATIVES TO DEPENDENCY, ECONOMIC AND POLITICAL SELF-CONFIDENCE, AND SOCIAL CONSENSUS

Negative incentives have been important fomenting factors in the development of political nationalism in Scotland and Newfoundland. Support for the SNP in the earliest part of the period can be explained almost entirely as a result of these. The analyses show, however, that as a rule, negative perceptions have only become accentuated, and the political nationalist discourse increasingly universal in the two societies, when perceptions of a possibly brighter future are added. In other words, whereas negative incentives coupled with a strong sense of national identity have mainly provided the necessary basis, positive incentives have often been decisive in setting in motion the development of political nationalist manifestations.

Positive incentives with regard to the development of political nationalism in Scotland and Newfoundland have mainly taken the shape of externally produced alternatives to economic and political dependency. Most actors did not actively advocate political nationalism until the viability of such alternatives outweighed the benefits of maintaining the status quo. In both Scotland and Newfoundland, oil and gas exploration was in periods seen as such a viable alternative to economic and political dependency. Although the *Scotsman* was autonomist prior to North Sea oil discoveries, devolution became much more of an issue in the paper in the early 1970s. The SNP and the Newfoundland PCs, in particular, made oil and gas exploration the fuel of political nationalism. The debate between centralist and autonomist discourses focused not on the existence of economic dependency or inequality – those factors were generally agreed on – but on the feasibility or viability of alternatives. Newfoundland autonomism can thus be seen largely to have risen and faltered with the prospects of natural resource development and ownership. This is an argument which is sustained by the rebirth in the early twenty-first century of autonomist politics in Newfoundland – heavily infused with oil revenue rhetoric.

When all possible alternatives to dependency and a strong federal government had either ceased to exist or become significantly diminished by the end of the 1980s, the PC government's autonomist policies ceased to appeal to Newfoundlanders – and even to the *Evening Telegram*. Not because they did not agree with Peckford's diagnosis of the illnesses, but because they could no longer agree with the proposed cure. The same can be said for the SNP and the devolution agenda in Scotland by the time of the Scotland Act referendum. By 1979, it was obvious that oil would not become the hoped-for Scottish cash crop, and it was no longer seen to provide an alternative to economic dependency on the UK and London. EC membership did not at this point appeal to the Scots, and European regional development funds were not regarded as an even remotely viable substitute for the continued Westminster block grant. With traditional Scottish industry in decline and Scotland lagging behind socio-economically, the constitutional status quo remained the best option. With the positive natural resource development prospects, both Scots and Newfoundlanders found new hope for better socio-economic conditions and a belief that Scotland and Newfoundland could catch up with other relatively wealthy parts of the state. Importantly, this was accompanied by a growing sense of being able to achieve this step without going cap-in-hand to Ottawa or London. With the appearance of alternatives came economic self-confidence and a gradual restoration of national pride.

Also important in this regard is the confidence provided by cultural achievements in the cultural revivals in Newfoundland from the 1960s, and in Scotland from the early 1980s. As ethno-cultural arguments were never made essential carriers of either Scottish or Newfoundland political nationalism, the cultural revivals in themselves were not such decisive factors as they might have become in more classic nationalist movements, but when a cultural renaissance occurred simultaneously with other positive fomenting factors, this added to a growing sense of general national confidence.

In the 1980s and 1990s in particular, a new viable alternative arrived in the Scottish case with the development of the European Community and increasing European integration. The SNP made 'Independence in Europe' sound to many Scots like a reasonable alternative to continued membership of the UK, and Labour and the Liberals along with the Scottish media hailed the economic safety-net provided by EC membership, which allowed for constitutional experiments to be carried out without these being detrimental to socio-economic welfare. European integration, in short, made it safer to support a political nationalist discourse. NAFTA, an altogether different kettle of fish, did not provide the same alternative to Confederation in which Newfoundland political nationalists could vest their hopes for increased autonomy. The near-total annihilation of the autonomist discourse in Newfoundland in the 1990s must be explained in large part by the fact that the existing situation remained to Newfoundlanders by far the best socio-economic option available.

As in the Scottish case, the existence of an inherent defeatist myth in Newfoundland culture must be dismissed as a largely insignificant element in the process of political nationalist decline. Tartanry and the myth of Newfoundland developed by the 'Newfcult' may have conferred upon Scottish and Newfoundland national identities images of the self which have worked against a sustained self-confidence and political nationalism. On the other hand, there can be little doubt that the myths and their images, no matter how false or degrading, have also ensured the existence of a distinct sense of national identity in both communities.

Increased confidence, be it of a political, cultural or socio-economic nature, in both societies had the profound impact of uniting the bulk of Scots and Newfoundlanders in political nationalism. What was produced as a consequence of shared perceptions of dependency, inequality and central government neglect, coupled now with the bright prospects of economic self-sustainability and confidence, was national consensus as to the means by which to change the unfortunate situations that Scotland and Newfoundland were seen to find themselves in.

The importance of the nationalising domain in a study trying to determine or map the development of political nationalism in societies like Scotland and Newfoundland has been underlined. But it has also been illustrated that populations are not mere empty vessels. National identity discourses and consequent political action are constantly negotiated, and as the 1979 Scotland Act and 1992 Charlottetown Accord referendums testify, no elite has the power to impose a certain persuasion on society. If such powers are taken for granted, the result is likely to be a pronounced discrepancy between dominant actors in the nationalising domain and the people. This discrepancy disappeared in Scotland during the 1980s, as cross-sphere and cross-strata co-operation emerged with the SCC and other political and cultural forums, and the general belief in the value of increased Scottish autonomy grew. Not only had the *Glasgow Herald* joined the *Scotsman* in the convinced autonomist camp, the political parties also exhibited more confidence in the project. Most importantly, the majority of the Scots now rejected the status quo because it made political and economic as well as emotional sense to do so. Newfoundland in the early 1980s experienced a similarly diminishing discrepancy, with the Liberals and the *Daily News* increasingly marginalised; but as large sections of Newfoundland society were alienated as a consequence of the lack of tangible results of autonomism, discrepancy reappeared, finally to produce an altogether different consensus among Liberals, the *Evening Telegram* and the majority of Newfoundlanders. Like the Scots, Newfoundlanders appear to have been moved, albeit in the opposite direction, by rational considerations regarding the socio-economic consequences of the choice of different options.

PRAGMATIC UNIONISM, CENTRALISM AND POLITICAL NATIONALISM

The overall impression of the causes of the rise and decline of political nationalism in Scotland and Newfoundland in the period under consideration remains one of pragmatic motivations. This is not to say that all actors only engage half-heartedly in political nationalism, or that emotions are of no relevance. However, compared to classic nationalist movements, the political nationalist movements in Scotland and Newfoundland clearly base the demand for constitutional change on well-considered calculations of the socio-economic and, to a lesser extent, politico-democratic pros and cons. Also, more than has historically been the case, popular support is determined by the ability of the actors of the nationalising domain to convince Scots and Newfoundlanders that the cost-benefit analysis comes out in favour of either improved or at least unchanged material conditions. No actors, including separatists, are willing to push forward on a political nationalist path unless the present level of social welfare can be met in the proposed, not too distant, future constitutional scenario. The Peckford governments pursued policies of welfare restraint in the 1980s, but the argumentation was always that once control over provincial resources and decision-making had been obtained, Newfoundland would prosper, and 'have-not' and inequality would be no more. What lies at the base of the pragmatic perception of union, influencing both the political nationalist and centralist discourses, is its contractual nature. As illustrated, the unions contracted by Scotland and Newfoundland were characterised by nationalists as marriages of convenience, not love. One should be careful not to disregard the genuine affection which had developed among many towards the supra-national state, but the fact remains that Confederation and Union are predominantly assessed in this period by Newfoundland and Scottish actors on the basis of the socio-economic conditions each manages to provide for its citizens.

For large parts of the period studied, most actors in the nationalising domain considered membership of Canada and the UK to be the best existing option. During these times no better alternative was believed to exist, so the demand for change would have to confine itself to what was possible within the existing framework of union. Separatism was thus rejected, as dissatisfied actors in the nationalising domain opted for a less radical form of political nationalism: autonomism. The SNP and the Party for an Independent Newfoundland can be argued to have chosen different paths. Still, separatism was for their part also always motivated by the belief in socio-economically viable alternatives.

As mentioned, agreement exists largely among all actors throughout the period about the character of Scotland's and Newfoundland's malaises, and their causes. Where actors differ is with regard to the preferred solutions. Not all actors perceive the same options to hold the same positive promises, but it is on the same kind of pragmatic considerations that they are accepted and rejected. The *Evening Telegram* expresses convinced centralism, fierce autonomism, and aggressive centralism over a period of little more than two decades, thus reflecting the popular point of view. When the best option for Newfoundland to prosper was a strong central government with the power to redistribute wealth, this was considered a valuable goal. When other alternatives came up, the value of a centralist government was perceived to fade, and autonomism became the creed. A similarly pragmatic assessment of the benefits of union and the viability of alternatives can be seen to explain why a seemingly soaring political nationalist discourse failed to produce a Scottish Assembly in the late 1970s, and why another managed to do so in the late 1990s. The autonomist stance of the Labour Party and the *Glasgow Herald* in the late 1970s and early 1980s must further be characterised as pragmatic, because it resulted from a less than convinced appreciation of constitutional change, advocated merely to avoid a more radical political nationalist discourse – as proposed by the SNP – from becoming hegemonic.

These conclusions may appear to mark off Scots and Newfoundlanders as coldly calculating people with little affection or consideration for anything but material needs. Such an impression would be false, of course. Although illustrating the pragmatic, socio-economic considerations and the perception of the contractual nature of union from which both the centralist and political nationalist discourses developed, this book also underlines the strength of national (i.e., Scottish and Newfoundland) identity in the three decades from 1967 to 1997. To Scots and Newfoundlanders, the media, and large majorities of intellectuals and politicians, Scotland and Newfoundland took first priority. Unique cultural identities existed, but it was issues of a socio-economic and politico-democratic character, created by the perception of decades of relative underdevelopment and the lack of influence to alter this state of affairs, which became the heavier weights on the balance.

AUTONOMISM IN THE TWENTY-FIRST CENTURY

In terms of the future of autonomism in Scotland, the re-establishment of the Scottish parliament in 1999 and, more importantly, its workings provided an interesting new situation. Would the supporters of the pragmatic autonomist movement be content with what had been achieved, and would, as a consequence, the Scots be 'happy Britons' again? Elements within the SNP – in official opposition in Scotland between 1999 and 2007 – have not been content with this level of self-government and have accused party leaders of having become too soft and devolutionist. Margo MacDonald and others of the old guard of the SNP have been arguing that the leadership of the SNP is being sucked into the unionist system. Having returned from early retirement to lead the SNP once again, Alex Salmond, however, has no intention of settling for the current degree of autonomy. In August 2007, his minority government set out its plans for a 2010 referendum on independence, while also leaving open the option of gradually increasing the powers of the Scottish parliament. As oil prices soared in the first decade of the twenty-first century, mainly as a result of the war in Iraq, the SNP brushed off the 1970s slogan to claim again: 'It's Scotland's Oil'. With the price of crude oil peaking at \$147 per barrel in 2008, once more oil resources seemed to constitute an alternative to economic dependence on others.

Support for SNP policies fell in the first years after 1999. The first Scottish parliament elections gave the nationalists less than a third of the vote, and in the 2003 elections support dwindled to 22 per cent. Although still sufficient to keep the status of official opposition, this result sent the SNP in search of more appealing policies – a search which included re-emphasising well-tried themes. The 2007 election finally saw the SNP climb to power with a third of the vote, just ahead of Labour. The strength of autonomism apparently still wavered with the sound of an oil boom, and the pragmatic nature of political nationalism in Scotland was yet again underlined. With the *Scotsman*, ironically, having turned into a harsh conservative critic of even the post-1999 scale of devolution, this leaves the *Herald* to potentially support a renewed struggle for further increased autonomy. Judging from editorial reactions to the SNP's return to oil-fuelled political nationalism, however, the nationalists are facing another uphill struggle to get the important media actors on their side. In a 2004 editorial, 'Shortsighted SNP', the *Herald* made its position clear: 'A smart, successful, sustainable Scotland needs people with vision able to take this country forward to a sustainable future based on a clear understanding of what that future holds for us. Unfortunately, the SNP just does not seem to grasp that a future funded by oil was last century's vision.'[3]

In Newfoundland, the Progressive Conservative Williams government believes a future funded by oil is anything but an outdated vision. On the Rock, autonomism has reappeared from its long winter sleep to challenge Ottawa on the old resource question. Some of the Peckfordian autonomist spirit was shown during the Liberal provincial government under Roger Grimes, which set up a Royal Commission on Renewing and Strengthening Our Place in Canada, but it was not until the change of provincial governments in 2003 that a political nationalist discourse can be said seriously to have reached for hegemony. Forty-nine per cent of the voters supported the reinvigorated Conservatives, who campaigned on the slogan 'No More Giveaways'. Hydropower and control over the fisheries are back on the agenda, but the main goal of the PC government is a bigger share of the wealth generated by offshore oil and gas – to be achieved mainly by dissuading federal government from clawing back increased revenues by diminishing Newfoundland's annual equalisation grant. After the October 2007 election, which saw the PCs take 70 per cent of the vote, and 43 of 47 seats in the Newfoundland Assembly, Premier Danny Williams has a strong mandate to try to wrest concessions from Ottawa. Importantly, the

Telegram, too, appeared to be warming up for a new round in the autonomist ring. Although somewhat reluctant to give its full support by the end of 2004, the paper shared Williams' perception of federal government: 'The irony is that this whole negotiation hinges on whether or not Prime Minister Paul Martin will keep his word . . . [I]t's obvious that someone is lying, and that trust is a commodity that Ottawa has fallen short in.'[4]

The increasingly dramatic rhetoric and symbolic actions indicate a deterioration of the federal–provincial relationship perhaps to the level of the early 1980s. Inspired, no doubt, by Brian Peckford's declared 'day of mourning' in 1982, and his decision to have the Maple Leaf flown at half-mast to protest against negotiations with Prime Minister Trudeau over oil royalties, in December 2004 Premier Williams ordered all Canadian flags to be removed from provincial buildings in Newfoundland, also to protest over the failure of negotiations with Ottawa on the oil issue. Considering the findings presented in this book, it is difficult to imagine anything of this sort taking place, in Newfoundland or in Scotland, had oil prices not increased so dramatically.

IN CONCLUSION

In the first chapter it was argued that in order to understand recent developments, which defy the application of standard theories and definitions, rather than 'What is nationalism?', the question should be: 'How does a particular kind of nationalism manifest itself in different societies?' The comparative analysis of Scotland and Newfoundland has given us some answers as to how national identity is constructed and how modern autonomist movements manifest themselves in these particular societies. Returning to some of the theoretical points raised, what can be extracted in the most general terms, perhaps to inspire similar studies of neo-nationalisms, is this: a feature which made both Scottish and Newfoundland autonomism distinguishable as political nationalism in this period was the implicit emphasis of uniqueness and of ethnicity as the legitimisation of political action in disputes with central government. This is an element shared with classic nationalist movements described in most theories. Another, not so common, dominant factor in these autonomist movements was an explicit accentuation of concerns about political and socio-economic advantages and disadvantages of political nationalism – that is, the stressing of pragmatic reasoning over ethno-cultural affection. Therefore, a characteristic feature was also the striving for decentralisation/devolution of political and economic power rather than full independence. This does not in itself explain the periodical success of autonomism, however. Autonomist and centralist discourses were constantly competing for hegemony, and it was clearly when the proper (political and socio-economic) alternatives to the constitutional status quo existed that political nationalism came to dominate. The analyses also illustrated how potentially fomenting actors (the nationalising domain) were far from determinative. Newspapers and other actors *reflected* as much as they *influenced* debates in society, and they sometimes altered points of view according to popular demand. Classic explanations – focusing on top-down 'instructive' processes while neglecting the bottom-up response – therefore failed to provide all the answers.

Those who set out to procure new knowledge about nationalist movements in modern liberal democracies in the age of globalisation should be prepared to venture outside the established theories. To be sure, autonomism studies should be inspired by theories of nationalisms of a different age. However, to truly come to terms with nationalism in a modern Western world characterised by rapid, unprecedented change, the politically expressed desire for national recognition demands specific focus on idiosyncratic identity-building processes and the porous nationalising domain of actors that reflect and influence them.

Notes

CHAPTER ONE: INTRODUCTION

1. Since 2001 the official name of the province is 'Newfoundland and Labrador'. Throughout this book, however, the shorter and more common 'Newfoundland' will be used to refer to the province.
2. Anderson, 'Introduction', 1–17.
3. Brubaker, *Nationalism Reframed*, 7.
4. Held, *A Globalizing World?*
5. Ritzer, *The McDonaldization of Society*.
6. Guibernau, *Nations Without States*, 101.
7. Keating, *Nations Against the State*, 126–7.
8. Quoted in Ignatieff, *Blood and Belonging*, 121.
9. McCrone, *The Sociology of Nationalism: Tomorrow's Ancestors*, 129; original emphases.
10. Gellner, *Nations and Nationalism*, 1.
11. Smith, *National Identity*, 91.
12. Meinecke, *Weltbürgertum und Nationalstaat*, 10–13.
13. Murray Edelman has argued persuasively for the role of art/culture in influencing and shaping politics, and it should be stressed that the distinction made here between cultural and political nationalism is not a rejection of Edelman's general idea that art/culture is more than merely 'ancillary to the social scene' or a reflection of the 'real' world (Edelman, *From Art to Politics*, 2).
14. Nairn, *The Break-up of Britain: Crisis and Neo-Nationalism*, 156.

CHAPTER TWO: NATIONAL IDENTITY-BUILDING

1. Cohen, 'Being Scottish? On the Problem of the Objective Correlative', 221.
2. Guibernau, *Nations without States: Political Communities in a Global Age*, 93.
3. Smith, *National Identity*, vii.
4. Krejci and Velímský, 'Ethnic and Political Nations in Europe', 209.
5. Renan, 'Qu'est-ce qu'une nation?'
6. Anderson, *Imagined Communities: Reflections on the Origin and Spread of Nationalism*.
7. Hedetoft, *Signs of Nations*, 21.

8. Hedetoft, 'National identitet som kulturel og politisk kategori i Vesteuropa', 119.
9. Smith, *National Identity*, 11.
10. Connor, 'Beyond Reason: The Nature of the Ethnonational Bond', 73; original emphases.
11. McCrone, *The Sociology of Nationalism: Tomorrow's Ancestors*, 29.
12. Cohen, 'Being Scottish? On the Problem of the Objective Correlative', 215–16.
13. Laclau and Mouffe, *Hegemony and Socialist Strategy*, 108.
14. Heywood, *Political Ideas and Concepts*, 101.
15. Gramsci, *Fængelsoptegnelser i udvalg*, 51.
16. Gramsci, *Fængelsoptegnelser i udvalg*, 283–4.
17. McCrone, *The Sociology of Nationalism: Tomorrow's Ancestors*, 30.
18. See e.g. Smith, *National Identity*, 17; Eriksen, *Ethnicity and Nationalism*, 24; Jørgensen and Phillips, *Diskursanalyse som teori og metode*, 57, 63–4.
19. Kapferer, *Legends of People, Myths of State*, 215.
20. Connor, 'Beyond Reason: The Nature of the Ethnonational Bond', 70.
21. Eriksen, *Ethnicity and Nationalism*, 62; original emphasis.
22. Eriksen, *Ethnicity and Nationalism*, 22.
23. In his *Signs of Nations* (1995), Hedetoft introduces a more elaborate and useful model of three modes: the 'exclusivist', the 'gradualist', and the 'exotic'.
24. Smith, *Nationalism and Modernism: A Critical Survey of Recent Theories of Nations and Nationalism*, 54, 52.
25. Gellner, *Nations and Nationalism*, 50–2.
26. Gellner, *Nations and Nationalism*, 51.
27. Gellner, *Nations and Nationalism*, 57.
28. Nairn, *The Break-Up of Britain: Crisis and Neo-Nationalism*, 100.
29. Gellner, *Nations and Nationalism*, 55, 57.
30. Renan, 'Qu'est-ce qu'une nation?', 17.
31. Gramsci, *Fængelsoptegnelser i udvalg*, 32–3.
32. An example of this is the 2 June 1992 Danish referendum on the Maastricht Treaty, which described the next set of steps to be taken to integrate member states further into the political and economic supra-national entity of the European Union. The Danish coalition government, headed by the Social Democrats, along with almost the entire opposition (of mainly Liberals and Conservatives) strongly supported a 'Yes'. So did a large majority of the media, the academics, the intellectuals and the business community. Nevertheless, the result of the referendum was a narrow 'No' victory. Another fine example of a majority of the population voting against the recommendations of the social and political elites would be the Canadian referendum on the Charlottetown Accord, also defeated in 1992.
33. Anthony Giddens, *New Statesman*.
34. Hedetoft, *Signs of Nations*, 328.
35. Hedetoft, *Signs of Nations*, 328; emphasis added.
36. Hroch, *Social Preconditions of National Revival in Europe*, 22.
37. Hroch, *Social Preconditions of National Revival in Europe*, 81, 23
38. Hroch uses Scotland as an example of exactly this belated type of national movement (*Social Preconditions*, 83).

39. Hroch, 'From National Movement to the Fully-formed Nation', 85.
40. Hroch, *Social Preconditions*, 3; Hroch, 'From National Movement to the Fully-formed Nation', 83.
41. Even if 'discover' is persistently placed in inverted commas (Hroch, *Social Preconditions*, 11; Hroch, 'From National Movement to the Fully-formed Nation', 84).
42. Gellner, *Nations and Nationalism*, 63.
43. Greenfeld, *Nationalism: Five Roads to Modernity*, 22.
44. The concept of the 'nationalising domain' obviously owes much to Jürgen Habermas' 'Öffentlichkeit' or 'public sphere' as developed in his seminal *Strukturwandel der Öffentlichkeit* from 1962.
45. It includes Max Weber ('The Nation', 25), Ernest Gellner (*Nations and Nationalism*, 60–1), Benedict Anderson (*Imagined Communities*, 47–65), John Hutchinson (*The Dynamics of Cultural Nationalism*, 254–7), Anthony D. Smith (*National Identity*, 92–6; 140–1), David McCrone (*The Sociology of Nationalism*, 53), Eric J. Hobsbawm (*The Age of Revolution*, 164), Miroslav Hroch (*Social Preconditions*, 16), Øjvind Østerud (*Hva er nasjonalisme?*, 56–8), Tom Nairn (*The Break-Up of Britain*, 117) and Elie Kedourie ('Dark Gods and their Rites', 205–9). The pages referred to merely indicate examples; all of these theorists have dealt with the question at length in much of their work.
46. Smith, *National Identity*, 93.
47. Østerud, *Hva er nasjonalisme?*, 57.
48. Smith, *Nationalism and Modernism*, 57; emphasis added.
49. Breuilly, *Nationalism and the State*, xii.
50. Breuilly, *Nationalism and the State*, 1.
51. Breuilly, *Nationalism and the State*, 1.
52. Breuilly, *Nationalism and the State*, 19.
53. Breuilly, *Nationalism and the State*, 47–51.
54. Calhoun, 'The National Identity of Newfoundlanders', 120.
55. Billig, *Banal Nationalism*, 98.
56. Billig, *Banal Nationalism*, 96.
57. Billig, *Banal Nationalism*, 93.
58. Siegel, *Politics and the Media in Canada*, 234.
59. Gellner, *Nations and Nationalism*, 51–2.
60. Smith, *National Identity*, 11.
61. Wagenberg et al., 'Campaigns, Images, and Polls', 143; original emphases.
62. McCron, 'Changing Perspectives in the Study of Mass Media and Socialization', 35, 38.
63. Hall, 'Introduction to Media Studies at the Centre', 117.
64. Gerbner, 'Mass Media Discourse: Message System Analysis as a Component of Cultural Indicators', 14.
65. Gerbner, 'Mass Media Discourse', 14–15.
66. Gerbner, 'Mass Media Discourse', 16–17. Gerbner continues to show how such a particular type of analysis, Message System Analysis, can be undertaken with this purpose. Message System Analysis is a useful method for data collection

and analysis with regard to the study of media discourse, and it has been
applied (with modifications) in the analysis of images of self and other in
Scottish and Newfoundland media.

67. Anderson, *Imagined Communities*, 37–46.
68. McLuhan, *Understanding Media: The Extensions of Man*, 159–61.
69. McLuhan, *Understanding Media: The Extensions of Man*, 161.
70. Anderson, *Imagined Communities*, 44–5.
71. McLuhan, *Understanding Media: The Extensions of Man*, 159, 192; original
    emphasis.
72. *Herald*, 17 March 2000; *Scottish Sun*, 14 April 2000; *Telegram*, 17 March
    2000.
73. Siegel, *Politics and the Media in Canada*, 1.
74. Cf. Joey Smallwood's use of radio broadcasts during the National Convention
    debates of the late 1940s.
75. Siegel, *Politics and the Media in Canada*, 32.
76. This may soon be changing as the ever-expanding Internet is becoming a force
    to be reckoned with. Most newspapers now have online editions, and they
    provide an increasing part of the public with daily information.
77. McLuhan, *Understanding Media: The Extensions of Man*, 193; original
    emphases.
78. MacInnes, 'The Press in Scotland', 146.
79. Sevaldsen and Vadmand, *Contemporary British Society*, 150.
80. Smith, *Paper Lions: The Scottish Press and National Identity*, 1.
81. Smith, *Paper Lions*, 6.
82. Meech and Kilborn, 'Media and identity in a stateless nation', 255.
83. Sevaldsen and Vadmand, *Contemporary British Society*, 149; MacInnes, 'The
    Press in Scotland', 139; Greenstein 1999, 4.
84. Meech and Kilborn, 'Media and identity in a stateless nation', 255.
85. Siegel, *Politics and the Media in Canada*, 104.
86. Steel lectured in a press release: 'A critical press will of course be vigilant on the
    activities of Parliament as a whole and of individual MSPs . . . But one unfor-
    tunate recent trend is what I call "bitch journalism" – practised by both sexes,
    where character assassination of a reckless and cruel kind is employed. Several
    MSPs of all parties have fallen prey to this, mainly in the tabloid press and
    notably in the *Daily Record*. In the case of that paper the institution itself has
    come under sustained attack on a level which is mendacious in the extreme.'
    (Scottish Parliament, 'Presiding Officer hits out'.)
87. Siegel, *Politics and the Media in Canada*, 101.
88. In 1992 the *Glasgow Herald* became *The Herald*
89. Meech and Kilborn, 'Media and Identity in a Stateless Nation', 256.
90. Smith, *Paper Lions*, 68. In fact, the *Glasgow Herald* was the only major
    Scottish newspaper opposed to any kind of devolution.
91. *Ibid.*
92. Smith, *Paper Lions*, 232; Marr, *The Battle for Scotland*, 125, 156.
93. Siegel, *Politics and the Media in Canada*, 128.

94. In his contribution to Rawlyk's *The Atlantic Provinces and the Problems of Confederation* ('Newfoundland and Canada'), Pat O'Brien has made a thorough and useful analysis of the perception of Confederation in Newfoundland media (the *Daily News* and the *Evening Telegram*) in the period 1967 to 1978. Unfortunately, O'Brien's investigation stops immediately before the point when political nationalism really takes off in the shape of the Peckford administrations of the 1980s. Still, O'Brien's analysis shows that with regard to the images of self and other projected in Newfoundland newspapers, the entire period from the mid-1960s to the late 1970s contributes significantly to an understanding of the processes involved in the development of a Newfoundland autonomist agenda.

95. 26,240 in 1971 and 36,150 in 1981 against the *Daily News*' 6,682 in 1971 and 10,775 in 1981 (Lawton, 'Contrary Agendas', 141; Siegel, *Politics and the Media in Canada*, 106).

96. Lawton, 'Contrary Agendas', 145–7; Ellison, *Historical Directory*, 33.

97. Hobsbawm, *The Age of Revolution*, 166.

98. Some literati, linguists and folklorists in both Scotland and Newfoundland would argue that Scots and Newfoundland English possess quite distinct characteristics, which unquestionably distinguish them from the English spoken in Mainland Canada and the rest of the UK, respectively. As true as this may be, it does not change the fact that neither Newfoundland English nor Scots can be considered 'heavy ammunition' in terms of political nationalism. Hugh MacDiarmid utilised language ('Lallans') in his attempt to ignite a Scottish nationalist movement in the early twentieth century, and failed. Gaelic in Scotland is spoken by such a small part of the population that it can not in any foreseeable future form the basis of a popular nationalist movement, as is the case, for instance, in Wales.

99. Balakrishnan, 'The National Imagination', 202.

100. Kapferer, *Legends of People, Myths of State*, 1.

101. Acton, 'Nationality', 31–2.

102. Kedourie, 'Dark Gods and their Rites', 205–7.

103. Hutchinson, *The Dynamics of Cultural Nationalism*, 308–11.

104. Hauge, *Den danske kirke nationalt betragtet*, 85. A new alliance was concocted between Protestantism and Danish liberal nationalism in the nineteenth century – an alliance personified in the Danish carrier of Herder's ideas of the *Volksgeist*, the nationalist pastor and poet N. F. S. Grundtvig. There is an internal (romantic) logic of the alliance: until the people (the *Volksgeist*) are free – introducing the people's language into the people's Church is a step in that direction – true Christianity can not be preached. This kind of logic is nowhere better expressed than in the name of the Danish state church, which is not really a *state* church but a *Folkekirke* (the 'People's Church').

105. Billig, *Banal Nationalism*.

106. Rothney, 'The Denominational Basis of Representation in the Newfoundland Assembly', 149.

107. Matthews, 'Perspectives on Recent Newfoundland politics', 129.

108. Matthews, 'Perspectives on Recent Newfoundland politics', 133.

109. Quoted in Matthews, 'Perspectives on Recent Newfoundland politics', 125.
110. Noel, *Politics in Newfoundland*, 138.
111. Harvie, *Scotland and Nationalism*, 147.
112. Walker, 'Varieties of Scottish Protestant Identity', 257–8.

CHAPTER THREE: SCOTLAND AND NEWFOUNDLAND IN COMPARISON

1. Cohen, 'Being Scottish? On the Problem of the Objective Correlative', 210.
2. Cohen, 'Being Scottish? On the Problem of the Objective Correlative', 214.
3. Cohen, 'Being Scottish? On the Problem of the Objective Correlative', 214.
4. In the Faeroe Islands a Home Rule Party has existed since 1906, and in 1948 the islands were granted home rule. Today a strong independence movement is likely to succeed in achieving some sort of further secession from Denmark for the 17 inhabited islands with a total area of only 1,399 square km and a population of 45,000. In 1967 Nauru, another small island society, became the world's smallest independent nation-state with an area of only 21 square km and a population of less than 10,000.
5. In 1983 the Newfoundland Court of Appeal ruled that Newfoundland had indeed been a sovereign state prior to Confederation with Canada (Hiller, 'Dependence and Independence: Emergent Nationalism in Newfoundland,' 264).
6. Sider, 'Culture and Class in Anthropology and History,' 171.
7. See e.g. Neary, *Newfoundland in the North Atlantic World*, 316–19; Jackson, *Surviving Confederation*, 61, 75–6.
8. O'Brien, 'Newfoundland and Canada, 1967–1978', 284.
9. Lynch, *Scotland: A New History*, 313.
10. McCrone, *The Sociology of Nationalism: Tomorrow's Ancestors*, 141.
11. In 1707 qualifications to vote lay only with major (male) landowners, and the Scottish Parliament which alone made the decision to join the United Kingdom of Great Britain was elected by less than 2,000 Scots. In contrast, the outcome of two public referendums in 1948 decided the fate for Newfoundland.
12. The famous ode 'Rule, Britannia' from 1740 which celebrates the expanding British Empire's great maritime and political power, was written by the Scottish poet James Thomson.
13. Harvie, *Scotland and Nationalism*, 126.
14. Quoted in Harvie, *Scotland and Nationalism*, 133.
15. Donaldson, *Scotland: The Shaping of a Nation*, 269.
16. Harvie, *Scotland and Nationalism*, 199.
17. Donaldson, *Scotland: The Shaping of a Nation*, 262.
18. Marr, *The Battle for Scotland*, 172.
19. Scottish Office, 'Scotland's Parliament – Your Choice', 4.
20. Scott, *Still in Bed with an Elephant*; an expression coined by the former Prime Minister of Canada Pierre Elliott Trudeau to describe his country's experience as a neighbour of the United States.
21. Cohen, 'Being Scottish? On the Problem of the Objective Correlative', 215.
22. Graesser, 'The Newfoundland 1982 Election Study,' Table 7.

23. See e.g. Martin, *No Fish and Our Lives*, and Palmer and Sinclair, *When the Fish Are Gone*.
24. Palmer and Sinclair, *When the Fish Are Gone*, 75.
25. Norrie and Owram, *A History of the Canadian Economy*, 417.
26. Norrie and Owram, *A History of the Canadian Economy*, 440.
27. Norrie and Owram, *A History of the Canadian Economy*, 443.
28. Government of Newfoundland, *Historical Statistics of Newfoundland and Labrador*.
29. *Globe and Mail*, 'Unemployment Rate Dips to Seven-Year Low'; Statistics Canada, 'Labour Force Characteristics'. Unemployment in Newfoundland was, however, spread unevenly: on the South Coast/Burin Peninsula, the unemployment rate was 34.8 per cent; on the Avalon Peninsula, enjoying an economic boom partly caused by oil development, the rate was down to 14 per cent (Statistics Canada, 'Labour Force Characteristics').
30. Statistics Canada, 'Labour Force Characteristics.'
31. *Report on Business*, 'The Rock's on a Roll'.
32. Norrie and Owram, *A History of the Canadian Economy*, 450–1.
33. Srebrnik, 'A Garden in Disorder?' Since 1996 a balance and a surplus have been achieved in the federal budget, which has had an effect on the proposed policies.
34. 'Runrig' refers to a specific feature of Scottish farming whereby the most was made of soil ill-fitted for agriculture.
35. McCrone, *Understanding Scotland*, 21–2.
36. Quoted in Nairn, *The Break-Up of Britain*, 171.
37. Meech and Kilborn, 'Media and Identity in a Stateless Nation', 258.
38. McCrone, *Understanding Scotland*, 99.
39. Cohen, 'Being Scottish? On the Problem of the Objective Correlative', 213.
40. Hearn, 'Scotland's Hidden Powers', 274.
41. Quoted in Kellas, *Modern Scotland*, 54–5.
42. Kellas, *Modern Scotland*, 55.
43. McCrone, 'We're A' Jock Tamson's Bairns'.
44. McCrone, 'We're A' Jock Tamson's Bairns', 113.
45. Donaldson, *Scotland: The Shaping of a Nation*, 117.
46. Hearn, 'Scotland's Hidden Powers', 286–7.
47. Keating, *Nations against the State*, 172.
48. Brown, McCrone and Paterson, *Politics and Society in Scotland*, 154.
49. Cohen, 'Being Scottish? On the Problem of the Objective Correlative', 216.
50. Dickson, 'Scotland is Different, OK?', 61.
51. Quoted in Rankin, *Rebus's Scotland: A Personal Journey*, 20.
52. Thomas, *The Divided Kingdom*; original emphases.
53. Calhoun, 'The National Identity of Newfoundlanders', 7. The abolition of the Union Jack as the provincial flag might serve to support this assertion with regard to a potential 'British' Newfoundland identity. In spite of the fact that Newfoundland has been exposed to considerable amounts of American culture *qua* the presence of US naval bases, the idea that an American identity should have a real presence in Newfoundland seems far-fetched too. Calhoun himself

later (Calhoun, 'The National Identity of Newfoundlanders', 179) appears to disqualify both these options.

54. McNaught, *The Penguin History of Canada*, 126.
55. Neary, *Newfoundland in the North Atlantic World*, 8. Newfoundland was covered by the 1931 Statute of Westminster, but prior to that enjoyed dominion-like status in the latter part of the 1920s.
56. MacLeod, *Connections: Newfoundland's Pre-confederation Links with Canada and the World.*
57. Tomblin, *Ottawa and the Outer Provinces*, 89–91; Srebrnik, 'A Garden in Disorder?'
58. This is a theme explored by Margaret Conrad in her 2003 David Alexander Lecture: 'Mistaken Identities? Newfoundland and Labrador in the Atlantic Region'.
59. Calhoun, 'The National Identity of Newfoundlanders', 109–110.
60. Paine, 'The Making of Peckford and the "New" Newfoundland', 8.
61. Hiller, 'Dependence and Independence: Emergent Nationalism in Newfoundland,' 265.
62. In 1990 the question was: '*Do you think of yourself as a Canadian first or as a citizen of your province?*'; in 1994, the question was slightly different: '*Do you think of yourself as a Canadian first, or as a resident of a particular region or province?*'
63. Calhoun, 'The National Identity of Newfoundlanders', 182.
64. Data Laboratories, 'Report of a Special Survey of Newfoundlanders' Attitudes Towards Confederation with Canada', 3.
65. Graesser, 'The Newfoundland 1982 Election Study', Table 8.
66. Corporate Research Associates, 'Atlantic Omnibus Survey', Table 168A.
67. House, *The Challenge of Oil*, 2–3.
68. See e.g. O'Dea, 'Newfoundland: The Development of Culture on the Margin', 73.
69. P. C. Mars, 'The All 'Round Newfoundlander' (1924), quoted in Byrne, 'The Confluence of Folklore and Literature in the Creation of a Newfoundland Mythology', 62.
70. Byrne, 'The Confluence of Folklore and Literature in the Creation of a Newfoundland Mythology', 60, 62.
71. Byrne, 'The Confluence of Folklore and Literature in the Creation of a Newfoundland Mythology', 63.
72. A closer examination reveals the regionalisation of Canadian politics in the period, and the great swings this caused between provincial voting patterns. Voters in Newfoundland were often in agreement with Ontario voters (1972, 1974, 1980, 1984, 1993, (1997)), while seldom in agreement with voters in Quebec and Western Canada – most clearly expressed from 1980 onwards.

CHAPTER FOUR: SCOTTISH NATIONAL IDENTITY AND NATIONALISM

1. Rönnquist, *Historia och nationalitet*, 148.
2. Scott's position is the most obvious case of what the Scottish literary critic G. Gregory Smith referred to as 'Caledonian antisyzygy': the division between

a rational British 'head' and a romantic Scottish 'heart' (Nairn, *The Break-Up of Britain*, 150).

3. Harvie, *Scotland and Nationalism*, 20, 34.

4. Watson, 'Maps of Desire: Scottish Literature in the Twentieth Century', 287.

5. A pseudonym for William Sharp.

6. Quoted in Watson, 'Maps of Desire: Scottish Literature in the Twentieth Century', 287.

7. 'Kailyard' translates as 'cabbage bed'.

8. Craig, 'Myths Against History: Tartanry and Kailyard', 11–12.

9. Quoted in Harvie, 'Scott and the image of Scotland', 174.

10. Harvie, *Scotland and Nationalism*, 192.

11. See e.g. McArthur, *Scotch Reels: Scotland in Cinema and Television*; Craig, 'Myths Against History: Tartanry and Kailyard.'

12. They set up the 'Scotch Myths' exhibition in Edinburgh in 1981.

13. Nairn, *The Break-Up of Britain*, 155–6.

14. Harvie, 'Nationalism, Journalism and Cultural Politics', 31.

15. Mitchell, 'Scotland in the Union, 1945–1995', 94.

16. With the Maastricht Treaty in 1993, the European Community (formerly the European Economic Community (EEC)) became the European Union (EU)

17. Keating, *Nations against the State*, 178–9.

18. Harvie, *Scotland and Nationalism*, 176.

19. Webb, *The Growth of Nationalism in Scotland*, 111.

20. Marr, *The Battle for Scotland*, 133.

21. Webb, *The Growth of Nationalism in Scotland*, 104; Harvie, *Scotland and Nationalism*, 176, 182.

22. Harvie, 'Industry, Identity and Chaos', 8.

23. Lynch, *Scotland: A New History*, 446.

24. SNP, 'General Election Manifesto', 4; original emphasis.

25. SNP, 'SNP & You: Aims and Policy', 4.

26. SNP, 'Return to Nationhood', 6.

27. SNP, 'Supplementary Manifesto', 1.

28. Rönnquist, *Historia och nationalitet*, 147.

29. Webb, *The Growth of Nationalism in Scotland*, 106; Marr, *The Battle for Scotland*, 119.

30. SNP, 'General Election Manifesto', 4.

31. SNP, 'SNP & You: Aims and Policy', 4.

32. SNP, 'SNP & You: Aims and Policy', 4.

33. SNP, 'SNP & You: Aims and Policy', 10.

34. SNP, 'Return to Nationhood', 11–12.

35. SNP, 'Supplementary Manifesto', 1–2.

36. Keating, *Nations against the State*, 169.

37. 47,000 people per year in 1965–6 (Webb, *The Growth of Nationalism in Scotland*, 120).

38. Harvie, *Scotland and Nationalism*, 187–8.

39. The Scottish Labour report submitted to the Kilbrandon Commission, quoted in Marr, *The Battle for Scotland*, 130.

40. In 1964 the Wilson government had the Scottish vote to thank for the Labour victory.

41. Keating, *Nations against the State*, 172; emphasis added.

42. Quoted in Marr, *The Battle for Scotland*, 155–6.

43. Webb, *The Growth of Nationalism in Scotland*, 102.

44. Breuilly, *Nationalism and the State*, 333–4.

45. McCrone, *The Sociology of Nationalism*, 137.

46. McCrone, *Representing Scotland*, 161.

47. McCrone, *The Sociology of Nationalism*, 142.

48. Harvie, *Scotland and Nationalism*, 180.

49. McCrone, *Understanding Scotland*, 212.

50. 30.78 per cent said 'No'.

51. Marr, *The Battle for Scotland*, 160.

52. Maxwell, 'The Scottish Middle Class and the National Debate', 134–5.

53. Marr, *The Battle for Scotland*, 161; Harvie, *Scotland and Nationalism*, 197.

54. Harvie, *Scotland and Nationalism*, 197.

55. Cohen, 'Being Scottish? On the Problem of the Objective Correlative', 215.

56. Scott, *Still in Bed with an Elephant*, 111; Keating, *Nations against the State*, 189.

57. Beveridge and Turnbull, *The Eclipse of Scottish Culture*, 1–6.

58. Nairn, *The Break-Up of Britain*, 162; 165.

59. Beveridge and Turnbull, *The Eclipse of Scottish Culture*, 2.

60. Beveridge and Turnbull, *The Eclipse of Scottish Culture*, 4.

61. Beveridge and Turnbull, *The Eclipse of Scottish Culture*, 5.

62. Beveridge and Turnbull, *The Eclipse of Scottish Culture*, 6.

63. Scott, *Still in Bed with an Elephant*, 33, 111.

64. Beveridge and Turnbull, *The Eclipse of Scottish Culture*, 14.

65. The obvious exception being the *Scotsman*'s referendum editorial (*Scotsman*, 1 May 1979), but it cannot be said to have been characteristic of political nationalist discourse.

66. Marr, *The Battle for Scotland*, 163.

67. Paterson, 'Are the Scottish Middle Class Going Native?', 10.

68. Paterson, 'Are the Scottish Middle Class Going Native?', 11.

69. Marr, *The Battle for Scotland*, 123.

70. Scott, *Still in Bed with an Elephant*, 32.

71. Keating, *Nations against the State*, 176.

72. The poll tax (or community charge) was introduced in Scotland in 1989, a year ahead of England and Wales. It was not a tax calculated according to personal income, but a fixed charge per head. Its socially unfair nature made the tax extremely unpopular, and large campaigns of non-payment resulted. The tax was later repealed.

73. Harvie, *Scotland and Nationalism*, 203.

74. Keating, *Nations against the State*, 173.

75. McCrone, *Understanding Scotland*, 142.
76. McCrone, *Understanding Scotland*, 173.
77. Nairn, *Faces of Nationalism: Janus Revisited*, 192.
78. Marr, *The Battle for Scotland*, 170.
79. MacInnes, 'The Press in Scotland', 145.
80. Keating, *Nations against the State*, 173–6.
81. Keating, *Nations against the State*, 181.
82. See for example Kieran Allen's *The Celtic Tiger? The Myth of Social Partnership in Ireland*, which challenges many established views of the causes and social consequences of Ireland's 'tiger economy'.
83. SNP, 'General Election Manifesto', 5, 10.
84. SNP, 'Supplementary Manifesto', 2.
85. SNP, 'Choose Scotland – The Challenge of Independence', 11.
86. SNP, 'Play the Scottish Card', 9.
87. SNP, 'Scotland's Future – Independence in Europe', 4–6.
88. SNP, 'Scotland's Future – Independence in Europe', 2.
89. Mitchell, 'Scotland in the Union, 1945–1995', 99.
90. Keating, *Nations against the State*, 179.
91. Labour Party, 'The Better Way for Scotland', 24.
92. Labour Party, 'Scotland Will Win', 12.
93. Labour Party, 'It's Time to Get Scotland Moving Again', 11.
94. Labour Party, 'It's Time to Get Scotland Moving Again', 23.
95. Labour Party, 'New Labour: Because Scotland Deserves Better', 37.
96. Paterson, 'Are the Scottish Middle Class Going Native?', 11.
97. Maxwell, 'The Scottish Middle Class and the National Debate', 151.
98. Keating, *Nations against the State*, 188.
99. Brown, McCrone and Paterson, *Politics and Society in Scotland*, 169.
100. Brown, McCrone and Paterson, *Politics and Society in Scotland*, 169; the survey results reproduced exclude Northern Ireland.
101. SNP, 'Choose Scotland – The Challenge of Independence', 5–6, 23.
102. SNP, 'Yes We Can Win the Best for Scotland', 18–19, Table 1.
103. Labour Party, 'The Better Way for Scotland', 1, 11; 'It's Time to Get Scotland Moving Again', 11.
104. The *Scottish Sun* changed its masthead text to: 'Fighting for Independence' (Marr, *The Battle for Scotland*, 215).
105. Hamilton, 'The Scottish National Paradox', 17.
106. SNP, 'Choose Scotland – The Challenge of Independence', 3.
107. SNP, 'Choose Scotland – The Challenge of Independence', 12–13.
108. SNP, 'Choose Scotland – The Challenge of Independence', 3.
109. SNP, 'Choose Scotland – The Challenge of Independence', 4.
110. SNP, 'Play the Scottish Card', 3, 6, 7, 11.
111. SNP, 'Independence in Europe: Make it Happen Now!', 2.
112. SNP, 'Yes We Can', 3.
113. SNP, 'Yes We Can', 17.
114. McCrone, 'The Local and the Global: National Identity in the New Scotland.'

115. Bond, 'Squaring the Circles', 30.
116. Brown, McCrone and Paterson, *Politics and Society in Scotland*, 162.
117. Keating, *Nations against the State*, 175.
118. Brown, McCrone and Paterson, *Politics and Society in Scotland*, 211.
119. See e.g. Labour Party, 'Scotland Will Win', 1.
120. Labour Party, 'The Better Way for Scotland', 28.
121. Labour Party, 'New Labour: Because Scotland Deserves Better', 16.
122. Labour Party, 'New Labour: Because Scotland Deserves Better', 5.
123. Labour Party, 'The Better Way for Scotland', 2.
124. Labour Party, 'The Better Way for Scotland', 5.
125. Labour Party, 'The Better Way for Scotland', 28.
126. Labour Party, 'Scotland Will Win', 2.
127. Labour Party, 'New Labour: Because Scotland Deserves Better', 3, 5, 32.
128. Labour Party, 'It's Time to Get Scotland Moving Again', 6.
129. Labour Party, 'New Labour: Because Scotland Deserves Better', 5.
130. Brown, McCrone and Paterson, *Politics and Society in Scotland*, 154.
131. Scottish Constitutional Convention, *Scotland's Parliament. Scotland's Right*, 34–5.
132. Keating, *Nations against the State*, 210.
133. McCrone, *Understanding Scotland*, 213.
134. Smith, *Paper Lions*, 3.
135. MacInnes, 'The Press in Scotland', 143.
136. Smith, *Paper Lions*, 15.
137. Paterson, 'Are the Scottish Middle Class Going Native?'.
138. Nairn, *Faces of Nationalism: Janus Revisited*, 192.
139. Maxwell, 'The Scottish Middle Class and the National Debate', 150.
140. Paterson, *The Autonomy of Modern Scotland*, 103–31.
141. Paterson, *The Autonomy of Modern Scotland*, 169–70.
142. The front page illustration of this particular issue shows a man happily waiting to be swept along by the home rule tide.
143. Marr, *The Battle for Scotland*, 229, 228.
144. Labour Party, 'It's Time to Get Scotland Moving Again', 6.
145. Quoted in Marr, *The Battle for Scotland*, 206.
146. Scottish Constitutional Convention, *Scotland's Parliament. Scotland's Right*, 6–7.
147. After the constituency, which its originator, Tam Dalyell, represented.
148. A new problem arose, as the Scotland Act 1998 defined the number of MPs at Westminster as equal to the number of Members of the Scottish Parliament elected under the majority in single-member constituencies system; the Scottish Parliament (Constituencies) Act 2004 ended this link.
149. Craig, 'Series Preface', in Smith, *Paper Lions*, vi.
150. Wallace, 'Introduction', 1.
151. Rankin, *Rebus's Scotland: A Personal Journey*, 119–20.
152. Quoted in Smith, *Paper Lions*, 23.
153. Craig, 'Series Preface', in Smith, *Paper Lions*, vi–vii.
154. Campaign for a Scottish Assembly, 'A Claim of Right for Scotland', 2.

155. Paterson, 'Liberation or Control?: What are the Scottish Education Traditions', 246.
156. Review of Scottish Culture Group, 'Scottish Culture and the Curriculum. Conclusion.'
157. *Cencrastus*, 'Revaluation', 3.
158. Harvie, *Scotland and Nationalism*, 208.
159. Keating, *Nations against the State*, 173, 192.
160. McCrone, *Understanding Scotland*, 212.
161. Hamilton, 'The Scottish National Paradox', 17.
162. Craig, interview by the author.
163. Craig, interview by the author.
164. McCrone, *Understanding Scotland*, 212.

CHAPTER FIVE: NEWFOUNDLAND NATIONAL IDENTITY
AND NATIONALISM

1. Quoted in Craig, *Lord Durham's Report*.
2. Hartz, *The Founding of New Societies*.
3. Hartz, *The Founding of New Societies*, 5; unfortunately, Hartz never defines the English-Canadian creed in one simple, similarly useful phrase.
4. Hartz, *The Founding of New Societies*, 11–12.
5. Ashcroft et al., *The Empire Writes Back*.
6. Hartz takes the edge out of this criticism as he argues that with the advent of globalisation (Hartz never actually uses the phrase 'globalisation', but speaks of the 'Return to Revolution'), the old national fragment is being seriously challenged. Not only by external forces, but also by new generations, forgetting the 'psychic magic, all of the wonderful metamorphoses accomplished by [their] predecessors' (Hartz, *The Founding of New Societies*, 20). Under such circumstances the fragment is likely to respond in an aggressively regressive manner, but the generation which has left the Platonic cave will continue to reject the national fragment creed.
7. Hartz, *The Founding of New Societies*, 34; McRae, 'The Structure of Canadian History', 234–47.
8. Hartz, *The Founding of New Societies*, 34; Gad Horowitz develops this part of the Hartzian thesis in *Canadian Labour in Politics* from 1968.
9. McRae, 'The Structure of Canadian History', 256–9.
10. Newfoundland's population growth: 1790: *c.*20,000; 1806: 27,000; 1815: *c.* 40,000; 1825: 58,000; 1832: 76,000; 1851: 102,000; 1861: 123,000 (Newfoundland and Labrador Heritage Web Site; Kerr, *Historical Atlas of Canada*, 53).
11. Francis, *National Dreams: Myth, Memory and Canadian History*, 52–87.
12. Noel, *Politics in Newfoundland*, 4; Thornton 'The Problem of Out–Migration from Atlantic Canada', 1999.
13. McRae, 'The Structure of Canadian History', 254.
14. Neary, *Newfoundland in the North Atlantic World*, ix.

15. I am aware that by making this claim I also exclude from Newfoundland collective identity the Labradoreans. Although to some residents of Labrador that might not be an unreasonable exclusion, this is not my purpose. However, studies of national identity must focus on dominant discourses, rather than minority views, and as such, the 'gulf' is a very real and relevant mental feature.

16. With Irish immigration following the Great Famine, this too would be characteristic of other parts of British North America. This wave of Irish immigrants, however, passed over Newfoundland. At the peak of Irish immigration to Canada in 1847 (when 54,000 Irish immigrants landed at the Port of Quebec), Newfoundland received only 1,000 (Cowan, 'British Immigration Before Confederation', 19–20).

17. Many Irish leaders in Newfoundland were actively engaged in O'Connell's struggle for emancipation (Greene, *Between Damnation and Starvation*, 69). According to Kevin Major, one of the leading reformers in Newfoundland, Patrick Morris was an 'associate and vigorous campaigner' for O'Connell (Major, *As Near to Heaven by Sea*, 203).

18. Greene, *Between Damnation and Starvation*, 49.

19. Major, *As Near to Heaven by Sea*, 196, 235.

20. Which means the assembly was elected from among the people of the colony. Still, the purpose of the assembly was mainly to assent to legislation produced by the Legislative Council which, together with the governor, remained appointed by the Crown.

21. Noel, *Politics in Newfoundland*, 7.

22. Brookes, 'Nation or Notion?'

23. The appointed Executive Council was replaced by a cabinet and ministers, holding office only as long as they enjoyed the support of a majority of the members of the legislative assembly. Therefore the government became 'responsible' to the assembly (and thus the people), rather than to the governor.

24. Noel, *Politics in Newfoundland*, 4.

25. Major, *As Near to Heaven by Sea*, 175–6.

26. Greene, *Between Damnation and* Starvation, 71–74.

27. McCann, 'Culture, State Formation and the Invention of Tradition', 89.

28. McCann, 'Culture, State Formation and the Invention of Tradition', 93.

29. One important other to confront would be France, on account of the unsettled question of the French Shore.

30. McCann, 'Culture, State Formation and the Invention of Tradition', 93.

31. Noel, *Politics in Newfoundland*, 24.

32. See e.g. Noel, 'How do Consociational Systems Begin?'

33. Major, *As Near to Heaven by Sea*, 281.

34. Neary, *Newfoundland in the North Atlantic World*, 5.

35. Quoted in Rothney, 'The Denominational Basis of Representation in the Newfoundland Assembly', 23.

36. Noel, *Politics in Newfoundland*, 25.

37. Quoted in Rothney, 'The Denominational Basis of Representation in the Newfoundland Assembly', 21.

38. In Europe, similar monuments celebrating and re-connecting nations with their past were erected. In Scotland, the Wallace Monument in Stirling and the Walter Scott Monument in Edinburgh are illustrative of the trend.
39. Peter Neary even refers to opposition towards the existence of French Shore rights as 'economic nationalism' (Neary, *Newfoundland in the North Atlantic World*, 5).
40. Noel, *Politics in Newfoundland*, 12. Also, St John's, which had grown to become the political and economic centre of the colony, faced east, physically closer to Dublin and London than to most parts of Canada.
41. Quoted in Major, *As Near to Heaven by Sea*, 292.
42. *Evening Telegram*, 21 April 1906.
43. Still, it meant that the pre-Confederation Newfoundland Dominion in 1983 could be recognised by the Newfoundland Court of Appeal as an independent state – only later to have this decision overruled by the Supreme Court of Canada.
44. Quoted in Neary, 'Newfoundland's Union with Canada', 379.
45. Brookes, 'Nation or Notion?'
46. Quoted in Doody, 'The Dominion of Newfoundland'.
47. Neary, *Newfoundland in the North Atlantic World*, 321–4.
48. Noel, *Politics in Newfoundland*, 257.
49. Noel, *Politics in Newfoundland*, 257.
50. Major, *As Near to Heaven by Sea*, 399.
51. FitzGerald, 'The True Father of Confederation?', 199–200.
52. Noel, 'Post-Confederation Society and Politics', 135.
53. Noel, 'Post-Confederation Society and Politics', 135.
54. Neary, *Newfoundland in the North Atlantic World*, 321.
55. Neary, *Newfoundland in the North Atlantic World*, 324.
56. Blake, *Canadians at Last*, xvii.
57. Major, *As Near to Heaven by Sea*, 401–2.
58. Noel, *Politics in Newfoundland*, 260.
59. Byrne, 'The Confluence of Folklore and Literature in the Creation of a Newfoundland Mythology', 64.
60. Byrne, 'The Confluence of Folklore and Literature in the Creation of a Newfoundland Mythology', 69.
61. O'Flaherty, *The Rock Observed: Studies in the Literature of Newfoundland*, 149.
62. O'Flaherty, *The Rock Observed: Studies in the Literature of Newfoundland*, 150.
63. Hiller, 'Dependence and Independence: Emergent Nationalism in Newfoundland', 267–9.
64. Byrne, 'The Confluence of Folklore and Literature in the Creation of a Newfoundland Mythology', 73.
65. Nairn, *The Break-Up of Britain*, 162.
66. Farley Mowat, perhaps the principal initiator of the Newfoundland cultural revival, did entertain secessionist views, but they were never on his part translated into serious politics.
67. O'Brien, 'Newfoundland and Canada, 1967–1978', 282.
68. Young, *Our Place in Canada*, 26.
69. In e.g. Gwyn, 'The Newfoundland Renaissance'.

70. Smallwood himself subscribed to cultural nationalism. He is perhaps best described as a unionist nationalist of much the same type as Walter Scott. This becomes clear when reading his *The Book of Newfoundland*, for which he wrote many of the chapters. Both these men managed to reconcile affection for their country's culture and heritage with their rational appreciation of modernisation and political and economic union.

71. Hiller, 'Dependence and Independence: Emergent Nationalism in Newfoundland', 268; Overton, 'Towards a Critical Analysis of Neo-Nationalism in Newfoundland', 237

72. Byrne, 'The Confluence of Folklore and Literature in the Creation of a Newfoundland Mythology', 74.

73. Byrne, 'The Confluence of Folklore and Literature in the Creation of a Newfoundland Mythology', 74.

74. O'Flaherty, 'Newfoundland, Writing in', 798.

75. His satirical short story 'The Quick and the Dead' is rich on the dry wit with which he illustrates outport life.

76. As illustrated by James Overton, Horwood's relationship with what he at one point referred to as Newfoundland's 'peasant culture' was complex. After being an unapologetic cultural nationalist in his early years, he would later, in the 1950s, declare that Newfoundland had little in terms of cultural heritage worth preserving; only then, in the 1960s, with Mowat, to rail against the destruction of a distinct Newfoundland culture by encroaching American cultural imperialism (Overton, 'Sparking a Cultural Revolution', 190–3).

77. Jackson, *Surviving Confederation*, 3–4; Jackson is nevertheless guilty of much the same kind of romantic nostalgia when he explains the true nature of outport life: '[T]he sea is in our blood . . . The Newfoundland outport is . . . the disgorging of the limitless bounty of the sea from longliners tied up alongside wharves and premises, and on the slopes behind, the typical circle of fences and simple salt-box houses. . .'. (Jackson *Surviving Confederation*, 11–12). The real issue for Jackson is the fashion in which Newfoundland culture is best protected from assimilation into Canadian culture: through preservation and celebration, or through radically engaging with it as a way of life.

78. Jackson, *Surviving Confederation*, 29, 30.

79. Strong, *Acts of Brief Authority*, 127–9.

80. Strong, *Acts of Brief Authority*, 168.

81. It would be a futile exercise to list the exact periods when this can be said to have been the case. In many situations the two also remained entangled, as was the case with Premier Joey Smallwood's attack on the International Woodworkers of America in the late 1950s, which was legitimised as a defence of Newfoundland tradition.

82. Political nationalism can also be argued to have caused the establishment of the short-lived United Newfoundland Party in 1959 (Calhoun, 'The National Identity of Newfoundlanders', 121).

83. Blake, *Canadians at Last*, 70.

84. Throne Speech, 30 November 1966.

85. Throne Speech, 24 February 1969.
86. Throne Speech, 18 February 1970.
87. Throne Speech, 18 February 1970.
88. Rawlyk et al., *Regionalism in Canada*, 102.
89. Throne Speech, 1 March 1972.
90. Throne Speech, 1 March 1972.
91. See e.g. 'Speech From the Throne', 19 April 1972, and 'Speech From the Throne', 19 November 1975.
92. *Daily News*, 'Happy Birthday, Newfoundland!', 1 April 1974.
93. Paine, 'The Making of Peckford and the "New" Newfoundland', 5.
94. Overton, 'Towards a Critical Analysis of Neo-Nationalism in Newfoundland', 226, 232.
95. Progressive Conservative Party, 'The Way We Want to Grow'.
96. Data Laboratories, 'Report of a Special Survey of Newfoundlanders' Attitudes Towards Confederation with Canada', 11.
97. See e.g. *Daily News*, 'He Didn't Say It!!', 11 February 1981; 'He's No Separatist!', 18 October 1983.
98. Throne Speech, 12 July 1979, 2, 9.
99. Throne Speech, 25 April 1985, 27.
100. Data Laboratories, 'Report of a Special Survey of Newfoundlanders' Attitudes Towards Confederation with Canada', 4, 5.
101. Throne Speech, 12 July 1979, 1.
102. Hiller, 'Dependence and Independence: Emergent Nationalism in Newfoundland', 268. Although the most important trend, this was not the nature of all Newfoundland political nationalism. The unsuccessful Party for an Independent Newfoundland chose to abandon Newfoundland culture as an argument in itself, and explicitly stated the attainment of control of natural resources as the only reason for the existence of the party (Warren, 'Newfoundland Separatism', 19).
103. Pollard, 'Newfoundland: Resisting Dependency', 85.
104. Graesser, 'The Newfoundland 1982 Election Study', Table 7.
105. Newfoundland ranked number one in Canada with regard to real per capita gross general expenditure from 1962 to 1972, but last or second to last in Canada with regard to real per capita revenue from own sources from 1957 to 1972 (Simeon and Miller, 'Regional Variations in Public Policy', 247, 250).
106. Pollard, 'Newfoundland: Resisting Dependency', 84–5.
107. Paine, 'The Making of Peckford and the "New" Newfoundland', 1981b, 1.
108. The Liberal Trudeau government was back in power in Ottawa, but in the Newfoundland provincial elections the Liberals won only 8 seats. The PCs won the remaining 44.
109. Smallwood allegedly coined the phrase, confidently encouraging Newfoundland fishermen to leave their traditional jobs in the fisheries to engage in other, more modern industries.
110. From 1954 the Centralization Program, from 1965 to 1970 the Household Resettlement Program.

111. Graesser, 'The Newfoundland 1982 Election Study', Table 7, 5.

112. *Daily News,* 'JRS: The Tide Has Gone Out', 26 June 1968.

113. Hiller, 'Dependence and Independence: Emergent Nationalism in Newfoundland', 268.

114. Overton, 'Towards a Critical Analysis of Neo-Nationalism in Newfoundland', 236–41.

115. House, 'The Mouse That Roars', 185, 187.

116. Peckford, *The Past in the Present,* 79.

117. Simeon and Elkins, 'Conclusion: Province, Nation, Country and Confederation', 298.

118. Throne Speech, 12 July 1979, 9.

119. Throne Speech, 10 May 1982, 8–12

120. Throne Speech, 25 April 1985.

121. Throne Speech, 10 May 1982.

122. Marshall quoted in Pollard, 'Newfoundland: Resisting Dependency', 86.

123. Throne Speech, 12 May 1982, 4.

124. Hiller, 'Dependence and Independence: Emergent Nationalism in Newfoundland', 263.

125. Brown, 'Sea-Change in Newfoundland: From Peckford to Wells', 204.

126. Paine, *Ayatollahs and Turkey Trots: Political Rhetoric in the New Newfoundland,* 3.

127. Jackson, *Surviving Confederation,* 83.

128. Lawton, 'Contrary Agendas: Political Culture and Economic Development Policies in Newfoundland', 96.

129. Quoted in Paine, 'Ayatollahs and Turkey Trots: Political Rhetoric in the New Newfoundland', 3.

130. Quoted in Calhoun, 'The National Identity of Newfoundlanders', 114.

131. *Daily News,* 'Peckford Breeding Separatist PCs!', 19 October 1983.

132. Liberal Party of Newfoundland and Labrador, 'Campaign '89: Policy Manual.'

133. For an account of the rise and decline of PIN, see *Daily News,* 'Otherwise PIN will fold!', 19 October 1983; *Evening Telegram,* 'Independent Newfoundland goal of new political party', 19 October 1983; *Daily News,* 'Separatist move about to collapse', 15 March 1984.

134. O'Brien, 'Newfoundland and Canada, 1967–1978', 330.

135. Throne Speech, 12 July 1979, 1–2.

136. Throne Speech, 10 May 1982, 1–6.

137. Throne Speech, 12 March 1984.

138. Throne Speech, 25 April 1985, 2.

139. Clyde Wells was a long-standing centralist. He had represented the Trudeau government in a Newfoundland Supreme Court case in 1980, arguing that federal government did not need the consent of the provinces, but was free to unilaterally patriate the constitution (*Evening Telegram,* 'Ottawa Says Provinces' Claims Not Justified', 13 February 1981).

140. Throne Speech, 25 May 1989, 1.

141. Throne Speech, 25 May 1989, 14.

142. The emphasis on resource development was also changed from oil and gas to fisheries.
143. Throne Speech, 25 May 1989, 10; emphasis added.
144. Throne Speech, 25 May 1989, 12, 14.
145. Government of Newfoundland, 'News Release'.
146. Government of Newfoundland, 'News Release'.
147. Young, *Our Place in Canada*.
148. Fossum, *Oil, the State and Federalism*, 205.
149. Summers, 'Resource Politics and Regime Change in the Federal Era', 24.
150. Throne Speech, 12 July 1979, 7.
151. Peckford, *The Past in the Present*, 61.
152. House, *The Challenge of Oil*, 44.
153. House, *The Challenge of Oil*, 61.
154. Graesser, 'The 1989 Newfoundland Provincial Election', 4–5.
155. Joey Smallwood would fly the Union flag at half-mast, protesting John Diefenbaker's stand on Newfoundland's Terms of Union. Similarly, in 1982, during negotiations with Pierre Trudeau over oil royalties, Brian Peckford ordered a day of mourning, and the Maple Leaf to be flown at half-mast.
156. CBC, 'Crowd Rallies behind Williams on Equalization', 11 May 2007.
157. Köhler, 'Go Ahead, Take Your Best Shot', 20.

CHAPTER SIX: IMAGES OF SELF AND OTHER IN SCOTTISH NEWSPAPERS

1. A note on data collection: articles have been selected via the use of indexes on the basis of expected importance of events covered – cf. focal points developed in previous chapters. Included in the Scottish data set are the *Scotsman*: 50 editorials, 21 front pages and other articles; *Glasgow Herald*: 62 editorials, 26 front pages and other articles.
2. *Scotsman*, 27 January 1968.
3. *Scotsman*, 12 January 1968.
4. *Scotsman*, 1 November 1973.
5. *Scotsman*, 2 November 1973.
6. *Scotsman*, 1 March 1979.
7. *Scotsman*, 3 November 1967.
8. *Scotsman*, 8 November 1967; 19 October 1973.
9. *Scotsman*, 17 January 1968.
10. *Scotsman*, 11 February 1974, I.
11. *Scotsman*, 3 November 1967.
12. *Scotsman*, 17 March 1972.
13. *Scotsman*, 19 January 1968, II.
14. *Scotsman*, 21 May 1968.
15. *Scotsman*, 20 March 1968, II.
16. *Scotsman*, 12 February 1974.
17. *Scotsman*, 19 January 1968, II.
18. *Scotsman*, 19 January 1968, I.

19. *Scotsman*, 21 May 1968.
20. *Scotsman*, 2 November 1973.
21. *Scotsman*, 16 March 1972.
22. *Scotsman*, 2 October 1968; 21 May 1968.
23. *Scotsman*, 1 November 1973.
24. *Scotsman*, 12 February 1974; 15 February 1974.
25. *Scotsman*, 7 June 1975.
26. *Scotsman*, 1 March 1979.
27. *Scotsman*, 3 November 1967.
28. *Scotsman*, 3 November 1967, front page.
29. *Scotsman*, 12 October 1974, II.
30. *Scotsman*, 5 March 1979.
31. *Scotsman*, 9 May 1968.
32. *Scotsman*, 5 May 1979.
33. *Scotsman*, 7 November 1967.
34. *Scotsman*, 20 May 1968.
35. *Scotsman*, 11 March 1974.
36. *Scotsman*, 11 March 1974.
37. *Scotsman*, 12 October 1974, II.
38. *Scotsman*, 3 March 1979.
39. *Scotsman*, 1 March 1979.
40. *Scotsman*, 3 March 1979.
41. In 1968 the *Scotsman* even published its own booklet, *How Scotland Should be Governed*, advocating devolution. The front page illustration is one of the British Isles divided into four regions: England, Wales, Northern Ireland and Scotland. The first print sold out within two weeks, and a second print had to be made to accommodate the demand.
42. *Scotsman*, 12 October 1974, II.
43. *Scotsman*, 3 March 1979.
44. *Scotsman*, 5 March 1979.
45. *Scotsman*, 4 February 1989.
46. *Scotsman*, 14 July 1988.
47. *Scotsman*, 31 March 1989.
48. *Scotsman*, 16 November 1988.
49. *Scotsman*, 11 March 1982.
50. *Scotsman*, 12 March 1987.
51. *Scotsman*, 8 December 1986.
52. *Scotsman*, 12 November 1988.
53. *Scotsman*, 4 February 1989.
54. *Glasgow Herald*, 1 March 1968.
55. *Glasgow Herald*, 7 July 1972, II.
56. *Glasgow Herald*, 17 March 1967.
57. *Glasgow Herald*, 1 March 1968.
58. *Glasgow Herald*, 2 January 1973.
59. *Glasgow Herald*, 5 June 1975.

60. *Glasgow Herald*, 3 May 1979.
61. *Glasgow Herald*, 4 November 1967.
62. *Glasgow Herald*, 8 October 1971.
63. *Glasgow Herald*, 21 July 1972.
64. *Glasgow Herald*, 2 January 1973.
65. *Glasgow Herald*, 12 February 1979.
66. *Glasgow Herald*, 3 May 1979.
67. *Glasgow Herald*, 15 February 1972.
68. *Glasgow Herald*, 1 November 1973.
69. *Glasgow Herald*, 4 May 1979.
70. *Glasgow Herald*, 10 October 1974.
71. *Glasgow Herald*, 17 March 1967.
72. Smith, *Paper Lions*, 68.
73. *Glasgow Herald*, 18 October 1973.
74. *Glasgow Herald*, 4 May 1973.
75. *Glasgow Herald*, 3 November 1967.
76. *Glasgow Herald*, 14 March 1974.
77. *Glasgow Herald*, 17 March 1967.
78. *Glasgow Herald*, 13 January 1968, II.
79. *Glasgow Herald*, 1 March 1968.
80. *Glasgow Herald*, 1 March 1968.
81. *Glasgow Herald*, 18 October 1973.
82. *Glasgow Herald*, 1 November 1973.
83. *Glasgow Herald*, 11 March 1974.
84. *Glasgow Herald*, 1 November 1973; emphases added.
85. *Glasgow Herald*, 15 February 1974.
86. *Glasgow Herald*, 14 March 1974.
87. *Glasgow Herald*, 8 October 1974.
88. *Glasgow Herald*, 5 June 1975.
89. *Glasgow Herald*, 7 June 1975.
90. *Glasgow Herald*, 12 October 1974, II.
91. *Glasgow Herald*, 12 February 1979, I.
92. *Glasgow Herald*, 12 February 1979, I.
93. *Glasgow Herald*, 1 March 1979.
94. *Glasgow Herald*, 25 September 1980, front page.
95. *Glasgow Herald*, 31 May 1980.
96. *Glasgow Herald*, 14 July 1988.
97. *Glasgow Herald*, 12 November 1988.
98. *Glasgow Herald*, 21 February 1981.
99. *Glasgow Herald*, 11 March 1982.
100. *Glasgow Herald*, 18 September 1982.
101. *Glasgow Herald*, 31 March 1989.
102. *Glasgow Herald*, 21 February 1981.
103. *Glasgow Herald*, 18 August 1986.
104. *Glasgow Herald*, 11 November 1988.

CHAPTER SEVEN: IMAGES OF SELF AND OTHER IN
NEWFOUNDLAND NEWSPAPERS

1. Another note on data collection: articles have been selected via the use of indexes on the basis of expected importance of events covered – cf. focal points developed in previous chapters. Included in the Newfoundland data set are: *Daily News*: 77 editorials, 13 front pages; *Evening Telegram*: 102 editorials, 22 front pages and other articles.
2. *Daily News*, 1 April 1974.
3. *Daily News*, 6 January 1967.
4. *Daily News*, 7 February 1967, II.
5. *Daily News*, 21 May 1980.
6. *Daily News*, 24 June 1980.
7. *Daily News*, 31 October 1972.
8. *Daily News*, 12 November 1980.
9. *Daily News*, 29 March 1974.
10. *Daily News*, 31 March 1967.
11. *Daily News*, 3 April 1967.
12. *Daily News*, 31 March 1969.
13. *Daily News*, 28 January 1971.
14. *Daily News*, 8 March 1984; 16 March 1984; 23 March 1984.
15. *Daily News*, 3 April 1967.
16. *Daily News*, 29 March 1974.
17. *Daily News*, 31 March 1969.
18. *Daily News*, 29 September 1969.
19. *Daily News*, 5 November 1980; 5 July 1977.
20. *Daily News*, 6 February 1968.
21. *Daily News*, 30 October 1980.
22. *Daily News*, 8 September 1967.
23. *Daily News*, 11 June 1969, II.
24. *Daily News*, 25 October 1977.
25. *Daily News*, 30 October 1980.
26. *Daily News*, 1 April 1974.
27. *Daily News*, 15 November 1977.
28. *Daily News*, 30 October 1980; 27 February 1981.
29. *Daily News*, 10 March 1984.
30. *Daily News*, 4 June 1984.
31. *Daily News*, 6 January 1967.
32. *Daily News*, 19 February 1980.
33. *Daily News*, 20 April 1980.
34. *Daily News*, 19 February 1980; 30 October 1980.
35. *Daily News*, 7 February 1967, II; 10 August 1967.
36. *Daily News*, 8 June 1970.
37. *Daily News*, 8 July 1971.
38. *Daily News*, 20 October 1971.
39. *Daily News*, 24 May 1973.

40. *Daily News*, 17 June 1975.
41. *Daily News*, 18 June 1979.
42. *Daily News*, 20 June 1979.
43. *Daily News*, 16 July 1979.
44. *Daily News*, 29 October 1980.
45. *Daily News*, 10 March 1984.
46. *Daily News*, 16 March 1984.
47. *Evening Telegram*, 30 June 1967, I.
48. *Evening Telegram*, 7 July 1967.
49. *Evening Telegram*, 5 March 1973.
50. *Evening Telegram*, 30 March 1974.
51. *Evening Telegram*, 30 June 1967, II; 7 July 1967.
52. *Evening Telegram*, 4 May 1977, I.
53. *Evening Telegram*, 14 December 1979.
54. *Evening Telegram*, 1 February 1973.
55. *Evening Telegram*, 29 February 1972.
56. *Evening Telegram*, 1 February 1973.
57. *Evening Telegram*, 22 January 1979.
58. *Evening Telegram*, 16 December 1968, II.
59. *Evening Telegram*, 20 January 1979; 22 January 1979.
60. *Evening Telegram*, 28 March 1977.
61. *Evening Telegram*, 23 April 1979.
62. *Evening Telegram*, 4 May 1977, II.
63. *Evening Telegram*, 1 July 1968; 31 March 1979.
64. *Evening Telegram*, 1 February 1973.
65. *Evening Telegram*, 1 July 1968.
66. *Evening Telegram*, 28 March 1977.
67. *Evening Telegram*, 23 May 1979.
68. *Evening Telegram*, 9 October 1967, I.
69. *Evening Telegram*, 12 February 1969.
70. *Evening Telegram*, 30 October 1971.
71. *Evening Telegram*, 19 March 1979; 27 March 1979.
72. *Evening Telegram*, 25 June 1980, front page.
73. *Evening Telegram*, 3 April 1981.
74. *Daily News*, 29 October 1980.
75. *Evening Telegram*, 19 June 1979.
76. *Evening Telegram*, 7 June 1980.
77. *Evening Telegram*, 3 October 1980.
78. *Evening Telegram*, 12 February 1985.
79. *Evening Telegram*, 31 March 1989.
80. *Evening Telegram*, 12 November 1980.
81. *Evening Telegram*, 18 September 1979.
82. *Evening Telegram*, 9 March 1984.
83. *Evening Telegram*, 7 April 1990.
84. *Evening Telegram*, 16 June 1990.

85. *Evening Telegram,* 7 May 1981.
86. *Evening Telegram,* 31 March 1989.
87. *Daily News,* 30 October 1980; *Evening Telegram* 29 October 1980.
88. *Evening Telegram,* 7 June 1980.
89. *Evening Telegram,* 13 July 1979.
90. *Evening Telegram,* 15 April 1981.
91. *Evening Telegram,* 7 May 1981.
92. *Evening Telegram,* 7 April 1982.
93. *Evening Telegram,* 9 March 1984.
94. *Evening Telegram,* 12 February 1985.
95. *Evening Telegram,* 19 July 1988.
96. *Evening Telegram,* 23 January 1989.
97. *Evening Telegram,* 17 April 1982.
98. *Evening Telegram,* 18 June 1990.
99. *Evening Telegram,* 3 April 1981.
100. *Evening Telegram,* 22 June 1990.
101. *Evening Telegram,* 29 May 1973.
102. *Evening Telegram,* 16 June 1990.
103. *Evening Telegram,* 24 June 1990.
104. *Evening Telegram,* 26 May 1989.
105. *Evening Telegram,* 7 May 1981.
106. *Evening Telegram,* 7 May 1981.
107. *Evening Telegram,* 7 April 1982.
108. *Evening Telegram,* 20 October 1983.
109. *Evening Telegram,* 14 June 1984; 21 April 1989.
110. *Evening Telegram,* 19 April 1989.

CHAPTER EIGHT: THE NATURE OF AUTONOMISM IN SCOTLAND
AND NEWFOUNDLAND

1. From the beginning of the period studied here to 1973, the Canadian economy experienced a boom, followed by recession in the period from 1973 to 1982. From 1982 to 1988 the economy recovered, only to enter recession again from 1989 to 1997.
2. Judging entirely by the continued gap between earnings, this is an argument with some validity. According to Statistics Canada, by 2005 the Newfoundland after-tax family income stood at $52,275, compared to the Canadian average of $67,567 (Statistics Canada, 2008).
3. *Herald,* 1 October 2004.
4. *Telegram,* 24 December 2004.

Bibliography

Acton, Lord John E. E. D. 1996. Nationality. In *Mapping the Nation*, ed. Gopal Balakrishnan, 17–39. London: New Left Review/Verso. Original edition, *The Home and Foreign Review* no. 1, July 1862.

Allen, Kieran. 2000. *The Celtic Tiger? The Myth of Social Partnership*. Manchester: Manchester University Press.

Anderson, Benedict. 1991. *Imagined Communities: Reflections on the Origin and Spread of Nationalism*. 2nd edn. London: Verso.

——— . 1996. Introduction. In *Mapping the Nation*, ed. Gopal Balakrishnan, 1–17. London: New Left Review/Verso.

Ashcroft, Bill, Gareth Griffiths and Helen Tiffin. 1989. *The Empire Writes Back: Theory and Practice in Post-Colonial Literatures*. London and New York: Routledge.

Balakrishnan, Gopal. 1996. The National Imagination. In *Mapping the Nation*, ed. Gopal Balakrishnan, 198–214. London: New Left Review/Verso. Original edition, *New Left Review* no. 211, May–June 1995.

Bell, Daniel. 1976. *The Cultural Contradictions of Capitalism*. New York: Basic Books.

Beveridge, Craig and Ronald Turnbull. 1989. *The Eclipse of Scottish Culture: Inferiorism and the Intellectuals*. Edinburgh: Polygon.

Billig, Michael. 1995. *Banal Nationalism*. London: Sage.

Blake, Raymond B. 2004. *Canadians at Last: Canada Integrates Newfoundland as a Province*. Toronto: University of Toronto Press.

Bond, Ross. 2000. Squaring the Circles: Demonstrating and Explaining the Political 'Non-Alignment' of Scottish National Identity. *Scottish Affairs* no. 32 (Summer): 15–35.

Boolsen, Merete Watt. 1991. *Forskningsværktøj, en indføring i sociologisk metode og statistik*. Næstved: Kontekst.

Brand, Jack. 1978. *The National Movement in Scotland*. London: Routledge & Kegan Paul.

Breuilly, John. 1993. *Nationalism and the State*. 2nd edn. Manchester: Manchester University Press.

Brookes, Chris. 1997. Nation or Notion?, *East of Canada: The Story of Newfoundland* [television documentary]. St John's: CBC Newfoundland.

Brown, Douglas M. 1990. Sea-Change in Newfoundland: From Peckford to Wells. In *Canada: The State of the Federation 1990*, ed. Ronald L. Watts and Douglas M. Brown, 199–230. Kingston, Ontario: Queen's University, Institute of Intergovernmental Relations.

Brown, Alice, David McCrone, and Lindsay Paterson. 1998. *Politics and Society in Scotland*. 2nd edn. London: Macmillan.

Brubaker, Rogers. 1996. *Nationalism Reframed: Nationhood and the National Question in the New Europe*. Cambridge: Cambridge University Press.

Burns, Robert. 1996. *The Complete Illustrated Poems, Songs and Ballads*, ed. Samuel Carr, 141–2. London: Lomond Books. Original edition, 1785.

Byrne, Pat. 1998. The Confluence of Folklore and Literature in the Creation of a Newfoundland Mythology within the Canadian Context. In *Canada and the Nordic Countries in Times of Reorientation: Culture & Politics*, ed. Jørn Carlsen, The Nordic Association for Canadian Studies Text Series, vol. 13, 55–77. Aarhus: Aarhus University [conference publication].

Calhoun, John H. 1970. The National Identity of Newfoundlanders. PhD thesis, University of Pittsburgh.

Campaign for a Scottish Assembly. 1988. A Claim of Right for Scotland. Edinburgh: Campaign for a Scottish Assembly.

Campbell, Terry and G. A. Rawlyk. 1979. The Historical Framework of Newfoundland and Confederation. In *The Atlantic Provinces and the Problems of Confederation*, ed. G. A. Rawlyk, 48–81. St John's: Breakwater.

Caughie, John. Scottish Television: What Would It Look Like? In *Scotch Reels: Scotland in Cinema and Television*, ed. Colin McArthur, 112–22. London: British Film Institute.

CBC. 2007. [Online]. Crowd rallies behind Williams on equalization [retrieved 11 May 2007]. URL: www.cbc.ca/canada/newfoundland-labrador/story/2007/05/11/rally-williams.html

Cencrastus. 1982. Revaluation. *Cencrastus* 10 (Autumn): 3.

Cohen, Anthony P. 1999. Being Scottish? On the Problem of the Objective Correlative. In *The Boundaries of Understanding: Essays in Honour of Malcolm Anderson*, ed. Eberhard Bort and Russell Keat, 209–28. Edinburgh: University of Edinburgh, International Social Sciences Institute.

Connell, Ian and Adam Mills. 1985. Text, Discourse and Mass Communication. In *Discourse and Communication: New Approaches to the Analysis of Mass Media Discourse and Communication*, ed. Teun A. van Dijk, 26–43. Berlin: de Gruyter.

Connor, Walker. 1990. When is a Nation? *Ethnic and Racial Studies* 13, no. 1 (January): 92–103.

——. 1996. Beyond Reason: The Nature of the Ethnonational Bond. In *Ethnicity*, ed. John Hutchinson and Anthony D. Smith, 69–75. Oxford: Oxford University Press.

Conrad, Margaret. 2002. Mistaken Identities? Newfoundland and Labrador in the Atlantic Region. *Newfoundland Studies* 18, no. 2, 169–74.

Corporate Research Associates. 1999. Atlantic Omnibus Survey: 1st Quarter 1999, Commissioned Results. N.p.: Corporate Research Associates and CBC (Canadian Broadcasting Corporation).

Cowan, Helen I. 1978. British Immigration Before Confederation, *The Canadian Historical Association Booklets*, no. 22. Ottawa: Canadian Historical Association.

Craig, Cairns. 1982. Myths Against History: Tartanry and Kailyard in 19th-Century Scottish Literature. In *Scotch Reels: Scotland in Cinema and Television*, ed. Colin McArthur, 7–15. London: British Film Institute.

——. 1994. Series Preface. In *Paper Lions: The Scottish Press and National Identity*, Maurice Smith, vi–vii. Edinburgh: Polygon.

——. 1999. Interview by author, 3 June 1999, Edinburgh. Tape recording.

Craig, Gerald M., ed. 1963. *Lord Durham's Report: An Abridgement of Report on the Affairs of British North America*. Toronto: McClelland and Stewart, 1963.

Daily News. 26 June 1968. 'JRS: The Tide Has Gone Out'.

——. 1 April 1974. 'Happy Birthday, Newfoundland!'

——. 11 February 1981. 'He Didn't Say It!!'

———. 18 October 1983. 'He's No Separatist!'
———. 19 October 1983a. 'Peckford Breeding Separatist PCs!'
———. 19 October 1983b. 'Quebec, Newfoundland Politics "Almost Identical":
    Neary'.
———. 19 October 1983c. 'Otherwise PIN Will Fold!'
———. 15 March 1984. 'Separatist Move about to Collapse'.
Data Laboratories. 1979. Report of a Special Survey of Newfoundlanders' Attitudes
    Towards Confederation with Canada. N.p.: Data Laboratories Research
    Consultants.
Dickson, Tony. 1989. Scotland is Different, OK? In *The Making of Scotland:
    Nation, Culture and Social Change*, ed. David McCrone, Stephen Kendrick and
    Pat Straw, 53–69. Edinburgh: Edinburgh University Press.
Donaldson, Gordon. 1993. *Scotland: The Shaping of a Nation*. 2nd edn. Nairn:
    David St. John Thomas.
Doody, Richard. 2001. The Dominion of Newfoundland. From Oldest Colony to
    Newest Province [online]. *The World at War*. [retrieved 23 December 2003].
    URL: worldatwar.net/article/newfoundland/.
Edelman, Murray. 1995. *From Art to Politics: How Artistic Creations Shape
    Political Conceptions*. Chicago: University of Chicago Press.
Edensor, Tim. 1997. Reading Braveheart: Representing and Contesting Scottish
    Identity. *Scottish Affairs* no. 21 (Autumn): 135–58.
Ellison, Suzanne. 1997. *Historical Directory of Newfoundland and Labrador
    Newspapers 1806–1996*. St John's: Queen Elizabeth II Library, Memorial
    University of Newfoundland.
Encyclopedia of Newfoundland and Labrador. 1991. Vol. 3, ed. Cyril F. Poole.
    St John's: Harry Cuff.
Eriksen, Thomas Hylland. 1993. *Ethnicity and Nationalism: Anthropological
    Perspectives*. London: Pluto Press.
(Evening) Telegram, 21 April 1906.
———. 19 June 1979. 'Now Peckford is Ready to Lead into the 80s'.
———. 13 February 1981. 'Ottawa Says Provinces' Claims not Justified'.
———. 19 October 1983. 'Independent Newfoundland Goal of New Political Party'.
———. 18 January 1985. 'Government Doesn't Consider Newfoundland Atlantic
    Province'.
———. 2000. No headline [online]. N.p.: *Telegram* [retrieved 17 March 2000]. URL:
    www.thetelegram.com/
———. 17 June 2000. 'DFO Abandons the Adjacency Principle'.
———. 27 October 2000. 'Day Takes Stock of Newfoundland'.
———. 24 December 2004. 'Failed Talks Lead to Big Chill'
Fairclough, Norman, and Ruth Wodak. 1997. Critical Discourse Analysis. In *Discourse
    as Social Interaction*, ed. Teun A. van Dijk, 258–84. London: Sage.
FitzGerald, John Edward. 1998. 'The True Father of Confederation'?: Archbishop
    E.P. Roche, Term 17, and Newfoundland's Confederation with Canada.
    Newfoundland and Labrador Studies 14, no. 2: 188–219.
Fossum, John Erik. 1997. *Oil, the State and Federalism: The Rise and Demise of
    Petro-Canada as a Statist Impulse*. Toronto: University of Toronto Press.
Fowler, Roger. 1991. *Language in the News: Discourse and Ideology in the Press*.
    London: Routledge.
Francis, Daniel. 1997. *National Dreams: Myth, Memory and Canadian History*.
    Vancouver: Arsenal Pulp Press.
Gellner, Ernest. 1983. *Nations and Nationalism*. Oxford: Blackwell.
———. 1994. Nationalism and Modernization. In *Nationalism*, eds John Hutchinson
    and Anthony D. Smith, 55–63. Oxford: Oxford University Press. Original
    edition, London: Weidenfeld and Nicholson, 1964.

——. 1996. The Coming of Nationalism and its Interpretation: The Myths of Nation and Class. In *Mapping the Nation*, ed. Gopal Balakrishnan, 98–145. London: New Left Review/Verso.

Gerbner, George. 1985. Mass Media Discourse: Message System Analysis as a Component of Cultural Indicators. In *Discourse and Communication: New Approaches to the Analysis of Mass Media Discourse and Communication*, ed. Teun A. van Dijk, 13–26. Berlin: de Gruyter.

Giddens, Anthony. 1998. *New Statesman*, 1 May.

Globe and Mail. 10 January 1998. 'Unemployment Rate Dips to Seven-Year Low.'

Government of Newfoundland and Labrador. 1994. *Historical Statistics of Newfoundland and Labrador*. St John's: Newfoundland Statistics Agency, November.

——. 1999. *1999 Budget Speech, Newfoundland and Labrador: 'Celebrating 50 Years'*. N.p.: Government of Newfoundland and Labrador, 22 March.

——. 2000. News Release [online]. N.p.: Government of Newfoundland and Labrador, 2000 [retrieved 16 October 2000]. URL: www.gov.nf.ca/releases/2000/exec/1016n04.htm.

Graesser, Mark W. 1982a. St. John's Political Attitude Survey. Department of Political Science, Memorial University of Newfoundland. March.

——. 1982b. The Newfoundland 1982 Election Study. Department of Political Science, Memorial University of Newfoundland. August.

——. 1991. The 1989 Newfoundland Provincial Election: A Case of Partisan Realignment? Department of Political Science, Memorial University of Newfoundland.

Gramsci, Antonio. 1991. *Fængelsoptegnelser i udvalg*, ed. Gert Sørensen, Copenhagen: Museum Tusculanums Forlag.

Greene, John P. 1999. *Between Damnation and Starvation. Priests and Merchants in Newfoundland Politics, 1745–1855*. Montreal: McGill-Queen's University Press.

Greenfeld, Liah. 1992. *Nationalism: Five Roads to Modernity*. Cambridge, Mass.: Harvard University Press.

Greenstein, Rachel. 1999. Perceptions of Audience and Political Coverage in the Scottish Press. Paper presented at the Department of Political Science, Edinburgh University, April.

Guibernau, Montserrat. 1999. *Nations without States: Political Communities in a Global Age*. Cambridge: Polity Press.

Gwyn, Sandra. 1976. The Newfoundland Renaissance. *Saturday Night* 91, no. 2: 38–45.

Habermas, Jürgen. 1971. *Strukturwandel der Öffentlichkeit. Untersuchungen zu einer Kategorie der bürgerlichen Gesellschaft*. 5th ed. Berlin: Neuwied. Original edition, 1962.

Hall, Stuart. 1987. Introduction to Media Studies at the Centre. In *Culture, Media, Language*, ed. Stuart Hall et al., 117–21. London: Hutchinson. Original edition, 1980.

Hamilton, Paul. 1999. The Scottish National Paradox: The Scottish National Party's Lack of Ethnic Character. *Canadian Review of Studies in Nationalism 26*, no. 1–2: 17–36.

Hartz, Louis. 1964. *The Founding of New Societies. Studies in the History of the United States, Latin America, South Africa, Canada and Australia*. San Diego: Harcourt Brace Jovanovich.

Harvie, Christopher. 1989. Scott and the Image of Scotland. In *Patriotism: The Making and Unmaking of British National Identity*. Vol. 2, *Minorities and Outsiders*, ed. Raphael Samuel, 173–92. London: Routledge.

——. 1991. Nationalism, Journalism and Cultural Politics. In *Nationalism in the Nineties*, ed. Tom Gallagher, 29–45. Edinburgh: Polygon.

258   Bibliography

—— . 1994. *Scotland and Nationalism: Scottish Society and Politics 1707–1994*. 2nd edn. London: Routledge.

—— . 2000. Industry, Identity and Chaos. *Scottish Affairs* no. 32 (Summer): 1–14.

Hauge, Hans. 1998. *Den danske kirke nationalt betragtet*. Frederiksberg: ANIS.

Hearn, Jonathan Scott. 1997. 'Scotland's Hidden Powers': History, Nation and Justice in the Scottish Autonomist Movement. PhD Thesis, City University of New York.

Hedetoft, Ulf. 1990. National identitet som kulturel og politisk kategori i Vesteuropa. In *War and Death as Touchstones of National Identity*. Papers on Languages and Intercultural Studies no. 14, Ulf Hedetoft, 99–123. Aalborg: The European Research Programme, Aalborg University.

—— . 1995. *Signs of Nations: Studies in the Political Semiotics of Self and Other in Contemporary European Nationalism*. Aldershot: Dartmouth.

Held, David, ed. 2003. *A Globalizing World?* 2nd edn. London: Routledge / Open University Press.

Herald. 2000. About the Herald [online]. N.p.: *Herald* [retrieved 17 March 2000]. URL: www.theherald.co.uk.

—— . 1 October 2004. 'Shortsighted SNP'.

Heywood, Andrew. 1994. *Political Ideas and Concepts: An Introduction*. Houndmills: MacMillan.

Hiller, Harry H. 1987. Dependence and Independence: Emergent Nationalism in Newfoundland. *Ethnic and Racial Studies* 10, no. 3 (July): 257–75.

Hobsbawm, Eric J. 1962. *The Age of Revolution: 1789–1848*. London: The New English Library, 1962.

—— . 1991. *Nations and Nationalism since 1780: Programme, Myth, Reality*. Cambridge: Cambridge University. Original edition, 1990.

Horowitz, Gad. 1968. *Canadian Labour in Politics*. Toronto: University of Toronto Press.

House, J. D. 1986a. The Mouse That Roars: New Directions in Canadian Political Economy – the Case of Newfoundland. In *Regionalism in Canada*, ed. Robert J. Brym, 161–96. Toronto: Irwin.

—— . 1986b. Oil And The North Atlantic Periphery: The Scottish Experience and the Prospects for Newfoundland. In *Contrary Winds: Essays on Newfoundland Society in Crisis*, ed. Rex Clark, 117–49. St. John's: Breakwater Books.

—— . 1998. *The Challenge of Oil: Newfoundland's Quest for Controlled Development*. Social and Economic Studies no. 30. St John's: Institute of Social and Economic Research, Memorial University of Newfoundland. Original edition, 1985.

Hroch, Miroslav. 1985. *Social Preconditions of National Revival in Europe: A Comparative Analysis of the Social Composition of Patriotic Groups among the Smaller European Nations*. Cambridge: Cambridge University Press.

—— . 1996. From National Movement to the Fully-formed Nation: The Nation-building Process in Europe. In *Mapping the Nation*, ed. Gopal Balakrishnan, 78–97. London: New Left Review/Verso.

Hutchinson, John. 1987. *The Dynamics of Cultural Nationalism: The Gaelic Revival and the Creation of the Irish Nation State*. London: Allen & Unwin.

Ignatieff, Michael. 1993. *Blood and Belonging*. London: BBC Books.

Jackson, F. L. 1986. *Surviving Confederation*. Rev. edn. St John's: Harry Cuff.

James, Paul. 1996. *Nation Formation: Towards a Theory of Abstract Community*. London: SAGE.

Jensen, Mogens Kjær. 1991. *Kvalitative metoder i anvendt samfundsforskning*. Copenhagen: Socialforskningsinstituttet.

Johnston, Richard. 1980. Federal and Provincial Voting: Contemporary Patterns and Historical Evolution. In *Small Worlds: Provinces and Parties in Canadian*

Political Life, ed. David J. Elkins and Richard Simeon, 131–78. Toronto: Methuen.

Jørgensen, Marianne Winther, and Louise Phillips. 1999. *Diskursanalyse som teori og metode*. Frederiksberg: Samfundslitteratur, Roskilde University.

Kapferer, Bruce. 1988. *Legends of People, Myths of State: Violence, Intolerance, and Political Culture in Sri Lanka and Australia*. Washington: Smithsonian Institution.

Keating, Michael. 1996. *Nations against the State: The New Politics of Nationalism in Quebec, Catalonia and Scotland*. Houndmills: Macmillan.

Kedourie, Elie. 1994. Dark Gods and their Rites. In *Nationalism*, ed. John Hutchinson and Anthony D. Smith, 205–9. Oxford: Oxford University Press. Original edition, London: Weidenfeld and Nicholson, 1971.

Kellas, James G. 1980. *Modern Scotland*. 2nd edn. London: Allen and Unwin.

Kerr, D.G.G. 1975. *Historical Atlas of Canada*. 3rd rev. edn. Don Mills, Ontario: Nelson.

Kornberg, Allan, William Mishler and Harold D. Clarke. 1982. *Representative Democracy in the Canadian Provinces*. Scarborough, Ontario: Prentice-Hall.

Köhler, Nicholas. 2006. 'Go Ahead, Take Your Best Shot'. *Maclean's* 31 July: 17–20.

Krejčí, Jaroslav, and Vítěslav Velímský. 1996. Ethnic and Political Nations in Europe. In *Ethnicity*, ed. John Hutchinson and Anthony D. Smith, 209–21. Oxford: Oxford University Press. Original edition, London: Croom Helm, 1981.

Labour Party. 1979. The Better Way for Scotland: The Labour Party Manifesto for Scotland 1979. Glasgow: The Labour Party in Scotland.

——. 1987. Scotland Will Win: Labour Manifesto, June 1987. Glasgow: The Labour Party, Scottish Council, June.

——. 1992. It's Time to Get Scotland Moving Again: It's Time for Labour. Glasgow: The Labour Party, April.

——. 1997. New Labour: Because Scotland Deserves Better. Glasgow: The Labour Party.

Laclau, Ernesto and Chantal Mouffe. 1985. *Hegemony and Socialist Strategy: Towards a Radical Democratic Politics*. London: Verso.

Laver, Ross. 1994. 'How We Differ'. *Maclean's*, 3 January: 8–11.

Lawton, William A. 1994. Contrary Agendas: Political Culture and Economic Development Policies in Newfoundland. PhD Thesis, University of Edinburgh.

Lenman, Bruce P. 1992. *Integration and Enlightenment: Scotland 1746–1832*. Edinburgh: Edinburgh University. Original edition, Arnold, 1981.

Liberal Party of Newfoundland and Labrador. 1989. Campaign '89: Policy Manual. N.p.: The Liberal Party of Newfoundland and Labrador.

Lynch, Michael. 1992. *Scotland: A New History*. 2nd edn. London: Pimlico.

MacInnes, John. 1992. The Press in Scotland. *Scottish Affairs* no. 1 (Autumn): 137–49.

MacLeod, Malcolm. 2003. *Connections: Newfoundland's Pre-confederation Links with Canada and the World*. St John's, NL: Creative Publishers.

Major, Kevin. 2001. *As Near to Heaven by Sea. A History of Newfoundland and Labrador*. Toronto: Penguin.

Marr, Andrew. 1992. *The Battle for Scotland*. London: Penguin.

Martin, Cabot. 1992. *No Fish and Our Lives: Some Survival Notes for Newfoundland*. St John's: Creative Publishers.

Matthews, Ralph. 1974. Perspectives on Recent Newfoundland Politics. *Journal of Canadian Studies* 9, no. 2 (May): 20–35.

Maxwell, Stephen. 1991. The Scottish Middle Class and the National Debate. In *Nationalism in the Nineties*, ed. Tom Gallagher, 126–51. Edinburgh: Polygon.

McArthur, Colin, ed. 1982. *Scotch Reels: Scotland in Cinema and Television*. London: British Film Institute.

McCann, Phillip. 1988. Culture, State Formation and the Invention of Tradition: Newfoundland 1832–1855. *Journal of Canadian Studies*, 23, nos. 1&2.

McCron, Robin. 1976. Changing Perspectives in the Study of Mass Media and Socialization. In *Mass Media and Socialization*, ed. James D. Halloran, 13–44. Leeds: International Association for Mass Communication Research.

McCrone, David. 1989. Representing Scotland: Culture and Nationalism. In *The Making of Scotland: Nation, Culture and Social Change*, ed. David McCrone, Stephen Kendrick and Pat Straw, 161–74. Edinburgh: Edinburgh University Press.

——. 1992. *Understanding Scotland: The Sociology of a Stateless Nation*. London: Routledge.

——. 1996. We're A' Jock Tamson's Bairns: Social Class in Twentieth-Century Scotland. In *Scotland in the 20th Century*, ed. T. M. Devine and R. J. Finlay, 102–21. Edinburgh: Edinburgh University.

——. 1998. *The Sociology of Nationalism: Tomorrow's Ancestors*. London: Routledge.

——. 1999. The Local and the Global: National Identity in the New Scotland. Paper presented as part of the *Colloque Annuel de Generation Québéc: 'Un Quebec ouvert sur le monde'*, Montreal, 24 April.

——. 2000. Opinion Polls in Scotland: May 1999–June 2000. *Scottish Affairs* no. 32 (Summer): 86–94.

McLuhan, Marshall. 1964. *Understanding Media: The Extensions of Man*. 2nd edn. New York: Mentor.

McNaught, Kenneth. 1988. *The Penguin History of Canada*. Rev. edn. London: Penguin.

McRae, Kenneth D. 1964. The Structure of Canadian History. In Louis Hartz, *The Founding of New Societies. Studies in the History of the United States, Latin America, South Africa, Canada and Australia*. San Diego: Harcourt Brace Jovanovich, 219–74.

Meech, Peter and Richard W. Kilborn. 1992. Media and Identity in a Stateless Nation: The Case of Scotland. *Media, Culture and Society* 14: 245–59.

Meinecke, Friedrich. 1928. *Weltbürgertum und Nationalstaat: Studien zur Genesis des deutschen Nationalstaates*. 7th edn. Munich.

Miller, William L., Bo Sarlvik, Ivor Crewe and Jim Alt. 1977. The Connection Between SNP Voting and the Demand for Scottish Self-Government. *European Journal of Political Research* no. 5: 83–102.

Mitchell, James. 1996. Scotland in the Union, 1945–1995: The Changing Nature of the Union State. In *Scotland in the 20th Century*, eds T. M. Devine and R. J. Finlay, 85–101. Edinburgh: Edinburgh University.

——. 1996. *Strategies for Self-Government*. Edinburgh: Polygon.

Mollins, Carl. 1990. 'An Uncertain Nation'. *Maclean's*, 1 January: 12–13.

Nairn, Tom. 1977. *The Break-Up of Britain: Crisis and Neo-Nationalism*. London: New Left Books.

——. 1997. *Faces of Nationalism: Janus Revisited*. London: Verso.

Neary, Peter. 1988. *Newfoundland in the North Atlantic World, 1929–1949*. Montreal: McGill-Queen's University Press.

——. 1999. Newfoundland's Union with Canada, 1949: Conspiracy or Choice? (1983). In *Atlantic Canada After Confederation. The Acadiensis Reader: Volume Two*, eds P.A. Buckner et al. 3rd edn. Fredericton: Acadiensis Press.

NLHW. 1997. [Online]. Newfoundland and Labrador Heritage Web Site [retrieved 29 March 2003]. URL: www.heritage.nf.ca/exploration/voluntary.html.

Noel, S. J. R. 1971. *Politics in Newfoundland*. Toronto: University of Toronto Press.

——. 1974. Post-Confederation Society and Politics. In *Perspectives on Newfoundland Society and Culture: Book of Readings*, ed. Maurice A. Sterns, 135–41. St John's: Memorial University of Newfoundland.

——. 2001. How do Consociational Systems Begin: Canada and Northern Ireland in Historical Perspective. In *Northern Ireland and the Divided World – Post-Agreement Northern Ireland in Comparative Perspective*, ed. John McGarry. Oxford: Oxford University Press.

Norrie, Kenneth, and Douglas Owram. 1996. *A History of the Canadian Economy*. 2nd edn. Toronto: Harcourt Brace.

O'Brien, Pat. 1979. Newfoundland and Canada, 1967–1978: The Newspaper Response. In *The Atlantic Provinces and the Problems of Confederation*, ed. G. A. Rawlyk, 282–333. N.p.: Breakwater.

O'Dea, Shane. 1994. Newfoundland: The Development of Culture on the Margin. *Newfoundland Studies* 10, no. 1: 73–81.

O'Flaherty, Patrick. 1979. *The Rock Observed: Studies in the Literature of Newfoundland*. Toronto: University of Toronto.

——. 1997. Newfoundland, Writing in. In *The Oxford Companion to Canadian Literature*. 2nd edn, ed. Eugene Benson and William Toye, 794–9. Toronto: Oxford University Press.

Old, Ian G. 2000. EEC Referendum 1975 [online]. N.p.: Scottish Politics Pages [retrieved 22 September 2000]. URL: www.alba.org.uk/.

Olorunsola, Victor A. 1972. *The Politics of Cultural Sub-Nationalism in Africa*. Garden City, N.Y.: Anchor Books.

Osmond, John. 1988. *The Divided Kingdom*. London: Constable.

Overton, D. J. B. 1992. Mass Media and Unemployment in Canada: The Politics and Economics of Stigma. In *Critical Studies of Canadian Mass Media*, ed. Marc Grenier, 29–46. Toronto: Butterworths.

Overton, James. 1979. Towards a Critical Analysis of Neo-Nationalism in Newfoundland. In *Underdevelopment and Social Movements in Atlantic Canada*, ed. Robert J. Brym and R. James Sacouman, 219–49. Toronto: New Hogtown.

——. 1986. Oil and Gas: The Rhetoric and Reality of Development in Newfoundland. In *Contrary Winds: Essays on Newfoundland Society in Crisis*, ed. Rex Clark, 150–75. St John's: Breakwater Books.

——. 2000. *Sparking a Cultural Revolution: Joey Smallwood, Farley Mowat, Harold Horwood and Newfoundland's Cultural Renaissance*. Unpublished manuscript. Memorial University of St John's.

Paine, Robert. 1981a. *Ayatollahs and Turkey Trots: Political Rhetoric in the New Newfoundland*. St John's: Breakwater.

——. 1981b. The Making of Peckford and the 'New' Newfoundland. Paper presented to the AASA, 27 March.

Palmer, Craig, and Peter Sinclair. 1997. *When the Fish Are Gone: Ecological Disaster and Fishers in Northwest Newfoundland*. Halifax: Fernwood Publishing.

Parti Québécois. 2000. Le projet souverainiste du gouvernement du Parti Québécois [online]. N.p.: Parti Quebecois, 1995. [retrieved 15 June 2000]. URL: www.premier.gouv.qc.ca/projet/ententef.htm.

Paterson, Lindsay. 1990. Are the Scottish Middle Class Going Native? *Radical Scotland* no. 45 (June/July): 10–11.

——. 1994. *The Autonomy of Modern Scotland*. Edinburgh: Edinburgh University Press.

——. 1996. Liberation or Control?: What are the Scottish Education Traditions of the Twentieth Century? In *Scotland in the 20th Century*, ed. T. M. Devine and R. J. Finlay, 230–49. Edinburgh: Edinburgh University Press.

Pattie, Charles, David Denver, James Mitchel and Hugh Bochel. 1998. The 1997 Scottish Referendum: an Analysis of the Results. *Scottish Affairs* no. 22 (Winter): 1–15.

Payne, Peter L. 1996. The Economy. In *Scotland in the 20th Century*, ed. T. M. Devine and R. J. Finlay, 13–45. Edinburgh: Edinburgh University Press.

Peckford, A. Brian. 1984. *The Past in the Present: A Personal Perspective on Newfoundland's Future*. St John's: Harry Cuff. Original edition, 1983.

Pollard, Bruce G. 1985. Newfoundland: Resisting Dependency. In *Canada: The State of the Federation 1985*, ed. Peter M. Leslie, 83–117. Kingston, Ontario: Queen's University, Institute of Intergovernmental Relations.

Progressive Conservative Party. 1979. The Way We Want to Grow: The Peckford Government's Program for the 80's. N.p.: Progressive Conservative Party of Newfoundland and Labrador.

Putnam, Hillary. 1994. *Words and Life*, ed. James Conant. Cambridge, Mass.: Harvard University Press.

Radical Scotland. 1991. Why This is the Final Issue. *Radical Scotland* no. 51 (June/July): 3.

Rankin, Ian. 2006. *Rebus's Scotland: A Personal Journey*. London: Orion.

Rawlyk, George A., Bruce W. Hodgins and Richard P. Bowles. 1979. *Regionalism in Canada: Flexible Federalism or Fractured Nation?* Scarborough, Ontario: Prentice-Hall.

Renan, Ernest. 1994. Qu'est-ce qu'une nation? In *Nationalism*, ed. John Hutchinson and Anthony D. Smith, 17–18. Oxford: Oxford University Press. Original edition, Paris: Calmann-Levy, 1882.

Report on Business. 11 October 1999. 'The Rock's on a Roll'.

Review of Scottish Culture Group. 1997. Scottish Culture and the Curriculum. Conclusion [part 4]. Edinburgh: Scottish Consultative Committee on the Curriculum.

Ritzer, George. 1993. *The McDonaldization of Society: An Investigation into the Changing Character of Contemporary Social Life*. Thousand Oaks, Calif.: Pine Forge.

Rothney, Gordon O. 1973. The Denominational Basis of Representation in the Newfoundland Assembly. In *Perspectives on Newfoundland Society and Culture*, ed. Maurice A. Sterns, 149–53. St John's: Memorial University of Newfoundland.

Rönnquist, Ralf. 1990. *Historia och nationalitet: Skotsk etno-territorialitet i ett historiskt perspektiv*. Lund: Lund University.

Scottish Constitutional Convention. 1995. *Scotland's Parliament. Scotland's Right*. Edinburgh: Scottish Constitutional Convention.

Scott, Paul H. 1998. *Still in Bed with an Elephant*. Rev. edn. Edinburgh: The Saltire Society.

Scottish Office. 1997. Scotland's Parliament – Your Choice. Edinburgh: Scottish Office.

Scottish Parliament. 1999. Presiding Officer Hits out at Misleading and Untrue Press Coverage. Parliamentary News Release, 6 September.

Scottish Sun. 14 April 2000. Title banner.

Sevaldsen, Jørgen, and Ole Vadmand. 1997. *Contemporary British Society*. 4th edn. Copenhagen: Academic Press.

Sider, Gerald M. 1986. *Culture and Class in Anthropology and History: A Newfoundland Illustration*. Cambridge: Cambridge University Press.

Siegel, Arthur. 1983. *Politics and the Media in Canada*. Toronto: McGraw-Hill Ryerson.

Simeon, Richard, and David J. Elkins. 1980. Conclusion: Province, Nation, Country and Confederation. In *Small Worlds: Provinces and Parties in Canadian Political Life*, ed. David J. Elkins and Richard Simeon, 285–312. Toronto: Methuen.

Simeon, Richard, and E. Robert Miller. 1980. Regional Variations in Public Policy. In *Small Worlds: Provinces and Parties in Canadian Political Life*, ed. David J. Elkins and Richard Simeon, 242–84. Toronto: Methuen.

Smallwood, J. R., ed. 1937. *The Book of Newfoundland*. Vol. 1: *Journalism in Newfoundland*, by T. D. Carew. St John's: Newfoundland Book Publishers.

Smith, Anthony D. 1991. *National Identity*. London: Penguin.
—— . 1996. Nationalism and the Historians. In *Mapping the Nation*, ed. Gopal Balakrishnan, 175–97. London: Verso.
—— . 1998. *Nationalism and Modernism: A Critical Survey of Recent Theories of Nations and Nationalism*. London: Routledge.
Smith, Maurice. 1994. *Paper Lions: The Scottish Press and National Identity*. Edinburgh: Polygon.
SNP (Scottish National Party). 1974. General Election Manifesto. Edinburgh: Scottish National Party, February.
—— . 1977. SNP & You: Aims and Policy of The Scottish National Party. 5th edn. Edinburgh: Scottish National Party.
—— . 1978. Return to Nationhood. N.p: Scottish National Party, November.
—— . 1979. Supplementary Manifesto of the Scottish National Party for the General Election Campaign of April/May 1979. Edinburgh: Scottish National Party, April/May.
—— . 1983. Choose Scotland – The Challenge of Independence: Manifesto of the Scottish National Party for the 1983 General Election. N.p.: Scottish National Party, May.
—— . 1987. Play the Scottish Card: SNP General Election Manifesto 1987. N.p.: Scottish National Party.
—— . 1989. Scotland's Future – Independence in Europe: Scottish National Party Manifesto: European Elections – 15 June 1989. N.p.: Scottish National Party.
—— . 1992. Independence in Europe: Make it Happen Now! The 1992 Manifesto of the Scottish National Party. Edinburgh: Scottish National Party.
—— . 1997a. Yes We Can: The Manifesto of the Scottish National Party for the 1997 General Election. Edinburgh: Scottish National Party.
—— . 1997b. Yes We Can Win the Best for Scotland: The SNP General Election Budget 1997. Edinburgh: Scottish National Party, April.
Srebrnik, Henry. 2000. A Garden in Disorder? Reaction to the Maritime Union Proposal on Prince Edward Island [online]. Paper presented as part of the 1996 Conference of the Atlantic Provinces Political Science Association, Acadia University, Nova Scotia, 27 October [retrieved 22 September 2000]. URL: http://ace.acadiau.ca/polisci/appsa/papers/paperC.htm.
Statistics Canada. 2000. Labour Force Characteristics (Population 15 years and Older) by Economic Regions, 3 Month Moving Averages, Unadjusted for Seasonality [online]. N.p., Statistics Canada, 2000 [retrieved 19 June 2000]. URL: www.statcan.ca/english/econoind/lferua.htm.
Statistics Canada. 2008. Income, Pensions, Spending and Wealth [online]. N.p., Statistics Canada, 2008 [retrieved 14 November 2008]. URL: www40.statcan.gc.ca/l01/indo1/l3_3868-eng.htm?hili_none.
Strong, Joan. 1994. *Acts of Brief Authority: A Critical Assessment of Selected Twentieth-Century Newfoundland Novels*. St John's: Breakwater.
Summers, Valerie A. 1992. Resource Politics and Regime Change in the Federal Era, 1949–1991. In *The Provincial State: Politics in Canada's Provinces and Territories*, eds Keith Brownsey and Michael Howlett, 9–30. Mississauga, Ontario: Copp Clark Pitmann.
Supreme Court of Canada. 1984. Reference re: Seabed and Subsoil of the Continental Shelf Offshore Newfoundland 1 S.C.R. 86, File No.: 17096.
Thomas, Colin. 1988. *The Divided Kingdom: Scotland – Identity in the Balance*. Directed by Colin Thomas. HTV Wales for Channel 4. Videocassette.
Thomsen, Jens Peter Frølund. 1997. *Moderne politikbegreber: introduktion til systemanalyse, marxisme og diskursanalyse*. Aarhus: Systime.
Thornton, Patricia A. 1999. The Problem of Out-Migration from Atlantic Canada, 1871–1921: A New Look (1984). In *Atlantic Canada After Confederation. The*

Acadiensis Reader: Volume Two, eds P.A. Buckner et al. 3rd edn. Fredericton: Acadiensis Press.

Throne Speech [TS]/Speech From the Throne. 1966. Delivered at the Opening of The First Session of the Thirty-Fourth General Assembly of the Province of Newfoundland. 30 November. N.p.: Queen's Printer.

——. 1969. Delivered at the Opening of The Third Session of the Thirty-Fourth General Assembly of the Province of Newfoundland. 24 February. N.p.

——. 1970. Delivered at the Opening of The Fourth Session of the Thirty-Fourth General Assembly of the Province of Newfoundland. 18 February. N.p.

——. 1972. Delivered at the Opening of The First Session of the Thirty-Fifth General Assembly of the Province of Newfoundland. 1 March. N.p.

——. 1972. Delivered at the Opening of The First Session of the Thirty-Sixth General Assembly of the Province of Newfoundland. 19 April. N.p.

——. 1975. Delivered at the Opening of The First Session of the Thirty-Seventh General Assembly of the Province of Newfoundland. 19 November. N.p.

——. 1979. Delivered at the Opening of The First Session of the Thirty-Eighth General Assembly of the Province of Newfoundland. 12 July. N.p.

——. 1982. Delivered at the Opening of The First Session of the Thirty-Ninth General Assembly of the Province of Newfoundland. 10 May. N.p.

——. 1985. Delivered at the Opening of The First Session of the Fortieth General Assembly of the Province of Newfoundland. 25 April. N.p.

——. 1989. Delivered at the Opening of The First Session of the Forty-first General Assembly of the Province of Newfoundland. 25 May. N.p.

Tomblin, Stephen G. 1995. *Ottawa and the Outer Provinces: The Challenge of Regional Integration in Canada*. Toronto: Lorimer.

van Dijk, Teun A. 1991. Media contents. The Interdisciplinary Study of News as Discourse. In *A Handbook of Qualitative Methodologies for Mass Communication Research*, eds Klaus Bruhn Jensen and Nicholas W. Jankowski, 108–20. London: Routledge.

Wagenberg, Ronald H., et al. 1992. Campaigns, Images, and Polls: Horseracism in Mass Media Coverage of the 1984 Canadian Election. In *Critical Studies of Canadian Mass Media*, ed. Marc Grenier, 133–44. Toronto: Butterworths.

Walker, Graham. 1996. Varieties of Scottish Protestant Identity. In *Scotland in the 20th Century*, ed. T. M. Devine and R. J. Finlay, 250–68. Edinburgh: Edinburgh University.

Wallace, Gavin. 1993. Introduction. In *The Scottish Novel Since the Seventies*, eds Gavin Wallace and Randall Stevenson, 1–7. Edinburgh: Edinburgh University.

Warren, Ted. 1983. Newfoundland Separatism: Relic from the Past or Omen for the Future? *Newfoundland Herald*, 5 November: 16–19.

Watson, Roderick. 1996. Maps of Desire: Scottish Literature in the Twentieth Century. In *Scotland in the 20th Century*, ed. T. M. Devine and R. J. Finlay, 285–305. Edinburgh: Edinburgh University.

Webb, Keith. 1978. *The Growth of Nationalism in Scotland*. Rev. edn. Harmondsworth: Penguin and Molendinar.

Weber, Max. 1919. Politik als Beruf. In *Gesammelte Politische Schriften*, 396–450. Munich: Duncker & Humboldt.

——. 1994 (1948). The Nation. In *Nationalism*, eds John Hutchinson and Anthony D. Smith, 21–5. Oxford: Oxford University Press. Original edition, London: Routledge and Kegan Paul.

Willings Press Guide. 1999. Vol. 1: *United Kingdom*. Teddington: Hollies Directories.

Young, Victor, et al. 2003. *Our Place in Canada. Summary Report of the Royal Commission on Renewing and Strengthening Our Place in Canada*. St John's: Office of the Queen's Printer.

Østerud, Øyvind. 1994. *Hva er nasjonalisme?* Oslo: Oslo University Press.

Index